This major new textbook addresses fundamental questions about the nature of the state in early modern Europe through an analysis of the most important continental state, France. Professor Collins abandons the traditional formulation of the absolute monarchy, and presents in its place a state that evolved to meet the needs of the French elites. French kings cooperated with local elites to create the model for all other continental European political units. Collins offers a detailed analysis of French society, to provide the broader context for the development of the French state. The state that emerges from this synthesis is one that relied more on persuasion and congruity of influence than on arbitrary authority, and Collins argues that fundamental changes in French society made the monarchical, ministerial state a dangerous anachronism by the 1750s. Its inability to reconcile problems about the definition of property or the conflict between individuals and corporate bodies led to a political impasse by the second half of the eighteenth century.

Dealing both with the changes in the idea of the state and with the evolution of the state institutions themselves, Collins offers a fundamental reinterpretation of the state in early modern France which addresses issues relevant to historians and students of political thought.

NEW APPROACHES TO EUROPEAN HISTORY

The State in Early Modern France

NEW APPROACHES TO EUROPEAN HISTORY

Series editors
WILLIAM BEIK   *Emory University*
T. C. W. BLANNING   *Sidney Sussex College, Cambridge*

New Approaches to European History is an important new textbook initiative, intended to provide concise but authoritative surveys of major themes and problems in European history since the Renaissance. Written at a level and length accessible to advanced school students and undergraduates, each book in the series will address topics or themes that students of European history encounter daily: the series will embrace both some of the more 'traditional' subjects of study, and those cultural and social issues to which increasing numbers of school and college courses are devoted. A particular effort will be made to consider the wider international implications of the subject under scrutiny.

To aid the student reader scholarly apparatus and annotation will be light, but each work will have full supplementary bibliographies and notes for further reading: where appropriate chronologies, maps, diagrams and other illustrative material will also be provided.

For a list of titles published in the series, please see end of book.

The State in Early Modern France

James B. Collins

Georgetown University

 **CAMBRIDGE**
UNIVERSITY PRESS

PUBLISHED BY THE PRESS SYNDICATE OF THE UNIVERSITY OF CAMBRIDGE
The Pitt Building, Trumpington Street, Cambridge, United Kingdom

CAMBRIDGE UNIVERSITY PRESS
The Edinburgh Building, Cambridge CB2 2RU, UK
40 West 20th Street, New York, NY 10011–4211, USA
477 Williamstown Road, Port Melbourne, VIC 3207, Australia
Ruiz de Alarcón 13, 28014 Madrid, Spain
Dock House, The Waterfront, Cape Town 8001, South Africa

http://www.cambridge.org

First published 1995
Reprinted 1996, 1999, 2001

A catalogue record for this book is available from the British Library

Library of Congress Cataloguing in Publication data
Collins, James B.
    The state in early modern Frnace / James B. Collins.
        p.   cm. – (New approaches to European history)
    Includes bibliographical references and index.
    ISBN 0 521 38284 X – ISBN 0 521 38724 8 (pbk.)
    1. France – History – Bourbons, 1589–1789.
    2. Monarchy – France – History.
    I. Title.   II. Series.
    DC100.C575 1995
    944'.03–dc20 94-33992 CIP

ISBN 0 521 38284 X hardback
ISBN 0 521 38724 8 paperback

Transferred to digital printing 2003

VN/CP

Contents

Illustrations

All illustrations reproduced courtesy of the Special Collections of Lauinger Library, Georgetown University. The maps are adapted from eighteenth-century originals found in Rizzi-Zannoni, *Atlas historique de la France Ancienne et Moderne* (Paris: Desnos, 1766). The use of maps contemporary with the period under discussion allows us to get some sense of how early modern French people perceived the shape of their country, but it does sacrifice a bit of accuracy in comparison with modern maps. The enclaves, for example, are not as precisely drawn as they might be: they tend to be a bit larger than they should be. Observant readers will notice that their boundaries vary from one original map to the next, even though the actual territory in question had not changed.

Preface

This book, although it has a single author, rests on the work of many scholars. One could not write a work of synthesis such as this one without drawing on the research of countless historians. Many of these people are my friends, as well as my professional colleagues; I express here my debt to them all, in both capacities.

The Baltimore–Washington area has a society of specialists of the Old Regime and the French Revolution who meet regularly to discuss each other's work; the group met and discussed an earlier draft of this work. The members who attended that discussion (as best I can recall) included Orest and Pat Ranum, who kindly offered their hospitality to us all, as well as: Tom Adams, Katherine Stern Brennan, Tom Brennan, Jack Censer, Bob Forster, Mack Holt, Emmett Kennedy, Sharon Kettering, Joe Klaits, Bob Kreiser, Gary McCollim, and Don Sutherland. I here express my sincere appreciation for their comments; I would like especially to thank Gary McCollim, who provided me with a copy of his excellent unpublished thesis on controller general Desmarets.

Others have read parts or all of the manuscript. Cambridge University Press sent the chapters to unknown specialists, as well as to the series editors. The many comments and corrections I received immensely helped my task. My graduate students – Sara Chapman, Joanna Hamilton, Brendan Hill, and Zoë Schneider – also read parts of the manuscript and offered useful comments from the student perspective. In France, Bernard Barbiche and I have often discussed the evolution of the Old Regime state; I have benefited greatly from his knowledge and insight, as well as from his friendship. The occasional forays into Breton and Burgundian sources owe much to my fruitful conversations with Alain Croix and Jean Tanguy in Brittany, and with Jean Bart in Burgundy.

Bill Beik originally proposed this book to me; I appreciate his confidence and hope that I have lived up to it. I want also to thank my editor, Richard Fisher, and the copy-editor, Karen Howes, for their assiduity and professionalism.

Lastly, I want to thank my family for their support. This is a book intended especially for students, so I thought it best to dedicate it to four of my favourite ones, three of them young learners and the fourth forever young at heart. To Anna, Liz, and Margaret from their dad, and to my mother, Constance Collins Cain, from her loving and grateful son.

Chronology of events

1589 Assassination of Henry III; accession of Henry IV (2 August)
1590 Battle of Ivry; Henry IV defeats the army of the Catholic League
1593 Henry IV abjures Protestantism
1594 Henry IV crowned at Chartres
1596–97 Assembly of Notables at Rouen
1598 Edict of Nantes – Henry IV recognizes Protestantism as a legal
    religion in France (with restrictions)
1598–1604 Wide range of reforming edicts issued by Henry IV;
    king institutes the *paulette*, guaranteeing hereditary of most
    offices
1600–01 War with Savoy; peace of Lyons gives Bresse, Bugey, Val-
    romey, and Gex to France
1601 Conspiracy of marshal Biron; Biron executed
1606 Conspiracy of duke of Bouillon
1607 Largest of Henry's Chambers of Justice, investigating financiers
1610 Assassination of Henry IV (14 May); Louis XIII becomes king; his
    mother, Marie de Médicis, becomes Regent
1614 Louis XIII declares his majority
1614–15 Meeting of the Estates General
1614–17 Endemic revolts of major nobles against Regent; they end with
    murder of Concino Concini (favorite of Marie de Médicis and
    dominant influence in government), carried out by Louis XIII and
    his friends
1617 Assembly of Notables, unsuccessful
1618 Thirty Years' War begins in Bohemia
1620 Navarre permanently united to French crown
1621–29 Internal war with Protestants; key event, capture of La
    Rochelle by the king (1628)
1624 Richelieu rejoins royal council
1626–27 Rebellion in Quercy
1626–27 Assembly of Notables at Saint-Germain, deliberations lead to a
    wide range of reforming ordinances, especially:

1629 Code Michau, massive recodification of French law and administrative practice

1629–30 Mantuan war against Spain

1630 Day of the Dupes (10–11 November); Louis XIII sides with Richelieu against Marie de Médicis and Marillac

1634 Large-scale introduction of intendants into the *généralités*; partial bankruptcy at expense of royal officers

1635 France enters the Thirty Years' War

1635–43 Peasant and urban revolts throughout the country; most serious are Croquants in the southwest, Nu-Pieds (1639) in Normandy

1636 Battle of Corbie; French repulse Spanish from Paris

1642 Death of Richelieu

1642 Intendants for first time receive right to apportion direct taxes

1643 Condé's army defeats Spanish *tercios* at Rocroi

1643 Death of Louis XIII; Louis XIV becomes king; his mother, Anne of Austria, becomes Regent, with Cardinal Mazarin as chief minister

1644–45 Extensive increase in legal privileges of robe nobility, particularly in Paris (in return for their support for Regency)

1647–48 Public order disintegrates in provinces; disorder spreads to Paris

1648 Peace of Westphalia ends fighting in Germany and war between Spain and United Provinces; France obtains Upper Alsace and certain rights in Lower Alsace

1648 Government conducts another partial bankruptcy

1648–53 The Fronde, a series of revolts by officers (1648–49) and by great nobility (1649–53); Mazarin exiled twice; intendants abolished (1648) then gradually reintroduced (after 1653)

1651 Louis XIV declares his majority

1654 Coronation of Louis XIV at Reims

1659 Peace of Pyrenees ends war between France and Spain; France obtains Perpignan

1661 Death of Mazarin (9 March); Louis declares himself chief minister and reorganizes royal councils

1661 Arrest of Fouquet; abolition of superintendancy of finances; Colbert becomes chief financial officer (but only obtains title of controller general in 1665); government carries out another partial bankruptcy

1661–67 Chamber of Justice to investigate financiers

1663–72 Great royal academies: painting (reorganized 1663), Sciences (1666), Académie Française (under royal protection beginning in 1671), architecture (1671), music (1672)

1666–74 Government-led research inquiry into the legitimacy of claims of nobility; nobles required to furnish written proof of their status

1667–68 War of Devolution; Peace of Aix-la-Chapelle (1668) gives France Lille and part of Flanders

1669–70 Great legal and administrative ordinances (forests and civil law, both 1669; criminal law, 1670)

1672–79 Dutch War; Peace of Nijmegen (1678) gives France small gains in the north and the Franche-Comté in the east

1673 Parlements lose right of preregistration remonstrances

1675 Papier Timbré and Bonnets Rouges rebellions in Brittany

1679–81 Chambers of Reunion gradually add parts of Alsace to France, culminating in occupation of Strasburg (30 September 1681)

1682 Four Gallican Articles

1682 Permanent move of Court to Versailles

1683–84 Conquest of Luxembourg

1685 Edict of Fontainebleau (Revocation of the Edict of Nantes) outlaws Protestantism in most of France

1689–97 War of the League of Augsburg (fighting begins 1688); at Peace of Ryswick (1697) France gives up Luxembourg, but is confirmed in its possession of Alsace

1693–94 Harvest failure leads to famine and mass starvation, especially in the Midi

1694 Dictionary of the Académie Française

1695 First direct tax levied on everyone except the clergy, the *capitation*

1700 Philip V, grandson of Louis XIV, inherits Spanish throne

1702–10 War of the Camisards (suppression of Protestants in the Cévennes Mountains)

1702–13 War of the Spanish Succession

1705–08 Disastrous French defeats at Blenheim, Oudenarde, Ramilies, and Turin

1709 Louis XIV unsuccessfully sues for peace; Louis appeals directly to the French people for their support in the war; French fight English and Dutch to a draw at Malplaquet

1709 Louis XIV closes Port-Royal convent (Jansenists)

1709 Bossuet's heirs publish his main political treatise on absolute monarchy

1709–10 Brutal winter in France leads to massive impoverishment, widespread starvation

1710 Revenue tax, the *dixième*, instituted; abolished when war ends

1711 Death of Dauphin

1712 Death of new Dauphin (duke of Burgundy) and his oldest son

1713 Peace of Utrecht; France loses territory in America; England obtains monopoly slave trade to Spanish colonies

1713 Papal bull *Unigenitus* condemns Jansenism's beliefs

1715 Death of Louis XIV (1 September); Louis XV becomes king and his uncle, Philip of Orléans, becomes Regent; Parlement of Paris overturns Louis XIV's will; Regent restores right of preregistration remonstrance to the Parlements

1715–23 Regency of Philip of Orléans; he attempts many reforms

1716–17 Chamber of Justice

1717–20 System of John Law: revises banking and financial practices; founds national bank; ends in bankruptcy

1722 Louis XV crowned

1723 Louis XV reaches majority

1726 Cardinal Fleury becomes chief minister

1726 *Livre tournois* fixed in value

1730 Open conflict breaks out again with Jansenists

1730 Orry becomes controller general

1733 War of the Polish Succession; Louis XV's father-in-law, Stanislas Leszczynski, obtains duchy of Lorraine and agrees to leave it to king of France when he dies

1738 Orry introduces *corvée* labor to maintain roads

1740–48 War of the Austrian Succession (French participation starts in 1741); France wins many battles but obtains no gains at the Peace of Aix-la-Chapelle

1745 Machault becomes controller general

1748–51 Creation of central technical schools: engineers (1748), military (1751)

1749 New, permanent tax on revenue, the *vingtième*

1752–57 Affair of the confession certificates

1756 Exile of Parlement of Paris

1756–63 Seven Years' War; France allies with ancient enemy, Austria, against Britain and Prussia

1757 Damiens attempts to assassinate Louis XV

1759 France loses Canada

1763 Peace of Paris takes Canada, Louisiana, and other colonies in the West Indies, Africa, and India from France

1764–69 Brittany Affair

1764–70 Choiseul and Praslin reorganize the Navy

1766 Seance of the Scourging (3 March)

1768 France obtains Corsica from Genoa

1770 Exile of Parlement of Paris; disgrace of Choiseul

1771–74 Maupeou "Revolution": Parlements abolished, law courts reorganized, venality of legal office eliminated; Abbé Terray reforms fiscal and tax systems

1774 Death of Louis XV; Louis XVI becomes king

1774 Maupeou and Abbé Terray disgraced

1774–76 Turgot as controller general; his reforms (abolition of guilds, free trade in grain) are retracted when he resigns

1775 Count of Saint-Germain abolishes king's military household, reorganizes the army

1776 Necker becomes director general of finances

1778 France allies with United States of America against Britain

1781 Necker reorganizes financial administration, which leads to his dismissal; after leaving office he publishes *Compte Rendu au Roi*

1783 Peace of Paris; United States achieves independence; France obtains return of some colonies (Sénégal)

1786 Free-trade agreement with Britain

1787 Assembly of Notables; king gives some rights to Protestants

1788 Wide range of fiscal and legal edicts; provincial assemblies begin to meet; Day of the Tiles (Grenoble, 7 June)

1788 Court of Peers calls for Estates General; king announces Estates will meet, eventually (8 August) declares opening date to be 1 May 1789; king exiles Parlement of Paris; Necker recalled

1789 Elections for Estates General; Estates opens on 5 May; three orders debate rules; eventually Third Estate constitutes itself as the National Assembly (17 June) and promises not to adjourn until it has written a constitution (Tennis Court Oath, 20 June)

Genealogy

Henry IV was married twice, to Marguerite of Valois, sister of his predecessor (Henry III), and to Marie de Médicis. He and Marie had five children: Louis XIII, Gaston of Orléans, Henriette-Marie (who married Charles I of England), Elisabeth (who married Philip IV of Spain), and Christine (who married Victor Amadeus of Savoy). Gaston married twice but had only one daughter, whose property reverted to the Crown in 1693.

Louis XIII married Anne of Austria, oldest daughter of Philip III of Spain. They had two children: Louis XIV and Philip of Orléans. Philip was married twice, to his first cousin, Henriette of England, and to Charlotte von der Pfalz. Their son Philip was Regent of France from 1715–23; their great-great-grandson, Louis-Philippe d'Orléans, became king of France (1830).

Louis XIV married his double first cousin, Maria Theresa of Spain. They had only one surviving son, Louis, called the Grand Dauphin. He died in 1711, before he could inherit. Two of his sons – Louis and Philip – had issue. Philip became king of Spain in 1700, founding the Spanish royal family of Borbon. Louis, duke of Burgundy, died in 1712. He had married a cousin, Marie-Adelaide of Savoy (the delight of Louis XIV's old age). Their eldest son died shortly thereafter, leaving the younger son (then titled duke of Berry) to inherit as Louis XV in 1715.

Louis XV married Maria Leszczynski, daughter of Stanislas Leszczynski, deposed king of Poland. Louis had been betrothed to the daughter of Philip V of Spain in 1721, but she was only three at the time. Fearing that Louis XV might die without male issue, the chief minister, the duke of Bourbon, renounced the Spanish marriage (nearly causing a war) and quickly married Louis XV to Maria Leszczynski. She had ten children, of whom seven survived, though only one son, Louis (born 1729). He was married twice, first to a princess of Spain, who died in childbirth, and then to Marie-Joseph of Saxony, who bore four sons who survived into adolescence. The eldest died a teenager and his brother Louis became the heir apparent (and Louis XVI). The two younger sons, the counts of Provence and Artois, inherited the throne after the French Revolution (as Louis XVIII and Charles X).

Glossary

abonnement – exemption payment. A province, such as Brittany, that wished to be exempt from a new tax could make an agreement with the king to provide a fixed amount of money each year in lieu of the establishment of the tax in question. This *abonnement* could apply to an entire province, to a single town, to a corporation (like the Clergy), or even to an individual.

aides – indirect taxes, primarily on sales and manufacture. The king, with the approval of an Estates General, established indirect sales and manufacturing taxes in the fourteenth century. These taxes, called the *aides*, lasted until the end of the Old Regime. They changed somewhat in the fifteenth century; under the Bourbons, the income from the *aides* came primarily from taxes on wine, fish, and wood.

Aides Générales – farm of all the *aides* levied in France, made permanent under Henry IV (see also General Tax Farm).

Assembly of Notables – group of notables invited by the king to discuss reform of the government. Assemblies met in 1583, 1596–97, 1617, 1626, 1787, and 1788. These Assemblies included royal princes, peers, archbishops and bishops, important judges, and in some cases, major town officials. Like the Estates General, they served a consultative purpose only. The king would issue a reforming edict (or edicts) after listening to their advice.

bailiwick – local royal court. The *baillis* (chief bailiwick officials, although very different than the direct English translation, bailiff, would suggest), called seneschals in most of southern France and in Brittany, dated from the thirteenth century, when they had been the king's local representatives. They originally had wide responsibilities in judicial matters, in executing royal policy, and in commanding the local noble militia. Over time, the functions divided into two parts: the *bailli*, almost always a member of the sword nobility, continued to have military responsibilities; the judicial functions devolved upon a professional court, called the bailiwick court (in the South, seneschalsy court), whose chief official was the lieutenant general of the bailiwick. He was joined by a small group of judges, by a *procureur du roi* (royal attorney), and by sergeants and clerks. Throughout France, the bailiwicks/seneschalsies formed the first layer of the royal judiciary.

ban et arrière-ban – noble feudal militia. The king had the right to call his vassals (the *ban*) and their sub-vassals (the *arrière-ban*) to provide military service. Louis XIII actually issued such a call in 1636, but, in most cases, kings preferred to commute service into a cash payment. The king could threaten to call the *ban et arrière-ban* as a way to extort money from the nobility.

bureau des finances – the collective group of treasurers-general of each *généralité*. In the late sixteenth century, the merger of the offices of treasurer of France (responsible for oversight of the royal demesne) and *général des finances* (responsible for oversight of royal tax collection) created regional bodies of treasurers-general, who kept watch over royal finances. Rather than acting separately, in individual sub-districts, the treasurers-general took collective responsibility for oversight. Their collective identity was called a *bureau des finances* – financial office. By the middle of the seventeenth century, most *bureaux des finances* had between 19 and 26 treasurers-general. Of the *généralités*, only Brittany had no *bureau des finances*.

cahiers de doléances – lists of grievances. For the Estates General, each parish drew up a list of its grievances, to be presented either to the king or to the bailiwick (or provincial) assembly charged with selecting the deputies to the Estates. These bailiwick assemblies also drew up *cahiers*, which they presented to the king. Provincial estates redacted similar documents at each session.

capitation – direct tax introduced in 1695. The original capitation levied money on all French lay people (the clergy bought an exemption), based on a series of 22 classes, ranging from the Dauphin (who paid 2,000 *livres*) to the lowliest shepherd (who paid one). Abolished and reestablished several times, the capitation often became a simple adjunct to the *taille* for peasants; among the nobility, despite the theoretical shift in its rules during the War of the Spanish Succession, the local documents suggest that the tax collectors continued to use a sort of class system basically similar to that of 1695.

Central Treasury (*Epargne*) – main receiving and disbursing center of the monarchy. The Central Treasury received a significant portion of royal revenue, although by no means did this constitute "net" income in any meaningful sense. The Central Treasurer (*trésorier de l'Epargne*) had to authorize virtually all spending; he rendered his accounts each year to the Chamber of Accounts. In order to limit the possibilities of fraud (and to raise more money from the sales of the offices), two or three men held the office of Central Treasurer, serving in a two- or three-year rotation.

Chambers of Reunion – special courts established by Louis XIV to legalize his seizure of territory on the borders of eastern France (especially Alsace).

Chambre de Justice – investigating commission, looking into the conduct of royal financial officials and tax farmers. The Crown regularly used such commissions to exact large fines from tax farmers and corrupt officials and to frighten officials into being more honest. In time, the *Chambre de Justice* became the device of choice for an incoming controller general to eliminate the financial network of his predecessor and introduce his own cronies. Colbert established this pattern with the great Chamber of the 1660s.

chevalier – literally, knight. This term originally meant a function, that of mounted fighter, but came to be used as a title by early modern times.

Cinq Grosses Fermes – the five main import–export tax farms, leased together under Henry III and permanently from the time of Henry IV. The *Cinq Grosses Fermes* later added taxes such as the levy on wine entering walled towns; they eventually formed part of the General Tax Farm (see separate entry).

commissaire – an individual operating on the basis of a royal commission. The king would issue a commission to, say, an intendant, limiting his jurisdication and his time in the position. When the commission expired, the official lost his job. A *commissaire* did not own his office, as an *officier* would do. Note that most *commissaires*, like the intendants, owned a venal *office*, such as that of master of request.

controller general – from the 1660s on, the chief operating officer of the French administration. The original controllers general supervised the activities of the Central Treasurer. When Louis XIV abolished the post of superintendant of finances (1661), he turned to Colbert, then an intendant of finances, to oversee matters. Colbert became controller general in 1665. In this post, he came to dominate the Royal Council of Finances and to obtain *de facto* control of royal finances. His successors as controller general kept that control, as well as primary authority for much of the internal administration of the country. The provincial intendants reported directly to the controller general.

corvée – originally labor performed on the lord's estate by his serfs, later by tenants. In the eighteenth century, the *corvée* was the obligatory repair work on royal roads performed by the rural population.

Council of Dispatches (*Conseil des Depêches*) – this body theoretically established internal policy for France. As noted in the text, it steadily lost authority during the reign of Louis XIV.

Council of State (*Conseil d'En haut*) – the highest royal council, this body established royal policy in both internal and external matters (although in theory largely about the latter). Its members, who alone had the right to the title royal minister, attended solely at the discretion of the king. No royal official had the *right* to sit on this council. The king usually invited the controller general, the four secretaries of state, and on occasion, some other trusted councilors to sit.

curia regis – the medieval household court of the king. Many government offices evolved from specific functions in the king's household. Thus the "count of the stables" (or constable) took care of the king's horses; he eventually became the head of the king's cavalry. As the cavalry dominated medieval armies, the constable later became the commander of the royal army.

dixième (tenth) – an income tax introduced during the War of the Spanish Succession. Louis XIV did not actually inquire deeply into people's incomes; the *dixième* in practice became another adjunct to the *taille* for those subject to the latter. For the privileged, the state usually relied on their personal declaration of income. The state abolished this wartime tax as soon as peace arrived. The same sort of tax returned in permanence after 1750, in the form of the twentieth (see *vingtième*).

douanes – import–export duties. The king collected import–export duties not only at the edge of the kingdom, but also at the edge of the area covered by the *aides*. Those provinces, such as Brittany, that did not pay the *aides* had to pay an equivalent tax at their borders on goods imported from the regions of France that did pay the *aides*.

dragonnades – quartering of troops, mounted infantry (dragoons, hence the name) in the houses of civilians, especially Protestants. Louis XIV used this tactic extensively in his campaigns against the Huguenots.

droits aliénés – alienated rights or surtaxes. The king sold the right to collect surtaxes to some of his officials. Thus he sold (through the mediation of a *traitant*) the local receivers the right to a surtax of 2.5 percent of all money they collected. They, in return, paid him ten times the annual value of that surtax. The king abolished the *droit aliénés* in 1634, but then began reselling them on a per-parish basis – thus *X livres* per parish for the officer, rather than a percentage of the total levy. This had the advantage of preventing inflation of the surtax, because, unlike the amount of taxation, the number of parishes remained stable.

Eaux et Fôrets – royal administration of Waters and Woods. The king had a special group of officers, many of them judges, for all disputes related to water and to woods. This administration employed foresters, as well as special judges (who sat at courts called the "Table of Marble") to hear disputes about hunting, about wood usage, and about fishing and water rights. In a society in which wood provided the main fuel as well as an important building material, management of the kingdom's forests was an extremely important task.

écuyer – squire. Unlike the English squire, a French one held hereditary nobility. The term *écuyer* was the lowest one in the French hierarchy of noble titles.

Edict of Fontainebleau – 1685 edict in which Louis XIV rescinded the Edict of Nantes and outlawed most Protestant worship in France (he made an exception for Lutherans in Alsace).

Edict of Nantes – 1598 edict of Henry IV allowing public Protestant worship in designated areas. This edict gave the Huguenots certain fortified cities, with royally funded garrisons, and established special courts to hear religious cases (the *chambres de l'édit*, which had both Huguenot and Catholic judges).

élu – local financial overseer. In the fourteenth century, when France first established direct taxation, the representative assemblies elected the local overseer of the collection, hence the name *élu* (literally, elected one). An *élu* had jurisdiction over a district called an *élection*; France had more than 150 *élections* by the middle of the seventeenth century.

Estates General – representative body for the kingdom of France. In medieval times, the so-called Estates General usually met in two separate bodies, one for the North (Languedoïl) and one for the South (Languedoc). In the fifteenth century, however, the Estates General came to mean the Estates of the entire kingdom. The Estates met in 1484, 1560–61, 1576, 1588, 1614–15, and 1789. All parishes had the right to send grievances, the so-called *cahiers de doléances*, to the Estates. The representatives of parishes often met together in bailiwick or castellany assemblies, to draw up regional *cahiers*. In the areas with provincial estates, such as Brittany or Languedoc, the provincial estates merely sent a delegation to the Estates General. The Estates General did *not* have legislative authority. Traditionally, the king asked their advice about reforms and then issued an edict after the meeting, incorporating his original proposals and some of their suggestions. Many French jurists claimed that only Estates General could vote new taxation. That sentiment had significant support in the late sixteenth century and again at the end of the eighteenth. The monarchy, however, never specifically accepted it; furthermore, it created many new taxes without the slightest recourse to the Estates General.

gabelle – salt tax. The king had a monopoly on the sale of salt in most of France. In northern France, he collected a large tax by means of distribution of salt from warehouses. This region was known as the *pays des grandes gabelles* (area of large salt taxes). In southern France, the king collected the tax when the salt left the areas of salt production (marshes near the Mediterranean); this region had the name of the *pays des petites gabelles* (area of small salt taxes). Some regions, such as Brittany, the Southwest, and the Cotentin peninsula (in Lower Normandy), either escaped such taxes altogether or levied special, low salt taxes. Early modern French people used the term *gabeleur* to describe anyone associated with collecting the salt taxes. This term of universal opprobrium was often used to describe any tax collector.

gages – annual payment to royal officer. The literal English translation, wages, does not accurately reflect the reality of *gages*. Officers received only their *gages* as official recompense for their office (except for judges, who had a right to officially established "gratifications," called *épices*), so it was, in a sense, their salary. Its amount, however, was determined solely by the official price of the office; most officers received one-tenth of that value as their annual *gages*. In short, *gages* represented their interest on the capital invested in the office.

Gallicanism – belief in the supremacy of the French Church in ecclesiastical matters. Gallicans believed that the Pope did not have final authority in the French Church. They believed that the king and the French Church itself should hold the dominant position in French Catholicism (without denying the special and extremely important position of the Pope). Gallicans strongly resisted any efforts to remove French ecclesiastical independence. The Parlement of Paris, which had final authority in French ecclesiastical cases (through a procedure called the *appel comme d'abus*), was always a stronghold of Gallicanism.

General Tax Farm – combination of all leased taxes in France. Under Colbert, the government created a single tax farm for all of the great indirect taxes: the *Aides*, the *Cinq Grosses Fermes*, the various *gabelles* (and, later, the royal demesne). This General Tax Farm provided half (at times more) of total French tax revenue. Colbert's successor abolished the General Tax Farm, as part of the effort to destroy his clientele, but the government soon restored it (to different hands, of course). The Farmers General ran the General Tax Farm in the eighteenth century. They dominated French government finance and played a central role not only in French politics but in French culture as well. Louis XV himself bought shares in the General Tax Farm (as did other members of the royal family).

généralité – regional financial district. Fourteenth-century France had only four *généralités*: Languedoc (southern France), Languedoïl (mainly the Loire valley), Normandy, and the north and northeast (called Paris-et-Outre-Seine). Each large district had an overseer in charge of its "general" collection, thus the name of the district (and the officer, called a *général des finances*). The Estates General originally selected these officials but, in the 1370s, Charles V converted them into royal councilors, thus putting their appointment in royal hands. Each new province became a new *généralité*; in the sixteenth century, the old *généralités* subdivided. By the middle of the seventeenth century, France had about 25 *généralités*.

Grand Conseil – a Sovereign Court dealing with special cases and with jurisdictional disputes. France had only one *Grand Conseil*, at Paris, which decided on the appropriate jurisdiction for a case when the disputants disagreed about the right court. Many French people had the right to be judged only in certain courts; thus a Breton could claim the right to be judged only by the Parlement of Brittany. A neighboring Angevin would demand that the case go to the Parlement of Paris; the *Grand Conseil* decided such disputes. It also heard other special cases, many of them with political overtones. It should not be confused with the royal council.

greniers – royal salt warehouses. In most of France, the king held a wholesale monopoly of the sale of salt. The salt tax monopolists (independent contractors, i.e., tax farmers) had to bring their salt to a royal warehouse, where a royal official, the *grenetier*, registered it and oversaw its later distribution to merchants. The tax farmers collected, on behalf of the king, a fixed amount on every *muid* of salt registered by the *grenetier*. The *grenetier* also served as the judge in the first instance of all small-scale lawsuits related to the salt tax. Each warehouse also had a controller, to check on the *grenetier*, and an official measurer of salt. All these offices were venal.

intendants – royal *commissaires* sent on mission to act on the king's behalf. The original intendants were either investigating commissioners, sent to given governorships in the late sixteenth century, or commissioners sent to royal armies. The state used intendants on a fairly regular basis in some areas (Languedoc, Lyons) after 1600, but most of the commissions still related to governorships or to royal armies until 1634. In 1634, Richelieu sent out intendants to the *généralités*, where they took on new administrative oversight roles. Those roles expanded after 1642, leading to violent conflicts with the officers. During the Fronde, the government had to abolish most of the intendants; it reestablished them after 1653. Royal armies continued to have "intendants of the army" throughout the seventeenth and eighteenth centuries.

intendants of finance – the central financial apparatus had a small number (ranging from two to eight) of intendants to assist and help oversee its operations. After Colbert's assumption of the office of controller general in 1665, the intendants of finance became full-fledged assistants of the controller general. They reported to the Royal Council of Finance and also participated in the lesser councils that did much of the preliminary work for the Royal Council of Finance. Readers should not confuse intendants of finance (a venal office) with provincial or army intendants (*commissaires*).

Keeper of the Seals (*Garde des Sceaux*) – the king of France could not dismiss his chancellor, who normally held the Seals of France. The office of chancellor lasted for life (unless one resigned, as did occur in the eighteenth century). If the chancellor lost favor with the king, the king could (and did) remove the Seals from his custody. The official charged with them took the title of Keeper of the Seals. In theory, if the king restored the chancellor to grace, he would dismiss the Keeper and return the Seals to the chancellor; in practice, the two officials sometimes shared responsibilities for months.

lettre de cachet – arbitrary letter of arrest. The king issued *lettres de cachet* to those in royal favor. Their abuse spread rapidly in the eighteenth century. Husbands used them to lock up their wives in convents; nobles used them to imprison merchants seeking payments; fathers used them to imprison their children for disobedience (often related to proposed marriages); some influential royal officials even sold blank *lettres de cachet*, allowing the buyer simply to fill in the name of the person to be arrested.

lettres de jussion – letters instructing a Parlement to register a royal edict without further discussion. Prior to and after Louis XIV, kings used *lettres de jussion* to overcome the objections of Parlements to royal legislation. Such legislation had to be registered in the official books of the Parlement to be law; save under Louis XIV, Parlements could delay such registration by sending the king remonstrances about the law in question. The king's first step to overcome remonstrances was a *lettre de jussion* (see also *lit de justice*).

lit de justice – royal sitting of the Parlement. In a literal sense, the "bed of justice" was the place where the king sat during such a session. By the seventeenth century, a *lit de justice* had become the final mechanism by which to overcome the resistance of the Parlement to legislation. The king came in person to the Parlement; in his presence, there could be no objections to his legislation. The Parlement then had to shift to indirect resistance to prevent the impact of the legislation. In the eighteenth century, that resistance sometimes took the form of judicial strikes.

livre tournois – French pound (literally, pound of Tours). France used the *livre tournois* as its official money of account (except in the period 1576–1602). The *livre* consisted of 20 *sous*, each *sou* (shilling) contained 12 *deniers* (pence). The *livre* did not exist as a literal coin, so its value could be adjusted up or down without actually changing the coinage (a practice widely used in the 1630s and 1640s, and again from about 1690 to 1725). I have used the French terms to avoid confusion with the English pound, which was worth much more than the French one.

mandements de l'Epargne – payment order from the Central Treasury. The Central Treasury paid most of its debts with paper. It gave an individual a payment order (*mandement*) drawn on a given receiver. The individual then had to go to the place in question to collect the money. Few creditors wanted to do so, so they sold the *mandements* to Parisian bankers (at a discount, of course). The Parisians then regulated accounts with the local receivers by means of letters of exchange.

maréchaussée – mounted constabulary. Originally, the mounted constabulary existed to oversee the behavior of royal troops within France. The constabulary was supposed to prevent conflict between such troops (always quartered on the population in those days) and the civil population. In time, the mounted constabulary became the national police force. In the eighteenth century, it had about 3,000 men to police the whole of rural France.

master of request – subordinate official of the king's council. The masters of requests prepared the documentation for all cases brought before the king's council. For most of the period in question here, the king had 72 to 80 masters of requests. He drew the vast majority of intendants from this group. It should be noted that the office of master of requests was a venal one, although it was held by commission, and thus the king had to approve any purchaser.

métayer – sharecropper. A *métayer* usually paid half of the net produce of the land as his or her rent. The net produce meant the total harvest, minus the seed set aside for the next year, the tithe paid to the Church, and in some cases, the taxes. The American term "sharecropper" conjures up images of impoverished Southern farmers; in France, however, the *métayer* was usually one of the richest peasants in the village.

minister of state – a member of the Council of State. Only those who participated in this Council (called in French the *Conseil d'En haut*) had the right to the title of minister. Ministers served entirely at the discretion of the king. Usually, he invited the four secretaries of state (War, Foreign Affairs, Paris-Royal Household-Marine, and Huguenot Affairs) and the controller general, with perhaps a few others. These officers had no *de jure* right to sit on the council, and the king could (and often did) make them wait for some time after their appointment as secretary before they joined the Council.

noblesse d'épée – nobility of the sword. This nobility, tracing its heritage back to the Middle Ages (the standard date was prior to 1400), also called itself the nobility of blood ("noblesse de sang"). In the eyes of early modern people, only sword nobles were "true" nobles. In practice, however, sword and robe families often intermarried. The sword nobility suffered dramatic casualties in three periods: the Hundred Years' War (1337–1453), the Wars of Religion (1562–98), and the later wars of Louis XIV (1689–1713). These losses mandated extensive ennoblements in the aftermath of the wars, because of the need to have a nobility large enough to maintain the social and political system of France.

noblesse de robe – nobility of the robe. Certain royal offices ennobled their possessors. These offices usually ennobled the office holder himself, but did not ennoble his family. Different offices had different rules for ennobling the family; many of them required that the family hold the office for three generations, over a period of at least twenty years. The government gradually loosened these rules over time, often in negotiations with the officers in question. Anne of Austria, for example, loosened the rules for ennoblement of councilors of the Parlement of Paris in return for their cooperation in breaking Louis XIII's will. Most nobility of the robe came from legal families; they rarely had an immediate contact with the mercantile bourgeoisie (from whose ranks their distant ancestors had often sprung).

Parlements – chief law courts. The Parlement of Paris dated from the thirteenth century; the provincial Parlements received royal sanction beginning in the early fifteenth century. In most cases, a province newly added to the kingdom received a Parlement because of the need to co-opt its local elite into the French and because each of these areas (such as Brittany or Normandy) had customary laws quite different from those of other regions of France, such as the area around Paris. These courts often took the place of local courts that existed before the royal takeover. The Parlements were the apex of judicial society. They heard on appeal all important cases: civil cases involving more than fifty *livres*; criminal cases involving the death penalty. Many privileged individuals had the right to be heard in the first instance in a Parlement. The Parlements also registered royal edicts and ordinances; without such registration, the edict or ordinance did not have the force of law. Except under Louis XIV, Parlements could delay registration by sending the king remonstrances (emendations). Under Louis XIV, they could only send such remonstrances *after* registration. The Parlement of Paris served as the final court of appeal for religious cases in France, through a procedure called the *appel comme d'abus*. Sitting in conjunction with the peers of France, as the Court of Peers, the Parlement of Paris also heard all cases related to peers.

parti – an agreement to collect a certain fee or tax. A *parti* differed from a *traité* (see below) only in that the individual who collected a *parti* was the person who had proposed the next tax. Thus the individual who proposed the *paulette*, annual fee for hereditary officers, was a *partisan*. The subsequent holders of the right to collect that fee (leased for nine years) were *traitants*.

paulette – annual fee paid by royal officials to guarantee heredity of office. The king introduced the *paulette* in 1602–04. Officers had previously to survive the sale of their office by forty days, lest the office revert to the Crown. If they paid the *paulette*, one-sixtieth the official value of their office, each year, they no longer had to worry about the forty-day clause. They had also to pay a lower transfer fee at the time of sale or inheritance (down from one-fourth to one-eighth).

pays d'élection – area with local financial districts (*élections*). This area covered about two-thirds of France; these regions had no provincial estates after 1657 (when Normandy, the last area that had both *élections* and estates, lost its estates).

pays d'Etats – regions with provincial estates. Through most of the period in question here, the *pays d'Etats* included Brittany, Burgundy, and Languedoc. Normandy lost its estates under Louis XIV; Provence and Dauphiné lost their estates under Louis XIII (although Provence kept an Assembly of the Communes, a meeting of the Third Estate that voted Provençal taxation). Newly added provinces, such as Artois, often had and kept provincial estates.

presidial – intermediary royal court. Henry II created the presidial courts to lessen the appellate burden on the Parlements and to raise money (from the sale of the offices). The presidials did not exist everywhere; in some regions, the existing bailiwick judges simply bought up the offices and combined the courts. The presidials heard appeals on small-scale civil cases, as well as certain other designated cases (such as appeals from the provostal court of the mounted constabulary).

procureur du roi – chief royal attorney prosecutor. All royal courts had a royal attorney, the *procureur du roi*, who presented the king's cases. He often had an assistant or two, known as the *avocat(s) du roi*. The distinction between the two often followed that of present-day British barristers (*avocats*) and solicitors.

régale – right to collect the revenues of a bishopric in the period between the death of the old bishop and the annointing of the new one.

rentes – annuities. The French government sold *rentes* (annuities) to help fund its debt. It guaranteed these annuities by means of revenues held by the town government of Paris (the *rentes sur l'Hôtel de Ville de Paris*), by the clergy, or simply by liens on regular indirect taxes. It also issued annuities guaranteed by the town governments of Rouen and Lyons. These original annuities were perpetual: the government never repaid the capital, but had to pay interest forever. The going rate of interest was usually the twelfth penny – 8.33 percent – but the government rarely paid more than half of the due amount. The owners of the annuities, the *rentiers*, expected to get only 4.16 percent. In the late seventeenth century, the government began to sell life annuities, carrying much higher rates of interest. These annuities expired with the person on whose life they were guaranteed (who did not have to be the actual holder of the annuity).

rescription – a sort of lien on a royal receiver's revenues. The royal receivers could lend the king his own money by issuing *rescriptions*. These papers sold at a discount, like *mandements*. They relied on the individual (i.e., personal) credit of the receiver. In effect, he advanced the king the expected return from the taxes in question; he collected the interest for this advance. In some cases, the receiver could advance the government cash in his possession that, in fact, was the government's own cash (but was not yet due). To suggest that the system was murky is an understatement. Controller general Desmarets organized a successful combined system of *rescriptions* with his *caisse Legendre*, guaranteed by the personal credit of the receivers general of all of France (see chapter 4 for details).

Royal Council of Finances (*Conseil Royal des Finances*) – the king always had a financial council. Prior to 1661, the superintendent of finances ran the Financial Council. After the disgrace of Fouquet, Louis XIV chose to abolish the position of superintendent and to establish a Royal Council of Finances (so called because the king himself attended). Both Louis XIV and Louis XV regularly attended this council, but its functions largely devolved upon the controller general, who often presented *faits accomplis* to his colleagues.

secretary of state – officer responsible for administration of a major element of the French state, such as Foreign Affairs. The four secretaries of state had responsibility for War, Foreign Affairs, Paris–Royal Household–Marine, and Huguenot Affairs. In addition to these functional divisions, the secretaries of state also had responsibility for specific geographic regions in France (not contiguous areas, but allocated by *government*). All Royal Council documents sent to the given area had to be countersigned by the relevant secretary of state. In the *pays d'Etats*, the provincial estates made sure to send a substantial '"gratification"'to their secretary of state (and another one to his chief clerk) to make sure that he handled their business in a timely fashion.

secretary of the king (*secrétaire du roi*) – venal office responsible, in theory, for redaction of royal documents. Secretaries of the king did actually draw up (or have their clerks draw up) royal documents, but most men holding this sinecure did not actually participate in the work. They sought out this extremely expensive office (250,000 *livres*) because it gave its occupier full family nobility. Although sword nobles decried the practice, in reality only the very richest commoners could afford to become a secretary of the king. The social mores of the time all but required that anyone with that much power had to be a noble, lest an alternative ruling elite come into being. Thus the office of secretary of the king served to perpetuate the monopoly of noble power, rather than to undermine it, as some have suggested.

seigneur – rural estate owner possessing feudal rights. A *seigneur* (in English, lord) owned a *seigneurie*, a collection of feudal rights over a given area and/or certain individuals. Such rights could include rights of justice (high, middle, and low: high justice gave the right to condemn to death; the others related to more mundane, but often more lucrative, civil and lesser criminal matters), milling or pressing monopolies, market oversight, and a wide range of other feudal rights. Many *seigneurs* also owned *sieuries*.

sieur – rural estate owner not possessing feudal rights. A *sieur* (in English, lord) owned an estate, that is, land, but did not own the feudal rights – such as justice – traditionally attached to a fief. Virtually all members of the robe nobility owned such estates, called *sieuries*. Many sword nobles also owned such estates.

subdelegate – local assistant of the intendant. At first informal commissions, the position of subdelegate became permanent in the eighteenth century. Most subdelegates were royal officials of another kind (such as a treasurer of France or an *élu* or a mayor), as well as holding the commission of subdelegate. Eventually, intendancies had districts called subdelegations.

taille – main direct tax. The original direct tax created in the fourteenth century had the name of *fouage* (from the word *feu* or hearth). In the late fourteenth century and early fifteenth century, its name changed to *taille*, from the verb to cut up or divide. The tax officials divided the *taille* among the *généralités*, then within that district according to *élections*, then within the *élections*, by parish. Within the parish, the parishioners themselves divided and collected the tax. They assessed primarily income from land, but also counted other revenues. In most of northern France, the system was the *taille personnelle*, so called because the personal status of the individual determined his or her eligibility or exemption. Nobles were exempt from the *taille*, as were the bourgeois of privileged towns (like Paris or Lyons); the tenants of such exempt people, however, had to pay the *taille* (the issue of noble "exemption" is discussed in chapters 1 and 3). In southern France – Languedoc, Provence, parts of the Southwest – the system was called the *taille réelle*, because the status of the land itself (which had been fixed in the thirteenth century) determined eligibility and exemption. Nobles owning "commoner" land had to pay the *taille réelle*. The term *tailles* refers to the mass of direct taxes, other than the capitation and later additions. The *tailles* included not only the *taille* itself (the name of one specific tax) but also such taxes as the surtax (*crue*) of 600,000 *livres*, the garrison tax, the mounted constabulary tax, the *taillon* (a special military tax), and the "great surtax" (*grande crue*). A person who had to pay the *taille* was called a *taillable*.

traité – an agreement to collect a certain fee or tax. The king had a wide variety of fees and taxes that he allowed others to collect for him. When he created a new office, for example, the king sold a *traité* to an investor (usually to a group of them), who paid him a fee in advance. He gave them a discount on the overall price (often called a rebate). The investors were the *traitants*.

traites – transit and import–export taxes. The king collected some of these taxes as part of his seigneurial rights but others belonged to taxes voted in the fourteenth century, such as the *traite foraine* (the levy on goods leaving the region in which the king levied the *aides*).

ultramontanism – doctrine supporting the supremacy of the Pope in the Catholic Church. Ultramontanists, like the Jesuits, supported the Pope's argument that he had the final say in all doctrinal matters. Their opponents argued that Church Councils had the final word. In France, the phrase "Church Council" essentially came to mean a Council of the French Church (see Gallicanism).

union des classes – theory that all of the Parlements were part of one

Parlement. This theory received some publicity in the sixteenth century but fell into disuse after the 1580s. The Parlements, particularly that of Paris, revived it in the 1750s. The Parlement of Paris traditionally quarreled with the other Parlements about a wide array of matters (especially jurisdiction); the union of classes enabled the Parlements to develop a united front against the royal government.

vingtième – twentieth, a tax on income introduced in the middle of the eighteenth century. This tax took effect during several wars, notably the War of the Austrian Succession (French participation, 1741–48), only to be abolished after they ended. In 1751, however, the state reintroduced the *vingtième* to help pay the debts of the previous wars. The *vingtième* then became permanent. Unlike the earlier *dixième*, the *vingtième* did not rely on simple declarations of income from the taxpayers. Non-*taillables* had to provide extensive documentation of their income (such as leasing contracts) to justiy their claims about the size of their income. *Taillables* seem to have suffered from the usual situation of having new direct taxes merely added on, as percentage surtaxes, to the *taille*. In time, however, the royal government sought (and obtained) more detailed records about *taillables*. By the 1780s, in many regions, local royal officials demanded land surveys and other detailed records in order to establish the *vingtièmes* of all French taxpayers.

Historical background: the growth of the French state to 1627

On the cover we see Henry IV, the last French king regularly to lead his cavalry charges, at the scene of one of his greatest triumphs, the battle of Arques in 1589. Henry and his forces wear the "modern" attire of light cavalry; his defeated opponents, led by the grandee duke of Mayenne, are dressed as heavily armored medieval knights.

Here we have in a single visual image the traditional version of the evolution of the French state between the sixteenth century and the Revolution: the "modernizing" monarchy overcoming the "feudal," backward nobility. As the painting suggests, some people (often in the pay of the king) promulgated this view as early as 1620 (the time of the painting). Generations of publicists and historians have worked very hard to maintain this image. They have often called this centralizing state the "absolute monarchy," because, they argue, the king's ability to act had no legal barriers. The king did not have to give a reason for his decision; he had merely to state, in the final operative phrase of so many royal documents, "for such is our pleasure."

To these historians, the "absolute monarchy" is an historical stage of statebuilding between the "feudal" monarchy of the Middle Ages and the constitutional governments of the past two centuries. They argue that the "absolute monarchy" attempted, unsuccessfully, to modernize the state. In this absolutist construct, the "bourgeoisie" provided the monarchy with its chief ally against their common main opponent, the nobility. Other historians, notably but not exclusively the Marxists, accept the concept of the absolutist monarchy, but argue that it was merely the recharged and strengthened final stage of the feudal monarchy.

At long last, however, the foundation of this historiographical edifice has begun to crack. In the remainder of this text, there will be virtually no references to the phrase "absolute monarchy": I will state simply here that I believe the prevailing historiographical concept of "absolute monarchy" is a myth, promulgated by the royal government and legitimized by historians. Like most myths, this one has a basis in fact: the

1

Old Regime French monarchy often acted with remarkable arbitrariness, especially in the eighteenth century.

The royal government did try to systematize the state apparatus but our contemporary definition of a "rational" or "modern" state is hopelessly anachronistic when applied to an early modern state. The idea that the nobility opposed the central government, most particularly that it offered an elaborated alternative system of government, one based on an earlier, more "feudal" model, is equally false. In rejecting this argument, I similarly reject the notion that the absolute monarchy was simply a strengthened final stage of the feudal monarchy.

Contemporaries had a simple definition of absolutism: it meant the king had absolute (unlimited) authority to make law. If we want to make the "bourgeoisie" (however defined) the ally of the monarchy against the nobility or if we want to claim that the absolutist monarchy represented the final stage of a feudal monarchy, we will have to bend reality. The state (and society) obviously had feudal elements – the ruling class remained landlords with feudal rights – but the increasing importance of non-feudal forms of property, including simple ownership rights over land, meant that the French state of the seventeenth century had to consider interests broader than those of the feudal nobles. The state also had to attack directly the key interest of the feudal lords by increasing its income from direct taxation, paid overwhelmingly by the tenants of those same landlords. Although the landlords remained the ruling class until the middle of the nineteenth century, the share of the land held by owners who did not possess feudal rights grew steadily in the last two centuries of the monarchy.

One's focus in statebuilding will, to a great extent, determine one's understanding of it. If we focus on the element of the state most controlled by the merchant class, the tax system, we will find a France in which the king seems allied with the merchants against the nobility. If we focus on the military, we will see the same old nobles largely in charge. If we look at the judiciary, we can recognize the compromise worked out with the landed elites, one in which the interests of landlords remained paramount. Royal judges had much closer ties, particularly class-based ties, to other landowning nobles than they did to the mercantile bourgeoisie.

If we cannot accept the idea of the absolutist state and reject the monarchy-against-the-aristocracy model, what then are we considering here? One group of French historians calls this state the "administrative monarchy." As a description of the state institution itself, that makes a great deal of sense; unfortunately, these historians rely on a description of social structure, emphasizing the old "society of orders" model that makes less sense. The French monarchy would seem to have gone through three stages from the thirteenth to the eighteenth centuries. The first stage, lasting until the end of the fifteenth century, might be called the *judicial* monarchy because the king's chief function remained that of judge. Moreover, he judged laws he had not made; in the eyes of contemporaries, he *discovered* the law, he did not make it. His main role thus involved mediating disputes among his subjects, especially his most powerful ones. The Hundred Years' War (1337–1453) did much to undermine this judicial monarchy, because it forced the king to create a whole series of new structures – a permanent army, lasting taxation, a state administration.

The second stage, the *legislative* monarchy, took firm root under Francis I (1515–47). He focused on *making* the law, not discovering it. This stage lasted until the early seventeenth century, when the monarchy's focus shifted to *administering* the law. In that sense, the phrase "administrative monarchy" provides an accurate description of the French state of the seventeenth and eighteenth centuries. That said, we must emphasize that the French state at all three stages of development contained elements of each type of monarchy. Medieval kings made law and they, and their officers, even administered it. Sixteenth-century rulers continued to judge and, increasingly, interfered in what had been local affairs. The Bourbon kings also judged and, of course, issued a wide range of laws. What they and their officials added to the definition of the state, however, went far beyond making law and judging; they actively interfered in more and more aspects of daily life. They made the state a part of everyone's daily existence; that, to me, defines the administrative monarchy.[1]

The French state evolved in clear directions between the early seventeenth century and the late eighteenth century. That state became stronger, in the sense that it could accomplish much more of what it set out to do. Action requires information; the state increasingly gathered (relatively) accurate information about its society. The state became more centralized: initiatives increasingly came from Paris, from one of the great ministries in charge of the administration of the kingdom. The government expanded outside its traditional areas of activity, into those activities we associate with the state. The state administration got much

---

[1] As for the differences between this newly intrusive Bourbon state and its nineteenth- and twentieth-century successors, one can point to several key distinctions, among them: (1) lack of active consent by the governed; (2) lack of a coherent definition of property; and (3) lack of the rule of law, in the sense of laws made by a representative body, as opposed to by the will of an individual. This last distinction should receive special emphasis, because it provides the basis for the original use of the term "absolutism" to describe the Bourbon state.

larger, involving substantial numbers of nobles, lawyers, merchants, and even ordinary farmers and artisans.

Allowing all these changes, however, the state also preserved many of its traditional qualities: it satisfied the needs of elites (still overwhelmingly landlords); it preserved order, above all property; it systematically sought to disempower women and to place them under male authority. This state struggled with the two overlapping social systems of early modern France: France had a society of orders, based on traditional socio-legal classifications, and a society of classes, based on economic activity and wealth.

These two societies often blended seamlessly; the ruling class, the landlords, was also, by and large, the ruling order, the nobility. Those who owned enough land would eventually end up as nobles. In other, fundamental ways, however, the two social paradigms proved irreconcilable. The society of orders rested on families and groups, often organized into corporations (the Church, the nobility, towns, guilds, etc.). That society rested on the fundamental principle that everyone was unequal, in law as well as in social life. The society of classes, however, rested increasingly on individuals, acknowledged as fundamentally equal in certain ways. In the philosophical sense, all men (men only) had reason; in the legal sense, the king sought to treat all French people as equally subject to his law, that is, he regularly sought to overcome or circumvent privileges. Those protected by such privileges (the corporations listed above) viewed them as "liberties."[2] The king thus struggled to preserve inequality and, simultaneously, to establish equality. In its effort to balance these contradictory elements, the French government created the prototype of the modern state.[3]

In order to understand how that state differed from its predecessors, we must begin with a brief summary of the institutional structure of the French state (c. 1625). Rather than introduce each major institution, one at a time, it is easier to provide an overview at the beginning. The study of

[2] When provincial estates or towns sought to have their charters renewed (obligatory at the beginning of each new king's reign because, in this state resting on *personal* ties, the new king was not bound by his predecessor's promises), they invariably requested that the king continue their "rights" (*droits*), franchises, and liberties. When the king wrote back agreeing to their request, he invariably referred to their "privileges."

[3] Before we go on, be forewarned against applying *our* ideas of consistency to Old Regime France; to understand it, one must accept contradictions and inconsistencies, the social and political reality of a system of this *and* that, not this *or* that. Lest we get too self-congratulatory about our rationalism, however, let us remember that our society contains a fundamental contradiction that would have baffled most early modern French people: we believe all people are equal, yet insist that the fruits of social labor should be unequally distributed. For early modern people, the fundamental belief that all people were unequal gave a logic to the empirical reality that some people had more than others.

the historical background will make clear the rational basis of these seemingly irrational institutions, which correspond to the political exigencies of French particularism. Rather than thinking of France as a coherent nation-state, we might do better to consider it a polyglot empire, with a wide range of local institutions adapted to the many local cultures.

The early development of French state institutions

What is the state? How difficult it is for us to imagine a world in which the concept of the state was so ill-defined. The early modern state had three basic attributes: (1) it promulgated and executed laws; (2) it fought wars; and (3) it raised money, primarily to pay for the wars. Many of our contemporary ideas of the responsibilities of the state – such as poor relief, education, or transportation – are anachronistic with respect to early modern states. In early modern France, the Catholic Church ran almost all education and doled out the largest share of poor relief. The king shared responsibility for the transportation system with a bewildering array of local authorities, including provinces, towns, landlords, and village communities. The royal government's efforts to improve that system proved sporadic at best. Military costs and debt service, the latter invariably the repayment of borrowings for earlier military expenses, formed the two largest governmental expenses. We might profitably begin, therefore, with a consideration of the origins of three royal institutions: the judiciary, the army, and the fiscal system.

The judicial system

The Bourbon monarchy inherited a bewildering variety of institutions and customs from the various monarchical configurations that France had taken since the time of Charlemagne. The weak kings of the ninth through eleventh centuries had had to share public power with an ever-widening group of individuals, who later became what we call the feudal nobility. Even in 1789, in the countryside, these people were often the first level of the "state." Several thousand feudal nobles had judicial rights, even extending to the right to condemn people to death (high justice). By the sixteenth century, however, a royal court, usually the local Parlement,* automatically heard on appeal all death sentences, so that only the king's own courts could actually order *and carry out* an execution. The nobles also held other rights that we associate with the state: policing markets, setting weights and measures, judging some land disputes, acting as courts of first (and even second) instance in almost all of the countryside. Seigneurial courts invariably served a peasant clientele.

The feudal nobles and the royal government perpetually quarreled over the precise division of their responsibilities. In the twelfth and thirteenth centuries, the king made a few inroads into the power of these local rulers, most notably in Louis IX's (1226–70) abolition of private wars and of trial by ordeal. The pace of change quickened sharply in the late thirteenth century, as King Philip IV (1285–1314) appointed the first non-clerical chancellor (1295), regularized the meetings of his chief law court, the Parlement of Paris, and instituted the practice of calling representative estates. These steps – secularization of the state, expansion of royal judicial rights, and the use of representative bodies to raise taxes – resembled those taken by other rulers of the time, such as the king of England.

The central state organisms grew out of the king's immediate entourage – the *curia regis** and his personal, household officers. All kings needed professional scribes; the earliest ones came exclusively from the clergy, thus the dual meaning of the French word *clerc*. The head of the king's chapel, the chancellor, therefore became the logical head of his scribes. The chancellor gradually accreted enormous powers and prerogatives. By the sixteenth century, he had become the official head of all royal councils. He also held an immovable office: the king could not remove a chancellor, other than by execution. When a king lost faith in his chancellor, he could only remove the royal seals from the chancellor's hands, giving them instead to a special, temporary official, known as the Keeper of the Seals.*

Just as the position of chancellor grew out of that of head of the king's chapel, so, too, did other important positions grow out of the great household offices, notably those of seneschal (food) and constable (horses). The seneschal eventually came to take over the administration of finances and the constable became the head of the royal army, more particularly of its cavalry. The men holding these positions, as well as the other great barons surrounding the king, formed the core of his itinerant court, the *curia regis*. This court originally focused on mediating disputes: more than half of the surviving charters from Philip Augustus's reign show the *curia regis* merely acting as witness to an agreement worked out by the parties themselves. By the middle of the thirteenth century, however, Louis IX appointed a permanent group of judges, the court began to hold scheduled sessions at Paris, and it kept archival records of its activities (the first of which, the *Olim*, dates from 1248).

By 1300, France had an established royal judicial system, headed by the chief offshoot of the *curia regis*, the Parlement of Paris, whose basic structure the king had laid out only in 1278. The *curia regis* began to divide into increasingly specialized segments after 1300. By the end of the fourteenth century, the king had established five types of sovereign courts: the *Grand Conseil*,* Parlement, the Chamber of Accounts, the Court of Aids, and the Court of Monies.[4] The latter three had specialized responsibilities (further discussed below); the Parlement had broad jurisdictional range, including civil and criminal cases and appeals from even ecclesiastical courts. The great nobility, the peers of France, sat by right in the Parlement and possessed the right to be judged only by it. The *Grand Conseil* judged special appeals and, as we shall see, certain political cases.

In most of France, the king carried out his justice through officials created during the twelfth century: the royal bailiffs or seneschals. They represented the king's authority – military and judicial – and so *executed* the king's will as well as serving as his local judge. This combination of judicial and executive responsibility permeated most French state institutions. Because the king of France had no specifically executive branch of government, no officials charged solely with executing his will (save the later tax collectors), he had always to rely on judicial officials to *execute* the law as well as to judge it.

The great semi-independent duchies and counties (like Burgundy, Brittany, or Flanders) had their own court systems. The local rulers often disputed the jurisdictional rights of the Parlement of Paris and, by extension, the king himself, in their areas. Their court officials tended to have titles similar to those used in France itself – bailiffs in the north, seneschals in the south or in Brittany.

The rapid growth of state power in response to the Hundred Years' War (1337–1453) led to an expansion of the number of royal courts. The kingdom also grew, adding such provinces as Guyenne (1451), Burgundy (1477), Provence (1482), and Brittany (1490–1532). These areas needed royal courts of their own, so the king either created a new Parlement or transformed an existing local court into a Parlement. He followed this practice with most territorial additions, so that provinces (such as Béarn, Artois, or Alsace) added after 1550 usually had a Parlement or other high court of royal justice.[5]

The subordinate jurisdictions also proliferated, to the extent that Henry II (1547–59) created an intermediate body of courts, the presidials,* to ease the burden of appeals to the Parlements. Throughout all but the last few years of the period under consideration here, most of France

---

[4] Because the king rendered sovereign judgments through the *curia regis*, its constituent elements came to be known as the Sovereign Courts.

[5] Under Henry IV, France had Parlements in Paris, Toulouse (created 1443), Grenoble (1453), Bordeaux (1462), Dijon (1477), Rouen (1499), Aix (1501), and Rennes (1554). Later kings added Parlements or similar courts at Pau, Metz, Douai, Besançon, Nancy, Colmar, Bastia, Arras, Dombes, and Perpignan.

had three basic judicial levels: bailiwick* (in the north) or seneschalsy (in the south); presidial; and Parlement. Some towns, notably those in the original Capetian demesne (the Ile-de-France, the Orléanais) and a few others, had a local royal provost, who shared jurisdiction over the town.[6] This pyramid of royal courts existed alongside *and* atop the seigneurial courts (much like the U.S. system of state and federal courts). A court case might start out in the court of a high justiciar, move to appeal in a superior jurisdiction seigneurial court, then to appeal to the bailiwick, thence to the presidial, and, finally, to the Parlement.

Financially, physically, and psychologically exhausted, our poor appellant might consider the case over after the Parlement had dealt with it, but the king's council or a special tribunal appointed by the king might intercede at the last minute. If the case involved a clergyman, he would have filed a countersuit in a religious court: the Catholic Church had a full set of courts of its own, for religious, moral, and, with respect to Church property and personnel, temporal cases. Religious cases often ended up on appeal in the Parlements, under a system called the *appel comme d'abus*. Had our original incident taken place in the woods, one appellant might have gone to the local seigneurial court but the other to the king's court of *Eaux et Forêts** (waters and woods).

Our simple pyramid model is very nice in theory but had little to do with everyday reality. The judicial system of seventeenth- and eighteenth-century France had endless problems of overlapping jurisdictions. In addition to the obvious division between seigneurial and royal courts, the Church had a system of courts, and the king had financial courts, mounted constabulary assizes, *Eaux et Forêts* courts, and a wide variety of special jurisdictions. Most major trading towns had merchants' courts, in which local merchants elected by their peers adjudicated disputes between merchants. Sea-going commerce could involve a merchants' court or the special royal admiralty courts (or both), as well as the regular royal court or courts and even, in rare cases, a seigneurial court. The real court system even included informal courts, such as those set up by guild masters or journeymen. The journeymen would model their proceedings on those of real courts; those punished by their fellows could be banned from a town or even from a trade. Such courts had no legal standing, but their judgments were quite effective.

At the northern city of Amiens in the late seventeenth century, the following courts held sessions:

---

[6] When the king obtained great feudal principalities, he also inherited their administrative systems. Thus in Brittany, the king maintained the provosts of Rennes and Nantes, the two most important Breton towns, which the Breton dukes had always directly administered through a provost rather than a seneschal.

royal judiciary	financial	non-royal
3 provosties	*élus*	municipal court
bailiwick	import–export	merchants' court
presidial	salt tax court	bishop's court
Eaux et Forêts	*bureau des finances*	
constabulary	local Court of Monies	

In some cases (especially financial ones), appellants might also go to the intendant, although he did not officially function as a judge.[7] These courts employed lawyers, clerks, court bailiffs, secretaries, and sergeants. The vast network of people working in the legal field mainly consisted of these small fry; even the judges usually owned a relatively petty office, worth perhaps 5,000 or 10,000 *livres*.* In contrast, an ennobling office, such as that of Parlementaire, would cost between 50,000 and 150,000 *livres*. Even within the judiciary, an enormous social and economic chasm divided the local bailiwick judge and a member of Parlement.

The thicket of jurisdictions, seemingly so absurd, in fact served a very important political purpose: it protected the contracts between the king and members of French society. France had no written constitution and only a few universally accepted constitutional principles. The laws regulating the succession gradually came to be considered fundamental laws: that the oldest legitimate male in direct male line of legitimate issue inherited the throne (the Salic Law); that the king had to be of legitimate birth; and that the king had to be a Catholic (this last accepted only in 1593). In keeping with the tradition of the distinction between king and Crown, constitutional law held that the king could not permanently alienate (sell or give away) the royal demesne, because the person of the king held only its use rights, not full ownership, which belonged to the Crown. Lacking a constitution, French people protected themselves through contracts, most particularly through group contracts. A citizen of Paris, a duke, a Breton – each had the right to trial only in a certain (favorable) court. Imagine the case of a poor Breton salt smuggler, captured on the boundaries of Brittany (where salt was tax free) and Anjou. The Parlement of Brittany would adamantly defend the smuggler's right to be tried in a Breton court, rather than in the special royal salt tax courts in adjoining Anjou. The poor woman (many women smuggled salt because the penalty – a sentence as a rower on the royal

---

[7] The list comes from P. Goubert and D. Roche, *Les Français et l'Ancien Régime* (Paris: Armand Colin, 1984), I, 279; they take it from the classic work of P. Deyon, *Amiens, capitale provinciale. Etude sur la société urbaine au XVIIe siècle* (Paris, The Hague: Mouton, 1967).

galleys – could not be applied to women) could expect much more leniency from the former than the latter.

Accustomed as we are to clear-cut distinctions among the judicial, legislative, and executive branches of government, these early modern French courts appear to be a curious amalgam of all three. Their executive branch responsibilities came about because the medieval king had no other officials to whom he could turn to enforce his decisions; their legislative powers also had medieval roots. Medieval society believed that the king *discovered* the law, so that the royal courts had the traditional function of determining what the (usually unwritten) law was. They faced a simple question: what was the custom of the region?

King Francis I (1515–47) tried to change the king's relationship to the law. First, he actively pursued the redaction of customary laws: once the royally appointed commissions wrote down the law, its limits could be defined and its gaps identified. Second, he promulgated a wide range of new laws and ordinances, such as the ordinance of Villars-Cotterêts (1539), which mandated the use of French in all lay courts. Third, the king and his officials argued that the main function of the king was to *make* the law, not to discover it. Chancellor Michel de l'Hôpital put the matter succinctly to the Parlement in 1561: "[T]he true office of a king . . . is to consider the times and to augment or mitigate the laws accordingly."[8] In 1564, the king even went so far as to change the calendar: the Edict of Paris shifted the first day of the year from Easter to 1 January.

In 1576, the great French political theorist Jean Bodin, in his *Six Books of the Commonwealth*, provided the first coherent theory of undivided sovereignty since Classical times: "the power of giving law to everyone in general and to each in particular."[9] In France, the king held this power, one that, as Bodin said, was "inalienable, indivisible, and perpetual." The king had an *absolute* right to make positive law. This attribute provided the basis of the term absolute monarch; indeed, Francis I was the first king regularly to use the term "absolute power" in royal edicts, standardizing a practice sporadically followed since the days of Charles VII.

In fact, the king's ability to make law had significant theoretical and practical limitations. On the theoretical side, divine and natural laws bound the king. Bodin and almost all others argued that the king had to obey God's law, so that, for example, he had to respect the property rights of his subjects. Many carried that argument to its logical conclusion: the

---

[8] S. Hanley, *The* Lit de Justice *of the Kings of France* (Princeton: Princeton University Press, 1983), 149.

[9] J. Bodin, *Les six livres de la République* (Geneva: Scientia Aalen, 1961; reimpression of Paris edition of 1583), 221.

king could not tax his subjects (that is, take some of their property) without their consent. The royal government, as one might expect, did not subscribe to this interpretation. It respected this principle only in provinces, such as Brittany and Languedoc, in which a contract protected the principle and in which the provincial estates consistently voted the king large sums of money. Even in the provinces without estates, however, the belief that the king could not violate God's law provided an important restriction on his power, in a society so completely imbued with religious values and in a monarchy relying on sacerdotal legitimacy.

Early modern people believed their political (and often social) order had divine sanction. In the wars of the early sixteenth century, nobles openly expressed sentiments about the good death – the duke of la Trémoille "often said that he did not wish to die elsewhere than in a bed of honor, that is, in the service of the king in a just war." The good death came when one died bravely, in battle, in a just war, so that one was "enveloped in good renown and in the love and grace of God."[10] The Wars of Religion undermined the very strong ties between the king and God; first the Protestants and then the radical Catholics argued that the individual had the right to obey his or her conscience, to serve God rather than the king.

The early Bourbon kings worked very hard to reestablish this sacerdotal sanction for their kingship. As in England, these renewed efforts at emphasizing the sacrality of monarchy tended to focus on the monarchy itself, rather than on the larger society of orders; that is, the state stressed the divine sanction for royal rule rather than the divine origins of the social order. The gradual desacralization of the monarchy, beginning in the second half of the seventeenth century and intensifying sharply after 1750 or so, led to the late eighteenth-century cacophony of complaint about absolutism. One could not expect a desacralized monarchy to respect limitations grounded in divine law.

In a practical sense, the king had to promulgate his laws; he did so by means of his court system: Parlements and bailiwicks. These courts, in theory, had no share in the king's lawmaking ability, yet one can easily understand how courts that promulgated the king's laws could just as easily issue executive decisions, *de facto* laws, on their own. Royal courts often had to act on urgent local matters that could not wait until they had written to the king and had a response (a process, we must remember, that for most of France took several weeks). They found royal edicts out of touch with local reality, and sent them back to the king with proposed emendations. In the 1640s and early 1650s, and again under Louis XV,

---

[10] The passages are taken from the memoirs of Louis de la Trémoille, written by Jean Bouchet, *Le panegyric du chevalier sans reproche* (Paris, 1837), 553 and 509.

Parlements often modified royal edicts before registering them, leading to protracted conflicts with the king. The long tradition of courts emending laws or issuing local ordinances eventually led, in the eighteenth century, to arguments that the Parlements shared in lawmaking power. Charles de Secondat, baron of Montesquieu, whose theories of the balance of power among the different branches of government so influenced the US Constitution, was a president of the Parlement of Bordeaux: he believed that the Parlements represented the *legislative* branch of government.

Some judges in these royal courts held legal nobility; collectively, contemporaries called these noble judges the nobility of the robe (*noblesse de robe*).* Because of the overwhelming correlation between function and status in medieval and early modern societies, the traditionally noble function of judge might ennoble its executor (medieval society held the function of judge in such high esteem that most medieval effigies of kings portray the king as a judge). Such ennoblement applied *only* to the highest-ranking judgeships, such as the offices in the Parlements or the Masterships in the Chambers of Accounts. Although the precise mechanism and rules for ennoblement varied from one office to the next (even from one court to the next for the same category of office), by the second half of the seventeenth century, the most common rule for the Parlementaires was that, to achieve full family nobility, the judge had to hold the office for twenty years or more, or die in office. In some provinces, such as Brittany, many sword noble (*noblesse d'épée**) families entered the Parlement, but these tended to be noble families that had previously been active in lesser courts or as lawyers. By the eighteenth century, robe (and some sword) nobles so dominated some Parlements (as in Brittany), that only nobles could sit as judges.

Who were these judges? The common historiographical presentation argues that they came from the "bourgeoisie," that is, mercantile families. Some sons of merchants or financiers did make the meteoric climb to a position in the Parlement, especially in Paris, but most Parlementaires came from families with at least two generations of work in the legal profession. The father of the Parlementaire, if not a Parlementaire himself, invariably owned a judgeship in a lesser royal court; the grandfathers were typically judges or lawyers. Because the richest royal financiers clustered in Paris, more of the Parisian judges came from that family milieu, but they still formed a distinct minority within the Parlement of Paris as a whole.

Royal judges owned land. All of them held the title of *sieur*,* a person who owned an estate that did not have seigneurial rights (such as courts of their own). Some royal judges, particularly the court leaders such as the Presidents or the royal attorneys, also owned *seigneuries*.* In the eighteenth century, at least in Burgundy, some of these higher judges received a title, such as marquis, viscount, or baron. Royal judges shared common economic interests with the sword nobility, in that they received a substantial share of their income from landed property. Judges differed from the purely landowning class in that they also obtained substantial money (usually more than half of their total income) from their offices and from royal annuity payments.

Royal judges received a Classical and legal education in their *collèges*, although relatively few of them actually attended a university. They tended, especially outside Paris, to live in their own closed little world. In provincial cities, they had their own quarter of the city, separate from that of the mercantile elite. Judges often married the daughters and sisters of their colleagues, a pattern that increased during the seventeenth century. At the Parlement of Brittany, equal numbers (about a third) of councilors married daughters or sisters of colleagues and of lower-court judges prior to 1625; between 1625 and 1675, however, more than 57 percent of the judges married within the Court (and only 20 percent married daughters of lesser judges).

Although judges shared with sword nobles their interests as land-owners, they often did not share with the higher echelons of the sword nobility interests related to feudal property. Parlements sought systematically to remove jurisdictional rights from seigneurial courts, which placed them in direct opposition to the old feudal lords.[11] This pattern of a mixture of shared and conflicting interests existed throughout French society, as we shall see. Simplistic models of French society, such as the argument that the king allied with "bourgeois" officers (including the robe nobility) against the nobility, are completely misleading.

The early seventeenth-century French judicial system had four basic elements, including: (1) the extensive overlapping of jurisdictions; (2) the tradition of judging as a noble activity; and (3) the confusion of judicial, legislative, and executive powers in the hands of judges. The judges included men from the highest social groups and small-town lawyers just starting the long social and occupational climb through the system. The fourth curious (to us) and essential characteristic deserves special emphasis: the judges, with rare exceptions (such as the First President or the chief royal attorney – *procureur du roi** – of the Parlements or the chief judge of the bailiwicks), owned their offices. The king could not remove any judge without reimbursing him for his office. Given the king's constant shortage of money, such a course of action was most unlikely.

The judges in the lesser judicial courts usually did not possess nobility,

---

[11] Here remembering that some Parlementaires themselves had seigneurial courts.

yet they too came overwhelmingly from legal families, not mercantile ones. The lesser courts included not only those, like the bailiwicks or presidials, serving the judicial system, but also those, like the *élus* or the *grenetiers* of the salt tax system, that served financial purposes. Officers like the *élus* and the *grenetiers*, while in emphasis overseers of tax collection, in practice also served as judges in the first instance for tax lawsuits. Officials in these tax courts, unlike those in purely judicial ones, had close ties to the mercantile elite.

The military

The military formed the second important governing apparatus. Here again, some elements of the royal army dated back to the Middle Ages. In the twelfth or thirteenth century, the king relied on his feudal militia (*ban et arrière-ban**, the calling up of his vassals and sub-vassals) to do their military service to him. This militia never adequately met the king's needs, a problem that became increasingly acute during the Hundred Years' War. Charles V (1363–80) created the first French standing army, based in the provinces: each province paid for the upkeep of its own soldiers, recruited, in large measure, from the local nobility. This arrangement lapsed after his death, but his grandson, Charles VII (1423–61), reinstituted a standing army of 9,000 men, the *compagnies d'ordonnance*, in 1445.

As in the case of the army of Charles V, the *compagnies d'ordonnance* tended to be stationed in a given province and to recruit heavily from the nobility of that region. The companies were little more than the armed clients of their noble commanders, so that the king often could not rely on the loyalty of his own army. The governors of major provinces each had a company. These governors, who represented the king's person in the area in question, served as the chief military commanders of those regions. They chose all military officers – commanders of fortresses, local royal lieutenants, officers in their company – in their region.

In the sixteenth century, the king often used mercenary troops, especially infantry, to supplement the companies; Henry II created three permanent infantry regiments (those of Picardy, Champagne, and Piedmont) in the middle of the century. By the end of the century, the king had perhaps 20,000 permanent infantrymen as well as 9,000 cavalry. The general population and this army did not get along very well (discussed further below), so that the king created (in the 1550s) a special force, the mounted constabulary (*maréchaussée**) to supervise the interaction between the people and the army. The constabulary soon came to function as a mobile police force. For larger police actions, the king still relied on the old noble militia, which could be quite effective in quelling disturbances. All noble fief holders would be called to a local feudal levy, to help restore order. In Brittany, each bishopric had a designated commander of its noble militia; in most areas, the king relied on the most powerful local noble to call out his clients as the militia. Each sizable town had a civil guard of its own, responsible for order within the town. When the militia or civil guard failed, the king would turn to his final recourse: the army.

Given the size of the country (both geographically and demographically), the France of Henry IV had quite a small military. Most of the royal fortresses and towns had tiny garrisons, commanded by a powerful local noble, serving either as governor of the town or commander of the fortress. The hierarchy of military offices included a general commander of all French forces, the constable, his assistants, the marshals, the colonel-general of the infantry, the admiral, the commanders of the companies, and those of the infantry regiments. The military hierarchy also included governors, their assistants – lieutenants general, some sub-regional lieutenants general, local lieutenants (*lieutenants particuliers*) – town governors, fortress commanders, and the chiefs of the noble militias. The two hierarchies overlapped extensively: governors invariably commanded companies; the top military commanders (the constable and marshals) often held governorships. As in the judiciary, rank and function had a strong correlation: to be a governor, one almost had to be a duke or a prince; to be a local lieutenant or a town governor, one virtually had to be a marquis (or count). Even the commanders of the local militias tended to have a title.

In the 1620s, the king reorganized the military. The *compagnies d'ordonnance* disappeared. The serving constable died in 1626; the king did not replace him. These steps reduced grandee independent power within the royal military but the grandees remained firmly in command at all levels, from the two greatest seventeenth-century French military commanders, the prince of Condé and marshal Turenne, down to regimental commanders. Great nobles maintained the ability to name the officers of their regiments (subject to royal approval) but the regiments never offered them the same freedom of action as the old *compagnies d'ordonnance*. Even within the more restricted regimental structure, the landed nobility continued to share in the king's power by its dominance of the military. Although they (especially at the highest ranks) received considerable amounts of money from the king for their service, many military officers obtained the bulk of their income from an outside source – their landed property.

The financial system

The tax system provided the money to pay for the military and the rest of the state apparatus. The mercantile elite provided the financiers who ran the tax system. The three main elite groups thus each controlled one segment of the governmental triad: the sword nobility ran the army, the legal class (with the robe nobility at its apex) ran the judiciary, and the mercantile elite ran the tax system. Although the financiers came from the mercantile class, royal tax officials rarely engaged in trade because the king forbade the combination of the two activities. On the grand scale, however, a royal monopoly provided the ultimate combination of financial and mercantile activity. The king would grant (to his financial backers) a monopoly on trade with a given region, such as the French colonies in the Americas; French mercantilism was less an economic than fiscal policy.

The permanent fiscal system went back to the 1360s, when Charles V created the basic triumvirate of French taxes: a hearth tax, a salt tax, and a sales tax. The hearth tax, first called a *fouage* and then the *taille,*★ had an intermittent existence from the 1340s until the 1440s, when it became permanent. The king collected the first national hearth taxes, established in the late 1350s and in 1363, in districts called *élections*, because local estates at first elected the person (*élu*★) responsible for oversight of the collection. He soon became an appointed royal official. The state established geographic districts based on ecclesiastical jurisdictions, so that bishoprics became *élections* and the parish became the local unit of collection. As the state grew stronger and its institutions developed a tradition of their own, the government created new *élections* that no longer followed ecclesiastical lines.

Although Charles V abolished the hearth tax on his deathbed, the precedents he established survived: most of the rules he set up lasted until the Revolution and even the terminology persisted, long after its meaning was lost. In the 1360s, Charles V fired the elected general overseers and replaced them with his own officials: henceforth, they took the name of *général* and the section of the kingdom over which they had power took the name of *généralité.*★ While the *général* supervised the collection of the "extraordinary" revenue (i.e., the money from taxation), another official, the treasurer of France, supervised income from the king's demesne.

These broad arrangements lasted until 1789. The *élus* supervised the local district (*élections*); a local receiver, also a royal official, obtained the money from the parish collectors (the parishioners always collected their own direct taxes); a third official, the controller, verified the receiver's accounts. In the early sixteenth century, Francis I expanded the network of *généralités,* so that they became regional districts, supervised by the treasurers-general (whose offices he combined), aided by a regional receiver general. Between 1542 and 1546, he reorganized the entire system, finally forcing these officials to take up residence in their *généralité* and to take responsibility for it alone. When the king later created additional treasurers-general in each *généralité,* the group (known throughout our period as treasurers of France) sitting together took the name of a *bureau des finances.* * The receivers general handled virtually all receipts in the early sixteenth century but they later lost control of the receipts from indirect taxes. By the end of the sixteenth century, the receivers general usually collected only the money from direct taxation and the demesne.

Francis introduced (1523) the last major element of the receiving system, the Central Treasury* (*Epargne*), which superseded the old private, personal treasurer. The Central Treasury became the sole central repository of all money collected in taxes, except for revenue from sales of offices. Francis also institutionalized the previously irregular practice of selling offices; the king himself now organized the sale of almost all judicial and financial offices, collecting a fee during private transfers (and the sale price itself for new or vacant offices); these revenues went to a special treasury created in 1524. Francis and his successors also created a central financial personnel system, starting with a general director and two intendants of finance. Over time, the king created two controllers general* (later reduced to one), six intendants of finance, and a superintendant of finances (1562).

This system grew exponentially in the sixteenth century. In 1520, France had 11 *généraux* and 11 treasurers; by 1620, it had 200 treasurers of France, and by 1640, about 500. The king also created alternative (i.e., serving in alternate years) receivers and controllers in all jurisdictions. In the 1590s, he created triennial receivers and controllers (although the existing two officers often bought and shared the third office). These massive sales of offices tied an ever-larger group of people to the interests of the state as an institution; they also produced substantial revenues.

The number of *élections,* and *élus,* rose dramatically: between 1520 and 1620, up from 78 to 143 and from 120 to 1,200, respectively. As with the judicial system, these officials performed more than one role: the *élus,* for example, also served as judges in the first instance of most tax cases. In cases involving large amounts (and therefore, a member of the elites), the appellants could appeal the *élus'* judgment to a Court of Aids (the most important of which sat in Paris). The *élus* judged without appeal all cases involving small amounts, originally for assessments of under five *livres,* a sum adjusted later for inflation; until 1625, that would have left more than two-thirds of the taxpayers entirely at the mercy of the *élus*. Another group of Sovereign Courts, the Chambers of Accounts, audited the books of all the receivers (of these and other revenues).

The peasants paid almost all of the direct taxes (*tailles*). Nobles and many urban dwellers held theoretical exemptions. The nobles had obtained exemption in the late fourteenth century, on the grounds that they paid the tax "of blood," that is, they served the king in the army. Although many nobles did serve, the exemption included others who did not; the real reason for the exemption was that, in the great conflicts among the town burghers, the peasants, and the nobles between 1355 and 1358, the nobles won. Tax exemption served as their reward. As these conflicts took place essentially in the north, it is not surprising that the exemption for nobles held true only there. In much of the south (Languedoc, Provence), the king raised the *taille réelle*, in which only noble land received tax exemption; in the north, the *taille personnelle* exempted nobles because of their personal status.

Nobles often enjoyed only a partial exemption. Nobles and those urbanites who owned rural estates often indirectly paid these taxes. If the exempt landlord worked his land with servants, he did not have to pay taxes; however, if he used a tenant farmer, such as a sharecropper (*métayer**), the tenant's share of the output was taxable. The available evidence suggests that the landlord often paid part of the tenant's taxes, especially in the case of sharecroppers or allowed him/her to deduct some of the taxes before paying the rent.[12] The exempt landlords therefore had a strong interest in maintaining low direct taxes: (1) because heavy taxes interfered with the ability of their tenants to pay rent; and (2) because the landlord often helped the tenant to pay the taxes.

The king had three other main forms of tax revenue: the salt tax (*gabelle**), sales tax (*aides**), and transit fees (often called *traites**). The *traites* evolved from the king's overlordship rights, but the Estates General of the 1360s had voted the sales and salt taxes. The *gabelle* rested on a royal monopoly of the sale of salt in most of France; certain areas

---

[12]   The argument for this assertion rests on the evidence provided in my book, *The Fiscal Limits of Absolutism* (Berkeley, CA: University of California Press, 1988), and in an article by Philip Hoffman on the Lyonnais. Villages drew up two copies of their tax rolls: one for the *élus* and one for the village collectors. Among the few village tax rolls that survive, most are the royal administration's copy, rather than the copy of the village tax collector. The collector's copy contained the *solvy*, the margin notations of actual payment, together with the name of the payer. In the Lyonnais and in the parish of Dournazac in the Limousin, the landlords paid one-half of the taxes of their sharecroppers. My own sense is that such a system was very widespread, indeed universal, because the sharecropping system split the costs – seed and tithe – between owner and tenant. I believe that tenants could not have paid the taxes on their own, particularly after 1625. Nonetheless, this assertion rests on very fragmentary evidence.

(those that produced their own salt, like Brittany, the Southwest, or the Cotentin peninsula) were exempt or paid special reduced taxes. In the rest of northern France (called for this purpose the *pays des grandes gabelles*), the king had salt warehouses (*greniers★*), staffed by a warehouse manager (*grenetier*), who was watched by a controller. The *grenetier* also heard local-level judicial appeals in most salt tax cases. In most of northern France, each household had to purchase an officially designated minimum amount of salt. In southern France (called the *pays des petites gabelles*), the king levied taxes on salt as it left its region of production; the salt then circulated freely in the region of the *petites gabelles*. The multiplicity of systems encouraged smuggling, which provided a substantial portion of the livelihood of the peasants in several regions of France. In time, the salt tax developed a sort of private army, called the archers of the *gabelle*. The universal detestation of the salt tax led the people to use the epithet *gabeleur* to describe any tax collector.

The sales taxes (*aides*) fell on a relatively limited number of goods; the overwhelming majority of income came from taxes on retail sales of wine (popularly known as *maltôtes*, thus the other typical derogatory name for tax collectors, *maltôteurs*). The state collected transit fees (*traites*) on goods moving inside the kingdom, from one province or region to another, as well as on exports and imports (*douanes★*). The sales and salt taxes existed only in the regions that had been represented at the Estates General of Languedoïl (northern France) meetings in the 1360s; all other provinces – Brittany, Burgundy, Dauphiné, Guyenne, Languedoc, Provence, and the provinces added after 1550 – had special sales and salt taxes of their own.

As with the salt taxes, the sales and import–export duties created ample opportunity for smuggling. At the borders of the region represented at the Estates General of 1360, the king levied import–export duties, even though the regions on the other side such as Brittany or Languedoc belonged to France. These provinces bore the name "the provinces reputed to be foreign." Provinces like Alsace, added during the seventeenth century or later, had yet another tariff system, that of the "provinces effectively foreign." In addition to all these royal taxes, goods in transit had to pay large numbers of transit taxes to towns and to feudal lords. Between Orléans and Nantes on the Loire, for example, boats had to stop more than twenty times to pay local transit fees.

As the list of local courts in Amiens cited above suggests, the king had a wide range of fiscal courts. Three Sovereign Courts dealt with fiscal issues. The Chambers of Accounts audited all royal accounts; after 1600, they also audited all municipal accounts. Receivers had to justify all expenditures with receipts and other supporting documents. Chambers of Accounts also registered royal financial edicts, much the way the Parlements registered legal ordinances. As in the case of the Parlement, the king created regional Chambers of Accounts in major provinces: Normandy, Brittany, Guyenne, Languedoc, Provence, and Burgundy. The Courts of Aids heard tax-related lawsuits; again, the king created several such courts, although they did not exist outside the region in which the king levied the taxes of the 1360s (thus Brittany and other later additions did not have Courts of Aids).[13] The Courts of Aids registered the enumeration of fiefs (*aveu et dénombrement*) required each time the fief changed hands; in those areas without a Court of Aids, such as Brittany or Burgundy, the Chamber registered the enumerations. The Courts of Monies dealt with currency matters, especially counterfeiting. The lesser financial jurisdictions included the *élus* and *bureaux des finances* for direct taxes, the *grenetiers* for salt taxes, and the special courts for transit and import–export duties.

This system, seemingly so complex and illogical, actually provided a very rational adaptation to the practical realities of the early modern state. Brittany, which produced massive quantities of salt, did not pay a salt tax; it would have been too difficult to enforce the monopoly sale. Instead, Brittany paid the heaviest wine taxes in France – wine (except in the bishopric of Nantes) had to be imported. Burgundy, which produced oceans of wine, did not pay many of the wine taxes; instead, it paid especially heavy salt taxes because all its salt had to be imported. In both cases, the king met his primary interest, obtaining the maximum possible revenue from the province and simultaneously allowing the local elite to choose the form of taxation to ensure the easiest possible collection.

The king collected the direct (*tailles*) and indirect (salt, sales, and transit) taxes in different ways. The peasants themselves assessed and collected their parish *tailles*. By the seventeenth century, the king established the principle of solidary constraint: he held the parish as a whole responsible for its total contribution. If one (or several) parishioners could not pay their contribution, the parish had to do it. Royal officials could seize property, except for work implements (plough teams included), to force payment or to sell.[14] The money then moved on to the local receiver, who spent a small portion of it, and to the regional receiver general, who spent a very large portion of it. He passed the remainder onto the Central Treasury accounts, although little cash (perhaps 20 percent of the total collection) moved to Paris.

---

[13] The taxes voted in the 1360s took the collective name of the *aides* (a word later used to describe only the sales taxes), thus the name of the *Cour des Aides*, Court of Aids.

[14] Needless to say, troops sent out to collect taxes often violated these rules and seized work implements.

The king leased out the right (called *parti* or *traité*) to collect the indirect taxes to tax farmers (*partisans* or *traitants*). They paid the king a fixed sum, in return for which they collected the tax in question. In the sixteenth century, the king secured loans from large syndicates of Italian and German bankers (at Lyons) by promising to repay them from the receipts of such taxes. When he defaulted on such promises in 1557–58, the syndicates demanded the right to collect the taxes themselves. From 1560 on, the king steadily centralized such tax farms; by 1605, the state had single units for the northern salt tax, most of the sales taxes (*aides*), and many transit taxes (the Five Great Farms). The king leased these new farms, unlike those of the sixteenth century, to French financiers, so that the main French capital market shifted from Lyons (dominated by Italians) to Paris.

The three elements of the French state gave it solid roots in French society. Each of the three dominant classes – nobility, legal men, and merchants – had an important role in running the state. The military included some 5,000–10,000 nobles; the royal judiciary had about 3,000 legal men holding office; and the financial system involved about 2,500–3,000 people from the merchant class. In each case, the systems had many additional temporary personnel. The military (itself numbering 30,000 men in 1605) could call upon noble militias and town civil guards; the judicial system included the thousands of seigneurial jurisdictions, the many royal sergeants attached to local courts, the thousands of lawyers (solicitors and barristers), and tens of thousands of petty clerks and scriveners; the direct tax system periodically used two, four, or even ten peasants in every parish literally to collect the money; and the indirect tax system (the private tax farmers) hired tens of thousands of clerks, collectors, and archers. If we count all these people as government personnel, the French state of 1620 used something like 150,000 to 200,000 people, or roughly 3 to 4 percent of the adult male population, on at least part-time basis. That said, one must strongly emphasize that in 1620 very few of these people worked as full-time government officials.

Centralization and consolidation, 1596–1627

French judicial and financial institutions grew dramatically in the sixteenth century; the military did not (although changes in weaponry did increase its cost substantially). The king created the presidial courts, added new Parlements and expanded old ones, and exponentially increased the financial apparatus. Many of these judicial and financial officials worked for the state on a daily basis, unlike the military men, who served on a much more irregular basis (the *compagnies d'ordonnance* often existed at full strength only four times a year, at the official pay musters). This unbalanced growth shifted the nature of government; the judiciary and the financial apparatus enabled the king to intervene regularly in everyday life.

Henry III (1574–89) tried to create a more activist state but the civil war, combined with the king's personality, made his reforms generally unsuccessful. His two chief efforts to reform the kingdom came in 1576, at the Estates General,* and in 1583, at an Assembly of Notables.* The recommendations of the Estates General led to the great royal ordinance of Blois (1579), which meticulously reformed many aspects of French institutional life; the political situation prevented its implementation. The king then ordered his treasurers-general to present him with extremely detailed reports about all aspects of the royal government in their généralités; he used these remarkable reports as the basis for the reforming efforts of the Assembly of Notables of 1583. Again, political events forced him to abandon the reforms and even, in 1586, to pursue policies (such as the sale of more offices) specifically condemned by the Assembly. The Assembly of Notables was an extremely important reforming institution; Henry IV and Louis XIII, and Louis XVI after them, all attempted to use it to make fundamental changes in monarchical government.

Henry IV and governmental reform

Henry IV (1589–1610) built on the invaluable precedents of Henry III. He, too, called an Assembly of Notables, which met in 1596–97 at Rouen. The monarchy had gone through its darkest days, the early stages (1589–94) of the League War between Catholic hardliners (the Leaguers) and a coalition of moderate Catholics (the Politiques) and Protestants. Henry IV was a Protestant in 1589; until his abjuration and conversion to Catholicism in 1593, many Catholics refused to accept him as king. He bought off the main leaders of the Catholic League between 1593 and 1596 (the final one, the duke of Mercoeur, in Brittany, gave up only in 1598). By late 1596, Henry IV could set the kingdom on a reformed, stable footing. He spent the next ten years restructuring the state, establishing the basic apparatus we will examine here.

Although France had been mired in a civil war off and on since 1561, there was, in reality, little danger that the state would revert back to a collection of feudal principalities paying only lip service to the king. The struggles among the three great families of the second half of the sixteenth century – Bourbon, Guise, and Montmorency – concerned control of the central government, not its dismemberment. Too many people had too large a stake in that government to allow it to break apart. They had massive clientage networks of people who worked for the government – in the army, the judiciary, and elsewhere. Government money funded these networks.

French ruling elites – nobles, judicial officers, and merchants – desperately wanted stability in 1596. The very nature of the state apparatus, however, helped to destabilize the country. As we have seen, the French military was not really a centralized army, but an amalgamation of units loyal to their commanders. When the king split with a major noble family, such as Guise, their military units could be expected to follow their commander – the duke of Guise or his brother, the duke of Mayenne, or cousin, the duke of Mercoeur. The other two legs of the government stool, the judiciary and the financial bureaucracy, had few sword nobles, but the officers often tended to be clients of the most powerful families in their province. At the Parlement of Rouen, for example, many of the judges were former lawyers of the most powerful local noble families, such as Longueville or Harcourt. Royal officials, for a complex amalgam of religious and political reasons, divided sharply in their support for Henry IV in 1589.[15]

The late 1590s were a time of hope and despair, in France as elsewhere. France and Spain signed the Peace of Vervins in 1598, the same year Henry IV issued his famous Edict of Nantes,* giving legal recognition to French Protestants. This dual peace came at a time of desperation for much of the country: 1597 brought the worst famine in memory in much of western France (as in England). Henry wisely forgave tax arrears for all years up through 1597 and set about the business of putting his house in order.

He had an enormous mess to clean up. Henry had a tenuous line of succession: his immediate heir was a cousin, the prince of Condé. Unhappily married to Marguerite of Valois, the sister of his predecessor, Henry had no legitimate children. He obtained a divorce from Marguerite and soon married Marie de Médicis, niece of the duke of Florence (not coincidentally a man to whom Henry owed vast sums of money). Marie bore him six children, of whom two sons, Louis and Gaston, and three daughters, Elisabeth (married to Philip IV of Spain), Christine (married to the duke of Savoy), and Henriette-Marie (married to Charles I of England), survived to adulthood. Henry also had to reassure royal officers of their positions and investments, regain the confidence of the Catholic Church, satisfy his supporters, and gain over his opponents, particularly among the high nobility.

[15] Research on this issue has demonstrated a confused pattern. Senior officials sided with the king and junior ones with the Catholic League at Dijon and Nantes. Rouen, however, had precisely the opposite pattern and Paris did not follow neatly either pattern.

The country staggered under broad devastation. Commercial activity had declined to two-thirds (or less) of its 1580 level; many areas, such as Burgundy, suffered complete depopulation; the peasants everywhere lived on the verge of starvation, fighting off wolves and wandering bands of furloughed soldiers. Many nobles and royal officers had been forced to pay ruinous ransoms during the civil war and towns and village communities everywhere faced debts of unprecedented magnitude.

Henry fought a brief, successful war in Savoy (1601) but otherwise kept the country at peace from 1598 until his assassination in 1610. These twelve years brought an amazing recovery, one that has ever after preserved for Henry a warm popular memory: he was the "Henri le Grand," the good king, the king who believed in "a chicken in every pot," the only king whose statue the crowd did not tear down in Paris in July 1789. Peace could take much of the credit, but Henry and his ministers, a forceful group, actively set out to strengthen royal government.

An astute politician, Henry moved to satisfy the main desires of all the major constituencies of French society. He converted to Catholicism in 1593, married a devout Catholic, and successfully sought better relations with the Pope. He also reassured Protestants, notably by the Edict of Nantes (1598), which guaranteed them the right to worship in the areas in which they then did so, allowed them their own fortified towns and royally funded garrisons for those towns. The Huguenots also took great comfort in the devout Protestantism of the king's chief councilor, Maximilien de Béthune, duke of Sully.

The king promised huge sums of money to the Catholic League's leaders, such as the dukes of Mayenne and Mercoeur. He paid them gradually, avoiding a sudden burden on the royal treasury and creating a long-term dependence on the king. In the case of Mercoeur, Henry forced the duke to order the marriage of his daughter (and heiress) and Henry's bastard son, César of Vendôme. When Mercoeur died in 1602, Vendôme inherited his father-in-law's liens on his father (and also ended up with the governorship of Brittany). Henry struck hard against the occasional grandee who got out of line, such as Marshal Biron, whom he executed in 1601, or the duke of Bouillon, whom he defeated and disgraced in 1606. After the disastrous anarchy of the civil wars, everyone wanted desperately to avoid disorder of any kind.

Henry also satisfied the demands of the royal officers. He reneged on many of his debts to them, particularly the back interest due on the royal annuities (rentes*), but, in return, he eliminated the greatest danger to hereditary offices by creating the paulette.* Prior to 1604, a royal officer who sold or transferred his office had to survive the transaction by forty days; if he did not, the office reverted to the Crown. Henry promulgated an official table of value of offices and stipulated that the officer had to pay one-sixtieth of that value each year to be exempt from the forty-day clause. In a world in which unexpected sudden deaths were commonplace, the *paulette* answered every officer's prayers. Pierre de l'Estoile, a Parisian bourgeois who kept a journal during the reigns of Henry III and Henry IV, tells us that on the first working day of every January legions of officers would line up in the mud to be the first to pay their annual fee.

The king also obtained another, more long-term benefit. By fixing the official value of the offices, he also fixed the value of their *gages*,* the annual payment that the officer received from the king. *Gages* provided the only "salary" which many of these officers received; they were not really a salary, but the interest the officer received on the capital invested in the office. The institution of iron-clad heredity helped fuel a dramatic price increase in offices (they doubled or tripled in the next twenty years); when the king sold new offices, at these inflated prices, he did not have to pay the *gages* on the amount of the sale price (10 percent for most offices) but the much lesser interest represented by the official price. By 1630, the king saved several million *livres* a year in interest by this policy.

The *paulette* also somewhat undercut the patronage role of the grandees because fewer offices became vacant by death. In contrast to the reduced role of the great nobles in influencing appointments, the role of the royal courts increased. The purchasers of offices in the sovereign courts (Parlements, Chambers of Accounts, *Grand Conseil*, Courts of Aids, and Courts of Monies) had to be accepted by the members of the court before they could effectively hold the office. In the early seventeenth century, these courts became much more independent in such matters, often successfully refusing to seat those who had purchased an office.

Henry reduced the theoretical interest rate on royal annuities to 8.33 percent; he reduced the real interest rate to 4.16 percent by "temporarily" paying them at half value. The royal officers held the lion's share of these annuities but they could take comfort in the fact that Henry actually paid this 4.16 percent, in contrast to the non-payment of annuities from about 1585 to 1598 or even 1600. Henry's actions drastically reduced his capital debt and his interest payments, yet satisfied his officer creditors. In that sense, the *paulette* was the political price Henry paid to reduce his debt burden and a financially astute way to reduce future interest payments.

Henry and the duke of Sully moved quickly to reform abuses in the tax-collecting system and to create a more orderly style of government. Henry sharply reduced direct taxation between 1597 and 1602 and established more effective collection rules in the parishes. Sully combined the many indirect tax farms into larger units (following the precedents of the late sixteenth century) and leased these large units – one each for salt, transit, and sales taxes – to *French* financiers. Indirect taxes did not go up after 1597, but indirect tax revenues jumped dramatically: although Sully's careful administration led to some of the increase, the overwhelming portion of the increase came about simply because of the revival of trade.

Henry and Sully, and their many capable collaborators such as Pomponne de Bellièvre (chancellor), Nicholas de Villeroy (secretary of state*), and Pierre Jeannin, improved many governmental services. Sully, in particular, was a precise, demanding administrator, and his energetic activities led to significant improvements in royal fortifications, in the royal artillery, and in transportation. Sully had an imperious personality and he often made intemperate remarks about abolishing meddlesome and ineffective institutions, such as provincial estates, but his only actual effort to abolish estates came in the Southwest, where they met as separate assemblies for the many tiny *pays* of the region. Some historians view Sully's efforts as a conscious attempt at "modernization," but there is little evidence to suggest he wanted to introduce widespread innovation.

Henry and Sully did, however, increase the power of the central government; they may not have represented "modernization" but they did represent centralization and standardization (although often in very old-fashioned ways, such as Sully's anachronistic accounting techniques). They improved the royal army, stabilized royal finances (including the creation of a cash treasure of five million *livres* in the Bastille), and effectively mediated the conflicting needs of the three major interest groups. All of these people wanted order and Henry gave it to them. The contrast between the peace and prosperity of 1602–10 and the war and misery of the late sixteenth century was obvious to everyone. When Henry died, the kingdom did not dissolve into civil war. Some of the nobles, notably the prince of Condé (the ranking adult royal prince), tried to take advantage of Louis XIII's (1610–43) minority to enhance their role in running the state, but they found few supporters. The royal army remained loyal, as did the overwhelming majority of the nobility. The royal officers held steadfastly with the government; in 1614, when Condé sent letters explaining his reasons for rebellion to the Parlement of Brittany, they forwarded the letters, unopened, to the king's council.

The economic and demographic growth of the period 1602–10 continued after Henry's death. The minor disturbances of 1614 to 1616 caused some highly localized damage, but overall the country remained peaceful and prosperous. In 1617, however, the Protestants became restive, leading to a series of military confrontations of varying intensity, peaking at the unsuccessful royal siege of Montauban in 1621–22. By the mid-1620s, the government had a virtual state of war with the Protestants, culminating at the successful siege of La Rochelle in 1627–28. The king's triumph over the Rochelais and their English allies ended the Protestants' ability to fight a civil war.

Our main story begins precisely here, in the late 1620s, as the French state gathered itself for the coming great struggle with Spain. The insecurity at the center was now over, as Louis XIII reached adulthood. The instability of the teens, with Louis's mother (Marie de Médicis) and a succession of favorites dominating the court, gave way to a firmer order. As the king became more independent, those at court jockeyed for position. Louis and a small group of collaborators murdered Marie's favorite, Concino Concini in 1617; his successor as favorite, the duke de Luynes, also died suddenly (although of natural causes). In the early 1620s, the king tried a series of ministerial changes at the top, as he vainly sought to put his finances and indeed the administration of the kingdom itself in order. These ministerial intrigues and attempted reforms took place within the context of the Protestant problem, which demanded both time and money, and of the steadily worsening international situation. The Dutch and Spanish had resumed their war in 1621 (after a twelve-year truce) and the Habsburg emperor, Ferdinand, defeated one Protestant opponent after another in the German fighting of the Thirty Years' War. The old threat of Habsburg encirclement seemed stronger than ever.

These international concerns overlapped with internal ones. Gradually, two distinct parties took shape: the Devout (*dévot*) party, led by Marie de Médicis and Michel de Marillac, keeper of the seals, and the Good Frenchmen, led by the new royal chief minister, Armand-Jean du Plessis, Cardinal Richelieu. The Devouts believed the king should eradicate Protestantism and then carry out the internal reform of the kingdom. These two policies blended easily together, because the Devouts were perfectly happy to see the Spanish Habsburgs defeat the Dutch Protestants and to see the Austrian Habsburgs stamp out Protestantism in Germany. By keeping France out of these wars, the Devouts could keep taxes down and work earnestly for internal reforms. Richelieu's party, in contrast, believed the Habsburg threat to be the most important one; although Richelieu favored internal reforms, he argued that they would have to wait until the Habsburgs had been defeated. As the outcome of this debate determined French policy through 1659, it is there we shall begin.

1   The crucible, 1620s–1630s

Devouts and Good Frenchmen

Louis XIII decided, in the fall of 1627, that he would personally supervise the critical siege of La Rochelle. He mustered a large army, about 30,000 men, and ordered the nobility of the nearby provinces of Guyenne and Poitou to meet him in front of the city. The governor of Poitou, the duke of la Rochefoucauld, arrived with a contingent of 1,500 mounted nobles; dismounting in front of the king, la Rochefoucauld told Louis that "there is not one of these men who is not my relative."[1] Shortly thereafter, Louis replaced him as governor.

Here, in a single incident, we have a summary of the basic problems facing the French state in the 1620s. The governor of a relatively small province is able, on four days' notice, to raise a private army of 1,500 mounted nobles, all of whom are his client-relatives. La Rochefoucauld's feat was hardly atypical: in 1621, the duke of Epernon, governor of Guyenne, raised a similar number of nobles for a campaign against Béarn; the duke of la Trémoille once raised 3,000 men in 24 hours. The grandees (*grands*) regularly traveled with armed noble entourages of 100 to 300 men; they had military clients throughout their governorships, although the southern provinces tended to have rival factions rather than one coherent clientage network. One can imagine the effect upon the deputies of the estates of Brittany of the arrival of the duke of Rohan and his 150 mounted clients or of the baron of Pontchâteau and his armed 100. In Burgundy, Languedoc, or Provence, the names would have been different (Condé, Montmorency, or d'Alais), but the situation was basically the same.

The purpose of Louis XIII's 1627 call to arms – the siege of La Rochelle – highlights the second great problem of the monarchy in the 1620s: the civil war with the Protestants. France suffered through a long

---

[1] Y.-M. Bercé, *Histoire des Croquants* (Paris, Geneva: Librairie Droz, 1974; available in English as *Peasant Rebellions*, Ithaca, NY: Cornell University Press, 1989), 120. The word "relative" here would mean related either by blood or by marriage.

(1561–98) religious civil war before the Edict of Nantes established some religious toleration. After the death of Henry IV (1610), the personal commitment of Marie de Médicis and of Louis XIII himself to Catholicism led to greater pressure on the Protestants, culminating in the royal declaration of 1617 that Protestant Béarn had to allow once again the practice of Catholicism. When the province resisted, Louis XIII marched an army to Pau (1620) to enforce his edict. In 1621, the king attacked another Huguenot stronghold, Montauban, but he could not take the city. The off-and-on civil war continued until 1627, when the king decided to put an end to the Protestant "state within a state" by making an example of La Rochelle.

La Rochelle ranked fourth among the French Atlantic ports, after Bordeaux, Nantes, and Rouen–Le Havre. It had extensive ties to Holland and to England, the two main Protestant powers, and broad trading privileges, including exemption from several import–export duties. La Rochelle held one of the 150 royally funded Protestant town garrisons. Nationwide, the Huguenots formed a fairly small minority – typical estimates are 10 percent of the population – but a majority of them lived in the Southwest. By taking La Rochelle, the king could cut off French Protestants from any hope of outside (notably English) aid. The fall of La Rochelle would mean the end of Huguenot independence.

The siege became a matter of international politics. The defeat of the English army at Fort Louis, the withdrawal of one English fleet, and the failure of a second to destroy the vast breakwater that Cardinal Richelieu had constructed at the entrance to the city's harbor, led to La Rochelle's fall in 1628. The city lost all its fortifications and privileges, but retained the right to public Protestant worship. The king reinstated Catholic worship, in a mass celebrated by Cardinal Richelieu himself. Although the internal problem seemed to have doctrinal clarity – Catholics versus Protestants – its international ramifications transcended denominational lines: the Calvinist Dutch sent a fleet to assist their ally, Louis XIII, not the Huguenots. The devoutly Catholic Spanish offered assistance to the Protestant duke of Rohan, who was fighting a group of royal armies in Languedoc. Richelieu was certainly not the only political leader of his day who allowed reason of state to overcome religious scruples.

The siege of La Rochelle, itself a critical event in the evolution of the French state, and the broader contest against the Protestants of which it formed a part, made up only one element in the much larger reconfiguration of the state and the government. More than fifty years ago, the great French historian Georges Pagès drew our attention to the late 1620s and early 1630s as a decisive moment in the *evolution* of the French monarchy. Recent scholarship has done much to confirm and expand Pagès's pioneering insights, although historians are sharply divided about the extent (and timing) of any substantive changes in the nature of the monarchy.

What sort of changes took place in the 1620s and 1630s? Did they alter the dynamic between French society and the state? What was the nature of French society? Did social changes mandate a new state structure? Let us begin with a brief description of the structures of French society, and work our way up to the state built upon them. The great debate of the late 1620s concerned whether to keep peace with the Habsburgs and focus on internal reforms, the position of the Devout party, or to focus on the international rivalry with the Habsburgs, the policy of the *Bons Français* (literally, Good Frenchmen). To make sense of that debate, and of the evolution of the French state, we need first to establish the broad outlines of French society in the early seventeenth century.

Early modern French society

The France of the 1620s covered much less territory than contemporary France. Its eastern boundaries stood much further west: Alsace still lay in the Holy Roman Empire; much of Savoy (and the county of Nice) were in Italian states; the Franche-Comté and the Charolais belonged to the king of Spain (as heir to the dukes of Burgundy); Lorraine, ruled by an independent duke, had an ambiguous legal status between France and the Holy Roman Empire; parts of French Flanders and Artois belonged to the Spanish Netherlands; the Perpignan and Cerdagne regions still formed part of Spain; the Pope and the prince of Orange owned enclaves in southern France (see map 1.1). The king of Spain ruled territories on three sides of France: Spain in the south; Milan and the Franche-Comté in the east; and the Spanish Netherlands (modern-day Belgium) in the north. His cousin, the Holy Roman Emperor, was titular ruler of most of France's eastern borderlands and the largest landowner in southern Alsace. The sixteenth-century Habsburg threat of encirclement remained in place in the early seventeenth century.

This truncated France had a population of some 18 million people in the 1620s; roughly 80 percent of these people lived in the countryside.[2] Paris had about 400,000 people; Lyons and Rouen over 75,000 each; Marseilles, Nantes, Rennes, and Bordeaux had 40,000 or more each. A third group of cities, places such as Angers, Amiens, Saint-Malo, Tours, Nîmes, Orléans, Dijon, Grenoble, Toulouse, Arles, Montpellier, and

---

[2] The 1994 borders of France held about 20 million people in the 1620s; roughly 2 million of them would have lived in Alsace, Flanders, the Franche-Comté, and other regions not part of the kingdom then.

Narbonne, each had 20,000–30,000 people. The country had a vast nesting of smaller towns, most of which held 7,500 to 10,000 inhabitants, but some of which had as few as 2,500 people. Although we might consider such a town to be quite small, in early modern Europe a town of 5,000 or 10,000 people was an important urban center. In France, such a town invariably had a royal court (even a presidial) and its economic tentacles reached deep into the surrounding countryside. Many villages had a semi-urban center, with artisans, lawyers, and even a school.

Historians often describe early modern France as a "stable, sedentary society" and as essentially rural, but one must consider the extent of urban influence in the countryside. Part of that influence destabilized the villages by attracting young people to the towns. This France was two societies, co-existing in a precarious, even frightening balance. The first society, the stable sedentary one, included the ploughmen, *métayers*, and landlords of the villages, and the merchants, legal people, and some shopkeepers and artisans in the towns. The artisans and shopkeepers lay at the margins of the stable society; they invariably referred to themselves as *gens de bien* (the worthy people) but elites did not so view them. The phrase *gens de bien* captures the wonderful ambiguity of social definitions in early modern France; it literally means the good or worthy people, yet *biens*, the plural of *bien*, means goods, as it does in English. The *gens de bien* were also those with property.

The second society, the unstable, volatile, mobile one, included the day laborers and small farmers of the villages and the wage laborers and some artisans (even shopkeepers) of the towns. Artisan masters and shopkeepers usually stood with the forces of order, defending their property (and the system that protected it). When they turned against the system, as happened periodically, local order usually collapsed. Two key variables, age and marital status, helped to define the boundaries between the two societies. Virtually all lay members of the stable society were married. The mobile people – many day laborers and journeymen – often were not. These day laborers and journeymen also tended to be younger than the members of the stable society.

The distinction married/unmarried was a vital one in early modern France, revolving as it did around male control of women. The enhanced efforts of men to subordinate women formed one of the most important elements of a specifically early modern European society. The state made strenuous efforts to expand the powers of fathers over their daughters, particularly with respect to marriage. Family disputes over marriages led to extensive use of one of the most odious of the abuses of the Old Regime, the arbitrary order of arrest (*lettre de cachet**). Fathers used *lettres de cachet* to imprison (in a convent) recalcitrant daughters; husbands used

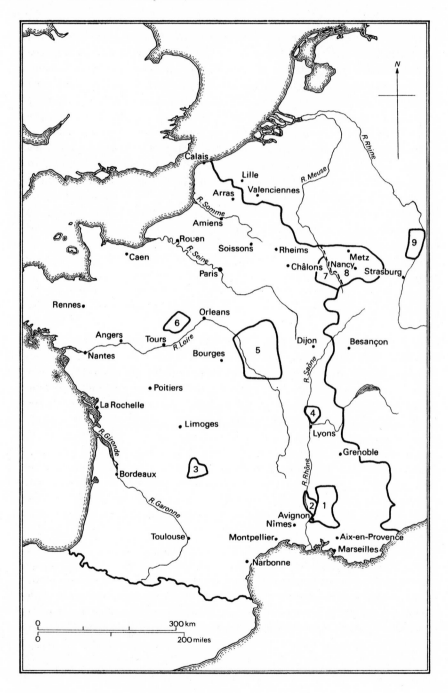

them to discipline "disobedient" wives.[3] Authorities singled out women for repression, but they had other targets as well. To a very large degree, these efforts at repression took place to preserve order, that is, to preserve the officially accepted version of how society was supposed to function. Male social elites viewed women as particularly disorderly, in part because of contemporary beliefs about female physiognomy, but disorder provided a threat to society no matter what its source. It could be a robe noble trying to become a sword noble or a peasant woman trying to marry a young man from outside her village: in either case, society had a battery of institutions and practices to prevent such "disorder." Movement of any kind, social or geographic, had to be prevented. In 1618, the king

[3] Families also used the *lettres de cachet* against sons, nobles used them against dunning merchants; in short, those in power used them to force others to do their will. In some cases, the king even sold such letters. The *cahiers de doléances*★ widely decried their existence.

Map 1.1   France in the middle of the seventeenth century: 1. Avignon and the Comtat Venaissin: property of the papacy. Periodically occupied by French troops but not permanently annexed to France until 1791; 2. County of Orange: property of the House of Nassau-Orange, *stadhouders* of the Netherlands. Ceded to France at Peace of Utrecht (1713); 3. Viscounty of Turenne: enclave belonged to the La Tour d'Auvergne family. Legally part of France, but exempt from some elements of royal jurisdiction. Inhabitants did not pay royal taxes. Annexed to France in 1733; 4. Principality of Dombes: owned by the Bourbon-Montpensier family. Under authority of the king, but legally separate from the kingdom. Annexed to France in 1762; 5. Duchy of Nivernais: property of duke of Nevers. Subject to jurisdiction of king; annexed to royal demesne under Louis XIV; 6. Duchy of Vendôme: royal appanage created for Henry IV's natural son, César of Vendôme. Legally part of France, but revenues and jurisdiction held by duke of Vendôme. Returned to royal demesne under Louis XIV; 7. Duchy of Bar: belonged to duke of Lorraine; in 1643, under occupation by French troops; 8. Occupied portion of duchy of Lorraine, owned by duke of Lorraine. Like Bar, occupied by French troops in 1643, thus the French cartographer considered it to have been part of France at that time, although it legally was not. The legal boundary of France, indicated by the broken/dotted line on the map, followed the Meuse River, with the exception of three enclaves around the cities of Metz, Toul, and Verdun; 9. Philippsburg enclave on the Rhine: France frequently occupied this small region as part of peace agreements (such as the Peace of Westphalia). The fortress of Philippsburg provided an early line of defense and a staging point for attacks into Germany. France had no real claims to sovereignty in this area. The city of Arras, shown as French on the map, legally belonged to the Spanish Netherlands; it had been captured by the French army in 1640, thus the cartographer's insistence on its inclusion within the France of 1643. The same is true for Roussillon and Cerdagne, on the Spanish border, not legally French until 1659. Source: Rizzi-Zannoni, *Atlas historique de la France Ancienne et Moderne* (Paris: Desnos, 1766), plate 27: "Tableau de la France sous Louis XIII."

ordered all recent immigrants to towns to register with town authorities because the newcomers "could engender and bring an alteration in the amity, concord, society, and good morals prevailing among the ancient inhabitants of the said towns." The newcomers had to provide evidence of their life, morals, and condition: that is, they had to show that they had a trade with which to earn a living and that they had an upstanding moral character.

Michel Foucault has called the seventeenth century the age of the "Great Confinement," a phrase that aptly describes the mentality behind elite responses to the poor (although we should not overestimate the practical extent of the actual confinement, which was rather limited). Early in the century, town governments and royal courts tried to regulate charity, limiting relief to the "genuine" poor. They recognized that "everyone wishes to give charity to the good and genuine poor but not to contribute to the disorders which always accompany begging." Later, society and the state took a progressively harsher view toward the poor and the mobile. The poor needed relief, yes, but they also needed supervision and control. "The work was divided into two categories: the business of social control, in the sense of the supervision and training of the able-bodied poor, and charity pure and simple, such as the care of the sick and the obviously helpless. The former became the preserve of men, the latter of women."[4] The poor would be set to work: at Rennes, in 1659, the Parlement mandated the creation of new hospitals to teach orphans and "genuine poor" a trade; the hospital would also have priests to provide the poor with religious instruction. Such supervision extended to the most minute of activities in towns, the seats of state activity. Royal (and urban) ordinances barred artisans from playing games during work hours: the provost of Nantes fulminated against the artisans and crafts-men of the city, who "passed most working days in cabarets, playing and getting drunk, instead of working, each at his trade, to make his living and serve the public." Authorities also closed taverns during church services in workers" districts, forced families to send children to school (and to learn a trade), forbade public dances (as "scandalous and dissolute"), outlawed charivaris, and exiled beggars, the unemployed, and prosti-tutes, the latter generally called "debauched and scandalous women of ill life." All levels of government struggled with their dual perception of such people, particularly women, as evil threats to society yet as objects of charitable pity.

These people lived at the margins of the idealized polity known as the society of orders. Everyone had a place and knew it; the trick was to get

[4] E. Rapley, *The Dévotes. Women and Church in Seventeenth-Century France* (Montreal: McGill-Queen's University Press, 1990), 77.

them to accept it. At its simplest, the society of orders divided people into three groups: the clergy (the first estate or order); the nobility (the second); and everyone else. This ancient Indo-European division of society into prayers, fighters, and workers became an important part of the French ideology of social polity in the eleventh century. This simplistic view of society evolved into a much more sophisticated and elaborated system of orders, but even the elaborate version maintained the fiction of the three orders. The Estates General of France (which sat in 1560, 1576, 1588, and 1614) met in three estates: clergy, nobility, and others. Lest we make too much of such distinctions, however, it should be emphasized that the provincial estates (in Brittany, Burgundy, etc.), which met regularly, did not meet precisely in this way. These estates followed the medieval practice of representation in three estates, in which the Third Estate did not represent "everyone else" but only the towns. In Brittany, in Burgundy, and in Languedoc, only certain specified towns had the right to send deputies to the estates. In these provinces, the peasants' sole representatives were their lay and ecclesiastical landlords, who attended by virtue of corporate right. In the south, however, the peasants often sent syndics to the estates (in Guyenne, Provence, and Dauphiné).

Each official order had profound internal divisions. The clergy was not a monolithic external force in French society. Its members had deep personal and social ties to other groups. Within the clergy itself, violent disputes divided the regular clergy (the monks and friars) and the secular clergy (the parish priests). The most violent contest pitted the Jesuits against the parish clergy, with the former arguing that parishioners could confess to them, and hear Mass and receive communion and all sacraments from them, rather than exclusively from their parish curé.[5] The loss of exclusivity posed a three-fold threat to parish priests: (1) it attacked their sense of the established order of things; (2) it attacked their sense of personal honor; and (3) it cost them money. The parish clergy and the monasteries each quarreled with the bishops, who in turn often fought with their cathedral chapters. Bishops generally came from noble families (both sword and robe); cathedral canons belonged to law/judicial families; parish priests often came from artisanal or petty merchant families. These lower levels of the clergy had little to say about religious affairs; at the Estates General of 1614, only one parish priest sat as a

---

[5] A designated individual – the *curé*, often selected by a bishop or by a noble parish patron – held the official "cure" of souls in a given parish. (The English term would be vicar.) The *curé* often had other assistant priests; in many cases, the chief among them, the *vicaire* (in English, curate; thus the obvious avoidance of the English terms in the text), performed the functions of "parish priest." Thus the *curé* was the official parish priest, but he was often not the parish priest in the literal sense of performing the priestly duties.

deputy for the First Estate. Bishops, abbots, and cathedral canons invariably represented the clergy at the various provincial estates and they dominated the periodic (every fifth year) national Assemblies of the Clergy. These Assemblies provided a venue to discuss doctrinal and political issues of interest to the clergy; they also voted the king an annual grant, the free gift (*don gratuit*) – the price of the continuing Church exemption from taxes.

In addition to these quarrels about matters of personal pride and income, the French clergy also had significant doctrinal and political divisions. France did not immediately adopt decrees of the Catholic Council of Trent (1559), which crystallized Catholic doctrine on the key issues raised by the Protestants. The Council reaffirmed the doctrine of justification by faith and by works, the efficacy of grace for works, the role of the institutional Church as intermediary between God and humans, the traditional seven sacraments, transsubstantiation, the special place of Mary in Catholic worship, and the magisterium of the Church.[6] Trent also sought to reform abuses within the Church and to improve its administrative practices. The Council mandated the keeping of parish registers (baptisms, marriages, burials) and sought to improve the education of parish clergy.

The Catholic Counter Reformation began to take root in France in the 1580s but did not really flower until the early seventeenth century (Assembly of 1611). The rise of the Devout party at Court coincided with greater religious fervor and a more demonstrative piety among religious people throughout France. Queen Mother Marie de Médicis, an Italian, led the Devout party, strengthening the connection between ultramontanism* and French politics. The opponents of the Devouts, the Good Frenchmen, obviously suspected the political motives of the religious reforms proposed by the Devouts. As "good" Frenchmen, they strongly supported the Gallican* tradition of French Catholicism, a tradition that worked against the acceptance of the Tridentine reforms.

The Jesuits, a Spanish order owing unquestioned obedience to their superiors and to the Pope (to whom they took a special oath of obedience), represented the most vivid challenge to Gallicanism. In the early seventeenth century, the Jesuits established *collèges* (preparatory schools) in many French towns, schools to which many elite families sent their children to get the best secondary education of the day. The kings had a

---

[6] Mainstream Protestants disagreed with Tridentine Catholicism on all these points. Protestants believed in justification by faith alone, in the direct connection between God and humans, and in fewer sacraments (usually two). They rejected transsubstantiation (disagreeing on what to put in its place), free will, and the special status of Mary. Many Protestant churches also rejected the saints. All rejected the magisterium of the Church, arguing instead that all doctrine had to come directly from Scripture.

series of Jesuits as private confessors, beginning with Pierre Coton, confessor of Henry IV and, later, of Louis XIII. The Jesuits usually stood for enhanced royal power; the ostentatious architecture of their churches mirrored an affinity for unambiguous manifestations of centralized power. Many monarchs, from Sigismund Vasa in Poland to Ferdinand II in Austria to Louis XIII in France, found such views attractive.

The renewed emphasis on spirituality and a more rigorous religion could, however, lead in other directions. In France as in other countries, among Protestants, Catholics, and Jews, the religious revival of the early seventeenth century often took the form of a movement toward intense personal piety and rigorous morality (Puritanism is one example among many). Some French theologians, notably the Augustinians (who dominated the Sorbonne), objected to the new Tridentine elements in Catholic theology, formulated by Jesuits such as Luis Molina. The practical rivalry between Augustinians and Dominicans, and Jesuits had theological parallels; in France, the key figure in the dispute was Corneille Jansen, briefly bishop of Ypres, a professor of theology at Louvain, and author of a violently anti-French pamphlet, *Mars gallicus* (1635), assailing the position of France and its Protestant allies on the eve of open French participation in the Thirty Years' War. This pamphlet likely had some role in the ongoing governmental perception (passed from Richelieu to Mazarin to Louis XIV to Fleury and Louis XV) that Jansenism posed a political, as well as religious threat to France.

Jansen and his followers, known as Jansenists, followed the Augustinian line rejected by the Jesuits. Jansenists, like Calvinists, believed in predestination and in what they called efficacious grace, the doctrine that God freely granted some the grace to effect their salvation yet denied that grace to others. Unlike Calvinists (and other Protestants), Jansenists clung to the Catholic doctrine of justification (salvation) by a combination of faith and good works. They therefore actively tried to carry out good works, in part by reforming the morality of others. Their intense moralism and emphasis on inward piety made them an easy target of ridicule, as anyone who has read Molière's *Tartuffe* can attest. Given their opposition to Jesuit theology, Jansenists naturally gravitated, in a political sense, toward those who supported Gallicanism, although the connection did not become a strong one until much later.

The Second Estate had similar internal divisions. The main demarcation lay along the line that split the grandees from ordinary nobles, but the levels of gradation within the nobility marked considerable differences in function, in income, and in power. At the top, the princes of the royal blood, such as the Condé family, and the duke–peers (great feudatories such as Rohan or Montmorency, lines descended from royal bastards, and certain foreign princes such as the duke of Lorraine) dominated the major military offices of the kingdom and maintained vast networks of clients. Beneath them, we find brokers, themselves clients of the grandees but patrons to their social subordinates. Noble titles – duke–peer, duke, marquis, count, viscount, baron, *chevalier*,* *écuyer** – descended to the level of humble rural squires, who often had little more income than neighboring ploughmen.[7] The capitation rates of 1695 (see chapter 3) give some idea of the enormous spread in wealth among these people: dukes paid 1,500 *livres* a year, whereas simple *écuyers* who did not possess a fief had to pay only 6 *livres*.

The grandees deserve special attention because of their dominance of the Second Estate. These great nobles had genuinely national interests, in part because they often owned large estates in different areas of the kingdom. A family such as Montmorency owned land in Languedoc (the family governorship), Brittany, Normandy, and elsewhere. The Condé family had estates everywhere in France – in Brittany, in Provence, in Picardy, in Berry, and in Burgundy. The Montpensier family, whose last heiress married Gaston of Orléans, possessed estates in the Auvergne, Poitou, Burgundy, Champagne, French Flanders, and in Normandy (where it held the county of Eu and the duchy of Aumale). These great families often held massive seigneuries, such as the duchy of Rohan in Brittany, which had seigneurial jurisdiction over more than 100 villages; indeed, the judgments of lesser seigneurial courts, even those of high justiciars, had to be appealed to his court. One branch of the Rohan family conducted marriage negotiations with the king of Sweden, who considered marrying his daughter to a Rohan. France had a small number of such great families; even if we consider those of somewhat lesser stature, their number likely did not exceed 250. In a political sense, these 250 families were the nobility.

The nobility of the robe straddled the line between the Second and Third Estates. At the Estates General of 1614, after a bitter dispute, the men of the robe had to sit with the Third; in 1789, everyone assumed they would sit with the Second (they did). The change alerts us to the increase in status of such people but should not obscure their importance in 1614. They, too, had a hierarchy. At the top, we see the Presidents of the Sovereign Courts, followed by the councilors of the Parlements, the Masters of Accounts, and the lieutenants general and seneschals of the lower courts.

The hierarchy of offices descended steadily from there, to positions such as king's attorney in some forgotten backwater bailiwick. The

---

[7] In France, below the level of duke, titles had no official hierarchy. See chapter 4 for further details.

patient vigils of Etienne Borrelly, a lawyer in the episcopal courts of Nîmes, for the newly appointed bishops of Nîmes – in one case including hiring a boat in order to deliver a flowery welcome speech to the bishop as he crossed the Rhône on his inaugural visit to Languedoc – led to his successful career as secretary-clerk of the bishopric. Borrelly never traveled further than Montpellier (and that at age 45!); he was literally dazzled merely to have seen the governor's wife, the marquise of Verneuil, sitting at the bishop's table.[8]

Borrelly, and thousands of small-fry commoners like him, provided the foot soldiers for the judicial ruling hierarchy. Nobles sat at the top of this hierarchy; by the middle of the seventeenth century, everyone accepted that fact (although many old nobles did not like it, and did not consider this nobility to be true nobility). Those at the bottom of the scale, like Borrelly, were, by general consent (and by law), commoners.

They lead us into the social vastness of the Third Estate, which included more than 95 percent of the population. The Third Estate included these lower-level officials and lawyers, merchants, shopkeepers, artisans, ploughmen, farmers, day laborers, and others less easily classified. In reality, these people, too, organized themselves into *corps*, literally bodies, which fought for privileges and recognition in the social hierarchy. This social hierarchy was a vital and tangible one; in the towns, parades followed strictly hierarchical marching orders. People fought (and killed) over the place of their *corps* in the parade. The craftsperson who belonged to the *corps* of his or her trade often belonged to its confraternity (lay religious group) as well; one of the chief functions of that confraternity was to bury its members. Even in death, one belonged to one's *corps*.

In the countryside, the Third Estate had four basic groups: day laborers, small farmers (*manouvriers*), ploughmen (*laboureurs*), and estate owners. In any given village, half of the taxpayers had no land, either rented or owned. Above them sat the small farmers, who rented a few acres, not enough to support themselves, but who also sold their labor (the man and woman) or its products (the woman). At the top of the peasant hierarchy sat the ploughmen, often called the *coqs du village*, the cocks of the walk. These peasant had a plough team (often leased from an estate owner), owned a small bit of land, and rented the estates of the various local landlords (often as *métayers*). At the tiny apex of village society came the estate owners themselves, who could be members of any of the three estates. The closer the village lay to a town, the more likely it was that townspeople, especially lawyers or notaries, owned the land.

[8] W. Beik, *Absolutism and Society in Seventeenth-Century France: State Power and Provincial Aristocracy in Languedoc* (Cambridge: Cambridge University Press, 1985), 54–55.

The social groups could be organized into classes, starting with those who sold their labor. These people tended to be young (between 15 and 30), unmarried, and mobile. Some of the men were learning a craft, first as an apprentice, then as a journeyman. Above them, we would find the small farmers and then the ploughmen in the countryside, the small artisans and shopkeepers, followed by the merchants, in the towns. French society had a fairly sharp demarcation line between merchants and artisans: artisans sold goods they had made; merchants sold goods made by others. Very few people crossed over this line.

As for the urban women, the young, single ones would be servants, regraters, spinners, or laundresses; they married in hopes of running a shop or a small business. Much like the contemporary French *boulangerie*, these shops usually had a man in the rear, producing the goods, and a woman in front, selling them and keeping the books.

In the countryside, the social structure had a similar reliance on age and marital status. Day laborers were usually young and unmarried (under 25); small farmers were married (it was all but impossible for single men to rent farms) and often just starting off, people in their late 20s or 30s; ploughmen were typically older, in their 40s, with much larger households (including servants and older children). Most villages had dynasties of ploughmen, yet young couples could aspire to a rise from day laborers, to small farmers, to ploughman and wife. The women followed an employment history quite similar to that of men: starting as servants in their late teens, marrying around age 25 (men about 28 to 30) to set up a small farm, and, if successful, getting one of the village's large tenancies by age 40 to 45.

At the top of the rural hierarchy stood the estate owners.[9] Some of these owners, the seigneurs, held feudal rights; others did not. Many wealthy landowners held a mixture of *seigneuries* and *sieuries* but social climbers usually owned only the latter.[10] In the seventeenth century, the French countryside began to shift slowly toward what we might call agrarian

[9] I am here using the term estate owners to distinguish them from all landowners; after all, many peasants owned a small plot of land. In theory, France had three types of estates: *seigneuries*, estates with feudal rights attached; *sieuries*, estates without feudal rights; and *allods*, estates of any size in the (southern) regions, which lay outside the feudal system. In northern France, the maxim of the law held "no land without lord"; in southern France, the customary law ruled "no lord without title."

[10] Terminology varied in different parts of France. In some areas, a *laboureur* was a day laborer, not a ploughman; in most regions, however, the term did mean ploughman. I have used it throughout in that sense. Similarly, as noted earlier, the term seigneur everywhere applied to a landlord with feudal rights. The French had another term, *sieur*, which also meant landlord; almost all theorists of the time, such as Charles Loyseau, used the term *sieur* to refer to an estate owner who did *not* have feudal rights. In keeping with the particularism of French society, however, in some areas a *sieur* might well be a feudal lord.

capitalism.[11] Even on seigneurial estates, the chief form of income tended to be land rent, rather than feudal dues. Everywhere, the portion of feudal dues declined as a share of income (and seigneurial courts declined in importance, especially after 1650 – see chapter 3).

The nature of rent tended to shift. In many areas, tenants paid a fixed amount of in-kind rent in the sixteenth century; in the seventeenth century, however, they increasingly paid a share (usually half) of the crop (after deduction of expenses such as seed, tithe, and taxes). After 1600, estate owners demanded fixed cash renewal payments; these payments grew substantially in size in the early seventeenth century. In the eighteenth century, more and more estate owners shifted entirely to cash rent. All estate owners shared common interests related to land rent income (interests such as keeping direct taxes low, because their tenants paid the taxes); some estate owners also had another layer of interest, related to feudal property. In many cases, non-feudal and feudal estate owners had conflicting interests, because the non-feudal estate owners had financial obligations to their feudal overlords, who possessed eminent domain rights over the land.

Urban elites often used the purchase of rural estates as part of their process of social climbing. Here again we can see sharp differences between the sixteenth and seventeenth centuries. Before 1600, merchant families often moved directly into royal courts; the merchant's son could buy an office in a Chamber of Accounts or even, on occasion, a Parlement. After 1600, however, the mechanism for social mobility at the highest levels of the robe slowed down. Families would send their sons to a *collège* to get the rudiments of a Classical and legal education. The family would also buy a rural estate. The son might then become a lawyer or perhaps buy a very petty royal office. His son might style himself *sieur* of "X" and would buy a more prestigious office. In some towns, he would seek an office of alderman, which carried the hereditary privilege for nobility in many large cities, such as Angers or Nantes.[12] Two or three generations of royal office, each one more exalted than the last, would lead to eventual transferral of all the family's wealth into land, royal debt, and offices.

---

[11] Let us not anachronistically push too hard on the "capitalist" nature of early modern agriculture. Estate owners showed limited interest in modernization and in the sort of agronomic practices that created the "Agricultural Revolution" in England, Holland, and Flanders. French villages also had very dense systems of protection of existing interests, so that outsiders (like the estate owners, who often lived in a town) had little chance of implementing radically new practices (such as new crops). Nonetheless, market elements, including cash, came to play an increasingly important role in the French agricultural economy during the seventeenth and eighteenth centuries. See below, chapter 4, for a fuller discussion of these issues.

[12] Older noble families particularly looked down on this form of nobility, called *noblesse de cloche* (literally, nobility of the bell tower).

Some families then left the royal judiciary but others maintained separate branches in the judiciary and the military. These powerful robe nobility families often owned estates (even *seigneuries*) that rivaled those of everyone but the richest sword nobles.

The ruling order, the seigneurs, had several defining characteristics: ownership of land, military service, noble heritage, and a distinctly noble ethos. Many nobles did not fit one or more of these characteristics but that did not disqualify them from membership in the ruling order. The staggering social mobility of the late sixteenth century meant that many seventeenth-century nobles could trace their noble lineage back only a generation; such mobility continued in the seventeenth and eighteenth centuries. The French nobility, far from being a closed caste, was a remarkably open elite. The mentality of the time required that a person of a given standing in the community have a certain social rank. If you owned enough land, you were virtually certain to become a titled noble. That mentality also required, however, that no one *admit* that social mobility was possible. The great difficulty was not getting into the nobility but becoming one of the 250 landed families who dominated every aspect of French life.

The economic classes overlapped with the social orders. The lay hierarchy of the society of orders ran from the nobility down to the legal families, to merchants, then to artisans and shopkeepers, and finally to those, such as day laborers, who did not belong to one of the *corps*, the corporations, that made up the society of orders. In the countryside, the people did not belong to such *corps*, yet the hierarchy looked quite similar: ploughman, small farmer, day laborer. In terms of a hierarchy of class, the estate owner stood on top, followed by merchants, and then those with a small stake of property, either an urban shop or a rural field.[13]

[13] What do I mean here by "class"? No one has ever provided an ideal definition of class, yet most historians use it as one of their categories of analysis. My understanding here is that class considers one's relationship to the means of production (how does one make one's living), one's wealth (the owner of a large estate does not necessarily have the same interest as the owner of a one-hectare plot), and, in some (alas undefinable) manner, one's cultural background. Land formed the main element of the means of production in early modern France. Estate owners drew the bulk of their income from rent created by ownership of land; merchants drew their income from commerce. Rich merchants and rich estate owners may have similar levels of income, but they do not belong to the same class because that income comes by means of different relationships to the main means of production. I believe the royal officers did not belong to the merchant class (often anachronistically called the "bourgeoisie") because they derived their income overwhelmingly from office and from land rent. In that sense, I believe they shared fundamental class interests with other estate owners, including seigneurs. Many estate owners, however, were not nobles. I would therefore argue that the nobles formed an estate but did not necessarily form a class, although the most powerful and richest nobles sat at the apex of both the ruling class, the large estate owners, and the ruling order, the nobility.

Those who relied on their labor for an income, whether in town or country, stood at the bottom.

In broader economic terms, we must think of France as a series of local economies, which often had little to do with each other. One of the most important developments of the period in question here was precisely the creation, in some parts of France, of a fairly integrated market, one tied into the larger world market centered in northwestern Europe (England, Holland, and northern France). Each region had a speciality: wine around Bordeaux, in Burgundy, in the Loire valley; salt around the marshes of the west or the south; grain in the open fields of the north and east; linen in western and northeastern Brittany and parts of Normandy; cloth in Amiens or Lyons. Most regions produced a bit of everything, so that they could be fairly self-sufficient. Grain held the first priority in almost all areas (except the wine regions), because bread provided the staple of the people's diet. The grain markets rarely had correlated prices before 1640. Even after 1640, France had several regional grain markets, rather than a single national one. Bread prices in Toulouse or Aix bore little or no relation to those in Paris. By the 1640s, however, we can find correlations between grain prices in many northern and western port cities. Old Regime France continued to be a much less integrated market than, say, eighteenth-century England, but large areas of France developed what for them were unprecedented levels of integration between 1625 and 1750. France increasingly came to have two economies, one tied to the world market and expanding, the other more isolated and even backward. For us here, the obvious question is, how is this economic development related to the evolution of the state.

State development in the 1620s and 1630s

The 1620s were a difficult period for France in every respect of human existence. The population, which had grown rapidly since 1600, suffered terrible epidemics in the mid-1620s, particularly in western France; no sooner had the epidemics subsided somewhat, than the famine of 1630–31 set in. The economy, which had expanded in the first two decades of the seventeenth century, slowed down in the late 1620s; in many areas, economic decline set in during the 1630s. The demographic and economic slowdowns exacerbated the sharply increased financial demands of the state. Direct taxation rose more than 100 percent between 1625 and 1634 and indirect tax rates, notably the price of monopoly salt, rose rapidly as well: the tax on a *muid* of salt rose from 600 *livres* in 1620 to 1,000 *livres* by 1640.

These developments fed on each other. Economic slowdown made

paying taxes that much harder; heavy taxes made investment, particularly for ploughmen, that much more difficult. Reduced investment further
cut productivity, and heavy direct taxes also competed directly with
rental income, so that landlords grew increasingly discontented with the
tax situation. The tension led to a series of violent local revolts. Most of
these uprisings involved a single town or a tiny sub-region: the peasants
or workers burned a tax official's house, sometimes murdering the official
or his clerks (the latter were the most vulnerable). In periods of grain
shortage, the lower classes turned on grain merchants, pillaging ships
exporting grain or confiscating grain in warehouses and selling it at the
regular price or giving it away. Some of the rebellions, however, were far
more ominous. Entire provinces, even regions, rose against the hated
"blood-suckers," that is, the tax collectors. Landlords and local elites
often encouraged such rebellions, although relatively few nobles actually
participated. (See chapters 2 and 3.)

Why did the late 1620s and early 1630s prove so decisive in the
evolution of the French state? We must consider a broad array of factors
to understand the necessity for change and to see the fundamental shift in
emphasis that took place between 1627 and 1634. First we have the
personality of the king, Louis XIII. Historians disagree sharply about
Louis's nature and abilities; his most recent biographer, Lloyd Moote,
offers a judicious general assessment that does much to illuminate the
political changes of Louis's reign. Moote believes Louis XIII was a
strong but not "charismatic" king. Louis XIII had very firm ideas about
the king's majesty: about his subjects' duty to obey him and about the
unquestioned nature of his authority. Perhaps the most succinct summary of those ideas was his remark to his bastard half-brother, César de
Vendôme (seven years his senior), when the latter begged forgiveness for
participating in a revolt in 1614: "Remember that your greatest honor in
this world is to be my brother."

Louis had a traumatic childhood. His father had often embarrassed the
young Louis by his adulterous ways; his mother encouraged Louis's
moralistic religiosity. Louis became king at nine and had to suffer
through the usual indignities of the child king, most particularly through
a fight among his relatives over control of his person and of the state itself.
The Queen Mother (Marie de Médicis) used Louis and his siblings as
policy tools. Following long-standing practices in such matters, she
created political marriages for Louis and his favorite sister Elisabeth: he
would marry Anne of Austria, eldest daughter of the king of Spain;
Elisabeth would marry the king's eldest son, soon to be Philip IV. Louis
reportedly cried for hours after his parting with Elisabeth on the Spanish

frontier; he did not transfer these affections to the young woman for whom she had been exchanged.

Louis chafed under the leash of his mother and her favorites. In 1610, he reportedly told his confessor and his mother after she had scolded him "that he would not always be so young and that (one day) they would remember having scolded him."[14] In 1617, at the age of fifteen, Louis and a handful of supporters organized the coup d'état against marshal d'Ancre (Concino Concini), favorite of Marie de Médicis. For the next four years, Louis relied heavily on his favorite, the duke of Luynes, who proved an ineffective leader. Luynes died of scarlet fever at the siege of Montauban. The old counsellors of Henry IV, Jeannin and Villeroy (both of whom had been royal advisors since the 1560s!), also died in rapid succession, leaving Louis without a unified, purposeful royal council. Despite the general governmental incompetence of the period 1617–24, we can see important continuities between that period and the succeeding one, most particularly in the assault against the Protestants, a personal initiative of the king. In 1624, the disarray in the king's council led to a complete reshuffling of his advisors; Louis invited several new members to the council, including Armand-Jean du Plessis, bishop of Luçon, recently named Cardinal Richelieu.

Richelieu's appointment was not, in itself, decisive; the cardinal represented a new group of capable advisors such as Keeper of the Seals Michel de Marillac, the superintendant of finances, marshal d'Effiat, and Richelieu's clients, Claude Bullion and Claude Bouthillier, who took over the financial administration after d'Effiat's death in 1632. Richelieu, originally a client of Marie de Médicis, served on the royal council in 1617, under Concini: his reentry into the royal council also symbolized the renewed influence of the Queen Mother on royal policy. In terms of policy initiatives, however, the three main reformers were Richelieu, d'Effiat, and Marillac.

What changes did they wish to make? Once they had decided upon policy changes, how could they carry them out? The first policy initiative was the definitive effort to destroy Protestant independence. Here Louis's advisors showed rare unanimity, but the king's own strong desire to teach the Protestants their duty to obey him undoubtedly provided the key factor. Louis XIII did *not* destroy Protestant freedom to worship; he forced the Protestant areas to allow Catholic worship and he insisted on the full *political* obedience of the Huguenots. As he wrote to constable Lesdiguières in 1621, "nothing should be more free than

---

[14] Cited in L. Moote, *Louis XIII. The Just* (Berkeley: University of California Press, 1989), 49.

consciences, which God knows how to move when it pleases him."[15] Those free consciences, however, should not release subjects from their duty to obey their king. In Louis's view, the ban on Catholicism in Béarn assaulted that same freedom of conscience Protestants demanded in the rest of the kingdom. Protestant fortified towns, like Montauban or La Rochelle, offered an open invitation to the Huguenots to disobey their king.

What other pressing issues faced the French government in the mid-1620s? Given the unstable political history of the previous sixty-five years, some effort to curb the power of the grandees had to rank high on the list. The permanent ministerial changes of 1624 included the elimination of the grandees, most notably the king's cousin, the prince of Condé, from the royal council. Condé had tried to be an independent power broker in the 1610s and early 1620s; by the late 1620s, he had become a client of Richelieu, a role he would fulfill admirably for the remainder of the cardinal's life. The chaotic state of the kingdom's finances dictated the necessity of fiscal reform. Fifteen years of ministerial instability had exacerbated administrative weaknesses and inconsistencies, so that the government desperately needed to establish a firm, consistent set of rules for its officials.

All of these problems were, in reality, one problem: the government had insufficient control of the state apparatus. Of the three elements of government – the military, judiciary, and financial – the grandees controlled the first, and the royal officers, now permanently entrenched by the *paulette*, the other two. The king had briefly suspended the *paulette* (1617–20) but the political need of support from the officers and the financial benefits of the *paulette* to the king's coffers forced him to reinstate it (for a substantial fee, to be sure) in 1621. Could the king rely on these officers in his efforts to reform the kingdom, once he had satisfied them with the *paulette*?

The immediate answer to such a question might well be no, just as the immediate reaction to military reform would be that the grandees and other high nobles could not be relied upon to implement needed changes there. In both cases, the targets of the reform would be themselves the reformers. As implausible as such a policy may seem, the king had no other choice. If the nobility did not run the army, who would? If the judges and financial officials did not operate those two elements of the state, who would take their place? Whatever the faults of these groups, many of their members were trained professionals: highly skilled soldiers and administrators. We cannot call the events of 1627–34 a revolution,

---

[15] *Ibid.*, 85.

because the same ruling elites remained firmly in place, but we can say that the changes of that period marked a definitive break with the past and the establishment of a new framework of government.

The Assembly of Notables, 1626–1627

The government sought the help of the elites through the mechanism of an Assembly of Notables. French kings had used Assemblies in 1583 and 1596–97 to help institute broad packages of reform (unsuccessfully in the first case, successfully in the second). Louis XIII had called an Assembly in 1617; given the disarray of the central government itself in 1617, the failure of that Assembly was a foregone conclusion. The intransigence of the judges in the Assembly, strongly defending their corporate interests, further assured its immediate failure. In 1626, however, the government was ready to enact serious reform and the elites, after fifteen years of relative disorder, were ready to support necessary reforms.

The Notables were hardly a representative body: they were the government's hand-picked assembly of members of the ruling elites – grandees (13), bishops (13), and important judges (29). Although many historians have treated this Assembly, and its predecessors, as unsuccessful because they failed to enact specific reforms, such accusations misunderstand the role of these Assemblies (or of Estates Generals). The Assemblies (and Estates) had no executive functions, nor did they possess any specific legislative powers; they served to offer informed commentary on government reform proposals and to make appropriate counter proposals. In the case of every successful Assembly or Estates, the king himself would issue a major ordinance or enact significant reforms, most notably the Edict of Blois (1579), in response to the Estates General of 1576, and the great Code Michau (1629), in response to the Assembly of Notables of 1626–27.

The king and the Notables agreed on four basic changes in French government. First, they agreed that the power of the Protestants had to be broken. There was no specific discussion of a march on La Rochelle, but the Notables firmly supported the king's desire to destroy the network of independent Huguenot fortresses. Second, the Notables, like those of 1596 and 1617, strongly criticized the grandees, particularly provincial governors. In 1626–27, the Notables particularly insisted that the king should regain full control of the military. Third, everyone agreed that the basic administration of the kingdom lay in disarray, so that a strong statement from the central government was needed to reestablish order. In most cases, this reaffirmation of government control required only the restatement of preexisting ordinances. Fourth, everyone agreed that the fiscal situation was catastrophic. The overwhelming majority of the Assembly's deliberations focused on this last issue.

The first problem took care of itself, with the king's victory in the long siege of La Rochelle. The second issue, the king's control over the grandees, was much more complex. Richelieu and others certainly understood that the defeat of the Huguenots was a prerequisite for limiting the grandees, but the Notables' demands alert us to the frequent clientage abuses in the French military. Four national positions gave their possessors effective control over appointments of military officers: the constable, for the cavalry and some other units; the colonel-general of the infantry; and the two admirals, for the navies of the Levant and Ponant (Atlantic). After the death of the constable duke of Lesdiguières in 1626, Louis deliberately refused to name a successor. The permanent abolition of this position came in 1643, when Louis, on his deathbed, signed an edict abolishing the posts of constable and of colonel-general of the infantry because:

We have recognized by experience on several occasions that these positions can cause great prejudice to the State . . . it being certain that the power of those who hold these positions to dispose of most of the important military commands gives them great credit and authority, and that they have often used the kingdom's own forces for their personal interests, against their duty and to the great detriment of the State.[16]

The reform of the military did not stop with the constable. In response to a demand from the Notables (one that mirrored royal desires), Louis abolished all admiralties and gave control of the French marine to a minister (Richelieu). He severely undercut the colonel-general's rights to name infantry officers and later abolished that post as well (although the final elimination of the position did not take place until the death of the duke d'Epernon, in 1661). The *compagnies d'ordonnance*, the aristocratic bands of retainers so loyal to their commanders, also faded out of existence. The general administrative rules of the army underwent massive change in the Code Michau of 1629, but the government could not fully implement these changes until much later. Most of the reform program of the 1660s merely restated the partially successful efforts of the 1620s.

Again following the advice of the Assembly, the king replaced royal governors who had displeased him (or Richelieu). Louis's half-brother, the duke of Vendôme, lost his position as governor of Brittany *at the demand of the Estates*, because of his role in the Chalais conspiracy of

[16] P. Viollet, *Histoire des institutions politiques et administratives de la France. Le roi et ses ministres pendant les trois dernières siècles de la monarchie* (Paris, 1912), 345–46.

1626. Vendôme's replacement, the loyal marshal Thémines, died within a year. After two years without a governor, the Estates decided that the province needed "someone in whose hands the province will be well protected," and they offered the position to Richelieu; he accepted (1630). Between 1625 and 1635, Louis changed governors in all of the major *pays d'Etats* – Béarn, Provence, Burgundy, Dauphiné, Languedoc, and Brittany – as well as in several other provinces – Picardy, Anjou, Touraine, and the Orléanais.

All of these changes did not mean, however, that the king had broken the power of the grandees; after all, a quarter of the members of the Assembly of Notables *were* grandees. The new governors immediately set to work to reinstitute clientage networks in their new provinces and in the regimental structure of the new army. These new clientage networks, however, owed allegiance to Richelieu (and the king). In most cases, they served as effective Richelieu clients, whether Condé in Burgundy or Schomberg in Languedoc. Although the grandees did use "their" troops against the government during the Fronde, the king was a minor at the time. After 1632, no grandee used royal troops against an adult king, striking evidence of Louis XIII's success in the changes of the late 1620s and early 1630s.

The grandees maintained command of the army, but to whom could the king give his troops, if not to the great nobles of the kingdom? The list of French generals of the seventeenth century reads like a who's who of the great nobility: Condé, Turenne, Luxembourg, Rohan, Harcourt, Schomberg. Their subordinate officers came from other distinguished families, although some relatively minor noble families achieved military distinction (even the office of marshal of France). In general, the king had to appoint a prince or duke as an army commander, just as he had to appoint someone of exalted rank to be a provincial governor. In a society so concerned with precedence and social distinctions, a royal governor of low social status could easily be humiliated by higher-ranking local notables: the king's majesty could not allow such a possibility. The king needed the grandees to help run the state, to fill certain positions; the grandees needed the king for income, for status, and for support of their political (and social) superiority. As the duke of Rohan wrote in 1617, "their [the high nobles] grandeur is that of their King; the *grands* are happier and more assured under a great King, than under those little sovereigns who fear everything."[17]

The reform of the non-military governing apparatus presented an overwhelming task. Could the officials then in place be relied upon to

---

[17] H. de Rohan, *Mémoires* (Paris: Foucault, 1822), I, 175.

carry out reforms? The central government took contradictory measures, at first expanding the authority of existing officials and then creating an entire administrative structure based on temporary royal commissioners called intendants. These officials came to be considered the archetypal symbols of absolutism, so we must pay particular attention to the circumstances that gave rise to their use.

The origins of the new state: the reforms of 1628–1634

In the aftermath of the Assembly of Notables of 1626–27, the government sought to reorder the entire administrative apparatus. The king restructured the military by phasing out the *compagnies d'ordonnance*, by abolishing the positions of constable and admiral, and by shuffling the line-up of governors. The Keeper of the Seals, Michel de Marillac, supervised a massive rewriting of French administrative law and procedure, known as the Code Michau. The Code covered everything from tax collection procedures in the villages to accounting rules to jurisdictional disputes.

Fiscal reform, the focus of the discussions of 1626–27, took place in an atmosphere of renewed financial pressure due to the La Rochelle campaign. The stepped-up war with the Protestants had greatly increased the king's financial needs as early as 1620; in response to that greater demand, the government restructured its debt, a move that had dramatic practical consequences for the tax system because the royal tax officials held most of this new debt.

The early modern French state forever lacked the ability to obtain cash income on short notice. A large segment of its revenue, from direct taxation, came in slowly and tardily. The monarchy forever searched for ways to obtain money faster and to borrow more efficiently. The confusion between loans to the king as an individual and loans to the state itself created difficulties for the government. In the sixteenth century, the king had borrowed from Italian and German bankers by means of offering them liens on tax revenues. After Henry II declared bankruptcy in 1557–58, the government had to change its borrowing methods. In the 1560s and early 1570s, the king offered his creditors tax farms of the indirect tax revenues. He also sold annuities (*rentes*) guaranteed by various revenues: tax revenues of Paris, the property of the Church, and indirect and direct royal taxes.

In the 1570s, the king turned the sale of these annuities into forced loans on royal officials. In the 1580s, Henry III stopped paying the interest on the annuities. Henry IV reduced the interest on these annuities but restored faith in them by actually paying that interest. In

1616, the government began a new method of borrowing money from the royal officers, selling surtax rights (the *droits aliénés**), at first taken from the traditional share of the village collectors (and thus not a tax increase). Starting in 1620, however, as part of a package of fiscal expedients created to finance the wars against the Huguenots, the king began to sell surtaxes that did add to the tax burden.

The mechanism of selling these surtaxes created immediate cash income. The king would sell the surtax to the tax official in return for a cash payment of ten times the annual value of the surtax. In this way, the king could anticipate the income from a large portion of the direct taxes. All of the doubling of direct taxes between 1625 and 1634 came about due to the sale of these surtaxes. Taxpayers greatly resented these surtaxes because they knew the tax officials, not the king, received the money. The estates of Normandy complained to the king in 1629:

If we complain, with reason, of the great and excessive *tailles* demanded of us, we have even more subject to redouble our complaints, in that they are levied and collected with surtaxes as excessive and onerous, or more so, than the *taille* itself, and this, in the name of a worthless group of officers . . . which, like caterpillars, . . . gnaw on and ruin your people.[18]

The local tax receivers (*receveurs particuliers*) and receivers general obtained the largest share of this money; given their critical role in the collection of the money, any effort to change the surtax system would create severe problems. Given that the projected levies of 1634 showed that 52 percent of the direct taxes would go directly to the officers for surtaxes, they offered a tempting target to a government desperate for money. The king decided to convert the surtaxes into annuities, thereby reducing the interest payments on the capital invested in them from 10 to 4.16 percent. In so doing, he reduced his interest payments on this form of debt from about 14 million to 4 million *livres*.

Popular opinion supported this step, but the tax officials had a different perspective. Given this massive evidence of bad faith on behalf of the government, could the king rely on these same tax officials to collect the even greater sums demanded of his subjects after 1634 (and, especially, after the entry into open war with Spain in 1635)? No. What then could the government do to assure itself of the continued flow of revenue?

This issue came up in the context of a much larger reorganization of government. The change in governorships, the military reforms, the new administrative code – all these belonged to an effort to restructure the state. Not surprisingly, the government first sought to use existing state

[18] C. de Robillard de Beaurepaire, *Cahiers des Etats de Normandie, règnes Louis XIII et Louis XIV* (Rouen: Société des Antiquitaires de Normandie, 1888), II, 150–51 (my translation). The fuller text is reproduced in Collins, *Fiscal Limits*, 136–37.

mechanisms to expand its power. The king expanded the powers of the treasurers of France in 1626, and greatly increased their numbers in a series of office creations between 1621 and 1630. He also tried to eliminate the distinction between the regions levying the regular taxes, called the *pays d'élection** after their local financial districts, and the regions that still had provincial Estates, collectively called the *pays d'Etats,** which had particularist tax systems.

The government began by creating *élections* in four of the five great provinces without them – Provence, Dauphiné, Burgundy, and Languedoc (following the example set in Guyenne in 1621). Aix, Grenoble, and Dijon exploded in rebellion. Richelieu, ever the pragmatist, compromised with the local elites: he abolished the *élections* of Provence, Dauphiné, and Burgundy in return for a payment of about 7 million *livres*. We see his pragmatism even more clearly in Brittany, into which he never tried to introduce the *élections* (why should he? he had become governor of Brittany in 1630, thus its special, and well-paid, protector), and in Languedoc. The dallying response to the compromise offered by Languedoc led its estates to support the 1632 rebellion of the governor, the duke of Montmorency (allied to the king's brother, Gaston of Orléans, in one of the latter's innumerable conspiracies).

After the king captured Montmorency during an attack on the royal army, he allowed the estates to purchase full exemption from the *élections* for 7 million *livres*. The king treated Montmorency with greater harshness, executing the hapless duke. As Richelieu noted in his memoirs, Montmorency's crime was not a simple case of a noble rebelling: "He caused a province to revolt by a resolution of the estates; this was never done."[19] This execution provided a dramatic political statement. Montmorency had been one of Louis XIII's closest childhood friends. His father and grandfather had been constables of France and governors of Languedoc (back to the 1530s). His sister, Charlotte, was the wife of the prince of Condé, second in line to the throne. In 1632, Montmorency's nephew seemed quite likely one day to be king. That such a man could lose his head on the block tells us how seriously Louis and Richelieu took the threat of a governor using provincial estates to abet a rebellion. Montmorency's fate did serve as a lesson to others; no one ever used provincial estates against an adult king again.

Quite apart from the difficulties of introducing existing institutions into provinces whose privileges specifically exempted them from those institutions, Richelieu saw the folly of using the network of royal officers to expand the king's power. Some of the *pays d'Etats*, such as Brittany

---

[19] Here Richelieu conveniently ignores the precedents of the League Wars, such as Mayenne in Burgundy.

and Languedoc, furnished substantial amounts of money to the royal treasury (and to Richelieu and his friends: the estates of Brittany voted the cardinal a biannual pension of 100,000 *livres* and gave his clients another 50,000). What is more, the estates of these two provinces had much better credit than the king, so they could borrow money at a much lower rate of interest (always an important consideration in French fiscal policy). Richelieu and his successors made extensive use of these favorable borrowing conditions.

From 1626 to 1630, the king consistently sought to expand the *existing* institutions, particularly the tax system. This effort failed, insofar as the king could not (or would not) expand the *élections* into the *pays d'Etats*. The decision to change the surtaxes into annuities guaranteed that most of the royal tax officials would be unwilling agents of augmented royal power. At the same time that the king issued the conversion edict on the surtaxes (February 1634), he sent out intendants* to supervise the tax collection precisely because he knew that the partial bankruptcy of 1634 had undermined the reliability of the existing tax bureaucracy.

What was an intendant? How did they differ from regular royal officials? They had been widely but irregularly used since the time of Henry II. The king would typically send one of the masters of requests* of his household to investigate problems in a given governorship or he might attach an intendant to an army in the field. The intendants, unlike the administrative officers, did not own their positions; in the language of the Old Regime, an intendant was a *commissaire*,* someone who operated on the basis of a limited commission, not an *officier*, someone who owned an office. The commission carried a specific definition of tasks and a time limit; when the task (or the time) ended, so did the commission.

The use of these officials became more regular in the first third of the seventeenth century. By the beginning of the century, the king had a regular intendant in Languedoc and another one in Lyons. For the other regions of the country, however, an intendant remained a temporary phenomenon at most; indeed, most provinces did not have even a temporary intendant between 1600 and 1620. Those intendants who did visit a given governorship rarely stayed more than a year or two; clearly they did not have real administrative functions.

The situation changed abruptly in 1634. The government now sent intendants to most of the *généralités*, not to governorships, in an effort to use them to oversee the financial administration, rather than simply as adjuncts to governors (or military commanders). For the next eight years, the king made regular use of intendants to oversee tax collections. They did not, however, actually run the tax administration. They investigated the local system and reported back to the central officials (Richelieu, chancellor Séguier, Bullion or Bouthillier) as to how things might best be improved. They also relayed messages from the ministers to local officials. As one might expect, the local officials resented the outside intruders, so that jurisdictional conflicts between intendants and financial officials and Parlements soon sprang up.

Although intendants, *as intendants*, held a commission rather than an office, they invariably came from officer families. Virtually all intendants also served as masters of requests, a venal office worth 150,000 *livres*. They came overwhelmingly from robe families (both noble and commoner). The king did not use the intendants to destroy the officers and establish "absolute" government. Intendants gave the king greater freedom of action; they did not allow him to move outside the structures of the social order of which they and their families formed so important a part. Their importance lay in the fact that they existed outside the realm of contract, and purely in that of law. The officers had a contract with the king, so his power, as expressed through them, remained within the traditional limits set by contracts. The intendants existed only in law, in the realm of which the king's power had no earthly limits, in which it was, in the terminology of the day, absolute. This connection made the intendants the inevitable focus of most complaints about "absolutism."

A brief summary of royal actions in this period demonstrates the dramatic changes of the late 1620s and early 1630s. In the military, the king abolished the offices of admiral and constable and greatly restricted (and then abolished) that of colonel-general of the infantry. He eliminated the *compagnies d'ordonnance* and removed the governors of each one of the major outlying provinces, from Provence to Picardy. In the civil administration (judicial and financial), he expanded the administrative and judicial competence of the treasurers of France and attempted to create *élections* in most of the kingdom. Burgundy, Languedoc, and Provence avoided *élections*, but the latter lost its estates; Normandy, Guyenne, and Dauphiné lost their estates and the latter two had to accept *élections* (Normandy already had them).

The king also introduced widespread use of intendants to oversee administration; these intendants soon quarreled with financial officers, with Parlements, and with some governors about the precise limits of their authority. At the same time he expanded the use of intendants, the king conducted a partial bankruptcy at the expense of the officers whom the intendants had been sent out to supervise.

These actions did not change the fundamental nature of government, because they left the same three groups in power. The king replaced one grandee governor by another (in some cases, they moved from one province to another). The regimental army had the same clientage system as the old *compagnies d'ordonnance* and local fortresses continued to be in the hands of the provincial governor's clients (often relatives). The sovereign courts forced the king to abandon his plans to abolish the *paulette* in 1630, although again the king exacted a large sum of money for this favor. The biggest losers of the period were some of the financial officials. In the system that fell into place after 1634, some officials from the existing tax system ended up with control of the entire system, while the others lost much of their power.

The Day of the Dupes

These internal reforms took place in an atmosphere of intense international conflict. French concentration on the civil war with the Protestants meant that France's involvement in the Thirty Years' War remained passive until 1629. After Louis captured La Rochelle, the Protestants no longer posed a threat; he immediately took advantage of this situation to pursue French interests in Italy. The Mantuan crisis (1629–30) pitted France against Spain in a contest over the northern Italy duchy of Mantua, astride one of the principal routes used by Spanish troops to move into Germany and the Low Countries. The possible heirs to the duchy included the French grandee, Charles, duke of Nevers, and two members of the Spanish royal family. The Habsburg Emperor, Ferdinand, refused to invest Nevers with the duchy of Mantua and a Spanish army soon besieged the main local fortress, Casale. Louis XIII and Richelieu agreed completely on an aggressive policy: the king set off for Italy immediately (in January 1629) and French troops rapidly took the great Savoyard fortress of Pignerolo. After another year of desultory fighting and tortuous negotiations, Nevers ended up with the duchy and the French and Spanish troops withdrew. The French used an Italian as their negotiator, Giuseppe Mazarini, later to become Cardinal Mazarin, and chief royal minister.

The Mantuan War, a major step toward a direct confrontation between Spain and France, shows the extraordinary complexity of the relationship between the king of France and his grandees. Nevers had been a Leaguer against Henry IV and revolted against the Regency government in 1614 and 1616–17. Yet the king of France fought a war to support Nevers's claim to Mantua. Why? After the 1616 rebellion, Nevers had become a loyal supporter of the king, who rewarded him with the governorship of Champagne, a position he filled quite ably. The king had even personally intervened, essentially on Nevers's behalf, in preventing a duel between the duke and the Cardinal de Guise in 1621. Nevers had the firm support of the Devout party; they had chosen him as commander of their new crusading order, the Christian Militia.[20]

Was Nevers entirely reliable? Certainly not, no more so than any other grandee. Did the king *have* to rely on such people in order to achieve his aims? Absolutely. Whatever his flaws, Nevers was a Frenchman, and a French grandee was a much more palatable ruler of Mantua than a member of the Spanish royal family. As was the case with so many grandees, Nevers had been a recalcitrant subject during the Regency but proved a loyal supporter of the king once Louis reached adulthood.

The secret to maintaining the loyalty of Nevers or of any other grandee was to establish strong personal bonds with him (or her), bonds which required that the king be an adult. Early modern European states relied on personal ties because of the profoundly personal nature of rulership. Even in contemporary times, the personality of U.S. president, a British prime minister, or a Russian leader has a significant impact on policy; in early modern times, with the belief in the sacerdotal nature of kingship and the tradition of close feudal ties between the king and his nobility, the personality of a given ruler or of a grandee had a dramatic impact on events. The clientage relationships of a king and his high nobles became particularly tortured during a royal minority, as in the period 1610–17 or again from 1643 to the mid-1650s. Grandees could revolt against a non-adult king, making the argument that they merely wanted to save the child king from evil advisors. In fact, the noble rebels of 1616–17 (including Nevers) surrendered immediately to royal troops when news of Louis's coup against Concini reached them. What these grandees wanted, of course, was to dominate the king themselves.

An adult king made matters much simpler but even he needed a firm succession to cut down on intrigues. Louis XIII did not have that luxury; until his son's birth in 1638, his brother Gaston (himself without male issue) was heir-presumptive, followed by their cousin, the prince of Condé (chief rebel of 1610–17). One of Louis's most important tasks was to assure the loyalty of these two princes. Richelieu understood such matters very well; he worked hard to maintain good relations with Gaston and made Condé one of his chief client-brokers. In the 1620s and early 1630s, Richelieu successfully established a clientage system throughout France, from the royal council to the outlying provinces. Gaston of Orléans and Marie de Médicis (the latter Richelieu's original patroness)

[20] The mysterious Christian Militia deserves more attention than it has received, because it demonstrates the complexity of the relationship between the Devout party and the Good Frenchmen. The chief organizer of the Militia, Father Joseph, held impeccable credentials as a Devout, yet he remained throughout his life the client (and gray eminence) of Richelieu.

deeply resented his success. Gaston worked unceasingly to undermine the cardinal's position; in 1629 and 1630, the Queen Mother joined those efforts, leading to a decisive showdown in late 1630.

The French government debated the direction it would follow after the Mantuan War throughout 1630, a debate that added a policy element to the personal struggle between Marie de Médicis and Richelieu. For two years, the Devouts and the Good Frenchmen had fought for control of the king's council. Marie de Médicis and the Marillac brothers urged the king to make peace with Spain and to relieve the suffering of his people. Richelieu argued that the power of Spain had to be broken, now or later. The king passed a difficult summer and fall in 1630, culminating with a harrowing illness in the last week of September. He received the last rites on 29 September; on 30 September, everyone expected Louis to die within hours. Miraculously (to contemporaries), the king's intestinal abscess broke and he recovered. Throughout the late summer and fall, his mother had been exceptionally solicitous of his health; she and her advisors, notably Michel de Marillac, constantly urged the king to sign a peace with Spain. The matter came to a head in a dramatic personal confrontation involving Marie de Médicis, Richelieu, and the king at Marie's Luxembourg Palace. Surely there are few historical events more melodramatic than the Day of the Dupes (10–11 November 1630).

The confrontation took place in four stages. On 10 November, Richelieu and Gaston of Orléans met with Louis XIII; the king forced his brother to make peace with the cardinal. That evening, at a meeting of the royal council in Marie's Luxembourg Palace, they decided to change commanders of the army in Italy: the new commander was to be Louis de Marillac, Michel's brother. Richelieu himself wrote to Louis de Marillac to inform the marshal of the decision and of the cardinal's agreement with it. After the council, the Queen Mother bluntly told Richelieu that she had "lost confidence in him" and stripped him of his many positions in her household (superintendant of the household, head of her council, and chief almoner). She reportedly told Louis that Richelieu was an ingrate, a deceiver, and a traitor. Louis told Richelieu that he should try on the following day to make amends with Marie.

Richelieu attempted to see the Queen Mother on the morning of the 11th but was told he would not be received. Further inquiries made it clear that she and Louis were in private conference and that every door leading to her apartments was locked and guarded. Richelieu remembered a secret passageway from Marie's private chapel, through a closet, into her private apartments. In his memoirs, Richelieu credits his good fortune to God's intervention, but Nicolas Goulas (a contemporary memoirist) is likely more accurate in noting that one of the cardinal's clients, Claire Bricet, chambermaid of the Queen Mother, had unlocked the door and sent word to the cardinal. Certainly Marie suspected Mme. Bricet, because she fired her five days later.

Richelieu's appearance startled the king and Queen Mother. He accused them of speaking about him, which the Queen Mother first denied but then admitted: "Why yes! We were indeed speaking of you and saying that you were the most ungrateful and wickedest of men." A violent confrontation ensued: Marie accused her son of preferring a lackey to her; Richelieu fell on his knees before the king, and burst into tears; Marie, too, sobbed uncontrollably. Louis demanded that Richelieu leave; when the king passed the cardinal in the courtyard of the palace a few moments later, he refused even to look at his supplicating minister. Everyone in Paris believed that Richelieu had fallen; his advisors urged the cardinal to flee to Le Havre (of which he was governor). Louis returned to the house in which he was staying and gradually recovered his composure. In the end, he decided to keep his minister: "Remain by my side and I will protect you against all enemies," he wrote to Richelieu.[21]

The king disgraced the Marillac brothers, not Richelieu. Michel de Marillac lost the royal seals and went to prison; he died there two years later. His brother, Louis, marshal of France, appointed commander of the army in Italy by royal letters of 10 November, was arrested by his colleague, marshal Schomberg, on order of letters dated the 11th. In early May 1632, despite a divided court decision about his fate, the government beheaded marshal Louis de Marillac on the *place* de Grève in Paris. Although these extraordinary events may seem like a key dividing point within the history of the French state, in fact, Louis XIII merely decided to pursue a policy he had already followed for four years or more. The break in continuity was not choosing Richelieu over the Devouts; the break would have been a Devout policy and the disgrace of the cardinal.

Sliding toward war, 1631–1635

In 1631 and 1632, Richelieu's policies went well. The satisfactory solution of the Mantuan question in 1630 had shifted everyone's

---

[21] Here I am interweaving two accounts of the Day of the Dupes, one of which provides the colorful eyewitness comments and the other the accurate chronology. The colorful language, and the quotations, come from V.-L. Tapié, *France in the Age of Louis XIII and Richelieu* (New York: Praeger, 1974; translation of 1967 Paris edn.), 233–35. Tapié follows the classic version of Louis Batiffol. Batiffol's chronology, however, does not bear scrutiny. L. Chevallier, *Louis XIII: roi cornélien* (Paris: Fayard, 1979), 379–95, provides the accurate chronology used here (placing the key meeting on 11 November rather than 10 November, as Batiffol and Tapié do). For a short summary in English, the reader should turn to Moote, *Louis XIII*, which relies on the more accurate Chevallier version.

attention to Germany. The Holy Roman Emperor Ferdinand II, allied with Maximilian, duke of Bavaria, had demolished his Protestant enemies in the 1620s. Maximilian's general, Tilly, had defeated the Bohemian rebels in 1620 and had combined with Ferdinand's generalissimo, Wallenstein, to crush the Protestant Germans and the forces of the king of Denmark by 1629. In that year, the Holy Roman Emperor issued the Edict of Restitution, requiring that all Church property seized since 1555 be returned to the Catholic Church. Meanwhile, to the west, the Spanish and the Dutch bogged down in an endless war of sieges for control of the area now known as Belgium.

The French supported the Dutch, the Danes, and German Protestant states with money. After the failure of Christian of Denmark, the French turned to another Scandinavian, Gustavus Adolphus of Sweden. France mediated a Swedish–Polish peace, and gave Sweden one million *livres* a year to maintain an army in Germany. Gustavus Adolphus proved as smashing a success as Christian of Denmark had been a failure. He drove the Imperial forces from the Baltic coast in a lightning campaign and crushed Tilly's army at Breitenfeld. Invading Bavaria (itself a French ally), he again defeated Tilly at the Lech and captured Munich. Shortly thereafter, following a series of skirmishes with Wallenstein's new army, the king defeated the generalissimo at Lutzen. Fortunately for the Emperor, Gustavus Adolphus wandered off into the mists of Lutzen and ended up in the middle of the Imperial army, where he was killed. When we consider the history of France in the 1620s or 1630s, we do well to remember that Louis XIII could easily have suffered the same fate (indeed, a man riding next to him was killed by a cannonball at Montauban). In an age of personal rule, the shift to Gaston would, no doubt, have altered French policies, although to what degree must remain anyone's guess.

Gustavus Adolphus's successes cost France much less than direct military action would have. His death destabilized the German situation but nearly two years passed before the critical battle of Nordlingen, in which the Spanish army, led by the Cardinal Infante, joined with the Austrians to annihilate the Swedes (September 1634). Two months later, the two leading German Protestant princes, the electors of Saxony and Brandenburg, signed a separate peace with the Emperor.

Like it or not, France had to face the fact that the preliminaries were over. France itself was the only power capable of standing up to the Habsburg combination of Spain and Austria. In February 1635, France signed an alliance with Holland, followed by a renewal of the Swedish arrangement in April. In between, Spain had seized the Catholic archbishop-elector of Triers, who was under the protection of the king of

France. France sent the king's herald to Brussels to declare war officially on the basis of this incident. The herald read his message, so redolent of the remnants of medieval thinking:

I come to seek you out on behalf of the king my master, my only sovereign lord, to give you to understand that whereas you have not seen fit to set at liberty My Lord Archbishop of Trier, an elector of the Holy Roman Empire, who placed himself under His Majesty's protection when he could not obtain it from the emperor or from any other prince: and whereas contrary to the dignity of the Empire and to the law of nations you thus hold prisoner a sovereign prince with whom you are not at war: His Majesty maketh known to you his resolution to have recourse to arms to obtain satisfaction for this offence which importeth each and every prince of Christendom.[22]

The herald scattered copies of the king's letter to the crowd, his trumpeter all the while blowing the chamade, and then rode back to France. At the border, he stopped to nail the proclamation of war to a post. It was the last heraldic declaration of war in western Europe.

[22] Tapié, *France in the Age of Louis XIII*, 331.

2   The twenty years' crisis, 1635–1654

War with Spain

From 1635 to 1659, France and Spain fought a war for political hegemony in western Europe. The effort required of the two states was such that it dismembered Spain, led to civil war in France, and induced governmental bankruptcies in both countries. Spain never recovered from the burdens it had to bear, slipping steadily in power after 1660. France emerged as the dominant power in Europe.

From our perspective, the outcome of this contest seems a foregone conclusion. France had a larger population and a much healthier demographic trend; France had a much more thoroughly integrated state than Spain; the French economy was varied and rich, that of Spain unbalanced and in decline. Contemporaries had rather a different view. Spain had the best army in Europe, the *tercios*, and the combination of Habsburg Spain and the revived Habsburg-ruled Holy Roman Empire seemed an overwhelming power. The Spanish could also draw upon the fabulous silver of Mexico and Peru to finance their armies. The king of Spain ruled the Franche-Comté, the duchy of Milan, and, through a vice-regent, the Spanish Netherlands as well. In short, he had France surrounded.

The war opened well for the French, with a victory at Avein (near Liège) and minor successes in the Rhine valley. Within weeks of its victory, however, the French army in Flanders melted away, unpaid and ravaged by disease. In early 1636, events began to confirm contemporary assessments of the two combatants: the Spanish army drove quickly into France, taking all of the fortifications in its path to Paris. In August 1636, the Spanish captured Corbie, the last fortress before the French capital.

Richelieu and the royal council unanimously agreed that they must leave Paris and head for the Loire valley. Louis XIII rejected this advice and ordered the council to prepare the defenses of the capital. The council members then acted with firm resolve, conspicuously riding through the streets to calm the Parisians. Royal troops moved quickly toward Paris;

thousands of nobles, called up by the feudal levy (*ban et arrière-ban*), came to defend the capital; the Parlement of Paris promised to help pay for troops; the common people of Paris volunteered to serve, leading Louis XIII to embrace the delegation of cobblers who brought him the news. The Spanish commander dallied at Corbie, unsure of his position (and worried by the rumors of a Dutch offensive to his rear). By September, Louis XIII had enough troops to go back on the offensive; by December, he had driven the Spaniards from France.

The ensuing military campaigns were remarkably indecisive. Each side had its share of successes and failures, a pattern that lasted from 1637 to 1659. The French in particular had a series of great victories – Rocroi, Lens, the Dunes – that they failed to follow up successfully. The two sides had the same basic weakness: domestic insecurity that made it impossible to raise enough money to pay their armies. Each side found it difficult to capitalize on their victories because they did not have enough money to pay their troops. Louis XIV himself, in his *Memoirs for the Instruction of the Dauphin*, wrote that "a thousand times we had the advantage but were unable to follow it up." Troops ravaged the countryside everywhere: the horrors of Grimmelshausen's tale of a simpleton could just as easily have taken place in eastern France as in Germany.

In France, the massive demands of the war led to equally massive demands for increased taxation. The new indirect taxes led to revolts throughout the kingdom, notably in the Southwest and in Normandy. The Southwestern revolts, known collectively as the risings of the Croquants, broke out in 1636 and 1637 in Périgord, in Bordeaux, in Angoumois, and in nearby areas. The local noble militia put down some of the risings, but other nobles supported the rebels; the Regent (Anne of Austria) did not pardon the compromised nobles of the 1643 rebellion in Rouergue until 1649. Louis XIII had to send royal troops to put down many uprisings. The Norman rebellion, the Nu-Pieds (barefoot) revolt, broke out in 1639, on the rumor that the state intended to introduce the *gabelle* into the Cotentin peninsula.[1] On 16 July 1639, a crowd at Avranches killed and mutilated a judicial official suspected of bringing copies of the edicts establishing the *gabelle*; they even defiled his grave in an attempt to frighten other *gabeleurs*. Little more than a month later, the artisans of Rouen murdered the clerk sent to establish the dyed cloth tax

---

[1] Part of the Cotentin belonged to one of the ubiquitous exceptional tax regions. People in Lower Normandy obtained their salt by means of boiling sea water trapped in shallow flats. This region had a tax system called the *quart bouillon*, because the king took one-quarter of the salt produced and did not tax the rest. Those who worked in the salt flats did so in their bare feet, hence the name of the rebellion.

and sacked the houses of the tax farmers. The bourgeois militia, called out to put down the disturbance, sided with the crowd and fought the royal troops, even murdering a royal captain in the church of Saint-Ouen.

By September 1639, the peasants had 20,000 men under arms, fully organized into companies that reported to regular musters. Order collapsed in the other Norman towns, notably Caen, which had had several risings in the mid-1630s. The urban disturbances died down during the fall, but the rural rebels remained in arms; the king eventually had to send an army of foreign mercenaries, for fear that French troops would sympathize with the rebels. Under colonel Gassion, they routed the peasants in a series of skirmishes near Avranches. His troops then looted and pillaged the town and surrounding countryside. In January 1640, chancellor Séguier came to Rouen, dismissed the Parlement and the other main courts of the province, removed the town council, and established a special commission to mete out exemplary punishments. This repression obtained some immediate money from the province (notably the fine of one million *livres* on Rouen) but the troops could not ensure the flow of tax revenues; in 1641, the *élection* of Valognes, on the Cotentin peninsula, paid only 17 percent of its taxes.

The non-payment of taxes became endemic in the late 1630s. In August 1639, the receiver general of Champagne complained that he had received *nothing* from that year's levy. Non-payment of taxes reached staggering proportions in the Southwest (Limousin, Périgord), in the Midi (Bourbonnais, Berry), and in Lower Normandy. Oddly enough, the *pays d'Etats* did pay their taxes, enabling the king to supply his armies in Languedoc, Provence, and Dauphiné, as well as to outfit ships in Brittany. Despite this minor financial success, the desperate straits of the French monarchy made military victory impossible. The constant internal disorder, reflected both in massive rebellions such as the Nu-Pieds and in the innumerable outbursts in every province and in many major towns, made sustained efforts against Spain out of the question.

Fortunately for the French, the Spanish government was in even worse shape. At this time, the king of Spain ruled the entire Iberian peninsula, which consisted of three separate kingdoms: Aragon, Castile, and Portugal. These areas had their own laws, their own *Cortes* (Estates), and their own languages. Castile furnished the bulk of the men and money for the war effort (the New World was considered an adjunct of Castile); the king's efforts to obtain more money from Aragon and Portugal helped to accentuate separatist feelings. In 1641, the dam broke: revolts broke out in Catalonia and in Portugal. The Portuguese succeeded in reestablishing their independence (lost in the 1580s) and the Catalans crippled the

Spanish war effort in the Pyrenees. The Catalan provinces split up, with Roussillon falling to a French army in 1642. The present Pyrenean boundary between France and Spain dates from the treaty of 1659, which legalized the French seizure of Roussillon and the Cerdagne, and established the tortuous serpentine dividing line that has persisted to this day, making it the oldest state boundary in continental Europe.

The major actors in this conflict disappeared in the early 1640s. Richelieu died in late 1642 and Louis XIII early in 1643; in Spain, the royal minister favorite, the count-duke of Olivares, was disgraced. Oddly enough, only six days after Louis XIII's death, the French and Spanish armies fought their most important engagement of the long war, at Rocroi (May 1643) in northern France. The young duke d'Enghien, soon to be prince of Condé, annihilated the main Spanish army, killing or capturing most members of the old-guard (that is, purely Spanish) *tercios*. Rocroi was, in a certain sense, a triumph for the French aristocracy, because Condé's (noble) cavalry struck the decisive blows in a series of wild charges against the Spanish cavalry and, in a flanking movement, against the *tercios*. In a broader tactical sense, however, Rocroi symbolized dramatic shifts in the nature of warfare; for that reason, it warrants a brief digression on the actual course of the battle.

The invading Spanish army under Don Francisco Melo de Braganza laid itself out in the classic three battles: cavalry on the left, mixed troops on the right, and the "invincible" *tercios* in the center. The *tercios* were large blocks of pikemen, with clusters of musketeers placed at each corner of each block. The French attack at Rocroi borrowed much from the successful tactics of Gustavus Adolphus. Condé and the French cavalry, stationed on the right, attacked the Spanish cavalry and put them to flight. In most contemporary battles, the cavalry would then have pursued their opponents, avoiding a direct confrontation with the deadly, impenetrable forest of pikes; Condé and Gassion (whom we have met above, crushing the Nu-Pieds) instead turned on the Spanish right and, in conjunction with the French infantry, routed it as well. The combined forces of the French army next attacked the *tercios*. The French artillery pounded the *tercios*, who made an ideal target, with their dense mass of men; when the artillery had dented the blocks, the French infantry attacked. After the combined infantry and artillery had weakened the *tercios*, Condé led a series of furious cavalry charges against the pikemen. His success was complete; the French killed or captured virtually all of the officers and obliterated the Spanish core of the army. Condé took so many prisoners that the towns of western France, required to maintain the prisoners after the battle, complained that their upkeep would bankrupt the town budgets.

Tactically, the battle confirmed the death of the old, pike-dominated armies of the sixteenth and early seventeenth centuries. The French army adopted three innovations of Gustavus Adolphus's Swedish army, using the combined arms of infantry, with a much higher ratio of musketeers to pikemen to increase its firepower; artillery, now including light field pieces; and lighter, more mobile cavalry who charged at full gallop into the gaps created by the greater firepower. Rocroi represented both a triumph of the past, of the aristocratic French cavalry, and of the future, the supremacy of gun over pike.

The Fronde

The Parlementaire Fronde

Back home, the king's death had its usual effect: the aristocracy began to quarrel over the spoils of state. First, there was the issue of who would become Regent for the boy king, Louis XIV (born in 1638). The Queen Mother, Anne of Austria, quickly won that contest with the support of the chief minister, Cardinal Mazarin, and of the Parlement of Paris. On his deathbed, Richelieu recommended Mazarin, who had been his trusted client after the Mantuan settlement, as his successor. Mazarin was also Louis XIV's godfather, a role of great importance after the death of Louis XIII in May 1643. The precise nature of Mazarin's relationship to Anne of Austria is unclear; her most recent biographer believes it to have been platonic rather than romantic, but surviving letters are open to both interpretations.[2]

The Queen Mother bought off the other chief claimant, the king's uncle, Gaston of Orléans: Gaston became governor of Languedoc and received money grants that enabled him to maintain his personal household staff of 400 people, as well as to add a wing to the chateau of Blois. Anne and Mazarin either co-opted Richelieu's clients, like chancellor Séguier, or disgraced them, like Sublet de Noyers. They replaced Sublet as secretary of war with the founder of another ministerial dynasty, Michel Le Tellier.

The deaths of Louis XIII and Richelieu enable us to see clearly the nature of the French state in 1643. First, we must recognize the extremely personal nature of power. The absence of an adult king crippled the government because of the importance of personal ties between the king and the grandees in maintaining political stability. The death of Richelieu, who had established an elaborate clientage network throughout the kingdom, exacerbated the problem. Richelieu's clients included

[2] R. Kleinmann, *Anne of Austria* (Columbus, OH: Ohio State University Press, 1985).

many of the kingdom's grandee governors: Condé in Burgundy, Schomberg in Languedoc, Conti (brother of Condé) in Picardy. Richelieu himself had governed Brittany, with the assistance of two of his cousins, the baron of Pontchâteau (from a powerful Breton family), and the duke of la Meilleraye, lieutenant general of the province, marshal of the army, and grand master of the artillery.

After Richelieu's death, Mazarin and Anne of Austria dismembered most of this network. Richelieu's creatures on the royal council divided into two factions, which helped to spread confusion in his regional networks. Anne of Austria and Mazarin, eager to placate potentially hostile grandees, restructured the governorships: in Languedoc, Gaston of Orléans replaced Schomberg (1644); in Guyenne, Bernard de la Valette became governor after the Parlement of Paris overturned his conviction for treason; in Brittany, Anne of Austria herself assumed the governorship, dispossessing la Meilleraye. Gaston, a lifelong enemy of Richelieu, restored the clientage network of the Montmorency family (governors of Languedoc until the execution of the duke for treason, in 1632); that is, he destroyed the power of all those who had supported Richelieu.

The special case of Bernard de la Valette illustrates the tenuous nature of state power in the 1640s, and the key role of specific individuals, usually grandees, in maintaining order. He proved to be Mazarin's worst choice for a new governor, because he sought only to settle scores with the Richelieu clients who had opposed his father. Richelieu had had a tumultuous relationship with the Epernon family, headed by la Valette's father, the duke of Epernon, long-standing governor of Guyenne (who was also, let us recall, colonel-general of the infantry, an extremely powerful post that Richelieu wished to abolish). La Valette even married Richelieu's niece in an effort to cement their ties. The old duke, however, a very difficult individual, frequently quarreled with Richelieu's other clients, notably the archbishop of Bordeaux, Henri d'Escoubleau de Sourdis. Sourdis received a long series of insults, even a physical attack, from Epernon's clients in the mid-1630s. The Epernon family fell into disgrace in the late 1630s, in part due to the military failure of Bernard de la Valette at the battle of Fuenterrabia.

At that disaster (September 1638), the three commanders had been the old prince of Condé, Bernard de la Valette, and the duke of Epernon's mortal enemy, Archbishop Sourdis of Bordeaux. When the early successes at Fuenterrabia ended in an ignominious rout of the French forces, Condé and Sourdis blamed la Valette, who fled to England. A special court tried and convicted him *in absentia*; the court sentenced him to death (a sentence carried out in effigy). The king named the old prince of

Condé governor of Guyenne. One can well imagine the intense hatred between the Condé and Epernon families after the events of 1638. Little wonder that the Fronde in Bordeaux was so protracted (see pp. 73–74).

Quite aside from the problems created by ill-chosen governors such as Epernon or Gaston of Orléans, the dismal financial situation made effective governance virtually impossible. By the late 1630s entire regions of the country no longer paid their taxes. The king's death and the great victory of Rocroi did little to improve the situation. The government so despaired of using the regular apparatus to run the country that it instituted a dual reform in 1642: it allowed the intendants to apportion and supervise the collection of the direct taxes and it allowed farming of those taxes. At the same time, the government reduced the *gages* and annuities of the officers to 50 percent (and later 25 percent) of their face value. Here we see the same mechanism employed in 1634: reduce the power of the officers and simultaneously attack their financial investments in the government.

Officer cooperation with the central government, already tenuous, collapsed. In 1643, in Berry, the king received none of the assessed 600,000 *livres*. Nearby, in the *élection* of Aurillac, only two of the ninety-six parishes had even drawn up their 1643 tax rolls by November; in the *élection* of Conches, the king received only 11,000 of the assessment of 380,000 *livres*; in Normandy, the *élection* of Mortagne had paid only one percent of its 1643 taxes by June. The lack of an adult king, the disintegration of Richelieu's carefully constructed patronage network, and the general sense that peace was at hand after the French and Swedish victories of 1642–43, combined to bring the government's finances to ruin.

The government greatly exacerbated its financial problems by mortgaging future revenues, to the extent that it had spent most of the projected income from 1644 by the end of 1642. A special effort in 1646 to achieve final victory brought this policy to its preposterous climax; the king's council demanded in 1646 that the receiver general of Poitou forward 962,850 *livres* from the receipts of 1651! The government, unable to collect its own taxes, tried to shift the burden onto private contractors: in return for a given amount, the financier would collect the direct taxes of a specific area. The king set the general amount and the intendant now set the amount for a given *élection*; the financier then had the right to try to collect the official amount. Any difference between what he paid the king and what he could collect was his profit (after deducting expenses).

In short, those receiving the taxes had become bankers to the king, providing him with advances against future revenues. He, in turn, gave them "interest" on these advances. By the late 1640s, this "interest" rate of 50 percent merely indicated that the receiver in question was only likely to be able to collect 60 percent of the assessment. No doubt competition for those taxes most likely to be collected – certain indirect taxes, the direct taxes of areas around Paris, in Upper Normandy, or in other areas in which troops could be used to threaten the population – was intense, while few people willingly risked their money on collecting the taxes of the Midi or other known trouble spots.

Time and again French and Spanish armies ran out of money and supplies; they responded by looting the countryside, whether in territory of friend or foe. The king admitted as much, telling the estates of Brittany in 1649 that "the ruin of the said provinces [of eastern France], occasioned as much by the damages caused by the troops His Majesty has been required to keep there as by the ravages of the enemy" meant he needed more money from unscathed areas such as Brittany. The instability of the provinces – the loss of control of the old clientage networks, the inability to collect the taxes, the alienation of the royal officers – gradually undermined the power of the central government.

Historians have long considered the Fronde, the civil wars of the period 1648–53, to have started in Paris and spread to the provinces. In fact, quite the opposite was the case: the Parlementary Fronde of 1648 was a case of the discontent of the provinces spreading at last to Paris. The first or Parlementary Fronde broke out because the officers of Paris had reached the same state of exasperation as their provincial colleagues. Anne of Austria bought the cooperation of the Parlement of Paris (and of the other major Parisian courts) by a series of favorable edicts in the mid-1640s. The Parlement helped her break Louis XIII's will and establish herself as fully empowered Regent; in return, she gave the officers of the Parlement nobility in the first degree: any judge serving at least twenty years or dying in office ennobled himself and his posterity. She later extended this privilege to the masters of requests of the king's household, to the masters of accounts of the Paris Chamber of Accounts, and to the leading officers of the Paris Court of Aids.

Meanwhile, in the provinces, the intendants (and some officers) fought most of the regular officers in a no-quarter battle for control of the kingdom. The archives of the period are filled with recriminations of the intendants against the officers and of the officers against the intendants. In some provinces, such as Provence, the situation deteriorated into severe factional fighting. In others, such as Languedoc, Richelieu's clientage network collapsed and the intendants, faced with the intransigence of the governor, Gaston of Orléans, and his clients, proved unable to carry out the government's orders. In Languedoc, the nadir came in

1645, when a popular rebellion broke out in Montpellier despite the opposition of both factions of the local elite.

The sovereign courts of Paris had their conflicts with intendants and financiers but they did not break with the government until the spring of 1648. The Parlement detested the financier Particelli d'Emery, who had been unofficial head of the king's finances since 1643 (and official head since 1647), particularly his cavalier attitude toward interest payments to royal officials. In the winter of 1647–48, the government made clear its intention to attack the investments of the officers on two fronts: reduced payment of *gages* and annuities, and elimination of the *paulette*. Jurisdictional quarrels were one thing (they lasted as long as the Old Regime) but an attack on the property of the officers could not be tolerated. Reducing *gages* and annuities, by paying them at half face value (or less), was also an old tactic: the king had used it in 1634 and again in 1642, to cite only two examples. These reductions reduced the officers' interest income but did not severely damage the capital invested in their offices. The abolition of the *paulette*, however, would reduce dramatically the value of their offices, thereby undermining their invested capital. As Machiavelli said, men sooner forgive the loss of their father than of their patrimony.

The Parlement protested vigorously against these fiscal innovations and against the steady stream of new taxes invented by the government. Their opposition to the new tariffs on goods entering Paris endeared the Parlement to the Parisian masses; many ordinary Parisians owned royal annuities, so that the Parlement also appeared as their champion in that cause (even though it was precisely its own heavy investments in such annuities that concerned the court). When the government issued an edict in April renewing the *paulette* in return for not paying the *gages* of royal officers (except Parlementaires), some members of the courts of Paris began to meet to formulate a combined response. In mid-May, the Parlement joined the other courts in establishing the Chambre Saint-Louis, which drew up a list of twenty-seven articles to submit to the king. These articles included the renewal of the *paulette*, the full payment of royal obligations, and the reduction of direct taxes by 25 percent; they also included a clause that required the government to get the approval of the courts before creating any new offices or levying any new taxes. The courts were even to execute these financial edicts. The courts demanded the abolition of the *acquits de comptants*, that is, the money spent solely at the king's discretion, with no official documentation to support its disbursement. All royal accounts, even those of the king's household, had to be audited by the Chamber of Accounts; in these audits, all expenses other than the *acquits de comptants* had to be justified by means of supporting documentation. The *acquits*, which had been some two million *livres* a year under Henry IV (a sum considered scandalous by the Chamber of his day), reached 52 million *livres* in 1644. Finally, the courts demanded the abolition of arbitrary arrest and detention beyond 24 hours.

Here one sees the confusing nature of the Parlements, pointed out in the introduction. The Parlement, in theory a purely judicial body, was, in practice, partly legislative and even executive. The courts demanded the abolition of the intendants, a further illustration of their unhappiness at the expansion of executive powers that escaped their oversight. It must be emphasized strongly that the courts acted thus in a period of a royal minority; moreover, they were certainly aware of the fact that Louis XIII had wished to establish some outside controls over his wife's Regency, because the Parlement itself had eliminated those controls. The Parlement strongly disliked the foreign triumvirate ruling France: a Spanish princess, Anne of Austria, and two "Italians", Mazarin and Particelli d'Emery (the latter, in fact, a Frenchman of Italian descent).

The Parlementary Fronde was not a constitutional war between proponents of mixed monarchy (the Parlement) and those of absolutism (Anne, Mazarin, and the boy king). The Parlement acted to protect its most vital economic interest – the preservation of its capital – and to eliminate some of the abuses of the financiers and royal ministers. The Fronde did not lead to the breakdown of order; rather, the breakdown of order led to the Fronde.

The government temporized with the courts, waiting for favorable news elsewhere. In late August, it came, with Condé's victory at Lens; at the *Te Deum* celebrating the victory, the government arrested the leaders of the Parlementary resistance, notably Claude Broussel. Broussel, one of the senior judges, was renowned for his honesty, learning, and, amazing to say, his relative poverty; he had considerable popularity in the city and wide respect in the court. Learning of his arrest, the Parisians erected over 1,200 barricades in the streets during the night of 26–27 August 1648. When Anne of Austria sent chancellor Séguier to the Parlement on the morning of the 27th, an irate crowd surrounded his carriage and forced him, his brother, and his daughter to abandon the carriage and hide in a nearby house. The crowd ransacked the house, searching for the chancellor (although they returned the pillaged items shortly afterward). The duke de la Meilleraye and a detachment of cavalry rescued the terrified chancellor.

Parlement set off as a body, 150 strong, to meet Anne at the Louvre. Soon a crowd of 20,000 marched behind them. When Anne refused to release Broussel unless the Parlement ceased its political activities, the Parlement set off for the Palace of Justice to discuss her terms. The crowd, led by the bourgeois militia of Paris, refused to allow them to pass through the barricades when the crowd learned that Broussel remained in jail. The Parlement then marched back to the Louvre, where it accepted Anne's terms. In reality, the two sides had agreed to discuss their respective demands. Anne and Mazarin wanted the Parlement to stay out of political matters; the Parlement wanted fiscal reform, the elimination of intendants, and an end to corruption in government. Anne eventually gave in on most of these points; the declaration of Saint-Germain (24 October) gave force of law to the May declaration of the Chambre Saint-Louis. In return, the Parlement registered without difficulty the Peace of Westphalia.

Far from establishing a permanent peace, the events of the fall of 1648 led to open war between the Parlement and some of the grandees, on one side, and the government and other grandees. The king and queen had to flee Paris, and then enrolled the prince of Condé and his army to besiege the city, controlled by the Parlement. This "war" lasted only three months and ended with the peace of Rueil (March 1649) that restored the situation of October 1648. The courts obtained the full implementation of the *paulette*, the abolition of the intendants, the permanent disgrace of d'Emery (and his replacement by the king's attorney of the Parlement, Nicolas Fouquet), the reduction of the direct taxes by 25 percent, and the power to oversee more fully the fiscal system. The grandee rebels received large pensions, various offices, and a full pardon. At the upper levels of society, there followed eight intrigue-filled but relatively peaceful months. In the provinces, however, it was a different matter.

The Fronde of the princes

Order broke down completely by late 1648. In the Loire valley, armed troops of mounted nobles escorted barges filled with salt past the checkpoints of the *gabelle*. They fought pitched battles with the archers of the *gabelle*, battles that involved hundreds of combatants on each side. The town government of Angers underwrote one such venture. In Provence, the Parlement and the governor conducted a civil war of their own, one that ended with the Parlement arresting the governor, the intendant, and the commander of the royal Mediterranean Navy. This quarrel, too, antedated the Parisian Fronde: when Mazarin attempted to create a second session of the Parlement of Aix, the Semester Parlement, the first man to buy one of the offices, Philippe Guiedon, was murdered while eating dinner in his inn (18 March 1648). Those loosely implicated in the murder included a who's who of Provençal judges. The news of the

Day of the Barricades in Paris only made matters worse, forcing the governor, the count d'Alais, to bring in 1,500 troops and to cancel the municipal elections. When the news of the royal family's flight from Paris reached Aix, d'Alais stepped up his military preparations. The Parlement responded by calling on its own supporters to put up barricades; the Parlementaires then brought in armed supporters from the surrounding countryside. The lieutenant general and the archbishop of Arles worked around the clock to negotiate a truce, at last succeeding. Two days later, however, a well-organized revolt captured d'Alais, Sève, and the duke of Richelieu, and murdered the usual collection of fiscal clerks and servants of judges in the Semester Parlement.

The vast majority of provinces, from Languedoc to Normandy (Brittany was a rare exception), had similar incidents. After the peace of Rueil, the government and the Parlement got on much better, but the prince of Condé grew increasingly restive because he had not received as much for his loyalty as he had wished. Titular head of the king's council, he managed to alienate virtually everyone by means of his arrogance and the avidity of his followers. By January 1650, the government had completely isolated Condé. Mazarin arrested Condé, his brother (the prince of Conti), and his brother-in-law (the duke of Longueville, governor of Normandy). Condé's sister, the resourceful Anne-Geneviève de Bourbon, duchess of Longueville, remained at large. She managed to start a revolt in Normandy and Condé's clients did the same in his governorship of Burgundy. In Burgundy, the Condé family had such complete control of the local administration that people applied the term "Frondeurs" not to those attacking the government, but rather to Mazarin's forces. The king's attorney general at the Parlement of Burgundy, Millotet, wrote in his memoirs that every judge, every abbot, every commander of a fortress, or governor of a town was a client of the Condé family; all of them, he wrote, owed their position to the direct intervention of the prince of Condé or of his father. Even in the 1660s, the great reforming intendant of Burgundy, Claude Bouchu, was a client of the Condé family.

The government had one great weapon against these clientele forces: the king himself. Mazarin and Anne of Austria sent him on many trips around France between 1650 and 1652. He visited Normandy (making a royal entry into Rouen to restore loyalty there) and Champagne. From Champagne he went to Burgundy, heartland of the Condé network. One town after another opened its gates to him. At Bellegarde (now Seurre) the rebel garrison agreed to a one-day cease-fire in honor of his presence. When the royal troops shouted, "Vive le Roi," in response to the news, the rebel troops stunned their officers by joining in. The garrison soon surrendered, its 800 soldiers joining the royal army. Mazarin wrote of the king's presence:

Without flattery, the King has conducted himself marvellously well on this voyage; the soldiers are extraordinarily satisfied with him; if it had been permitted, there is no place he would not have gone. The enthusiasm of the soldiers was such that, if he had commanded it, I believe they would have eaten the doors of Bellegarde with their teeth.[3]

Louis XIV was only twelve, yet the personal loyalty to the king already could overwhelm other obstacles.

The king moved from Burgundy to Guyenne, marching toward Bordeaux. He was less successful there; the city at first refused to open its gates to him when he arrived in August 1650. Bordeaux was a unique case during the Fronde because of the complexity of its political situation. When the Parlement of Paris rescinded Bernard de la Valette's sentence of treason on 16 July 1643 and he succeeded to his father's position as governor of Guyenne, he unleashed a reign of terror against his father's enemies. The intendant of Guyenne, René Voyer d'Argenson, wrote to Mazarin that la Valette "lives only for vengeance . . . his implacable and overly haughty attitude caused a great part of the disorders which afflicted Guyenne."[4]

La Valette's (now duke d'Epernon, after his father's death in 1642) purge of the Condé–Richelieu clients created an atmosphere of intense hostility within the local ruling elite. That Sourdis remained archbishop of Bordeaux did not ease matters. In the late 1630s, la Valette had also alienated the local population by his role in the bloody suppression of the uprisings, so he had virtually no support within the region. He was a loyal client of Mazarin, but he was the worst possible man on whom to rely in a time of crisis because so many elements of Guyennais society – the Parlement, the archbishop of Bordeaux, the old clients of Richelieu, and the ordinary people – detested him. When the Fronde broke out, this vast coalition quickly drove la Valette from the province, leaving Mazarin with no one on whom to rely in Guyenne.

La Valette later served Mazarin admirably as governor of Burgundy. In 1651, as part of his efforts to destroy the Condé clientage network in Burgundy, Mazarin named la Valette governor of the province. The duke captured rebel fortresses and reached an effective working relationship with the Parlement. That la Valette should be so hopelessly ineffective in Guyenne and yet completely successful in Burgundy underlines the profoundly personal nature of power in this society. The capabilities of

[3] F. Bluche, *Louis XIV*, trans. M. Greengrass (Oxford: Basil Blackwell, 1990), 91.
[4] R. Mousnier, *Lettres et mémoires adressés au chancellor Séguier, 1633–1649* (Paris: Presses Universitaires de France, 1964), 2 vols., I, 102–03.

the individuals wielding power formed only half of the equation; they had to be people who could work effectively with the local ruling elite.

La Valette's flight from Guyenne left a power vacuum; when Condé split with Mazarin, the princess of Condé came to Bordeaux to demand the aid of the inhabitants. Given the hostility of the Parlement of Bordeaux, and of the city's ordinary citizens, to la Valette (and his patron Mazarin), their support for the princess was a foregone conclusion. When the king's army reached the city, however, a sharp split developed in this coalition. Many in the Parlement wanted to open the gates to the king, fearing the consequences of locking the king himself out of the city. The popular groups tended to back the Condé position, but they eventually acceded, allowing the king to enter on 1 October (perhaps, as many historians have suggested, because the citizens of Bordeaux wanted to bring in the grape harvest!).

The following summer, the dispute between the princely party, still allied with the popular coalition, and the Parlement broke out again. This time the general population of the city also organized into factions, one of the merchants and another of the *menu peuple* (little people: artisans, laborers). A combined group of merchants, lawyers, and petty judges, and artisans created a new assembly in Bordeaux, called the Ormée, after the elm grove in which it held its first meetings. The Ormée supported Condé and soon gained control of the city. The most radical group of the Fronde, they produced pamphlets with vaguely democratic and republican sentiments (offering faint echoes of contemporary events in England that so distressed French ruling classes), and sometimes attacking (and looting) the houses of the rich. As one might expect, the Parlement and, eventually, the princely party grew increasingly restive with their radical allies. A year later, the royal army sent to besiege Bordeaux found many allies within the city, which surrendered after a brief resistance. The government executed the leaders of the Ormée and the city lost several of its privileges. The Parlement spent several years in exile at Agen, there to ponder the folly of open resistance to their king.

Bordeaux was not the only city to resist the king. In Provence, the constant factional fighting favored first one side, then the other. During the Fronde itself, the faction of Antoine de Valbelle, scion of the leading family of Marseilles, defeated the forces of Louis de Valois, count of Alais (grandson through illegitimate line of King Charles IX), governor of Provence. Valbelle's loyalty to Mazarin during the Fronde led the cardinal to grant him the right to reorganize municipal elections in Marseilles, in a manner such as to guarantee the control of his faction. When the new governor of the province, the duke of Mercoeur (son of Henry IV's bastard, César of Vendôme), and the First President of the

Parlement, the baron d'Oppède, interceded with Mazarin to return the municipal election rules to the old standard (and used those rules to elect anti-Valbelle candidates in 1656 and 1657), Valbelle responded by inciting a rebellion. His forces quickly restored the revised rules and elected his clients in 1658 and 1659. After further factional fighting, the Valbelles left the city. When Louis XIV visited Marseilles in 1660, he offered the city the extraordinary insult of refusing to enter by the city gate; instead, he entered through a breach in the walls, like a conqueror. The king quickly changed the municipal election rules, permanently eliminating the local nobility (and their leader, Valbelle) from any important role in the municipal government.[5]

The widespread factional fighting so evident in Marseilles or Bordeaux exacerbated the international situation. During the king's 1650 visit to Bordeaux, a Spanish army, led by one of the two greatest French generals of the age, the viscount of Turenne, invaded from the north. Turenne had joined the rebels because of his infatuation with the duchess of Longueville. In Paris itself, the coadjutator archbishop, the (soon-to-be) Cardinal de Retz, agitated against Mazarin. Mazarin at last gave in to the coalition (precisely the same one that had acted against Condé in January 1650), and fled Paris in February 1651, moving to Bruhl, near Cologne. The coalition, as one might expect, disintegrated fighting over the spoils. Some of the main conspirators, such as the duchess of Chevreuse (from the very high-ranking Rohan family, former first lady of Anne of Austria), went back over to Mazarin's side. The Parlement and even Retz and Gaston of Orléans joined in against Condé, who fled Paris for Bordeaux in September 1651. In December, Mazarin marched on the capital with a small army.

The Parlement and the Cardinal de Retz had no use for either Condé or Mazarin. The other Frondeurs, such as Turenne, tended to rejoin the cardinal. On 1 July 1652, Turenne trapped Condé's rebel army against the walls of Paris, but Gaston of Orléans's daughter, Anne Marie Montpensier de Bourbon, called the Grande Mademoiselle, ordered the garrison of the Bastille to turn its guns on the royal army and opened the Saint-Antoine gate to Condé's army. A month later, Mazarin went into exile again (at Bouillon), hoping to achieve the compromise of the king and Queen Mother returning to power without him. In October, the king returned to Paris; four months later, Mazarin came back as well. In the interim, the king had arrested the Cardinal de Retz and Condé had made an alliance with the Spaniards. The rules of the game had changed by

---

[5] This tale and the earlier ones about Provence come from S. Kettering, *Patrons, Brokers, and Clients in Seventeenth-Century France* (Oxford: Oxford University Press, 1986), 77–85 on Valbelle.

1652; the Frondeurs could no longer argue so persuasively that the boy king was misled by evil advisors: Louis XIV had declared his legal majority on 7 December 1651, in a special *lit de justice* (royal seance) in front of the Parlement of Paris.

The three Frondes – Parlementaire, grandee, and religious (discussed below) – were not an effort to change the existing system of government. The thousands of anti-government pamphlets, the Mazarinades, did not propose a return to a "feudal" monarchy or the establishment of a republic. As Christian Jouhaud has said of the Mazarinades: "This Fronde of words was not a Fronde of ideas."[6] The pamphleteers, reflecting the thoughts of their grandee masters, demanded the resignation of Mazarin and his replacement by Condé or Retz or some other grandee. The Fronde was not a revolutionary movement seeking to change the form of the French government nor was it a last-gasp protest by the "feudal" nobility against the emerging "absolute" monarchy; it was a struggle for control of the state by specific individuals or groups of individuals.

The Parlementary Fronde appears to have been the most radical in possibility because the courts demanded (and received) so many new powers that the full implementation of their program would have changed the nature of the monarchy. Yet we must remember that the Parlement acted during a royal minority, a traditional period of Parlementaire offensive. It is anachronistic to see the outward similarities of Parlementaire actions and arguments of 1648 and of the late eighteenth century as evidence of a continuous Parlementaire program of constitutionalism. The Parlement certainly wanted to expand its power and to reduce the power of its opponents (such as the intendants), yet this same radical Parlement meekly accepted the gradual repudiation of the Rueil agreement by the legally adult king after 1652. They did so because the government respected the legitimacy of many of the Parlementaire criticisms and because the government satisfied their most urgent demand: renewal of the *paulette* and the consequent stabilization of the value of their capital assets (offices). The government also began (slowly, to be sure) to pay once again its financial obligations to officers and bond holders.

The religious Fronde

This progress should not mask the considerable difficulties that remained at the time of Louis XIV's coronation. Tax strikes continued: in the

[6] C. Jouhaud, *Mazarinades: la Fronde des mots* (Paris: Aubier, 1985), 237.

généralité of Moulins, back taxes due totaled 8.4 million *livres* by 1654. The religious Fronde intensified in Paris. The Cardinal de Retz, a personal enemy of Mazarin (whom he had hoped to succeed during the height of the Fronde), had become titular archbishop of Paris after the death of his uncle (with whom he shared the see) in 1653. The government did not recognize Retz as archbishop of Paris, keeping him under arrest through most of the 1650s and keeping up a steady pressure on the Pope to disassociate himself from Retz. Retz, for his part, had the power to put Paris under the interdict: that is, he could forbid the performance of all sacraments within his archbishopric. His parish priest allies (more than three-quarters of them supported Retz rather than the government) would certainly have obeyed his orders, and they would have received political support from the Parlement, which contained many judges sympathetic to Jansenism.

Retz and the parish priests had allied themselves with the Jansenists, against their mutual sworn enemies, the Jesuits, allied with the government. Jansenism, which had many sympathizers in the Parlement, thus came to be identified with an anti-government position, even though the religious Jansenists did not really pursue political goals. Jesuit attacks on Jansenists such as Antoine Arnauld (a professor at the Sorbonne and member of a powerful robe family) led to a spirited counterattack by the great mathematician Blaise Pascal, whose *Provincial Letters* lambasted the Jesuits for their lax morality and their "situational ethics" with respect to the Gospel's moral teachings. Pascal brought Parisian elite opinion strongly over to the side of the anti-Jesuits. The complex network of problems created during the Frondes – the jumbling together of different intellectual currents such as Jansenism, Gallicanism, and anti-Jesuit sentiments, with the temporary political conflicts of the early 1650s – would intermittently bedevil the monarchy for another 130 years.

It is traditional to see a decisive break in the reign of Louis XIV in 1661, when Mazarin died and the king took personal control of the government. Attractive as that approach may be, we are better served by moving our attention back into the 1650s because of the strong continuities between the late 1650s and the 1660s. The period between the second return of Mazarin (February 1653) and his death (1660) is usually treated as an afterthought, as neither part of the Fronde era nor part of the glorious rise of Louis XIV. Such a focus, however, is too personal, too Parisian. There was a significant shift in the provinces in the mid-1650s. The chaos of the late 1640s and early 1650s abated. Political stability returned in many (but not all) areas. Broader social and economic indicators turned up once again: births began to rise, deaths to decline; trade volume went up, improving indirect tax receipts as it rose; royal demands for taxation declined and leveled off – lower rates meant greater compliance and, probably, higher real returns.

Rather than wait for Louis's assumption of ministerial power in 1661, let us begin our examination of his reign with a far richer, more powerfully symbolic act: his coronation.

3   Louis XIV and the creation of
the modern state

"Vive le Roi!"

On 7 June 1654, Louis XIV, Anne of Austria, Cardinal Mazarin, and virtually all of the great nobles of France gathered in the Gothic cathedral of Notre Dame in Reims for the king's coronation. The grandees performed their official functions at the great ceremony: the count of Vivonne, first gentleman of the king's chamber, removed Louis's cloak; the duke of Joyeuse, grand chamberlain, put on the king's slippers; the king's brother, Philip, duke of Anjou, put on the king's spurs. The bishop of Soissons, standing in for the archbishop of Reims (the see was then vacant), blessed the king's sword, reputed to be that of Charlemagne himself. The bishop then vested Louis with his sceptre and the crown of Charlemagne. Preceded by the peers of France, Louis slowly mounted the special stairway to his throne, there to receive, one by one, the homage of each peer of the realm.[1]

The grand ceremonial of the coronation did not stop there; the assembly had to sing a *Te Deum*, followed by a mass. At the mass, we see Louis's special status symbolically defined: like the clergy, alone among the lay people, he receives the communion in two kinds. Kingship remains profoundly sacerdotal; the king is not really a priest, yet he has the aura of ordination after his coronation and anointing with the miraculous oils. These oils, kept in a special ornate cruet in the sacristy of Reims, are miraculously replenished before each coronation; no human has added fluid to replenish the oil used in the previous coronation (or so contemporaries believed). The sacred oils testify to the sacerdotal quality of kingship. In recognition of his new, sacred character, two days later the king performs the age-old ritual of healing the king's disease, scrofula. Two thousand people infected with scrofula are brought to him to be touched; by his touch, they will be healed. The same day, Louis will pardon 600 prisoners, the first evidence of his intention to fulfill his coronation oath promise to offer mercy to his people.

---

[1] Bluche, *Louis XIV*, 20–25.

Here we see the king's three contracts: with God, with the grandees, and with his people. The contract with God provides the underlying basis for the others. We see the king anointed by the Church, supported by his grandees, and acclaimed by his people, at the end of the ceremony, when the bishop of Soissons intones, "long live the king," and the doors of Notre Dame are opened to allow those inside (the nobles) and those outside (the people) alike to shout: "Vive le Roi!"

The sacralization of the coronation ceremony offers the ideal symbol of the nature of royal power. The king's power emanates from God, although more in the sense of the king as God's *anointed* rather than God's *appointed* representative. The sacred basis of this power binds the king as much as it frees him. We see the latter quite clearly – one easily describes power grounded in divine approbation as absolute – but religion also set limits to the king's power. The king, as God's representative on earth, is, above all men, subject to the laws of God; those laws, like the Decalogue, establish clear limits to the king's power. To take only the three most relevant commandments, the king cannot covet the property of his subjects, he must not bear false witness, and he must follow only the true religion. To contemporaries, this second restriction, the sanctity of the oath, of the promise, of the *contract*, provides the most important check on the French monarchy.

The coronation ceremony itself includes the personal homage of the peers of France; homage binds the lord as well as the vassal. Each promises to the other; the promise binds the king as well as the duke. Similarly, the king has contracts with all of his powerful subjects: with the clergy, whose liberties and immunities the coronation oath itself specifically guarantees, with towns, provinces, and corporate groups of all kinds. The king has a contract with the kingdom; following the precedent established at the ceremony of Henry II (1547), Louis XIV "solemnly marries his realm" when he accepts the royal ring. As the "oldest son of the Church," the king bears singular responsibility to respect these contracts, to bear true witness in his dealings with all subjects. Those outside the circle of specific contracts seek protection in the oath's promises of peace, mercy, and justice, and in the king's responsibility, as a "husband," to protect his wife (the kingdom).

The king's coronation promises to do justice and to give mercy underlay the social order. Justice meant, above all, the preservation of each in his or her place in the order of society. Like most people of his time, Louis XIV had a singular obsession, one exacerbated by the Fronde, with the preservation of order. The king had an overwhelming mandate for the restoration of the "natural" order of society. By restoring everyone to their legitimate place in society, the king could establish justice.

The contemporaries of Louis XIII felt he had too strong a commitment to justice, that he ignored the second promise of his coronation oath: to show mercy. Louis XIV quickly demonstrated his willingness to temper justice with mercy. He pardoned most of the Frondeurs and gave many of them important royal positions. The viscount of Turenne became commander of the royal army; the king even pardoned the most hardened Frondeur, the prince of Condé, who added treason (seven years fighting on the side of the Spanish against an *adult* king) to the crime of rebellion. Others Louis treated only with justice: the duke de la Rochefoucauld and the Cardinal de Retz. Retz is the most famous victim, long imprisoned and eventually forced to relinquish his archbishopric of Paris. Some have argued that Mazarin's intense personal hatred of Retz led him to demand of Louis that he never pardon Retz, but the king needed no urging; he believed that Retz had attacked the sacerdotal nature of kingship. Retz and the Parisian parish priests, by their religious rebellion against the king, in effect denied his special sacral position. Louis long remembered this threat to the essence of his kingship. The connection between religion and kingship remained very strong throughout his life.

We should not, however, deny the king's profound personal dislike of Retz. Louis XIV had a very strong personality, one that reacted viscerally to specific individuals, such as Retz or Fouquet, whom he felt had affronted his royal dignity. Louis learned his lessons from a variety of masters. From his tutor, Mazarin, he took a profound suspicion of faction and of threats to the royal power and/or the royal dignity. Richelieu, Mazarin, and Louis XIV all agreed on this last element: they saw affronts to the royal dignity as *political* statements. From his mother, Anne of Austria, he took the Spanish love of ceremonial; Louis XIV carried the elaborate punctilio of the Spanish court one step further, to the regimented daily ballet of Versailles. The Spanish ceremonial blended perfectly with the French concern about dignity; by establishing an extraordinarily elaborate system of courtesy (Court etiquette), the king could impose respect for his dignity, and, by extension, royal power, in the most mundane daily act.

Louis also had a strong cultural attachment to his nobility: he once said his greatest title was to be first nobleman in his kingdom. The nobles liked to consider the king as *primus inter pares*, even after that fiction made little political sense. Louis wanted to establish the special (superior) qualities of royal blood, so he changed the ceremonial order at Court in favor of his bastards, yet he belonged to that same noble culture he thereby attacked. The king surrounded himself with his great nobles, not only to emasculate them politically but simultaneously to use their grandeur to cast favorable light upon his own and to provide himself with an ideal social setting in which to live. Louis loved the classic noble pursuits: the hunt, war, romantic affairs. The king's taste for elaborate balls and for art and music no doubt received considerable impetus from Mazarin, under whose patronage Italian culture (especially music and theatre) flourished. Surely he also learned from Mazarin the political uses of art.

Like most nobles of his time, Louis acted larger than life; Louis lived through the *geste*, and the *défi*, the challenge. Many of Louis's contemporaries, like the duke of Saint-Simon, left memoirs. Those who observed the king all spoke of his grandeur, of his commanding presence, and of his impeccable manners. The memoirists of Louis's early years invariably commented on his physical attractiveness; the king himself thought highly of his legs, whose shapeliness he liked to flaunt in official portraits.

We cannot understand Louis XIV without considering this noble cultural influence – his need for the grand gesture, for the challenge, for putting himself in the line of fire during the battle, for the passionate love affair. One side of Louis's personality wanted to be the first nobleman of his kingdom. Louis's chief general, viscount Henri de Turenne, whom contemporaries viewed as the perfect gentleman, served as Louis's model in noble comportment as well as in warfare. Mme. de Sévigné tells us of a two-hour discussion she had with several friends about Turenne's qualities:

Everyone spoke of the innocence of his morals, the purity of his intentions, his humility, far removed from any sort of affectation, the solid glory of which he was full, without show or ostentation, loving virtue for itself, without looking for the approbation of others: a generous and Christian charity.[2]

Louis aspired to many of these qualities, although no one would have suggested that he attained Turenne's level of innocence.

He engaged in a series of love affairs throughout his early life. His wife, Maria Theresa of Spain, did not match her husband's physicality. She had little of Louis's grandeur or his attractiveness; she did not share his passion for dancing (he himself regularly danced in the ballets put on for the Court). Maria Theresa, a devout Catholic, perhaps encouraged Louis's religious bent, although his personal morality violated Church law. Louis always treated Marie Theresa with public respect; according to his most recent biographer, despite his romantic liaisons, Louis returned each evening to the queen's bedroom.

Looking for a more compatible partner in his role as leader of Court

[2] Mme. de Sévigné, *Lettres*, ed. Gérard-Gailly (Paris: Bibliothèque de la Pléiade, 1953), I, 805–06, letter 332.

society, Louis had a series of mistresses and favorites. His first love, Marie Mancini, niece of Mazarin, had to be separated from him for political reasons. After his marriage to Maria Theresa, he soon fell in love with Louise de la Vallière, who remained his favorite from 1661 to 1667. Louis then switched his affections to Françoise-Athénaïs de Rochechouart-Mortemart, marquise of Montespan, who remained his titular favorite (the king had other, temporary liaisons) until 1681. The marquise of Montespan came from a distinguished noble family; unlike the relatively unpretentious Louise de la Vallière, Montespan played a major role in setting tastes and in promoting her own cultural agenda. She also produced a large number of children, eight, of whom four survived into adulthood. The king legitimized all these children; three of them married into the royal family (two to the Condé branch and one to Philip of Orléans, later Regent of France) and one into the Noailles family. Louis had other favorites, such as Anne de Soubise (Rohan) during these years, but they never attained the official status granted to Montespan or la Vallière. Montespan eventually lost favor to the woman she employed as a governess for her royal bastards: Françoise d'Aubigné, better known as Mme. de Maintenon (on whom, see chapter 4).

In keeping with Louis's own view of propriety, however, he never openly flaunted the sexual side of these relationships and maintained the greatest possible discretion about the precise nature of his relationship to all of his favorites.[3] The women also sought to atone for their private immorality with moral action. Both la Vallière (who refused Louis's suggestions that she marry because she did not want to become an adulteress) and Montespan (who was married) eventually retired to nunneries. Louise de la Vallière even wrote a devotional tract, *Reflections on the Mercy of God, by a Penitent Woman* (1680).[4]

The noble Louis played a dominant role in his personality. Although we tend to think of Louis as the Sun King, because he liked to have himself portrayed as Apollo, in fact the most common royal image was Mars, not Apollo: of the 318 medals struck during his reign to honor Louis, 218 portrayed him as the god of war and only 17 as the god of the sun.[5] Many seventeenth-century European kings, from England to Muscovy, used the sun king image. Louis's fascination with Mars speaks to his need to tie himself to that most noble of occupations, fighting.

In his pleasures, in his life of *geste*, Louis XIV was profoundly noble; in

---

[3] Anne de Soubise offers the best example of the king's discretion. To this day, no one has found any irrefutable evidence that she and Louis actually had an affair.

[4] Louise de la Vallière managed, throughout her liaison with the king, to remain on excellent terms with the queen. For details on the king's personal life, see Bluche, *Louis XIV*, ch. 14.

[5] Bluche, *Louis XIV*, 235.

his working life as king, however, Louis had an entirely different persona. Louis reveled in the minutiae of government. He actively participated in the three royal councils, working each morning (and many an afternoon) at the *métier* of king. Louis warned his son against the (noble) prejudice about concerning oneself with money, against the idea that it was "baseness" for the king to deal directly with money. Louis wisely told the Dauphin that "there is no project in which finances do not enter" and further that "there is not one subject that does not depend absolutely and essentially" on sufficient funds. The king had to know for himself how matters stood.

Louis understood perfectly the limitations on his options. He instructed his son that:

Neither you nor I, my son, can search out for these positions [minister] those whose distance or obscurity keep them from our view, whatever capacity they might have. We must by necessity choose from among a small number that luck presents us, that is, who are found already in important offices, or who by their birth or their inclination are closely attached to us.[6]

Louis sought always to make sure his assistants could never develop independent power bases on their own. He respected the separate functions of these ministers or courts (like the Parlement) but he wanted all power to come from him. He believed "nothing is more dangerous than weakness" and he sought always to maintain his (and the state's) position of strength. He took a Hobbesian or Machiavellian view of human nature. Speaking again of choice of ministers, he told his son: "[D]o not fool yourself, you are not dealing with angels but with men, whom excessive power will almost always in the end give some temptation to use it."[7] In Louis's view, he himself could never be so tempted because he understood that the good of the state (and thus of its people) was the very foundation of his own good; ministers, in contrast, often acted to obtain personal rather than public good.

Louis had to balance his desire to be *the* noble and his necessity to be king. When news of Turenne's death reached the Court, the nobles reacted with the customary histrionics. Turenne's nephew, the cardinal of Bouillon, did not eat for two days and spent those forty-eight hours crying and wildly throwing himself about. Others wailed and cried, contemplating suicide, much as Charlemagne's companions acted in the eleventh-century *Song of Roland* when they heard of Roland's death. Louis XIV, however, reacted with stoicism, giving the necessary orders for his armies; only when he retreated to his private apartment, away from

---

[6] Louis XIV, *Mémoires*, ed. J. Longnon (Paris: Taillandier, 1978), 45 and 108 (on finances).

[7] *Ibid.*, 109. The quotation about weakness comes from the "Réflexions sur le métier du Roi," written in 1679; the quotation can be found in the Longnon text, 279.

the Court, did Louis break down to mourn the death of his beloved mentor. Louis's restraint illustrates his campaign to curtail the culture of *geste* (he effectively eliminated its most violent manifestation, dueling) and replace it with one of self-control, a control the state could then use for social and political ends.

What was precisely the *métier* of a king in the late 1650s or early 1660s? The king's first responsibility, as Louis himself tells us, was to preserve order; without order, the state itself would collapse. Let us begin our examination of Louis's changes in the French state with the organization of government at the beginning of his reign, and the changes he wrought in 1661.

The organization of government under Louis XIV

If age is venerable in men, it seems to me even more so in these so ancient bodies.　　　　　　　　　　　　Louis XIV, speaking of the Parlements

What was the state of the kingdom and its government in the middle of the 1650s? Civil and foreign war had devastated much of the kingdom, save the west. The great famine of 1659–62 short-circuited the antici-pated peacetime recovery. Despite the famine, French commercial activity recovered in the late 1650s and, after the famine, even more strongly in the early 1660s. The government encouraged monopoly companies for overseas trade (all of which failed), a policy symbolic of the new element that revolutionized the French economy in the eighteenth century. Bordeaux, Rouen, Nantes, and La Rochelle began to develop trade to the West Indies, particularly in the 1660s. Sugar refineries popped up in these cities, a harbinger of the colonial boom to come. Other sectors of the economy, such as the textile trade of the northern towns, did not recover so well. Exports of cheap wine also suffered when northern European consumers turned to grain-based alcohol instead of spirits distilled from the wines of the Loire or of Languedoc.

The return of relative peace and order and the concomitant regulariz-ation of taxation provided the most important economic changes of the late 1650s and early 1660s. The excessive fiscal demands of the 1640s and early 1650s disappeared; when tax rates declined, taxpayer cooperation increased. Non-payment of taxes dropped sharply after 1654, in part because of much lower assessments. The new superintendant of finances, Nicolas Fouquet, again paid the scheduled interest, which made it easier to continue to borrow money. Fouquet also sought to place more of the interest burden on corporate bodies, such as the estates of Languedoc or the clergy. Irregularities and collection difficulties diminished but did not disappear in the late 1650s; by the 1660s, the king collected the assessed amounts for direct and indirect taxes. The government worked out an effective mechanism to meet its mutual interests with financiers.

Sequential bankruptcy, effected by stages in 1648, 1652, and 1661–67, provided the necessary preliminary to this arrangement with the tax farmers. The king coupled this bankruptcy with the greatest of the *Chambres de Justice** (investigative commissions), which threatened prosecution and imprisonment of virtually every royal tax official who had handled large amounts of money. The prosecutions rarely took place; instead, the king settled for the usual expedient of levying enormous fines on the financiers. These fines tended to be reduced over time but they remained, by far, the heaviest ones ever assessed by the *Chambre*. The *Chambre* had four major effects: it improved royal public relations (everyone hated the financiers); it raised a lot of money; it created a new climate in which to establish a more solid fiscal system; and it allowed Colbert, the next chief financial officer, to replace Fouquet's financial network with his own. These elements can perhaps best be seen in the most famous case associated with the *Chambre*, the disgrace of Fouquet himself.

The disgrace of Fouquet

Nicolas Fouquet came from a family of Parisian and Breton judges. The family made its earliest fortune trading silks and other goods in Angers but moved into the judicial world in the middle of the sixteenth century. Nicolas Fouquet's grandfather and two great uncles served as Parlementaires; one great uncle, Christopher Fouquet, president *à mortier* of the Parlement of Brittany, married Isabelle Barrin, granddaughter of André Ruiz, one of the greatest international financiers of the sixteenth century. Nicolas's father, François, married Marie de Maupeou, a member of one of the leading Parisian robe noble families (whom we shall encounter again in chapter 6); her brothers and cousins sat in three Parisian Sovereign Courts. In short, Nicolas Fouquet came from an unimpeachable background of robe nobles and financiers. He married in the same milieu, first to the daughter of a Breton Parlementaire and then to Marie Madeleine de Castille, cousin of the Central Treasurer and of the receiver general of the clergy.

Fouquet served as king's attorney at the Parlement of Paris, and, like his father, as a master of requests in the king's household. He had close ties to Mazarin, who used him as an intendant in the early 1640s. Fouquet failed in Dauphiné (rioters at Valence nearly lynched him) but he redeemed himself by good service as intendant of the army of Picardy in

1647 and as intendant of Paris during the first Fronde, when he gained a reputation as a skilled fiscal official and as a loyal client of Mazarin. In 1653, when the post of superintendant of finances became vacant, Mazarin named Fouquet as one of the co-holders (with Abel Servien, who died in 1659).

Fouquet came up with expedients sufficient to keep the monarchy afloat during the final six years of the war with Spain. By paying interest, Fouquet kept up the flow of new investments in government loans, loans largely provided by Fouquet's own circle of friends and family among the financiers and the Parlementaires. The interest rates often reached 20 percent (on occasion as much as 50 percent), but such levels represented a combination of real interest and of a risk premium; the king secured many of the loans on unreliable, hard-to-collect taxes. Fouquet also broadened the practice of farming the direct taxes, so that he could shift the burden of collection onto the financiers (invariably royal direct-tax system officials).

The Peace of the Pyrenees (1659) allowed tax levels to decline. Certain royal officials – Mazarin above all – profited from the reduction in spending by demanding repayment for old Crown debts. Mazarin or another powerful courtier could purchase Treasury papers, such as debts assigned to a given tax revenue in (say) 1651, for a fraction of their face value; with the right political connections, he could then insist that the king make good on these (legally valid) debts. At his death, Mazarin owned nearly 6 million *livres* of Treasury paper; his total estate added up to 38 or 39 million *livres*, the largest private fortune ever to exist in Old Regime France. In a kingdom starved for cash, Mazarin left nearly 9 million *livres* of cash to his heirs (among them Louis XIV); he left another 4.4 million *livres* worth of jewels. Because he lost his entire fortune during the Fronde, Mazarin must have amassed this sum after 1653, much of it in 1659 and 1660.

Two people knew the details about these dubious financial dealings: Fouquet and Jean-Baptiste Colbert, the intendant in charge of the cardinal's private fortune. When Mazarin died, Fouquet and Colbert fought to gain control over the kingdom's finances; Colbert won. Fouquet's outlandish lifestyle did not help his chances. Shortly after Louis XIV had decided to arrest Fouquet, the superintendant invited the king to a ball at the chateau of Vaux-le-Vicomte. The splendor of the ball – in sharp contrast to the economies necessary in the king's own household – so enraged the king that he decided to arrest Fouquet then and there; only the intervention of the Queen Mother, who argued that the king could not be so ungracious a guest as to arrest his host, postponed Fouquet's disgrace.

He arrested the superintendant a few weeks later, at Nantes, far from Court, and convened a special tribunal to try him. Fouquet's trial proved an embarrassment. He successfully refuted virtually every charge against him; indeed, public opinion thought he had made a mockery of his judges. Even the chief royal prosecutor, Lefèvre d'Ormesson, came to believe in Fouquet's relative innocence. Alas for Fouquet, the alternative to conviction was a posthumous trial of Mazarin, the king's beloved godfather and mentor. The court sentenced Fouquet to perpetual banishment, voting 13–9 against the death penalty sought by Colbert (whose uncle, Henri Pussort, chaired the tribunal and voted for the death penalty). The king later changed Fouquet's punishment to life imprisonment; his family managed to salvage some of his fortune (although not the chateau at Vaux). Fouquet's architects and artists – Le Vau, Le Notre, and Le Brun – went to work for the king, to produce a larger Vaux: Versailles.

Ministers and councils: the reforms of 1661

Fouquet's disgrace left Colbert in charge of the king's finances, although Colbert did not receive the title of superintendant of finances; he merely retained that of intendant of finances (in 1665, he became controller general of finances). Colbert had to share ministerial power with two others, Hugues de Lionne, the specialist on foreign policy, and Michel Le Tellier, the war minister. The long-serving chancellor Séguier saw his influence gradually diminish. Louis declared himself the chief minister; he never appointed anyone to that post.

Historians have long seen a break in Louis XIV's reign in 1661, pointing to the abolition of the position of chief minister, to the death of Mazarin and the king's assumption of "personal" power, and to the defeat of Fouquet by Colbert as the chief elements in a dramatic shift away from the turmoil of the 1650s to the stability of the 1660s. Louis himself encouraged this view, with the statement in his *Memoirs* that, when he came to full power in 1661, "Disorder reigned everywhere" (38). The situation was far from ruinous; in fact, the government had overcome the chaos of the Fronde between 1653 and 1661.

The solutions to the financial problems began in the mid-1650s, with Fouquet's insistence on paying interest to keep open the credit markets. Similarly, the king's relationship with the Parlement and other courts cannot be said to have shifted markedly in 1661 but rather in the mid-1650s. As the Burgundian intendant Claude Bouchu (son of the previous First President of the Parlement) wrote to Cardinal Mazarin in April 1660: "As for the speeches that may be made in Parlement, they merit neither to be written about nor to be responded to . . . noises from

Parlement are no longer in season."[8] The intendants had filtered back into the provinces after 1653 and the king's relationship with the various provincial estates improved markedly after his majority. Royal demands on the estates declined; the king no longer had any serious difficulties with representative bodies.

Louis XIV did restructure his government when Mazarin died (9 March 1661). First, the king himself became chief minister. Second, Louis restricted entry into the Council of State* (*Conseil d'En haut*).[9] He threw out the princes of the blood, the Queen Mother, a host of officials, and even the chancellor of France, who was, in theory, the head of all royal councils. The new Council of State had only four members: Fouquet (superintendant of finances), Michel Le Tellier (secretary of state for war), Hugues de Lionne (secretary of state for foreign relations), and the king himself.

These three ministers of state* (the term henceforth referred only to those invited to the Council of State) and the king met three times a week. This council took most important policy decisions, but two other councils, one existing and one new, also played key roles. The Council of Dispatches* (*Conseil des Depêches*), consisting of the king, the chancellor, the superintendant of finances, and the four secretaries of state, met twice each week to discuss internal affairs. The critical change in the composition of this council was that the king himself now attended, rather than leaving the chairmanship to the chancellor.

After Fouquet's fall (September 1661), the king created the third, new council: the Royal Council of Finances* (*Conseil Royal des Finances*). The Royal Council of Finances replaced the older Council of Finances, which had consisted of the superintendant of finances (Fouquet) and his assistants, the intendants of finance (not to be confused with the provincial intendants). Louis reduced the number of intendants of finance from twelve to two. The Royal Council of Finances, which met twice each week, henceforth consisted of the king, three councilors, one of whom had to be an intendant of finances, the newly created "Head of the Royal Council of Finances," and, if the king so chose (i.e., not purely by right), the chancellor. These three *royal* councils (i.e., councils in which the king himself sat) had subordinate councils to help them with their work: the Council of Litigants, the *Conseil Privé* on matters such as jurisdiction, two financial councils, the Council of Conscience or of religion (for benefices), and the Council of Commerce (1664–76 and after 1701).

---

[8] C. Arbassier, *L'absolutisme en Bourgogne: L'Intendant Bouchu et son action financière, 1667–1671* (Dijon: A. Picard, 1919), 25.

[9] So called because it met on the first floor of the palace, instead of on the ground floor, as all other councils did.

Louis XIV was the only Bourbon king of France to participate regularly in the financial council; the others left the technicalities of finance to their ministers. Nonetheless, Colbert did the background papers for this council and remained its driving force until his death in 1683. Even after Colbert's death, the controller general dominated the Royal Council of Finances. In fact, by the end of the reign, this council often acted as a rubber stamp, merely approving what the king and the controller general had already decided in private conference.

Like the Royal Council of Finances, the Council of Dispatches lost power during Louis XIV's reign. In theory, the Council operated the internal administration of the kingdom, especially the nuts-and-bolts correspondence with the many royal and corporate officials, handled through the four secretaries of state. During Louis XIV's reign, the Council of Dispatches steadily declined; it met twice a week in 1661 but only once every two weeks by 1700 and once a month by 1715.

Real power ended up with individual ministers, the controller general, and the Council of State. This Council – Le Tellier, Colbert, and Lionne – made most of the important policy decisions but its power came in part from the great individual authority of its members. The controller general (Colbert) ran the financial system, with the aid of the intendants of finance. He also increasingly had the day-to-day direction of affairs because of the relationship of almost all governmental activities to financial matters. Under the guise of reforming the tax system, Colbert could order every sort of investigation. As minister in charge of the Navy, he ordered an extensive census of all shipping on the Atlantic coast (1664–65).[10] As minister of trade, he urged the king to enact new trade legislation (the disastrous tariffs of 1667) or to charter monopolistic companies, such as the ill-fated Company of the North.

The extraordinary concatenation of powers in Colbert's hands facilitated the intermixing of financial, political, and mercantile policy. Colbert at first merely had ministerial responsibility for many tasks. He added official titles throughout the 1660s and 1670s: Colbert became superintendant of royal buildings (1664), controller general (1665), secretary of state for the Royal Household and the Navy (1669), and grand master of mines and manufactures (1670). He used these different positions to follow integrated financial, commercial, and manufacturing policies. After his death, the three key positions – controller general (for financial policy), superintendant of buildings (for manufactures), and secretary of state for the Marine and the Colonies (for commerce) – fell

---

[10] In 1664, the responsibility for the Navy lay divided between two *secrétaires d'Etat* (one in control of the Mediterranean, the other of the Atlantic); however, as early as 1661, Colbert had taken effective control of the Atlantic Navy.

into separate hands, so that Colbert's successors had more difficulties following a united policy on all three fronts. Colbert strongly believed that the state should encourage both trade and manufacture, by means of tax incentives and issuance of monopolies. These monopolies rarely had the approval of the merchant community; in fact, Colbert had great difficulty finding subscribers for them. He obtained almost all of the money from tax farmers and financiers.

Historians call Colbert's combination of government finance and manufacturing and commercial policy mercantilism. In its purest theoretical form, mercantilism conceives of the state as a merchant, seeking always to achieve a surplus of exports (sales) over imports (purchases). Colbert believed that a stronger manufacturing base would achieve three positive ends: (1) it would reduce dependence on imports of manufactured goods (especially from Holland); (2) it would provide employment to the mass of underemployed French people; and (3) it would increase tax revenues. He further believed that higher French tariffs against goods (mainly from Holland) would encourage French manufacture and shipping. In the following such policies, he resembled his contemporaries in England, who also excluded Dutch ships carrying non-Dutch goods after 1657.

Mercantilism involved a wide range of government-sponsored economic activities. Colbert acted forcefully in four distinct areas: (1) external trade; (2) colonial development; (3) internal trade and transportation; and (4) manufacturing. He tried to promote external trade by a mixture of monopoly trading companies, such as the Company of the North (for trade with eastern Europe and Russia), and a substantial tariff on imported manufactured goods, a tariff system that included a penalty fee, 50 *sous* per ton, on goods entering French ports on ships other than those from their country of origin. The tariff of 1667, which raised duties on many goods by 100 percent, helped lead to the Dutch War of 1672. In the end, Colbert had to back down and reduce the tariffs to their pre-1667 level. The Company of the North, like so many of the monopolies, failed, unable to compete against the Dutch and English. The Dutch War destroyed both the Company of the North and the Levant Company.

The colonial companies – the West India and East India Companies – likewise had a checkered history. Once again, war with the Dutch had disastrous consequences, although these two companies survived into the 1680s. In general, monopoly policies did not work; in the West Indies, for example, colonists sought goods outside the monopoly network. Even Colbert had to admit that a certain level of free trading would lead to faster development.

In internal matters, Colbert's record appears more mixed. Once again, we find him leasing manufacturing monopolies to his cronies, like the ubiquitous François Bellinzani. The manufactures Colbert subsidized – textiles, both cloth and tapestries – did make some long-term progress. Some royal works, such as the Gobelins tapestry manufacture, survived into the eighteenth century, turning substantial profit for their owners and providing an important source of employment. The king bought much of their production for his palaces, especially Versailles: from 1664 to 1683, he spent about 3.5 million *livres* on Gobelins tapestries alone.

Other manufacturers received special royal encouragement (such as tax abatements) or even direct subsidies, such as the payments to the General Hospital of Paris, which employed several thousand stocking makers. Colbert's admirers often point to the substantial gains in French textile manufacturing between the 1660s and the 1720s, and, especially in the eighteenth century, as evidence of the success of his mercantilist manufacturing policies. Given the far greater increase in some other countries (notably England), without such government intervention, the connection between Colbertian mercantilism and French manufacturing success in the eighteenth century remains rather tenuous. The rousing success of textile manufacture in Languedoc, for example, likely owes something to the encouragement offered by Colbert during the difficult 1670s, but the overwhelming increase of the eighteenth century (from about 3,900 to more than 99,000 pieces exported) had little to do with monopoly manufacture.

Colbert's efforts to improve internal communications similarly present a mixed picture. He funded one extraordinary venture, the Canal du Midi, which linked the Atlantic and the Mediterranean by means of a canal connecting the river system of Bordeaux with that of the Languedoc ports. The idea of Pierre-Paul Riquet, this 175-mile canal took 15 years to build and cost 17 million *livres*, making it the greatest public works project ever undertaken by the French monarchy. Colbert also spent money on other internal transportation improvements and sought to eliminate tolls on rivers and bridges. He had only partial success in these endeavors; the transportation network improved but little and he could only reform, not destroy, the internal tolls so pernicious to commerce. He also failed in his efforts to introduce some regional standardization into the system of weights and measures.

We cannot look upon Colbert's mercantilism as representative of broad-based French mercantile interests. French merchants well understood that they needed products imported on Dutch ships and that the French merchant marine would not be able to provide these goods. Only the French monopoly companies would profit by protectionism. These companies had fiscal rather than mercantile purposes. The four great companies (of the North, the West Indies, East Indies, and Levant) obtained their capital almost exclusively from financiers and from the king: less than 15 percent of their capital came from merchants. The same names – Bellinzani, Coquille, and the others – recur in every mention of either trading monopolies or manufacturing ones. Colbert's tariff policy had less to do with economic than with financial interest: like his state finance system, it was a family, not a national, affair.[11]

Lest we overstate the power of Colbert, we would do well to remember that the military, too, reached everywhere. Le Tellier and his son, the marquis de Louvois (associated in his father's job in 1667 and sole minister of War from 1677 to 1691) could claim broad supervisory powers over royal armies, provincial and town governors, and money collected for military expenses.

The decline of the chancellor's authority in 1661 did *not* mean that the old corps of officials lost its role in running the kingdom. The survival (and publication) of the records of the controller general's office has often led historians to assume that the old officers declined under Colbert. In this historiographical tradition, only now coming under attack, the replacement of government by venal officers with government by commissioners formed the basis of royal absolutism. Venal officers *owned* their offices; they could not be "fired," nor could the king abolish their offices without compensating them in full. In contrast, when the term of the commission ended, the commissioner lost his job. What is more, such commissioners served always at the king's discretion; he could revoke the commission at any time. The officers, on the other hand, owned their offices and could not be displaced. The shift from officers to commissioners, so the argument goes, heralded the birth of the absolutist state.

A simple examination of the structure of Louis XIV's state should alert us to the inadequacies of such a theory. It had perhaps 300 full-time commissioners (*commissaires*) and other non-venal officials. The latter included the First Presidents and the *procureurs du roi* of the Sovereign Courts and the chief judges of the bailiwicks; the former consisted primarily of the 30 to 35 intendants (chosen from among the 80 masters of requests of the king's household; the position of master of request was a venal office). In contrast, the state apparatus included approximately 45,000 venal offices. Louis could not run the state without the cooperation of many of these officers. Louis and his ministers co-opted some of

---

[11] Daniel Dessert used this phrase to describe the Colbert family's control of the financial system, but his work shows how it can well be used to apply to the monopoly system as well, given the close connection between the two. See D. Dessert and J.-L. Journet, "Le Lobby Colbert, un royaume ou une affaire de famille?," *Annales E.S.C.* (1975), 1303–36; and D. Dessert, *Argent, pouvoir et société au Grand Siècle* (Paris: Fayard, 1984).

the old officers into the new system, while striving to marginalize the political and administrative role of the others.

The ministerial state: war and foreign policy

The military reforms of Louis XIV had their roots in the 1620s, when Louis XIII either abolished or restricted the three main independent positions: constable, admiral of France, and colonel-general of the infantry (not finally abolished until 1661). By Louis XIV's time, the king had full authority to name all significant military commanders: in the Navy, all officers of command; in the army, all officers ranked colonel or higher. The king had always had full authority to name the military governors of provinces or towns. In practice, the king had far less leeway in military appointments than it would seem. The king rarely removed a provincial governor, except in cases of wholesale changes (such as the purge of 1628–32); in general, the son of the old governor became the new one. A provincial governor virtually had to be at least duke and peer of France, which limited the king's possible alternatives.

Town governorships passed from father to son. These local military families usually intermarried, creating a united local ruling military caste. In Brittany, the northern coast had three major fortresses: Saint-Malo, Morlaix, and Brest. Hercule-François de Boiséon, governor of Morlaix in the middle of the century, was the son and grandson of Morlaix's previous governors, grandson (through his mother, Jeanne de Rieux) of the governor of Brest, and brother-in-law of the governor of Saint-Malo, Malo II, marquis de Coëtquen. Malo II de Coëtquen married (1662) Marguerite de Rohan-Chabot, a member of the leading Breton family.

Within the army, regiments passed from father to son or, at the very least, remained in the same family. Louis XIV fully understood such limitations. He once remarked that he could not appoint someone from a new family to the command of a certain regiment because all of its officers were either relatives or clients of its current commander; if he appointed someone from another family to the command, the entire officer corps of the regiment would resign. Louis accepted the domination of the nobility within the army; however, the government did increase its control and gradually convinced the nobility to accept the basic principles of standardization. The insignia of the noble commander came to be replaced by those of the king. By the end of Louis's reign, the French army had uniforms and standard-issue weapons, and, wonder of wonders, marched in step. To project these changes back into the 1660s or 1670s, however, would be a serious anachronism. It took a full half-century for the military reforms started in the 1660s to bear fruit.

France had a more streamlined and better supplied army in the late 1660s and early 1670s than during the Thirty Years' War. This revitalized army provided an effective instrument of policy. Louis fought four major wars during his reign: the War of Devolution (1667–68), the Dutch War (1672–79), the War of the League of Augsburg (1689–97), and the War of the Spanish Succession (1702–13). The outcome of the wars grew progressively less successful but the two early wars ended with substantial French gains.

Louis XIV's early wars, 1667–1679

The France of 1667 territorially resembled that of 1635: no Artois, no French Flanders, no Franche-Comté. The main territorial gains at the treaties of 1648 and 1659 included Roussillon and the Cerdagne (in the Pyrenees), ten towns (the *Décapole*) and associated territories in Alsace, and the Landgravates of Upper and Lower Alsace. France remained quite vulnerable to attack from the east and north. The two largest French cities, Paris and Lyons, sat uncomfortably close to territories controlled by the Habsburgs.

The Peace of the Pyrenees did not aggrandize France as much as one might have expected, given its clear victory in the war. One offshoot of the Peace was the marriage of Louis XIV to his double first cousin, Maria Theresa, eldest daughter of the king of Spain. Her dowry provided the pretext for the War of Devolution. She had renounced all rights to her father's estate at the marriage, but Spain had not paid her enormous dowry, so France felt it had a legitimate claim for territorial compensation. The customary law of Brabant and adjoining areas gave the children of the first marriage all of the father's property – the so-called clause of "devolution" (hence the name of the war) – so that Maria Theresa, not the infant Charles II, Philip IV's son by his second marriage, should inherit.[12] That the law of devolution had never previously been applied to ducal succession mattered little to French jurists.

The international situation – Holland and England were at war (1665–67) – favored French action in the Low Countries when Philip IV died. Louis massed an army of 70,000 men on the northern frontier in May 1667; in the next six months, his troops captured most of the important cities of Walloon Flanders: Douai, Lille, Courtrai, and Tournai among them. In the southeast, the prince of Condé led an army into the Franche-Comté, quickly capturing (January 1668) its three major towns: Besançon, Dôle, and Gray. The main French army, under

---

[12] Maria Theresa was the daughter of Philip IV and his first wife, Elisabeth of France (Louis XIII's sister). Louis XIV's mother, Anne of Austria, was Philip IV's sister.

Turenne, wintered in the suburbs of Brussels and Ghent. Louis negotiated with Holy Roman Emperor Leopold I to divide the Spanish inheritance in the event of Charles II's death (expected daily, as he was in poor health). In January 1668, they agreed to partition the Spanish empire, with the Habsburgs getting Spain, much of northern Italy, and the New World; the Bourbons would get the Spanish Netherlands, the Franche-Comté, Navarre, the Philippines, Sicily, and Naples. Throughout his life, Louis would consistently seek the main prize: the Spanish Netherlands.

The vision of a French Antwerp drove the warring Dutch and English into each other's arms in July 1667. At the beginning of 1668, the two maritime powers and their interlocutor, Sweden, signed the Triple Alliance, effectively agreeing (in secret clauses) to ally against France if Louis did not make peace with Spain. Louis's negotiators did not wish to fight all Europe at once; they agreed to accept limited compensation in the Low Countries, although the fortresses in question stood far from the existing French frontier. Louis returned the Franche-Comté to Spain. Louis's brilliant engineer general, Sébastien Le Prestre, better known as marshal Vauban, immediately fortified the new cities, creating what contemporaries called the "iron belt." These conquests in the north created a much more stable frontier; the earlier first line of defense had depended too much on Amiens, the only first-class barrier to attack on Paris. With the line Courtrai–Lille–Tournai–Douai firmly in place, France's northern border now was safer from assault.

Despite this territorial gain, the benefits of the peace of Aix-la-Chapelle (1668) did not match the war's successes. Louis and his ministers immediately set out to complete the work begun in 1667. The United Provinces provided the obvious target; if the French could divide the Dutch from the English and from the smaller German states, they could obtain their goals. Such a policy reflected a change in long-standing French international alliances; France and the United Provinces had been allies against Spain since the 1560s (before the United Provinces, as such, even existed), and France had allied with the German Protestant states against the Habsburgs since Francis I. The new international order reflected three elements of French thinking on foreign policy: (1) that Spain had lost its ability to threaten France seriously; (2) that the commercial rivalry with Holland demanded concerted government action (Louis instituted a stiff tariff against the Dutch in 1667, five years before the Dutch War started); and (3) that France needed to expand and stabilize its northern frontier, in order to protect Paris. The lands Louis wanted belonged to Spain, but the main opposition to his plans came from Holland and the small German Protestant states, all recent French allies. Indeed the Rhineland principalities, which had been allied with France in the League of the Rhine since 1658, allowed their alliance system to lapse in 1668 because of concerns about French aggressiveness. The Dutch War demonstrates French acceptance of the fact of a new structure of international relations after the collapse of Spanish power.

Each of Louis's main ministers desired and effectively prepared for the next war. Colbert wanted to break the Dutch grip on European trade; Louvois wanted to expand French territory and to use the army he so painstakingly recreated; Lionne wanted to create a new and stable international system, one that solved in France's favor the vexatious problems created by the anachronistic Spanish presence in the Low Countries. Colbert continued his reform of the financial system and built up the Navy. Louvois improved the army, particularly its system of advanced stores. Lionne and his agents sought everywhere to isolate the Dutch.

Lionne had complete success: Charles II of England signed a secret agreement with Louis, agreeing to supply his navy and 6,000 soldiers for a campaign against the Dutch (June 1670). The minor German states, above all the ecclesiastical electorates in the Rhine (through whose territory the French army had to pass in order to avoid crossing the Spanish Netherlands), also allied with France. The Holy Roman Emperor agreed to remain neutral, if there was no fighting on Imperial soil. By the spring of 1672, Lionne's actions isolated the Dutch. Unfortunately for Louis, Lionne died in September 1671. Louvois replaced him briefly, until the permanent replacement, Simon Nicolas Arnauld, marquis of Pomponne, could return from a mission in Sweden. Pomponne proved a less capable diplomat. In the critical year of 1672, French diplomacy, so subtle and effective before 1671, lost direction and finesse.

The Dutch War (1672–79) had several causes. On an individual level, Louis sought personal glory; he wanted to achieve deeds worthy of his personal greatness. Economically, the French and Dutch had fallen out over the disastrous French tariff of 1667, which substantially raised duties on all goods brought on Dutch ships. Louis, following French foreign policy objectives that dated back to the Burgundian settlement of 1477, also wanted the Franche-Comté, control of Lorraine, and a definite settlement to his claims on Alsace. In the north, even considering the improvements of 1667, the border stood very close to Paris. Flanders had legally belonged to France throughout the Middle Ages; the king of France renounced his suzerainty over it only in 1559.

The conquest of Flanders and Brabant, especially the port of Antwerp, offered a very attractive prize. For the Dutch, the prospect of the reopening of Antwerp (the estuary had been closed by the Dutch fleet since the 1580s), as part of an expanded France, formed their worst nightmare. Louis's effort to obtain control of the Rhine dated from more recent times; indeed, the seizure of German-speaking Alsace, one of the core lands of the Holy Roman Empire, made little sense in "national" terms. France had no real claim to Alsace; its successes there greatly alarmed the small German states, as well as the Emperor.

The preliminaries started in 1670, when the French army occupied Lorraine, because the duke had failed to turn over Nancy, as mandated in the peace of Aix-la-Chapelle. The main battle began in March 1672, when the English and French jointly attacked Holland. Once again, the vastly superior French forces routed their opponents. Turenne and Condé captured one fortress after another and outmaneuvered their opponents, notably William of Orange, crossing the Rhine in early June. Louis made two blunders in that month, mistakes that would haunt his policies for years to come. First, he ignored Condé's advice to send several regiments of cavalry to take Amsterdam in the wake of the complete collapse of the Dutch forces after the crossing of the Rhine. Second, he rejected the Dutch peace terms offered at the end of June. The Dutch offered the territory south of the Meuse (the so-called Generality Lands), the various towns Louis had captured, and ten millon *livres*. Shortly after the rejection of the peace terms, the Orangist crowd in Amsterdam murdered the de Witt brothers, placing William of Orange, Louis's most determined adversary, in full control of Holland.[13]

The diplomatic failure makes more sense when we consider that the Dutch could not really offer Louis what he wanted. He did not want the Generality Lands or the money; he wanted Flanders and Brabant. The Spanish, not the Dutch, controlled those two provinces, so the Dutch could not very well sign them over to Louis. Louis's real aim in the Dutch War was the recognition of French claims to the Spanish Netherlands. He pursued those aims by invading Holland but the Dutch cut the main river dikes, flooding the entire province. Louis did capture the great fortress of Maastricht (1673), a scene celebrated in a famous tapestry of the king supervising the siege, but the French had obviously failed to defeat the Dutch.

In 1673, the main focus of the war shifted to the German lands. Louis marched into Alsace, forcing the *Décapole* to accept French garrisons (August); another French army captured Trier in September. These gains overextended French resources, and Imperial forces under Montecuccoli drove Turenne from the Main River valley and captured Bonn.

---

[13] John de Witt, head of the peace party, held the most powerful position in the Estates General of the United Provinces. William of Orange, *stadhouder* (head of state and commander of the military, yet not quite a king), opposed the peace.

In 1674, France's carefully constructed alliance system collapsed: England (February), Münster (April), and Cologne (May) all signed separate peace agreements and Brandenburg, which had withdrawn from the anti-French alliance in June 1673, returned to the fray in July 1674.

The Dutch now had the king of Spain, the elector of Brandenburg, and the Holy Roman Emperor as allies; the French had only Sweden. The peace negotiations at Cologne, so promising in August 1673, collapsed in February 1674, when the Emperor abducted one of the diplomats, Wilhelm Egon von Fürstenburg, a French agent. Those negotiations provide a fitting symbol of how times had changed since June 1672: at the first peace conference, the negotiations collapsed because the French demanded too much; at Cologne, the negotiations trailed on because the Dutch proved too exigent.

As the war wore on, the combatants wore down. A sniper killed marshal Turenne during a reconnaissance patrol (July 1675) and Condé, worn out by years of campaigning, retired to his estates. Their great Imperial adversary, the count of Montecuccoli, soon followed, declaring, "a man who has had the honor of fighting against Mohammed Coprogli, against M. le Prince, and against M. de Turenne, could not compromise his glory against men who are only beginning to command armies."[14] French armies won most of the battles, culminating with the surprise capture of Ghent in 1678, a campaign led by the king himself. The French Navy, so thoroughly pummeled up to 1674, managed several dramatic successes at the end.

The many French military successes did not lead to a complete victory at the peace of Nijmegen (1678) but France did consolidate substantial gains, by far the largest territorial (and population) additions to France during the last 250 years of the monarchy. Historians often speak of the "failure" of Louis's Dutch War, yet in an immediate sense Louis achieved enormous territorial success. He obtained recognition of his complete sovereignty over the *Décapole* of Alsace, as well as of his rights as Landgrave in Upper (southern) Alsace, and several trans-Rhenish fortresses (notably Freiburg and Kehl). He kept the Franche-Comté, pushing the borders of France up toward the Rhine and thereby consolidating his position in Alsace. He traded Courtrai, Oudenarde, and Charleroi for Valenciennes, Cambrai, and Ypres, and kept Lille and Douai. The new northern frontier ran from Ypres, through Lille, and on to Valenciennes, forming a more contiguous, solid barrier to invasion (one that Louis immediately sent Vauban to fortify). Louis obtained *de facto* control of Lorraine when its duke refused to sign what he viewed as a

---

[14] Bluche, *Louis XIV*, 373.

humiliating treaty, allowing the French to occupy Nancy and Longwy. Louis even rescued his defeated ally, Sweden, which regained all of the considerable territories it had lost to Denmark and Brandenburg. The Dutch also regained their lost territories, notably Maastricht, and obtained the recision of the hated tariffs of 1667. In short, a war that began as a conflict between France and Holland ended up with Spain as its chief loser. In a political sense, however, the treaty did not bode well for France, because Louis had alienated many of France's traditional allies in the Rhineland and created a climate in which France would be isolated in future international disputes.

Diplomacy and religion in the 1680s

France remained largely at peace from 1679 until 1689, interrupted only by a brief campaign in 1683–84. Louis took advantage of the ambiguities created by the Peace of Westphalia (1648) and that of Nijmegen on his eastern frontiers. The Westphalian treaties had given France titular control of ten cities in Alsace (the *Décapole*), their dependencies (undefined), and of certain other properties belonging to the Habsburg family. Unfortunately, the treaties also implied that these territories would maintain their juridical ties (their *immédiateté* in the official language) to the Holy Roman Empire. Louis created special courts, the Chambers of Reunion,* to clarify the precise status of different areas. After his occupation of the *Décapole* towns in 1673, they lost all independence; the precise boundaries of their areas of control (and thus of Louis's sovereignty), however, remained unclear. The Treaty of Nijmegen recognized Louis's full sovereignty over the *Décapole* but did not clarify their territorial claims. Louis stepped up the proceedings of the Chambers of Reunion in 1679 and 1680, aggressively pursuing his claims to all of Alsace except Strasburg.

In the summer of 1681, Louis sent Louvois and an army of 30,000 men to capture Strasburg, which they did without firing a shot (30 September 1681). The city had allowed Imperial troops to garrison it during the Dutch War and Louis had no intention of allowing the main Rhine crossing to remain independent. He guaranteed all of the city's privileges, although he insisted that the town had to allow the Catholic Church to retake possession of the cathedral. The bishop, Franz Egon von Fürstenburg, celebrated mass in Louis XIV's presence on 24 October 1681. The capture of Strasburg completed the French conquest of Alsace begun at the Peace of Westphalia.

French claims to the area, however, remained tenuous, so Louis immediately sought to solidify his position. He turned his eyes next to

Luxembourg. The preoccupation of the Holy Roman Emperor with the Turkish invasion of 1683 gave Louis his chance; he massed troops against the Spanish Netherlands, quickly taking Courtrai and moving up to Brussels. Spain capitulated and Luxembourg became French.

These dramatic successes on the eastern edges of the kingdom could not overshadow two diplomatic failures: the estrangement from the Pope and the absence of French troops in the lifting of the Turkish siege of Vienna (1683). The second matter mainly involved prestige: alone among the major continental powers, France sent no troops to the great crusading army that repulsed the Turks. The absence of a French contingent badly damaged the king's standing, particularly in the Catholic world. That Louis precisely then (summer of 1683) captured Luxembourg, did little for his reputation as the "Most Christian King."

The split with Pope Innocent XI had more serious consequences. The quarrel began in 1673 when the king issued an edict expanding his right of *régale*,* long established in northern France, into southern France. The *régale* gave the king the right to collect the revenues of all vacant sees and to nominate to certain other Church benefices (such as abbeys) in the absence of a serving bishop. The Pope opposed the edict. Louis tried various forms of pressure against the Pope in the late 1670s. They had fallen out over the refusal of two Jansenist bishops to accept the king's declaration on the *régale* because they feared his Jesuit confessor would have the ability to name holders of benefices. The bishop of Pamiers, Etienne-Françoise de Caulet, refused to recognize those churchmen appointed by the Crown under the *régale*; when his superior, the archbishop of Toulouse, sided with the king, Caulet appealed to the new Pope, Innocent XI (1676–89), who supported his position.

In response to Innocent XI's strong assertions of papal superiority over all temporal rulers, Louis XIV solicited aid from the French clergy. He turned first to the interim commission of the clergy, then to a special group of bishops living in Paris. They recommended a full Assembly of the Clergy (a body that met every five years, primarily to vote the king a gift); the king summoned an "extraordinary General Assembly representing the Council," implying a Church Council without calling one. The General Assembly followed a line slightly independent of the king's intentions, one that reflected the disputes among his own councilors about how to proceed.

Led by Bishop Jacques-Bénigne Bossuet of Meaux, they issued the famous Four Gallican Articles: (1) that the Pope had authority only over ecclesiastical matters; (2) that ecumenical Councils had authority superior to that of the Pope; (3) that the special rules of the Church of France were inviolable; and (4) that the Pope held supreme authority in matters of faith, *unless* overruled by an ecumenical Council. Charles-Maurice Le Tellier, archbishop of Reims, son of chancellor Le Tellier and brother of Louvois, strongly supported the hard line. The king tried unsuccessfully to mollify the Pope, following a policy urged on him by Colbert (one that would embarrass archbishop Le Tellier and hence Louvois). When Louis named two of the offending members of the Assembly to bishoprics, Innocent XI refused to confirm them.

This climate of hostility worsened in 1687, when the Pope (following a precedent set with other embassies) abolished the diplomatic immunity of the French embassy quarter at Rome after the death of the ambassador, the duke d'Estrées (brother of a cardinal). Louis responded by sending a boorish new ambassador, the marquis de Lavardin, who deliberately exacerbated the situation. The Pope excommunicated Lavardin; the king refused to see the papal nuncio. This diplomatic impasse contributed greatly to the next European war, which began in part as a dispute between the French and Austrian candidates for the bishopric of Cologne (see chapter 4).

How does one assess the long-term impact of the Four Articles crisis, given the difficult of assigning priorities to the related elements of the religious problems of the second half of the seventeenth century? Louis XIV faced three religious problems during his reign: (1) the Huguenots; (2) the Jansenists; and (3) the Pope. The Pope provided an ally against the other two threats, yet Louis often relied on Jansenists (and their sympathizers) in the Parlement of Paris during his conflicts with the Pope on Gallican issues.[15] The Revocation of the Edict of Nantes (1685), making Protestantism illegal in most of France, came in the midst of the *régale* quarrel. Although the Pope approved the elimination of the Protestants, he showed no special enthusiasm for the Revocation, nor did it modify his attitude toward those responsible for the Four Articles.

These religious quarrels diminished the sacrality of the monarchy. The French political nation, particularly the judges, held uniformly Gallican views; they believed French Church Councils superior to the Pope in matters concerning French Catholicism. Many judges, especially those in the Parlement of Paris, also had Jansenist leanings. The king's weaker ties to the Pope meant that he could not use papal assistance to buttress the religiously based elements of his power, while his opposition to Jansenism threatened to drive a religious wedge between him and powerful elements in the royal judiciary.

[15] Here remembering that in the *régale* controversy, the Jansenist bishops of Alet and Pamiers took the *anti*-Gallican position and the Jesuits supported the Gallican one. Remember that the broad alliances described here did not always hold together and that specific issues could make for strange bedfellows.

The Edict of Fontainebleau* (1685)

Since 1598, France had had two recognized religions: the official state religion, Catholicism, and a legally authorized, although restricted, Calvinist minority, the Huguenots. In the 1560s the latter may have made up as much as 25 percent of the French population, but their numbers declined steadily at the end of the Wars of Religion (1561–98). Under Henry IV, France had about one million Protestants but the number declined to 765,000 in 1660 and to 735,000 by 1680, due to the reduced number of urban Protestants. Huguenots remained a substantial presence in the Midi, particularly in the Cévennes Mountains and nearby towns, such as Nîmes.

The Edict of Nantes (1598) had guaranteed the Huguenots limited freedom of worship: they could worship in areas in which they already did so; they could have special fortified towns (with government-funded garrisons); they could openly practice their faith, so long as they did not proselytize and did not try to start new congregations in purely Catholic areas (special provisions specifically banned them from within the town limits of Paris and certain other episcopal cities).[16] The king also established a special court, the *chambre de l'édit*, of mixed Catholic and Protestant judges to hear cases involving disputes about Protestantism. The Protestant churches, like their Catholic counterparts, also held periodic national assemblies, to deal not only with doctrinal matters but also with political ones (notably relations with the government). Louis XIII undermined some of the provisions of the edict. His invasion of Béarn and his conquest of La Rochelle led to the loss of the fortified towns and to the collapse of the Huguenots as a military threat by 1628.

Louis XIV stepped up the pressure against the Huguenots. He made every effort to restrict the practice of Protestantism. The king's strong anti-Protestantism mirrored that of many of his contemporaries; the Calvinist Protectorate in England, and its execution of Charles I (1649), gave Protestantism, and Calvinism especially, a bad name in French royalist circles.[17] Louis did everything he could to make daily life more difficult for Huguenots. He effectively banned them from public office and then gradually extended that ban to a range of guilds and professions. He forbade Protestant civil registries, forcing the Huguenots to obtain baptism in a Catholic church. He closed most Protestant schools, outlawed psalm singing (except in Protestant churches and in private

---

[16] The Protestants of Paris had to worship at a temple in the outlying village of Charenton.
[17] Charles I's wife, Henriette-Marie, was Louis XIV's aunt. She fled to France and received widespread popular support, including special grants from the provincial estates of Brittany and Languedoc.

homes), and limited the number of Protestants who could gather together on private occasions. The government offered incentives, such as three years of tax exemption, to all those who would convert to Catholicism. The *chambre de l'édit* took an increasingly hard line against Huguenots; in 1679 the king abolished the *chambre*, merging it with the Parlement of Toulouse, a hotbed of rabid anti-Protestantism.

In 1681, the king introduced a new tactic: the *dragonnades*.* In Poitou, the king boarded troops (dragoons) in the homes of Protestant families; until the family converted, the dragoons would stay in the house. The tactic produced a wave of emigrations. Armed confrontations between southern Huguenots and Catholics between 1681 and 1685 exacerbated the situation. On 17 October 1685, the king signed the Edict of Fontainebleau, revoking the Edict of Nantes and outlawing Protestantism in most of France.[18] The king sent the dragoons into the Midi and Languedoc, the two centers of French Protestantism. Louis gave the Protestants three choices: fight, convert, or (for ministers) emigrate. Most chose to convert or to emigrate (which was illegal for laypeople), although many of the converted maintained a secret Protestantism. The most violent episode of the conversion came later, during the war of the Camisards in the Cévennes.

Protestant business people – merchants and artisans – took their skills to Holland, England (and its colonies, such as South Carolina), and Prussia; combined with the king's ban on trade with England, the emigration did considerable economic damage to France. The Revocation also proved a public relations disaster for Louis. His brilliant Court of the 1660s and 1670s had done much to increase French prestige abroad and to foster the image of Louis as patron of the arts and, in a certain way, of progress. The Revocation created a new image of Louis, that of ruthless tyrant, of regressive autocrat. The Protestant countries (England and Holland) with whom Louis would soon be at war expended enormous efforts to promulgate precisely that image of the king.

The Revocation of the Edict of Nantes, in the Edict of Fontainebleau, traditionally stands as a prime example of royal absolutism. English travelers invariably used the Revocation to emphasize the arbitrary nature of French government; historians generally have followed their lead. Yet the Revocation did not occur in a vacuum. Louis had very strong support, particularly in the southern heartland of Protestantism, from Catholic

---

[18] Louis made special provisions for the Lutherans of newly conquered Alsace, whom he specifically exempted from the edict in instructions to the intendant. The government did apply discriminatory measures against rural Lutherans in Alsace but left the Lutherans of the critical city of Strasburg alone. There, the government encouraged immigration of Catholics, which eventually changed the religious make-up of the city. Calvinists, who made up about 5 percent of the population of Strasburg, received no protection.

laypeople. The estates of Languedoc banned Huguenots both from their meetings and from the diocesan assemblies (1648). The *chambre de l'édit* turned strongly against the Protestants after 1660. In 1660–62 alone, the *chambre* banned Protestant worship in 135 communities.

The Catholic population everywhere took the offensive, destroying Protestant temples (at Nîmes and Montpellier), filing lawsuits to eliminate Protestants from all corporations, be they municipal, guild, or royal. After the king merged the Chamber of the Edict with the Parlement of Toulouse in 1679, Protestants lost what little legal protection they had; indeed, the Parlement now demanded repressive anti-Huguenot edicts from the king.[19]

The high level of religious fervor represented a carry-over from the early seventeenth century. In the middle of the century and at its end, several outstanding Catholic holy leaders created an atmosphere of renewed religiosity. Vincent de Paul founded (1625) an order of priests to make religious missions to the countryside. Squads of priests would descend on a village to hear confessions and preach the official high-church Catholicism of which so many peasants remained ignorant. He also founded an order for women, the Daughters of Charity, dedicated to helping the sick and the poor. Thousands of women, many of them from robe, sword, legal, and mercantile families, combined in new ways, as religious women acting in public, not living in cloisters. These religious women provided most of France's poor relief and care for the sick, and educated tens of thousands of young girls in the basic elements of reading, writing, and household skills.

In a sense, the attitudes of Louis and of society toward the poor mirrored those they had toward Protestants. In the name of religion, the state tried to incarcerate the able-bodied poor. Louis saw the Protestants, like the able-bodied poor, as threats to order. He had no compunction about taking whatever repressive measures seemed necessary to restore order but we must not jump to the conclusion that such repression represented absolutism. In annihilating Protestantism just as in locking up the poor, Louis could count on a broad coalition of support from the ruling elites. Indeed, they demanded no less of him.

Internal administration: a revolution in government?

The royal triumvirate – Colbert, Louvois, and Lionne – divided responsibilities in such a way that we perceive the internal administration of the kingdom to be Colbert's exclusive preserve. Louvois (and his father, Le

---

[19] See Beik, *Absolutism and Society*, 297–302, for details. Not all Languedoc officials shared the Parlement's enthusiasm for repression; the governor, duke of Noailles, preferred accommodation to violence.

Tellier) had more internal authority than one might suspect, particularly by means of the provincial governors and lieutenants general (who were military officers). Even the intendants wrote regularly to Louvois; they, too, had extensive military responsibilities.

The internal regulation of the kingdom had three parts: the financial system, the judicial apparatus, and the policing of order. Colbert had chief responsibility for the financial sphere; he, together with the chancellor, for judicial matters; and he and Louvois jointly for the maintenance of order. The dual responsibility for order is often forgotten, yet the surviving documentation from the period's one great popular rebellion, the Papier Timbré and Bonnets Rouges of Brittany (1675), demonstrates the extent to which local officials wrote to both Colbert and Louvois. The individual identity of given officials also mattered: when the chancellorship passed from Séguier to Le Tellier, the alliance between the army and the chancellor's office grew tighter.

Finances

We know surprisingly little about local administration in a period universally regarded as one of dramatic changes in that respect. The best study of a local financial system remains Edmond Esmonin's 1913 work on the administration of direct taxes in Normandy.[20] Esmonin demonstrates the extent to which the intendants and the existing financial administration (treasurers of France, *élus*, receivers) created a more efficient system. The receivers came to be local bankers (following the trend of the 1640s); each village, too, had what amounted to local bankers – its collectors. Direct taxation remained remarkably stable throughout the 1660s and 1670s: it increased after 1673, up in the *pays d'élection* from the 35 million *livres* of the 1660s to a peak of 42 million *livres* during the Dutch War, but dropped to the pre-war level in 1680. Although assessments declined from the extreme levels of the 1640s, actual payments likely increased because the royal administration managed to collect the full amount.

The state obtained other direct tax revenues from the *pays d'Etats* – Brittany, Burgundy, Languedoc, Provence, and the various areas added under the Bourbons. The lines between direct and indirect taxation blurred in these regions; in Provence, each commune collected its assessment based on taxes of their own choosing (most chose a mixture of direct and indirect taxes). In Brittany, the king collected about

---

[20] E. Esmonin, *La taille en Normandie au temps de Colbert* (Paris: Hachette, 1913).

950,000 *livres* in regular direct taxes and in sales and transit levies (Brittany paid no salt tax). The main source of revenue came from the estates of Brittany, who voted a biannual "free gift" of two or three million *livres* paid for mainly (85 percent) by wine sales taxes. During the Dutch War, the king threatened to create new taxes and offices, and to investigate the sales of royal demesne lands (since 1547): the 1673 estates voted 5.2 million *livres* to exempt Brittany from these edicts. In Languedoc, taxes also jumped in the 1670s, up from about 3 million to 4.8 million *livres*.

The full collection of the *taille* revenues always remained one of Colbert's main concerns. In 1670 he wrote the intendants:

[C]onsider this work [just apportionment of the *tailles*] as the most important of all those consigned to your attention, because it concerns the recovery of the largest income meeting the expenses of the State and the giving of justice to the people in that which is most important to them, their goods.[21]

Colbert constantly warned the intendants about the evil agents in this process, the *élus*, who themselves named the parish collectors (the parishioners were supposed to elect them) and allowed their protegés to siphon off funds by means of unauthorized surtaxes. The regional supervisors, the treasurers of France, had an equally unsavory reputation with Colbert. "For a long time, the government had been resigned to the negligence of the treasurers of France, and it had searched for a means to assure a good apportionment of the *taille* without their assistance." Colbert advised Mazarin as early as 1659 that the only way to collect the *tailles* was to shift full supervisory authority to the intendants and to reward those "who get the taxes paid most punctually and who most diligently send the money to the Central Treasury."[22]

The direct tax system operated on a straightforward basis. The peasants themselves named four to eight collectors, who took a 2.5- to 5-percent commission and passed the money along to the *élection* receiver. He spent some of the money, mostly on payments to officers for their *gages* and annuities, and gave the rest of it to the receiver general. These people, the receivers general, had the real power. They controlled about 90 percent of the direct tax income. They passed very little cash to Paris, perhaps 15 to 20 percent (about 6 to 8 million *livres*); the king spent the rest of the money by assigning expenditures to the receipts of a given receiver general. The Central Treasurer (*trésorier de l'Epargne*) issued

---

[21] P. Clément, *Lettres, instructions et mémoires de Colbert* (Paris: Imprimerie Impériale (6 vols.), then Imprimerie Nationale, 1861–73; reprint edition of 1979), 7 vols., II, 72–73.
[22] *Ibid.*, VII, 177. Both quotations cited in Esmonin, *La taille*, 49.

these assignations in the form of rescriptions★ or treasury orders (*mandements de l'Epargne★*).[23]

Prior to 1661, the superintendent had to sign all orders for payment; after 1661, Louis himself signed all such orders. Three officers – the two intendants of finance★ (not to be confused with provincial intendants) and the controller general – monitored the Central Treasurer's behavior. The intendants of finance became powerful members of the Council of Finances by the 1640s and increased in number (to twelve). Colbert, himself an intendant of finance, encouraged Louis to reduce them back to two in 1661. Colbert later (1665) became controller general, becoming a sort of combined interior minister and finance minister, a role the controller general kept until the end of the Old Regime.

This small group of men – the Central Treasurers, the intendants of finances, the receivers general, the treasurers of the estates of Brittany and Languedoc, the receiver general of the clergy, the treasurers of War, of the Navy, and of the Royal Household, and, after 1665, the controller general – dominated French government finance. These financiers ostensibly controlled only the direct tax system, yet they also dominated the tax farms for the indirect taxes. They, their relatives, and their clients controlled all the indirect taxes and the monopoly trading companies as well.

One example among many will illustrate the interconnections. Claude Coquille, nephew of intendant of finances Denis Marin, married Michelle Cormier, cousin of two receivers general. Mme. Cormier's daughter by her first marriage wed another receiver general. Coquille himself became a receiver general of Paris and, as a devoted client of Mazarin and Colbert, rose to become secretary of the Royal Council of Finances. Coquille took part in several tax farms in the 1650s and 1660s; he even belonged to the syndicate that farmed the right to collect the fines of the 1661 Chamber of Justice (although he was one of its targets). He later joined in the first syndicate for the General Tax Farm★ (1669) and invested in four monopoly companies. After Colbert's death, Coquille found himself the target of a less sympathetic investigation; he died penniless in a monastery.[24]

This small group of financiers needed firm control over the apparatus of government to make its system profitable. They strongly supported the greater use of intendants, under the direct supervision of the controller

---

[23] All receivers of money – *élection* receivers, receivers general, the Central Treasurer, other treasurers – served in a triennial rotation. Those not serving spent most of their two years of non-service justifying their expenditures to the appropriate Chamber of Accounts and running their tax farms.

[24] Dessert, *Argent, pouvoir et société*, 562–63.

general Colbert, himself head of the financial syndicate. The increased role of the intendants in the collection of direct taxes represented one of the most important permanent changes of Colbert's administration.[25] The intendants interfered in the most minute aspects of the taxing process: naming of parish collectors; parish assessments; the relationship between production and taxation; local abuses of officers, whether permanent like the *élus* and the *élection* receivers or temporary like the peasant assessor–collectors. To suggest that the intendants could do all this on their own, however, is to misunderstand fundamentally the nature of the task at hand. France had more than 30,000 parishes: could 30 or 40 men really supervise the tax collection in each of them? The more relevant question is, who did they get to help them? They used local officials, either royal, like the dreaded *élus*, or local, like mayors (many of whom held a venal royal office).

Colbert did not approve of this practice but he had to go along: intendants throughout the kingdom needed local informants and assistants. These assistants often became temporary official subordinates, or subdelegates.* Colbert constantly sought to limit the commissions of such men, and even to abolish their use; in the long run, he failed. Everywhere subdelegates began to proliferate; soon intendancies had official constituent units, subdelegations; the subdelegates later (1690s) became permanent officials.

The creation of this new layer of administration did not mean the abolition of the old ones. The *élus* and treasurers of France continued to have important oversight functions, as the constant complaints about them by the intendants make clear. Taxpayers who moved after paying their taxes had to register their receipts with the *élus* to avoid paying in the new parish. The *élus* also retained their judicial functions; they heard, without possibility of appeal, all tax cases involving small amounts of money. Again, we must be careful not to see "absolutism" in the reduced executive role of officials such as the *élus*; they maintained extensive powers because of the combination of legislative, executive, and judicial powers vested in them. The *élus* lost many of their executive powers but their judicial authority remained relatively untouched by Colbertian reforms. Their judicial supervisors, mainly the Courts of Aids, similarly maintained jurisdictional rights over tax cases, as their surviving archives amply demonstrate. The intendants merely provided a parallel administrative path, one followed primarily by the rich or by entire corporations or communities.

[25] Here remembering that the government used the intendants for the same purpose from 1642 to 1647/48; as was so often the case, a failed initiative established precedent for a later success.

The obvious question remains: how did Colbert and his intendants manage to achieve anything at all, let alone run the kingdom in what was, for the time, a remarkably orderly and efficient fashion? In the financial sphere, Colbert built on the work of Fouquet. After 1659, the government greatly lessened its reliance on off-budget expenditures and loans. Off-budget expenses dropped from 88 million *livres* in 1659 to 30 million *livres* in 1660 and to only 7 million *livres* a year between 1663 and 1670, rising slightly during the Dutch War (to about 10–11 million *livres* per year). Income from extraordinary affairs (agreements with financiers, often simply loans) declined from 57 million *livres* in 1657 to 9.6 million *livres* in 1661.

The shift in 1659–62 reflected both the peace and the dramatic changeover from Fouquet's financial network to that of Colbert. Colbert quickly reorganized the indirect taxes, leasing them to networks of his clients. The great *Chambre de Justice* broke the financial power of Fouquet's network, while leaving Colbert's cronies relatively untouched. As in the time of Henry IV, peace worked its economic magic. Revenues from the two taxes most reflective of commercial activity – sales and transit levies – increased from about 5.5 million *livres* in 1653 to 23 million *livres* in 1665. The lease price on salt taxes (*gabelles*) increased by 5 million *livres* between 1656 and 1663.

In the late 1660s, Colbert introduced another innovation with long-term consequences on French state development: the General Tax Farm. Since the time of Henry III, the government had tried to establish larger tax farms, culminating in Sully's creation of single unit tax farms for the sales taxes (*Aides Générales*★), some of the transit taxes (*Cinq Grosses Fermes*★), and the northern salt taxes (*Grandes Gabelles*). Colbert took this procedure one step further: he combined these three tax farms (and several lesser ones) into the General Tax Farm. In 1668, the financial syndicate offered 39.1 million *livres*; by 1681, they paid 57.8 million *livres* for a lease that included the royal demesne as well as the indirect taxes. The General Tax Farm united the financiers of Paris and, to a lesser extent, those of the provinces. The great tax farmers sold shares in the syndicate to a wide range of people, including the highest nobility.

These tax farmers had close ties to Colbert; the tax farmers of the 1660s and 1670s, like Claude Coquille, invariably belonged to Colbert's network. He protected them from full prosecution in the 1660s, made sure they obtained the tax leases, and turned first to them when the king or one of his projects (such as the monopoly companies) needed money. When Colbert died (1683), his clients, like Coquille or Bellinzani, suffered disgrace and, often, financial ruin. A new controller general meant a new network of financiers, a pattern that would continue until the end of the Old Regime. State finances thus always meant personal finance – the financial network of the controller general himself.

Colbert's network included many of the receivers general. The relative efficiency of the group of the 1660s and 1670s can be judged by the period's comparative absence of "extraordinary affairs." The king raised several new indirect taxes (on stamped paper, pewter, and tobacco) in the 1670s but he did not have to resort to the desperate measures – massive tax increases and endless creations of new offices – that marked the 1640s, 1650s, and later, the last two decades of Louis XIV's reign. The much lower financial demands of the Dutch War (compared to those of 1689–1713), however, must get a large share of the credit.

The struggle between the intendants and the officers of the old financial system lasted throughout the Old Regime. Many of those participating had positions on both sides of the dispute; that is, the intendants, the subdelegates, and their assistants all tended to be royal officers. Colbert had very ambitious goals for the new administration. Each year he sent detailed instructions to the intendants. In 1680, for example, he wrote:

His Majesty wishes that as soon as you receive this letter, you begin the visit of each *élection* of your *généralité*; that, during this visit, you examine with great care the quality of the land, the nature of the cattle, the manufactures, everything that may contribute in each *élection* to bring in money; that you examine with the same care everything which might contribute to augmenting both the raising of cattle and manufactures, even to establishing new ones.[26]

The intendant also had to visit several of the main towns each *élection* (other than those visited in 1679), there to receive complaints and to interrogate the parish collectors and the most important other local inhabitants. The list of detailed instructions ran to four or five pages.

The archives demonstrate that the intendants did do a remarkable amount of such work: Bouchu (in Burgundy) wrote to Colbert in 1667 that "for six years, there has not been a single day in which I worked less than 12 hours, and more things pass through my hands than those of all the sovereign companies." The monarchy had always sought to obtain information about its resources but the nature of the information and the method by which it was collected changed considerably under Colbert. In Burgundy, beginning in the 1550s, every ten years or so, local officials went to each parish in the province to collect information related to the hearth count for the direct taxes. With the notable exception of 1610–11, when the First President of the Chamber of Accounts of Burgundy decided to take a housing census, the investigators of the period 1550–1656 offered impressionistic comments about the parishes.

[26] G. B. Depping, ed., *Correspondance administrative sous le règne de Louis XIV* (Paris: Imprimerie Impériale, 1850–55), 4 vols., IV, 38.

Colbert had no interest in impressionistic comments; he wanted statistical data. The investigators of the 1670s and later followed a preestablished questionnaire, one probably devised by the intendant under Colbert's supervision. Each commissioner asked the same questions in each parish: how much is the tithe; to whom is it paid; what are the crop yields; how many plough teams does the parish have; who owns them; how many widows are on the tax roll; what are the tax assessments; who are the collectors? In the 1670s and 1680s, some investigators demanded a head count of all animals in every parish. The peasants rightly suspected the fiscal purpose of such information. Colbert wanted information to see how the state could improve the economy, by raising standards of living and, thus, more importantly, state revenue.

Colbert's efforts to use this information to reform the French economy did not succeed. In Burgundy, he sought to create new manufactures and to dig canals or clear channels in the province's rivers. In 1666, the intendant Bouchu wrote of the latter scheme: "[T]here is no one in these provinces [Champagne, Burgundy, Lyonnais] either intelligent enough or rich enough to carry out such enterprises; for such a great design, we must find someone from Paris." The establishment of manufactures fared no better. In 1671, Colbert's special commissioner, François Bellinzani, intendant of commerce, wrote: "[There is] little disposition among the inhabitants to undertake or to facilitate manufactures because of their laziness and of the opinion they hold, without wishing to be disabused of it, that such establishments are not to their advantage, so that one must resolve oneself to do them good in spite of themselves."[27]

Little wonder that Colbert's economic plans came to so little. Seventeenth-century merchants (and others with capital) believed strongly in their version of the "free" market. Even nobles, such as those in the estates of Brittany, supported the principle of the free market and opposed government monopolies and other economic activities: in meeting after meeting, they demanded from the king the "entire liberty of commerce." Merchants and nobles constantly opposed monopoly companies. The Bretons applauded the government's foundation of a Company of the West Indies at Lorient, but they did not favor giving it monopoly trade with the New World (a position they first adopted with respect to trade with Canada in the sixteenth century). Like most "free" market advocates, these same merchants saw no contradiction in seeking (and sometimes getting) special privileges or rules for themselves and their products.

The surviving administrative correspondence of the Old Regime

---

[27] *Ibid.*, IV, 52, for the first quotation; III, 881–82, for the second.

testifies to the entirely new spirit that pervades the exchanges among Louis XIV's ministers, particularly Colbert and Louvois, and their subordinates. Roger Mettam has written of Louvois that he had "an almost obsessive desire to gather more and more information about the problems which faced him"; one could say the same of Colbert.[28] Both clearly understood that the first precondition of modern government is information. They set out to obtain massive amounts of detailed, statistical information in order to act more efficiently. They succeeded beyond the wildest imagination of any seventeenth-century governmental official but they could not use this information in the way in which a modern government would. They may have wanted to carry out certain reforms, and may further have known that the kingdom possessed the practical means to do so, but their sphere of action remained severely limited by the traditional restrictions, both practical and theoretical, on the French monarchy. Bouchu's boast to the contrary notwithstanding, the traditional *corps* of officers still dominated everyday administration.

Judicial reform

The extensive use of clients to circumvent the regular financial administration (here remembering that the clients often belonged to that system) had its parallels in the other elements of internal government: the judicial system and the policing of order. The judicial system relied on a massive network of courts: royal, seigneurial, ecclesiastical, urban, mercantile, corporate, and informal. The Parlements sat at the apex of the systems, even the ecclesiastical one. The king could not effectively supervise thousands of judges by means of his intendants (who had virtually no judicial authority); indeed, one of Louis's most important overtures to the judges involved the effective removal of the intendants (and even the royal councils) from judicial process. Evocations of cases from the Parlements to royal councils declined sharply; the king grew increasingly reluctant to overturn judgments issued by the Parlements, who, in turn, stopped their interference in state affairs, notably finance. Again, as with the *élus*, the king greatly reduced the executive (and, in this case, the legislative) power of the officials, while he simultaneously increased their judicial role.

The king created (1665) a special commission of royal officials and a few lawyers to reform the judicial system. The commission did not include a single Parlementaire. Its head, Henri Pussort, uncle of Colbert, led two years of discussions, after which the king invited the First President and

---

[28] R. Mettam, *Power and Faction in Louis XIV's France* (London: Basil Blackwell, 1988), 225.

several judges from the Parlement of Paris to participate. The 1667 ordinance on justice reformed the system of appeals, mandated the keeping of civil registers for the state, and eliminated various judicial abuses. The king changed rules on evocations and jurisdictional disputes (1669), and revised the criminal code (1670). Colbert also spearheaded the creation of new regulations on woods and waters; his woodlands policy became firmly established, and remains the basic law of France to this day.

The French legal system represented the conflict of two distinct notions of right, one founded on law, the other on privilege (literally, private law). The conflict between these two definitions of right meant that specific rights, such as property, had confused definitions. Most French villages had communal property, over which the village community, the seigneur, and individual landowners might have conflicting rights. The village (and seigneur) even had some rights over "private" (that is, individually owned) property: the village animals had the right to pasture in most fallow fields; the villagers collectively had the right to glean each other's property; the seigneur often collected small feudal rights from property on which he or she derived no ground rent. As one might expect, these conflicting rights gave rise to endless lawsuits; given the inherent contradiction between the rights based on law and those based on privilege, each side could reasonably claim to be in the right and, moreover, could often find a court to agree.

The effort to mediate the endless conflict between law and privilege failed. In 1677 and in 1699, for example, the king tried to regulate the issue of village common lands; he failed. Private owners, basing their rights on law (on the principle that they owned the property in question and therefore had control over its use), conflicted with village communities and with seigneurs, who based their claims on customary rights (villages) and on privileges (seigneurs, whose claims dated from medieval feudal arrangements).

The reform stumbled on that most basic of Old Regime contradictions: the definition of property. The judicial system remained remarkably inefficient, in the sense of expeditiously and finally solving civil lawsuits, precisely because property had several definitions. Privileges protected these different sorts of property (including judges' offices), preventing the free rule of law. The Parlement, ostensibly the chief court of law, in fact always acted to preserve the system of privileges, from which its members derived so many benefits, including the very possession of their offices. Thus in the eighteenth century, the Parlement could serve as an effective barrier against rule by administrative fiat (absolutism) yet could not serve as the mechanism by which the rule of law would be introduced, as we shall see.

Each Parlement had dozens of judges; each court had separate chambers for civil and criminal cases, for appeals and inquiries, and for special cases, such as those involving high-ranking nobles or ecclesiastical cases. The senior and most powerful judges sat on the *Grand'Chambre*. The Parlement of Burgundy, one of the smaller ones, had in 1699 10 presidents, 70 councilors, 3 royal lawyers, 58 lesser officials (clerks and bailiffs), and an attached chancery with another 25 officers. Ninety lawyers had the right to practice in the court. Nearby, the Chamber of Accounts judged and audited all accounts: its personnel included a First President, 57 important officials, and a host of petty ones.

How did the king and his ministers keep control of the Parlements?[29] They could ask the intendants to draw up assessments of the judges, as Colbert did in the early 1660s. In Burgundy, intendant Bouchu contrasted the First President, Brulart, who, though of "good sense" had "mediocre abilities and great presumption," with Second President Fyot, who was a "good man and full of affection for the king's service."[30] Bouchu's memoir (all the relevant intendants did a similar one) shows us the mechanism of control: isolate key individuals in the court to carry out the king's wishes. The First Presidents (a non-venal charge) and the king's own lawyers had an especially important role in the process. King's attorneys and barristers often made the jump directly to president of a high court, such as a Parlement or a Chamber of Accounts.[31] They and their families provided many of the masters of requests of the royal household from whose ranks the king selected virtually all intendants. Many intendants were the sons of Parlementaires, even of First Presidents: in Languedoc, the intendant of 1673–85, Henri d'Aguesseau, son of the First President of the Parlement of Bordeaux, gave way to Nicolas Lamoignon de Basville (served 1685–1719), son of the First President of the Parlement of Paris.

At the lesser courts, the king followed the same procedure. He would rely on the chief judge of the bailiwick (non-venal) or president of the presidial. The presidials typically had 3–5 other high judges and 10–20 ordinary ones, as well as king's attorneys and lesser personnel, among them perhaps 40–60 sergeants. The bailiwick courts had 6–10 judges, together with support staff. Many of them provided highly professional,

---

[29] Under Louis XIII, France had nine Parlements: Paris, Toulouse, Bordeaux, Aix, Grenoble, Rennes, Rouen, Pau, and Dijon. He added a Parlement at Metz. Louis XIV added Parlements at Besançon and Douai, and courts in Artois, Alsace, and Roussillon that held the basic attributions of a Parlement without the title.

[30] Brulart actually had some considerable ability; he and Bouchu, whose father had earlier been First President, simply detested each other.

[31] Barristers (*avocats*) pleaded the king's cases; attorneys/prosecutors (*procureurs*) prosecuted and prepared cases.

loyally royalist service; the king relied on them to carry out his wishes. Others among them, like many of the judges assessed by Bouchu, had "limited capacity" or "were little affectioned for the service of the king." The royal administration had to create a solid core of loyal, capable judges at each court.

Clientage and control: the Breton revolts of 1675

The best situation involved an effective cooperation among the governor, the intendant, and the Parlement in the *pays d'Etats*; in the *pays d'élection*, the absence of a clear locus of local power sometimes made it more difficult to obtain effective cooperation. The government used a combination of officials, from the governor to the lieutenant general of the bailiwick to a few of the treasurers of France. The intendants would co-opt some of these people – often treasurers of France, local judges, or mayors – by making them subdelegates. In Burgundy, the ancient clientage ties binding the governor (Condé), Parlement, and intendant made for effective action in a variety of endeavors, such as the elimination of communal debts in the 1660s.

So well-knit a clientage network in a given province demonstrates the idealized version of effective governance; the reality in most provinces proved much easier. The southern provinces – Provence, Languedoc, Guyenne – suffered from endemic local clientage conflicts until the 1660s. The virtual elimination of such feuding represented Louis XIV's greatest success in southern France. He accomplished this feat by enticing the most important members of the elite to Paris, by paying large sums of money from royal taxes to members of the elite (thereby giving them a stake in the payment of taxes), by giving special honors (such as membership in the Order of the Holy Spirit) to six of the leading nobles of Languedoc, by enhancing the powers of the Parlements in Toulouse and Aix, and by everwhere reinforcing both hierarchy and the respect for it.

The king took firmer control of the great men (and women) of each local area: in Languedoc of the great nobles, the leading clergymen, the First President of the Parlement, and even of the main local financiers, such as Pierre-Louis Reich, *sieur* de Pennautier, treasurer of the estates of Languedoc and, later, receiver general of the clergy of France. These power brokers, in turn, had greater control over their clients. The broker went to Court to seek favors for him or herself or, more often, for followers and relatives. Everyone used these networks, trying to place clients throughout the administrative apparatus of state. When the broker wanted to get something done, he turned to his clients, not necessarily to his "official" subordinates or to the appropriate regular channels of action. The king also used local monies, such as those raised in Languedoc, to reward the local elite, who received between a third and a half of the revenues.

Colbert and Louvois both used clients to carry out policy. Preserving order formed a joint concern, touching as it did on military and financial considerations. In order to see how the system of government worked in the field, let us briefly examine the most serious breakdown of order in the period 1654 to 1689: the Breton revolts of 1675. These revolts did not seriously threaten the state but they provide a prototypical example of how Louis XIV's government actually functioned.

The Papier Timbré rebellion broke out in April 1675, when the lawyers at the Parlement in Rennes and local shopkeepers, upset at new taxes on paper, pewter, and tobacco, sacked the tax collectors' offices. The lawyers and artisans of Nantes followed suit a few days later, even holding the bishop captive for a day. Rennes remained uneasy for several months, with another major outbreak in June. In rural Cornouaille, the Bonnets Rouges rose up, burning chateaux, murdering a few nobles, and laying siege to several towns. Unlike other French peasant rebels, the Bretons targeted the nobility and the lawyers, not royal direct taxes (which were relatively light in Brittany). The king eventually sent several thousand troops to quell the disturbances.

How did the rebellion break out? How did the king's ministers act to suppress it? First, the rebels struck during a local power vacuum: the governors of the province and its two main towns were absent and its long-standing clientage networks stood in disarray. In the Parlement, the First President, Claude d'Argouges, had taken over in 1661 from Jean Blanchard, whose family had held the office from 1571 to 1661 (save for 1587 to 1598). The Blanchards had extensive respect in the court and powerful ties in the province; d'Argouges, for all his pretensions to be descended from Norman nobility, came from a family of Parisian financiers. At Nantes, the new mayor, Jean Regnier, alone among the seventeenth-century mayors, did not come from one of the traditional Nantais elite families. His two predecessors, Gratien Libault, and, especially, Jean Charette, came from prominent Nantais families; the Charettes had provided seven mayors between 1580 and 1680. The accounts of the pacification strongly imply that Regnier could do nothing; Charette and the commander of the chateau of Nantes, the count of Morveaux, restored order.

Colbert relied on d'Argouges to maintain order in the court and the province, writing in September 1673 about the creation of the stamped paper tax: "[I]t is sufficient to know that it is you who presides over the Parlement of Brittany, to be persuaded that the stamped paper tax is well established and that all of the affairs of the king that depend on your authority will go as well."[32] Colbert misjudged the situation; on a heavily aristocratic court such as the Parlement of Brittany, an outsider, one who owed his position to Anne of Austria and to his family's prowess as financiers, could not maintain order. D'Argouges paid for his failure; Louis XIV recalled him in 1677, replacing d'Argouges with his kinsman from the powerful Phélypeaux clan.

In a larger sense, how did the government try to regain control of the situation? The various officers immediately returned to their posts. The two key military officials, the duke de Chaulnes and the marquis de Lavardin, took control of Rennes and Nantes, respectively. Who were these two men? Charles d'Albert d'Ailly, duke de Chaulnes, governor of Brittany, grandson of Louis XIII's favorite Luynes, had close ties to the most powerful Breton family through his aunt, Marie de Rohan, duchess de Chevreuse. He had equally close ties to Colbert, whose eldest daughter, Jeanne-Marie, married Chaulnes's nephew, the duke of Chevreuse; Chaulnes stood as godfather to their first child. Chaulnes himself married Elisabeth Le Féron, daughter of the provost of the merchants (chief town official) of Paris, member of a financial family well attached to the Colbertian network. She was related, by blood or marriage, to many powerful families, among them the Phélypeaux. Chaulnes also borrowed money from Colbert (50,000 *livres* in 1663).

Henri-Charles de Beaumanoir, marquis de Lavardin, married to Chaulnes's aunt, came from the same circles. Lavardin's mother wrote to Colbert, of the birth of Lavardin's daughter in 1668: "I give you an account, monsieur, of all these particulars, as one would to our good head of the family, whom we respect and dearly love, and to whom we are obliged to give information about all that transpires in a house that belongs to him."[33] Lavardin's daughter by his second marriage also married a d'Albert.

These two men, so obviously clients of Colbert, held offices in the military hierarchy; that is, they should have reported to Louvois, not to Colbert. The administrative correspondence from 1675 shows a very different pattern, one that bears out the role of clientage rather than function. Chaulnes wrote four times as many letters to Colbert as to Louvois. The letters to Colbert are often very detailed and quite long; the letters to Louvois are invariably short and directly related to one specific point. As for Lavardin, only three short, critical letters from Louvois to the marquis survive. One lonely letter from Lavardin to his superior, Louvois, stands in sharp contrast to the ten long, detailed letters that he

[32] Clément, *Lettres*, II, 292–93.
[33] *Ibid.*, VII, 356–57, letter of 2 September 1668.

sent to Colbert between April and July 1675. Brittany as yet had no intendant, so Colbert had to use other means to his end: he obviously relied on d'Argouges, Chaulnes, and Lavardin. When d'Argouges lost control of the situation, Colbert turned to Chaulnes, even though the duke's position, military governor, put him in the orbit of Louvois.

Chaulnes and Lavardin played important roles in many areas of French administration; each served as ambassador to Rome. Chaulnes seems to have had closer ties to Louvois; he borrowed money from him, as well as from Colbert. The surviving correspondence does not reveal much criticism from Louvois's local clients, such as the *commissaire des guerres*, Jonville, about Chaulnes, as opposed to Jonville's regular excoriation of Lavardin. In one of his most revealing letters, Jonville tells Louvois that Lavardin alienated everyone at Nantes by his pretentiousness. When Lavardin insisted that his guards stand at attention (and not at ease) in the choir during his inaugural mass as governor of Nantes, the bishop informed him that only the king had that privilege. Lavardin would not back down, so the Cathedral canons refused to sing the responses at the mass. The bishop had no choice but to say a low rather than a high mass, publicly humiliating Lavardin.[34]

When the estates of Brittany sought the king's forgiveness for the revolt, they chose a delegation of their most powerful, well-connected members: Sébastian de Guémadeuc, bishop of Saint-Malo (client of Colbert and close collaborator of Chaulnes throughout 1675); the duke de Rohan; and Jean de Charette, seneschal of Nantes. All three of these men had impeccable royalist credentials and close ties to powerful figures at Court (in Rohan's case to the king himself, who was then infatuated with the duke's cousin, Anne de Soubise). For all the rhetoric about absolutism, when it came time to accomplish serious matters, everyone concerned understood that what mattered was the tie of one man or woman to another.

Culture and the state

Louis XIV left the administrative reform of the kingdom to his capable subordinates; he himself took a principal role in the dramatic new interference of the state in the production and dissemination of culture. Kings had always been important patrons of the arts but Louis XIV took this patronage to a new plane. The king left no cultural sphere untouched. He attracted the leading painters, sculptors, musicians, playwrights,

---

[34] This skill at alienating people (Jonville gives other examples) led to Lavardin's dismissal in the fall of 1675; perhaps it also explains Louis's choice of the marquis as his ambassador to Rome in 1687, when the king wanted to annoy the Pope.

architects, historians, and even pamphleteers to his service. The early stages of Louis's personal reign, chiefly the 1660s, formed a period of astonishing cultural productivity. These artists established French culture as the dominant high culture of Europe, a position it would retain for centuries afterward. In music and dance, the French Court revived opera and ballet. The king's architects (and sculptors and landscapers) created Versailles, the model palace imitated by Europe's Old Regime rulers, who constructed their own magnificent residences, such as the Schonbrunn Palace in Vienna. French propagandists, using every literary medium, from the humble pamphlet to the weighty official histories sponsored by the king, spread Louis's fame everywhere that elites read French.

The early stages of Louis's reign represent the Golden Age of French theatre, even of French literature as a whole. Molière and Racine dominated the theatre. Molière aimed his wit at the foibles of human nature; his comedies attacked the pretensions of many of his contemporaries, not least among them the Jansenists so hated by the king. Little wonder that Louis would find these comedies so much to his taste, beginning with the *Précieuses ridicules* (1659) and ending with the *Malade imaginaire* (1673). Molière's contemporary, Jean Racine, dominated the stage in the 1670s, primarily with his classic tragedies, such as *Andromaque*. Racine later (1677) became the official royal historian, lending his talents to those of the poet Nicolas Boileau. Racine never published his history of Louis XIV; instead, at the end of his life, he worked on the story of one of the king's worst enemies, the abbey of Port-Royal, center of the Jansenists.

A remarkable list of authors flourished in the 1660s and 1670s. La Rochefoucauld published his first book of *Maxims* in 1665; La Fontaine brought out his *Fables* in 1668; Mme. de Sévigné's first *Letters* concern the trial of Fouquet; Mme. de Lafayette published the first modern French novel, *The Princess of Cleves*, in 1678. The list continues into the 1680s and early 1690s, with a shift toward popular scientific writers such as Bayle and Fontenelle and toward the systematizing synthesis so desired by the king, one perhaps best represented by the *Universal Dictionary* of la Furetière (1690).

La Furetière's work represented precisely what the king desired when he created or amplified the collection of academies designed to dominate French intellectual life. He imitated Mazarin, in bringing the Academy of Fine Arts (painters and sculptors) under his control in 1661. He chartered the monopoly Comédie Française (one of two theatre companies legally allowed to perform in Paris); financed the publication of the *Journal des savants* beginning in 1665; created the Academy of Sciences (1666) and the Academy of Music (1669); and, at Séguier's death (1672), assumed patronage of the Académie Française, ever after the official guardian of the French language and, by extension, French culture as a whole. A royal Academy would now officially declare the meaning of words themselves; while popular discourse could (and did) maintain its own stock of words and meanings, political discourse took place in a royally sanctioned language. The Académie published the first official dictionary in 1694.

Here we see the meaning of "absolutism": the king interfered directly in the broadest possible spectrum of life, even in the dissemination of ideas. He successfully modified modes of life, restructuring culture itself. Louis did not act alone, nor did he act outside broader evolving social and cultural patterns, but he did accelerate their evolution. The shift of the Court to Versailles (from its temporary headquarters at Saint-Germain-en-Laye) enhanced royal control over the evolution of Court society because in the new, larger palace, the members of that society actually lived in the king's own house. Court society moved away from Paris, although the leading aristocrats kept most of their possessions in Paris residences, not in their tiny Versailles apartments.

Louis sought to create order in everything, from politics to daily life. In his own daily life, he enforced a level of structure that boggles the modern imagination. Each morning at his rising (the *lever*), he received his garments from specified people – the lord chamberlain (or a royal prince) brought Louis's dayshirt, the first valet helped with the right sleeve, the first servant of the wardrobe with the left – in a ceremony deliberately reminiscent of the coronation. Louis's day passed in such ceremonies, which served an avowed political purpose, as he told the Dauphin in terms reminiscent of Machiavelli:

Those people are gravely mistaken who imagine that all this is mere ceremony. The people over whom we rule, unable to see the bottom of things, usually judge by what they see from outside, and most often it is by precedence and rank that they measure their respect and obedience.[35]

How clearly we can see the connection between the explicit sacrality of the coronation ceremony, with its changeless order (changeless precisely because of its sacred character), and the implicit sacrality of the ceremonial enforced at Versailles. By creating an unchanging order in daily life, the king implied that everything, in the most tiny element of royal life (such as getting out of bed), had a sacred character. He further implied the sacredness of the ceremonial order itself and of the social and political order epitomized in it.

[35] Cited in J.-F. Solnon, *La Cour de France* (Paris: Fayard, 1987), 335.

He and the Court society helped to create a new civility, a new structure of manners. Just as Louis encouraged the clear, *authorized* definition of words (in the Academy's dictionary of 1694), so too, he encouraged the precise definition of forms of behavior. He promulgated such behavior himself, by his own precise actions, and his impeccable manners and politeness. For those of his subjects who could not witness Louis themselves, there were manuals of manners, such as that of Antoine de Courtin, the *Nouveau traité de la civilité qui se pratique en France parmi les honnestes gens* (1675). Courtin (brother of a royal diplomat) provides one of the first detailed prescriptions for modern table manners, much as they are still practiced today. One takes one's hat off at the table; one uses a fork, "because it is . . . very indecent to touch greasy things or sauce or sirop, etc. with one's fingers." One should not spit in the presence of people of quality nor throw unwanted food morsels from one's mouth to the floor, as people had once done (indeed as recently as the sixteenth century in polite society). Yet Courtin went beyond such general maxims, revealing the intricate detail, the order, of even the tiniest act: one took an olive with a spoon, not a fork, lest people laugh at one's maladroitness.[36]

Such strictures spread, as we know, from the Court to the proper houses of Paris, of other towns, eventually to society at large. Most people did not need to know the "proper" way to take an olive, yet gradations in level of adoption of these manners, of this civility, helped to establish class lines in later society. The word civility itself combined a meaning related to the actual rules of politeness, presumably attainable by all, and a meaning related to those who *could* act with civility, i.e., a meaning applicable only to a small number, to those who belonged to the right social groups. These rules of politeness helped to reinforce the social and political order of Louis XIV's France, as Louis's remarks to his son pointed out. The internalization of the rules (and the pressure to conform to them in order to *appear* to belong to the right social group) strengthened the state, as well as the social order.

The good Louis and the bad Louis?

Louis XIV enjoyed remarkable success in the 1660s. Culturally, in the theatre, literature, architecture, music, and the sciences, France had never known such prominence. The economy recovered from the problems of the 1630s through 1650s, although the level of recovery varied sharply from region to region. Taxation declined, levels of tax payment increased; order returned to France. The edifice constructed in

---

[36] R. Muchembled, *L'invention de l'homme moderne* (Paris: Fayard, 1988), 245.

the 1660s survived the turmoil of the 1670s, when a long war with Holland strained French finances and damaged the economy. Louis did not obtain all that he wished at the 1678 peace negotiations but he did achieve notable successes in the north and especially in the east, where he soon became master of Alsace and even of Luxembourg and part of the east bank of the Rhine.

The élan of the king's early years, however, began to wane. Many of his greatest collaborators died between 1675 and 1691: Turenne (1675), Condé (retired 1675, died 1686), Colbert (1683), Louvois (1691). The theatre passed from the comedies of Molière to the tragedies of Racine. The Court gradually moved from Saint-Germain-en-Laye, on the edge of Paris, to Versailles, some twenty miles away (permanently in 1682). The king developed diplomatic problems with the Papacy and created internal religious turmoil by revoking (1685) the Edict of Nantes, thus banning Protestants from the kingdom. At the turn of the year 1688–89, his greatest enemy, William of Orange, *stadhouder* of the Netherlands, became William III of England, expanding a war that would last, with a brief intermission, from 1689 until 1713.

These developments took time; Louis did not enjoy immense success from 1661 to 1683 (the dates of Colbert's ministry) and then suddenly embark on a series of ill-advised, unsuccessful policies. France had enormous material advantages over its European rivals in the 1660s and 1670s: a large and growing population, a coherent national territory, a comparatively modern state apparatus with unparalleled ability to raise money, a powerful army, and even a strong king. Those advantages disappeared in the late 1680s and early 1690s. The population stopped growing; the personal union of the Netherlands and England created a fiscally powerful opponent, with capital resources greater than those of France; the opposition had a strong leader in William III; other armies carried out reforms similar to those in progress in the French army.

All that said, the king himself changed considerably in the 1670s. His tastes, as well as the public's, changed from comedy to tragedy. He eschewed the lavish balls of the 1660s, when he escorted a series of dazzling mistresses to such events as the gala of the enchanted island, which lasted for an entire week in May 1664. In the late 1670s, Louis turned increasingly to a new mistress, Françoise d'Aubigné, known as Madame de Maintenon. She served as governess to the royal bastards in the early 1670s but later became Louis's mistress and, in secret, his second wife. She encouraged the king's turn away from the wild life of the 1660s and toward a more pietistic personal existence. The king, having created order out of chaos, became more and more conservative; he wanted to preserve order, not create it. His perception, amply outlined in his memoirs for the Dauphin, that he inherited a disorderly, even chaotic France, gave way to a sense of satisfaction at having created a world of unparalleled rigidity – the Court society of Versailles. He grew increasingly unwilling to leave that society; after the Dutch War, save for the campaigns of 1690–91, he rarely led his armies, which had been one of the joys of his early years.

In hindsight, 1689 marks not a magical turning point between the good Louis and the bad Louis but the beginning of a second Hundred Years' War (1689–1815) between France and England, with the final result – an English victory – reversing the outcome of the earlier one. The shock of the war's first two segments, the Wars of the League of Augsburg (1689–97) and of the Spanish Succession (1702–13), demolished the order Louis had so painstakingly constructed in the previous thirty-five years.

4   The debacle

War against Europe

[1688] France was in perfect tranquility: we knew as arms only those instruments necessary for turning over the earth and for building; we used the troops for those purposes . . . to change the course of the Eure so that the fountains of Versailles could play continuously.[1]

Mme. de Lafayette, like so many observers, reveled in that sweet spring and early summer of 1688. The king's sister-in-law, Elisabeth Charlotte (Liselotte) von der Pfalz, so often upset in those years because of affairs in her native Palatinate, seems positively giddy in a letter to her half-brother Karl Ludwig:

My dearest Carllutz. It has been a few days since I received your welcome letter of 23 April, but it has been impossible for me to answer it before now. For I was at Versailles when I received it, and since we had not been there for a whole month, I received so many visits and also participated so assiduously in the hunting that I had no time myself in which I could write.

Less than three months later, her beloved Karl Ludwig would be dead, a victim of fever at the siege of Negroponte, fighting on the side of France's enemies. Her son, the future Regent of France, would soon be in nominal charge (under the actual command of marshal Boufflers) of the armies that savaged the Palatinate in her name, in one of the most famous military atrocities of the seventeenth century, one not forgotten even today in the Rhineland. She had told Philip at his departure that "if it were for me to decide, you would not go, for I confess to you that I can only have pain and no joy in seeing that my name is used to ruin my poor fatherland."[2] The joylessness would not be Liselotte's alone.

The War of the League of Augsburg, which lasted from 1688 (officially 1689) to 1697, proved only the first of two devastating conflicts in the last

---

[1] Mme. de Lafayette, *Mémoires de la Cour de France pour les années 1688 et 1689*, ed. A. Petitot (Paris: Foucault, 1828), 3.

[2] E. Forster, ed., *A Woman's Life in the Court of the Sun King. Letters of Liselotte von der Pfalz, 1652–1722* (Baltimore: Johns Hopkins University Press, 1984), 57 and 58, letters of 17 May and 26 September 1688.

stages of Louis XIV's reign. The second war, that of the Spanish Succession, lasted from 1702 until 1713. In both cases, France fought a massive European coalition, headed by England, Holland, and Austria, including their German and other allies, although in the second war France had allies: Spain, Bavaria, and Cologne. Severe famines, in 1693 and 1709, added to the desolation of the wars. At the end of the War of the Spanish Succession, Louis suffered the personal tragedy of watching his son, two grandsons, and elder great-grandson die within months of each other, indeed his heir grandson and great-grandson in the same week, of measles. The royal succession, seemingly so secure in 1710, thus devolved upon a five-year-old when Louis XIV died in 1715.

Militarily defeated, in apparent economic ruin, in governmental bankruptcy, the succession disrupted by three untimely deaths, staggering to recover from a demographic catastrophe – France in 1715 appeared to bear little resemblance to the triumphantly supreme power of 1688. Yet France survived all of this, including a Regency, far better than anyone would have suspected; its resilience in every facet of life still strikes the imagination almost three centuries later. Perhaps things were not so dark as we have imagined; let us begin with an open mind, to examine the changes Louis wrought, often in spite of himself, in the final decades of his reign.

The War of the League of Augsburg, 1689–1697

The political situation of the mid-1680s boded well for France. Louis had annexed Alsace and Luxembourg. The king of England, James II, openly professed Catholicism; he easily put down the Monmouth rebellion in 1685, apparently securing his throne against Protestant challenge. The Ottoman Empire's army besieged Vienna in 1683, giving promise of keeping the Habsburg focus on their eastern frontier, rather than the Rhineland.

The political situation changed rapidly between 1685 and 1688. Louis's enemies likely believed that he sought to extend France's northern and eastern borders to the Rhine. With Alsace and Luxembourg in hand, Lorraine all but legally his, and an advanced set of French fortresses in the southern Netherlands, Louis seemed poised to achieve such a goal after the Truce of Regensburg (1684), which recognized French rule for twenty years in the territories newly acquired. Between 1685 and 1688, however, France's position slowly unraveled. In England, James II and his second, Catholic wife had a son, who now became heir apparent, supplanting his Protestant half-sisters, Mary and Anne. In Germany, Elisabeth Charlotte's childless brother Karl, elector of the Palatinate, died in May 1685.

Louis immediately demanded a share of Karl's inheritance on her behalf, in order to weaken the position of the new elector, Philipp Wilhelm of Neuburg, the Emperor's father-in-law. In 1688, the French backed Cardinal Wilhelm Egon von Fürstenburg in his unsuccessful attempts to obtain two vital archbishoprics, those of Liège and Cologne. Enemies of France had now secured the electorates of the Palatinate and Cologne, and the archbishopric of Liège, which surrounded the new French duchy of Luxembourg. Habsburg success thus imperiled Louis's two most signal gains of the 1680s, Luxembourg and Strasburg.

The Holy Roman Emperor made short work of the Turks at Mohacs (1687) and Belgrade (1688) and quickly turned his attention to France, on whom he declared war. Louis seized the papal enclave around Avignon and sent troops into the Rhineland. The atrocities committed by the latter galvanized German opinion against France. The minor German princes, even Protestant ones, promised support to the Emperor; Bavaria, a traditional French ally, also rallied to the Emperor.

Across the Channel, matters went just as poorly. On 15 November 1688, William of Orange, *stadhouder* of the Netherlands, landed in England and displayed his new banner, the arms of the House of Nassau quartered with those of England. James II had ignored Louis's warning of the impending Dutch invasion, sure that he could easily defeat the rebels, as he had crushed Monmouth. Within six weeks of William's landing, however, James had to leave England for France. For France, these English events spelled disaster. Louis XIV already faced a substantial alliance of German powers in a showdown over the electorate of Cologne; French troops ravaged the Palatinate at that very moment. Holland, led by William and the Grand Pensioner Heinsius, stood with the Habsburg Emperor against France. The addition of England made Louis's opponents truly a Grand Alliance, one whose core elements – England, Holland, Austria, and the Holy Roman Empire – remained united in the great conflicts of 1689–97 and 1702–13.

Louis housed James and his wife Mary in the chateau of Saint-Germain and then supplied him with weapons, some troops, and a naval escort to Ireland, where James hoped to rouse the Catholic population on his behalf. At the parting of the two kings, Louis told James that his fondest wish for James was never to see him again. Alas poor Louis, that wish did not come true; James rushed pell-mell into a disastrous defeat at the Boyne (July 1690). Two years later, the French attempted a direct assault on England but the combined Dutch and English fleets bottled up and destroyed the French Navy on the coast of Normandy (Barfleur/La Hogue), thus preventing the crossing of the army. James never again seriously threatened William's position.

French armies had great success in Flanders, where marshal Luxembourg won famous victories at Namur (1692), Steenkerke (1692), and Neerwinden (1693); in Italy, where marshal Catinat conquered the duchy of Savoy and the county of Nice; and in Spain, where a French army took Barcelona. The French Navy had a wide variety of successes, from Lagos to Texel; French privateers, such as Jean Bart and Duguay-Trouin, ravaged English and Dutch commerce (although English and Dutch privateers did the same to French shipping). The fighting expanded beyond Europe, especially to the New World, making the War of the League of Augsburg (known as King William's War in North America) the first world war between European colonial powers. Fighting in the colonies would soon bear as much on the outcome of the wars as land battles in Europe itself.

No war so clearly demonstrated the folly of open battle. The French won virtually all of the set-piece battles, yet obtained little advantage from any of these "great" victories. Luxembourg captured so many flags at Neerwinden that he draped the entire nave of Notre Dame of Paris with them at the victory Mass. So many flags, so much glory, yet two years later, after Luxembourg died, his successor, marshal Villeroy, an incompetent courtier who owed his position to his friendship with the king and his personal influence with Mme. de Maintenon, lost the key city of Namur, whose capture by Louis himself had engendered so many commemorative medals, poems, and public displays.

The last year or two of the war droned on in desperate conditions, with each side more concerned about supplies than about fighting. Despite the loss of Namur, from a military standpoint the War of the League of Augsburg looked pretty much like a French victory. The Peace of Ryswick effected a wide compromise. Surprisingly, Louis gave up land in the negotiations, returning the duchy of Luxembourg and several Flemish towns to Spain, abandoning all his trans-Rhenish fortresses, and even letting Savoy retake Pignerolo (French since 1629). France eliminated the tariff barriers erected against Dutch and English shipping and goods. Louis received firm recognition of his position in Alsace, including vitally important Strasburg.

Why did Louis sign so disadvantageous a peace, when his land forces seemed to have won the war? Three factors stand out as key elements in his decision. First, France suffered from financial exhaustion. Here we can see a fundamental weakness of the French monarchy, one that would hamstring its efforts in the eighteenth century: the inability to borrow money efficiently. Tax revenues did not begin to cover military costs. England and Holland borrowed at much lower rates of interest, through their national banks (the Bank of England was founded during the war).

Second, the king believed he could afford to be flexible, because the key issue remained the inheritance of the childless king of Spain. Ryswick formed part of a broader package of negotiations that focused on the Spanish succession, to which Louis's grandson, Philip, duke of Anjou, had the best legal claim. Third, the enormous casualties of even the victories, such as Steenkerke or Neerwinden, where the two sides lost nearly 20,000 men killed, could not be sustained. The French army could ill afford such constant losses, particularly among its aristocratic officers. Louis strongly encouraged aristocrats to serve in the army and thousands (including the princes of the blood, whose personal charge had turned the tide at Neerwinden) did so. "My God! Madame," wrote Mme. de Sévigné, "so many dead, so many wounded, so many consolation visits to make, and yet this combat (Neerwinden), which people first called an advantage that cost us too much, has finally become a great victory."[3] Perhaps she and her friends had it right the first time.

Court life and the aristocracy

Mme. de Sévigné and her friends take us away from the military battlefield and into the social one: the world of Court. Many of the battles had the same warriors, the aristocratic generals who commanded France's armies. The most notorious courtier general was surely marshal Villeroy, whose incompetence so damaged France in two wars, but even the most successful French military leaders played the game at Court.

By the mid-1680s, that Court had settled in the magnificent new palace of Versailles. The king occasionally vacationed at other palaces around Paris, particularly Marly, but he avoided Paris itself. In Versailles, the king laid out architecturally many of his socio-political ideas. He had built "without contradiction the most beautiful thing of its sort in the universe," the Hall of Mirrors; he created a combination of public and private space even in his bedroom, so that the high nobility could assist at his ceremonial rising (*lever*) and evening retirement (*coucher*); he built apartments for a Court of thousands, who would wait upon him at all times.

The ceremonial, too, reflected an ever more rigid hierarchization of function and status. The memoirs of the period contain many stories about disputes over who sat where, on what, and when. Because they invented much of the ceremonial as they went along, each new situation (such as the visit of the king and queen of England after James's exile) created new ceremonial disputes, particularly among princesses of the

---

[3] Mme. de Sévigné, *Lettres*, 835–36.

blood and duchesses. Affairs of state could be seriously put back by ceremonial disputes. When Philip d'Orléans (the king's brother) and Elisabeth Charlotte wanted to visit their daughter, the duchess of Lorraine, Louis forbade it on grounds of ceremony. Elisabeth Charlotte tells the tale:

the difficulty is that the Duc de Lorraine claims that he is entitled to sit in an armchair in the presence of Monsieur (Philip) and myself because the Emperor gives him an armchair. To this the King replied that the Emperor's ceremonial is one thing and the King's another, and that, for example, the Emperor gives the cardinals armchairs, whereas here they may never sit at all in the King's presence.[4]

According to Louis, the duke of Lorraine had the right only to a stool; Philip convinced his brother that the duke could have an armless chair. When Lorraine refused, Philip suggested that he and his wife follow the example of the king of England, who claimed that Philip and Elisabeth had the right only to stools in his presence (they claimed a chair), and therefore used himself only a stool in their presence (forcing them to do the same). Louis vetoed so perilous a compromise and Monsieur and Madame stayed home.

Court life included a constant series of such controversies over stools and chairs, over place in line or at table, over one's salutation in a letter or in public. Two dukes refused their induction into the main royal chivalric order because of a dispute over precedence. The prince of Condé, a prince of the royal blood, required the following salutation at the end of a letter:

> I am with profound respect Monseigneur
> Your Serenest Highness's
> very humble and very obedient servant

One would assure a bishop that one was his "very affectioned" servant, unless he were also a duke, in which case you were his "very obedient" servant. Molière parodies the process in a famous scene from *Le bourgeois gentilhomme*, in which an upstart social climber offers a progressively higher payment to a dancing master each time the man addresses him by a more prestigious title (ending with Monseigneur, a title reserved for the highest aristocracy). Parodies aside, the words "Monsieur" and "Monseigneur" had very specific social meanings; woe betide the individual who misused them. Prior to Louis XIV's curtailment of duels, the deliberate misuse of such words often served as the pretext for them.

The aristocracy at Court spearheaded the social conversion of mores in

---

[4] Forster, *A Woman's Life*, 116, letter of 11 October 1699.

Old Regime France. They internalized the extreme ceremonial of the Court and converted that ceremonial courtesy into an entire code of daily manners and morality. If the ordinary merchant of Paris could not aspire to the same "courtesy" as the duke or duchess, he or she could emulate them in their "civility." The latest fashions, sartorial or intellectual, would come from Versailles to Paris, spreading thence to the main provincial cities. At the same time that the Court originated such trends, however, Parisian society itself offered a new social world: the salons.

These salons brought together a wide range of individuals, although all of them from elites. Women led the salons and actively participated, during the late seventeenth century, in the intellectual activities. The literary circle associated with Mme. de Lafayette, author of *The Princess of Cleves*, a novel set at the Court of Henry II, Mme. Scudéry, and Mme. de Sévigné proved to be the precursor of a wide-ranging and long-lasting phenomenon. The salons reached their peak somewhat later, in the middle of the eighteenth century, yet salon culture played a key role in diffusion of new tastes – in literature, in fashion, in manners, in food, even in ways of thought – under Louis XIV. Parisian salons provided a counterpoint to the Court, with its rigid hierarchies, because salon goers assessed their co-participants on ability, above all on wit and social grace.

High society, at Court or in the salon, judged everyone, even kings. James II did not make the best of impressions; Mme. de Lafayette tells us that on his first day at Saint-Germain, "the figure of the King of England was not imposing to the courtiers; his speeches made even less of an effect than his person." James apparently had the ill grace to recount even the most vulgar indignities he had suffered; what is more, he recounted them poorly. Indeed, "the more the French saw of the King of England, the less they complained about the loss of his kingdom."[5] Court society, not merely the king, judged one's behavior. Women made such judgments; they made or broke the reputation of many a courtier. These new men had to possess a mixture of qualities. They had to fight and to show martial qualities but they had also to demonstrate to Court society, especially the women, their mastery of the new courtesy. In many cases, such as that of the prince of Condé, these old aristocrats received an education that would put a *robin* to shame. Few inept courtiers (marshal Vauban was one) overcame the lack of social graces to receive high office.

The salons took place in the homes of rich women, be they from judicial, financier, or old aristocratic families. The participants included leading writers of the time, as well as many of the Court aristocrats. These aristocrats did not spend all of their time in Versailles; most of them

[5] Mme. de Lafayette, *Mémoires de la Cour de France*, 64.

rented, or occasionally bought, a large town house (called an *hôtel*) in Paris. They divided their time between the two places, to the extent possible. Under Louis XIV, people spent more time at the palace than they would later on, when the focus of Court life shifted into Paris (under Louis XV). Aristocrats had to see and be seen by Louis XIV, lest they lose their ability to distribute patronage. They became the moons to Louis's sun, reflecting his light to those around them.

This Court society had three distinct male elements: the "old" aristocracy; the administrative elite; and the great financiers. All three groups combined scarcely totaled 600 families. We have long been blinded about their interpenetration by the multi-volume memoirs of the duke of Saint-Simon about life at Louis's Versailles. Saint-Simon constantly fulminates against the "vile bourgeoisie" running the country, casting aspersions on the lineage of men such as Louvois or Colbert, even on the background of high magistrates whose family had served for 200 years or of military officers, such as Villeroy, whose great-grandfather, even though secretary of state to every king from Henry II to Louis XIII, had been born a commoner. Saint-Simon should not be taken too seriously in such matters. French society did condemn social climbers but rare was the family that shied away from a financially advantageous match with the daughter of a great financier or an extraordinarily wealthy judge. The matter was much more complex than it first seems.

This new elite intermarried to a great extent. Substantial amounts of money changed hands: the dowry of a daughter of a president *à mortier* of the Parlement of Paris typically ranged from 300,000 to 600,000 *livres* by the late seventeenth century; that is, she received about the same amount as a duke's daughter. The balance should not surprise us; about half the time, she married a noble's son. A Parisian Parlementaire himself married the daughter either of a colleague, of an aristocratic noble or of a great financier (this last increasingly popular, a way to solidify the family's financial situation). Each group tended to live in a separate area of Paris: the nobles near what is now the Palais Royal, the financiers on the rue Saint-Honoré, judges near the law courts. They maintained their social distance in many ways, yet they also intermingled, intermarried, and formed political and social alliances.

The great powers of the kingdom – the duke–peers, the royal ministers, and the main financiers, like Samuel Bernard – tended increasingly to form detailed and complex alliances. Colbert and Louvois each received the title of marquis, as did their sons; however, their daughters, following the basic rule of women marrying up in Court society, married into the peerage.[6] One of Louvois's sons-in-law, the duke of

---

[6] Mettam, *Power and Faction*, 197–202.

Villeroy, came from a family who rose from simple judges (the middle of the sixteenth century) to duke–peer (1661) by means of high royal office (secretary of state, governor of the Lyonnais) and by the happy appointment of a Villeroy as Louis XIV's childhood governor. Although Saint-Simon and his ilk might cast aspersions on the length of the marshal Villeroy's genealogy, in practice Court society accepted the marshal, who had been, moreover, a personal friend of the king since his childhood. Over time, a mixture of royal bastards, secondary nobles, often those who had been childhood friends of the reigning king, and high administrators added a steady stream of new recruits to the ranks of the highest aristocracy.

Yet Louis effected a subtle change here. During his reign, he created twenty-three duke–peers, most of them in 1661–63 or in 1708–15. He used peerages to reward the families of the highest state officers, such as those of Richelieu, Mazarin, Villeroy, and chancellor Séguier. The other created peers of Louis's reign, with two exceptions, came from ancient noble families such as the Harcourt, d'Antin, d'Aumont, Boufflers, and la Rochefoucauld.[7] Louis greatly shifted the composition of the peerage, adding a renewed emphasis on the French nobility itself. In 1589, of the 35 lay peers of France, 10 came from the royal family and 14 others from princely "foreign" families (notably that of Lorraine, which held 5 peerages); only 11 simply noble families held a peerage. By way of contrast, in 1715, among the 65 lay peers, 48 came from French noble families. Louis thus greatly expanded the number of peers (up from 50 to 65 in his reign) and made the peerage a more specifically noble, rather than princely institution.[8]

If we take each of the three elites in turn, we can see that their numbers remained quite limited. How many people belonged to the high aristocracy or even to the secondary nobility? France had 50 lay peers in 1643 and 65 in 1715. Below these great aristocrats came the secondary nobles, marquises or counts. Even these titles were rare. The memoirs written by various intendants give us some idea of the rarity of the main titles: duke, marquis, and count.

The structure of the nobility comes through clearly in the capitation records. Louis introduced the capitation* in 1695 (details pp. 165–67); all laypeople, including nobles, had to pay according to a fixed system of twenty-two "classes." Nobles paid according to their title, which the

---

[7] The senior branch of the la Rochefoucauld family already held a peerage; the king created a second one for the cadet branch. Contemporary attitudes about such matters are perhaps best expressed by Séguier, who declined a peerage for himself but suggested that his son-in-law, from the ancient Breton house of Pontchâteau (and a cousin of Richelieu), receive it instead. Louis granted the chancellor's request.

[8] J.-P. Labatut, *Les ducs et pairs de France au XVIIe siècle* (Paris: Presses Universitaires de France, 1972), 69ff.

Table 4.1 *Titled nobles in selected provinces, late seventeenth century*

	Princes/dukes	Marquises	Counts
Touraine	6	18	9
Maine	3	18	9
Anjou	5	10	7
Poitou	6	25	5
Bourbonnais	1	6	6
Berry	1	2	0
Champagne	5	12	13

Sources: J.-M. Constant, 'Un groupe socio-économique dans la France de la première moitié du XVIIe siècle: la noblesse seconde,' in *L'état et les aristocraties*, ed. P. Contamine (Paris: Presses de l'Ecole Normale Supérieure, 1989), 297, memoirs of 1664; for Champagne, J.-P. Brancourt, *L'Intendance de Champagne à la fin du XVIIe siècle* (Paris: CTHS, 1983), 1698 memoir.

system assumed (correctly in almost all cases) would correspond to their landed revenue. Excluding members of the royal family, the landed nobility fell into six categories:

Category of noble (capitation class)	Individual payment in *livres*
dukes and princes (class 2)	1,500
chevaliers of the Order of the Holy Spirit (class 3)	1,000
marquises, counts, viscounts (class 7)	250
gentlemen seigneurs of parishes (class 9)	150
gentlemen holders of fiefs and chateaux (class 15)	40
gentlemen without fief or chateau (class 19)	6

The capitation records for Normandy demonstrate the extent to which, numerically, the lower categories dominated the nobility. In the five *élections* of Rouen, Pont de l'Arche, Eu, Pont Audemer, and Neufchâtel, the capitation records of 1703 indicate the very small numbers of nobles holding fiefs and the even smaller numbers of those with jurisdiction over a parish. In Pont Audemer, of the 238 nobles listed on the roll, only 48 possessed a fief and 29 others a parish. No one held a title. In Neufchâtel, only 71 of the 118 parishes had a resident noble: that group included two marquises, one count, and only seven other seigneurs of parishes. In the county of Eu, among 108 nobles, 11 held a parish (including 3 marquisates) and 21 others a fief, leaving 76 with only the legal status as noble.[9]

The highest families – the dukes – tended to come from the old nobility.

[9] Archives départmentales (AD) of the Seine-Maritime, C 311.

In Champagne, the five duchies belonged to three ancient families – two to Montmorency–Luxembourg, one each to Aumont and Choiseul – and to the heirs of Mazarin. The 13 counties belonged overwhelmingly (12) to old noble families. The marquisates, however, belonged equally (six each) to old noble families and to those ennobled by office (including two in the Le Tellier family). The sole county in *robin* hands belonged to Jérôme-Ignace de Goujon de Thuisy, a master of requests who enjoyed unusual royal favor: Louis XIV made Thuisy a marquis in 1680 and raised Autry from a barony to a county for him in 1695. Here we see a fairly standard pattern: save for the dukes, the nobility (unlike the English) had no real hierarchy of titles. The older titles – dukes and counts – tended to belong solely to old, military families; the title marquis belonged in many regions, as in Champagne, to a mixture of old and new nobles.[10]

Entire bailiwicks could have only one or two major nobles. These nobles often served at Court or in the army. In the Burgundian bailiwick of Saint-Jean de Losne, for example, the only marquis was Jean François de Champlecy, master of the wardrobe for the king's brother. The 1697 capitation roll for nobles in the bailiwicks of Dijon, Nuits, Beaune, Saint-Jean de Losne, and Auxonne listed 158 fief holders, among whom one finds only two counts, six marquises, and four barons. Two of the marquises and all of the barons were judges at the Parlement of Burgundy, which leaves only six representatives of the old titled nobility in the entire region.[11] In Champagne, all four dukes lived either at Court – Mazarin and Aumont, first gentleman of the king's bedchamber – or served in the army – marshal Luxembourg and Choiseul, lieutenant general of the king's armies and also lieutenant general of Champagne and governor of Troyes. At Court, these duke-peers participated in the intermingling discussed above: Aumont married one of Louvois's daughters; Luxembourg's son married the daughter of the duke of Chevreuse.

In general, a duke had to live at Court; to be a duke-peer was more than a title, it was a public office. When the government drew up a list of *per diem* allowances for its officials away on business, the highest allowance went to the Crown officers (constable, chancellor, etc.) *and* duke–peers. Except for duke–peers, only regular officials (governors, judges, etc.) received such money.

These aristocrats often had a national perspective on events; indeed, we

[10] There was some inflation of titles in the eighteenth century, as we shall see in chapter 5. In the Middle Ages, a marquis did have precedence over a count but the distinction seems to have been lost over time.

[11] The king's lieutenants in the region, titled nobles all, resided in Paris and paid their capitation there: AD Côte d'Or, C 5598.

may say that only they and the administrative elite could have a genuinely national outlook on state affairs. They obtained this national perspective through their vast range of interests, not only in the state itself but in land. A great noble such as the prince of Condé owned land all over France: around Condé itself, in Picardy; Chantilly, in the Ile-de-France; in the Burgundian governorship; the county of Clermont-en-Argonne; in Berry; parts of the great barony of Laval in Anjou, Maine, and Brittany; the list goes on and on. The family amassed a huge landed fortune during the seventeenth century, with large estates in several provinces, as well as a political clientele in several governorships (notably Burgundy). These great aristocrats obtained substantial income from their estates – in Condé's case several hundred thousand *livres* a year – but they also relied on massive infusion of state cash to sustain their lifestyle: Condé's total income came to over a million *livres* a year, of which royal grants made up half.

Here we see the rationale for one's presence at Court. Those whom the king did not see, he did not reward. Rewards came in the broadest possible range of categories: commands in the army; governorships; offices for clients; pensions; gifts (especially for dowries); even land. All of the great nobles and many of the secondary ones attended Court in the hopes of obtaining a reward. The cost of staying at Court, however, proved considerable; the hoped-for reward became ever more necessary the longer one stayed at Court, exhausting the proceeds of one's estate income (forcing some to borrow to keep up appearances). An income of 30,000 *livres* a year made you an extremely rich man on your provincial estate but only a minor player at Versailles or Paris. Thus Louis XIV accentuated the long-standing pattern that only the richest nobles served either in the army or in the civil administration. The poorer half of the nobility, with rare exceptions, could not afford to do either.

These poor nobles often resented the rich members of the other two elite groups, the administrators (and judges) and the financiers. The administrators came overwhelmingly from within the royal judiciary, especially from the Paris high courts. The king chose his intendants from among the masters of requests of his household; the masters of requests often came from a Parlementaire family. Certain of these families served the king in high office for generations on end. The Phélypeaux clan, for example, began as simple councilors at the presidial of Blois in the early sixteenth century. They moved to a series of high offices in Paris by the seventeenth century: Central Treasurer, secretary of state, presidency of the Chamber of Accounts, intendant of Paris. Under Louis XIV, of course, members of the two branches of the family held secretariats of state; one of them, Pontchartrain, became controller general and, later, chancellor.

Other major Parlementaire clans showed similar longevity. Five consecutive generations of the Lefèvre de Caumartin family served as masters of requests of the king's household, from the 1560s through the eighteenth century. One of them held the post of Keeper of the Seals (1622); two others served as ambassadors. The last of the group of five, Antoine Louis Lefèvre de Caumartin, married Elisabeth Fieubet, daughter of another master of requests and heir of a family that included a Central Treasurer (1620s) and several masters of requests and Parlementaires. The Lefèvre d'Ormesson clan (no relation) dated its rise to a sixteenth-century intendant of finances. The members of the family served as president of the Chamber of Accounts, as intendants, as masters of requests, as Parlementaires, as councilors of state, and as intendants of finance throughout the seventeenth and eighteenth centuries. They intermarried with other similar robe families, such as the d'Aguesseau. Anne Lefèvre d'Ormesson, whose father was a master of requests, married Henri François d'Aguesseau, whose father and grandfather had been presidents of the *Grand Conseil*, intendants, and, in the grandfather's case, First President of the Parlement of Bordeaux. Henri François d'Aguesseau himself served as *avocat du roi* and then as *procureur du roi* at the Parlement of Paris; in 1717, he became chancellor of France. When his Gallicanism displeased Philip d'Orléans, the Regent took the seals from him (1718) and gave them to Marc René Voyer d'Argenson, who had been a master of requests and lieutenant general of Paris. Voyer d'Argenson's family, too, included several generations of masters of requests and two ambassadors. He married one Marguerite Lefèvre de Caumartin. As for d'Aguesseau, he remained chancellor until 1750.

This tight little elite of judges and administrators did not form a closed caste. One notes in the descriptions above the occasional appearance of financiers: the Fieubet and Phélypeaux families had Central Treasurers, and many other Parlementaire clans had ancestors who had been intendants of finance or, in the distant sixteenth century, *grenetiers* or other low-level financial officials. The rich financiers continued to make their way into the administrative elite throughout the seventeenth and eighteenth centuries, although the pace does not seem so frenzied as in the sixteenth. For the most part, financial families married each other; in the eighteenth century, for example, members of families of the Farmers General did so about half the time. But the richest financiers married into the highest ranks of the other two elites. Antoine Crozat, one of the richest financiers of Louis XIV's time, married his daughter into Turenne's family and two of his sons into other ducal families (Luynes and Montmorency). Samuel Bernard, Louis's greatest banker during the War of the Spanish Succession, married his female heirs into great families. One granddaughter married Chrétien de Lamoignon, a President of the Parlement. Their son, Chrétien II, later became Keeper of the Seals (we will hear more about him in chapter 6). A second granddaughter married into a ducal family (Ventadour), while a daughter married Mathieu Molé, another President of the Parlement; like Lamoignon, he came from a distinguished robe family.

If we move outside Paris, we can see how the legal elite revolutionized French society in the provinces. The traditional leaders of that society had been the titled nobility: the dukes, counts, marquises, and barons. These people dazzled local society with their elaborate lifestyle. They held mini-courts, attracting leading cultural figures to visit them at their chateaux (Molière, for example, toured France in the middle of the century with his theatre company, playing mainly in noble houses), and offering a level of entertainment otherwise unthinkable outside Paris prior to the eighteenth century.

The steady shift of titled nobles to Paris and Versailles, however, dramatically changed the social structure of provincial France. With the leading sword nobles no longer in residence, leadership of provincial society shifted to the robe nobility, particularly to the Parlementaires. Again, the capitation rolls tell much of the story. The capitation required masters to pay the tax for their servants, so the rolls list people's servants. Who had the great provincial households? At Dijon, the two largest households belonged to: (1) First President Bouchu of the Parlement – two coachmen, a master of the *hôtel*, a secretary, a valet, a cook, three female servants, seven lackeys, a postilion, and a Swiss guard at his front door (one of two in Burgundy; the other also worked for a Parlementaire, president *à mortier* Le Grand); and (2) the king's military lieutenant for northern Burgundy, Louis, count of Amanzé – one coachman, a gardener, a "gentleman," a master of the *hôtel*, and twelve others.

The two great courts – the Parlement and Chamber of Accounts – neatly reflected the social hierarchy of Burgundy. Almost all presidents in either court had a coachman and a cook. Three-fourths of the councilors in the Parlement had a coachman and two-thirds had a cook, whereas only half of the slighty less prestigious masters of accounts had such servants. The lowly auditors, whose office did not ennoble its owner, usually had to settle for a single female servant: only one of the thirteen auditors had a cook and none had a coachman.

The roll of the nobility for the entire province of Burgundy shows only twenty-nine people with a coachman; of them, seven were Parlementaires and another four royal officials (three of them lieutenants general of a bailiwick court). In other words, the members of the Parlement of Burgundy owned three times as many coaches as all the nobles of the province combined. The overwhelming majority of the sword nobles had but a single female servant. Louis XIV had decapitated the old nobility in the provinces. The rich, titled nobles now lived overwhelmingly at Court (indeed many of the listings for titled persons on the capitation rolls are for widows, who had retired to the family estate). Society still needed a visible elite, one to dominate the social, cultural, and political aspects of local life. The royal judiciary took over this role.

Louis XIV may have deprived his Parlements of their overtly political role when he removed their right of preregistration remonstrance, but he expanded their political clout in the provinces by removing the only competing elite. When a carriage forced a pedestrian to jump aside in Dijon or in Rouen, you could be virtually certain that a Parlementaire was inside. When the Regent (Philip of Orléans) restored the remonstrance powers of the Parlements (1715), he gave back political power to a very different group than had lost it in the 1660s. By 1715, the Parlementaires and the other royal judges had almost complete control of provincial society. Outside Paris and Versailles, royal judges, not titled nobles, stood at the apex of civil society, so that re-empowering them created a uniquely powerful opposition to ministerial government, as we shall see. In the late seventeenth and eighteenth centuries, the king codified their precedence by granting titles – usually marquis or baron – to the leaders of the judicial elite, particularly the presidents of the Parlements.

In Paris itself the three elites – the aristocrats, the great administrators, and the main financiers – provided the core apparatus with which Louis XIV governed France. Louis changed the king's relationship with these people in fundamental ways. First, he deliberately sought to have them close to him, at Court, as a way to lessen their independence. He did not want to weaken them, merely to make them more dependent on him. Second, he used them to create a new sensibility, a new order of mores, a greater sense of discipline in French society. Third, he attracted most of the leading figures of French society to Versailles and Paris, which meant that debates about France's political system would take place at the center. Change would be enforced from the top down and from the center out. Rather than engage in civil war, as they had done in the sixteenth and part of the seventeenth century, those interested in taking over the state would now act within the Court system to establish their clique as the ruling one. Thus the new controller general would, like Colbert, Le Peletier, or Desmarets, introduce his own network of financiers as soon as he took power.

The elites themselves created a climate of change. Women had long played an important role at the French Court. The Regencies of the period 1560–1660 all fell to Queen Mothers (all foreigners at that).

French aristocratic women sponsored and themselves participated in cultural and intellectual life. Louis XIV sought always to keep women out of policy decisions, yet all his contemporaries commented on the influence of Mme. de Maintenon, particularly in matters of religion. More importantly, women had an enormously powerful function as social police – what they said of a man's character mattered a great deal in his success in the world of Court. Women often organized the Court factions (Mme. de Maintenon headed one of the three main factions, if we can believe Saint-Simon). Despite this indirect influence, however, women wielded virtually no direct power. Louis sought always to limit women's legal rights and to establish fathers as familial parallels of his own paternal power within the kingdom.

The appearance of stability notwithstanding, Louis and his ministers attempted radical reforms in the final decades of the reign. Court life changed – the king danced his last ballet as a performer in the early 1680s; institutions changed – the old system seemed to falter in the 1690s, under the strain of war; personalities changed – Louis had to initiate a new group of collaborators. The changes often failed, just as those of the 1630s failed; however, as in the case of the reforms of the 1630s, those of the 1690s and 1700s bore fruit later on. The monarchy relied on precedent; change took time. In almost all cases, the first efforts at reform would fail but the effort itself would establish a precedent that would enable later ministers (often the subalterns of the original reformers) to succeed. Let us turn next to Louis's efforts at reorganization.

Desperate measures and reform: institutional change, 1683–1721

The 1680s and early 1690s brought considerable administrative turmoil to France because of the rapid turnover of personnel. Colbert, the controller general and minister of the Marine, died in 1683; his successor-son as minister of the Marine, the marquis of Seignelay, died in 1691. Le Tellier, by then chancellor, died in 1685, followed six years later by his son Louvois, the minister of War and the dominant royal councilor of the 1680s. The three chief positions – controller general, chancellor, and minister of War – therefore each changed hands in the space of eight years. Louis XIV himself was the only member of the Council of State of 1682 still there ten years later. We can easily forget the simple human contrast between the stability of Colbert's tenure as head of finances, from 1661 to 1683, and the rapid turnover of the ensuing ten years. Colbert's successor, Claude Le Peletier, resigned as soon as the war started, perhaps because, as one contemporary wrote, he had too "tender

and timorous a conscience" to do what was necessary. His replacement, Louis Phélypeaux, count of Pontchartrain, lasted ten years, giving
way to Michel Chamillart, and he to Nicolas Desmarets (Colbert's
nephew).

Here we must stop, however, because the traditional historiography
would have us see only the instability of the late 1680s and early 1690s,
when Louis had three controllers general in six years, three chancellors in
eight years, three ministers of War in ten years, and three ministers of the
marine in eight years. Once again, Saint-Simon's memoirs cast a long
shadow: he vilified the ministers of the later period of the reign. The
classic Lavisse *Histoire de France* enshrined that view:

During the final 30 years of the reign, which were almost all years of war, no great
change took place in the political and administrative institutions, but the regime
of the absolute monarchy and of centralization strengthened and developed
itself.[12]

Louis reorganized the government between the death of Colbert (1683)
and the death of Louvois (1691), replacing his cohort of capable ministers
– Colbert, Le Tellier, Louvois, Seignelay, Colbert de Croissy – with new
collaborators: Pontchartrain, controller general, minister of the Marine,
and later chancellor; Barbézieux, war minister; Colbert de Croissy and
later Torcy at the foreign office; Colbert's son-in-law, the duke of
Beauvillier, as minister of State. Louis allowed the Dauphin (1691) and
the Dauphin's eldest son, the duke of Burgundy (1703), to sit on the
council. These new councilors enjoyed a long tenure: Pontchartrain
lasted from 1689 to 1714, the Dauphin and Beauvillier from 1691 until
their deaths (1711 and 1714). The king even created new councils, such as
the Council of Commerce, when he felt it necessary. This body, made up
primarily of elected merchant deputies from the major French commercial towns, offered a wide range of advice to the controller general – on
taxes, trade, and industry. The king did not attend this council, but he
often followed its advice.

Family continuity remained remarkable. Three families – Colbert, Le
Tellier, and Phélypeaux – dominated the six great offices of state (the four
secretaries of state, the controller general, and the chancellorship), from
1671 to 1715 (Table 4.2). Louis made four exceptions to this rule: Michel
Chamillart, controller general and secretary of state for War (1699–1708
and 1701–09, respectively); two long-serving judges raised to the chancellorship, d'Aligre (1671–77) and Boucherat (1685–99), neither of whom
sat on the Council of State; and Arnauld de Pomponne, secretary of state

[12] E. Lavisse *et al.*, *Histoire de France*, VIII: *Louis XIV – la fin du règne* (Paris: Hachette,
1911), 147.

Table 4.2 *Great offices of state, 1670–1715*

Office	Colbert family	Louvois family	Louvois client	Phélypeaux[a] family
Controller general	1685–83 1708–15		1683–89	1689–99
War ministry		1643–1701	1709–15	
Foreign affairs	1679–1715			
Huguenots				1629–1715
Ministry of the Marine, of Paris, and of the Royal Household	1669–90			1690–1715
Chancellor		1677–85		1699–1714

[a] The Phélypeaux family had two branches: the la Vallière branch held the secretariat of state for the Huguenots; the Pontchartrain branch held the other positions.

of Foreign Affairs from 1671–79.[13] Poor Chamillart, the king's personal friend and billiards companion, relied heavily on members of the Colbert and Louvois clans to run his two ministries. Desmarets served as his second-in-command at the controller general's office after 1703 and replaced him in 1708; Voysin, a Louvois client, took over the ministry of War in 1709.

The ministry of War passed through three generations of the Le Tellier family; after the death of the last one (Barbézieux, 1701), leadership of the military lobby passed to his brothers-in-law, the dukes of la Rocheguyon (later duke of la Rochefoucauld) and of Villeroy (son of the inept marshal). When the male line of the Colberts ran out, the late controller general's sons-in-law, the dukes of Beauvillier and Chevreuse, and his nephews, Torcy and Desmarets, took over. The Phélypeaux provided secretaries of state to every Bourbon monarch. Indeed, at the end of Louis's reign, the key division within the ministries pitted Desmarets and Torcy (of the Colbert clan) against Pontchartrain and la Vallière (of the Phélypeaux). On the Council of State, however, Desmarets, Torcy, and Beauvillier gave the Colbert clan three of the five ministerial seats in 1713–14 (Pontchartrain and Voysin held the others).

Can we call a government in which three families monopolized all important ministries a modern, bureaucratic government? In many ways we can. The extensive family links should not blind us to the play of powerful interest groups within France. Surely we can recognize the importance of a military lobby, led by the Louvois clan. Louvois took a hard line in the 1670s and 1680s; Barbézieux was the hawk of the 1690s;

[13] Louis disgraced Pomponne in 1679 but rehabilitated him in 1691. He rejoined the Council of State, without portfolio, and remained a member until his death in 1699.

Villeroy and la Rocheguyon insisted on saving Philip V in the 1700s. That the minister of War should be the head of the hawkish clan will come as no surprise to anyone familiar with contemporary politics. That his chief allies would come from the military aristocracy should be equally obvious.

The finance minister, on the other hand, longed for peace: war disrupted tax collection and placed intolerable strains on existing resources. Colbert, Croissy, Beauvillier, and Chevreuse – the line of accommodation ran, too, along family lines. In so saying, we must not ignore the deep intellectual roots of the quarrel, which had its origins in the contest of the Devouts and the Good Frenchmen in the 1620s, about whether to pursue peace and internal reform or war and political gain. The devout Beauvillier relied heavily on clergymen such as Bishop Fénelon, and he played a key role in soliciting the disastrous papal bull, *Unigenitus*. The king sought to balance these conflicting interests with his own – with his desire for glory, with his solicitude for his subjects, with his coronation promises, and with his own increasingly pious tendencies.

The duke of Orléans, Regent of France after Louis's death in 1715, tried to destroy the ministerial system and the power of the great clans. First, he effectively abolished the ministries by creating a new group of councils, the Polysynody: the new councils took authority over a mixture of old jurisdictions – War, Finance, Conscience, Marine, and Foreign Affairs – and new ones – Interior and Commerce. The Regent agreed to reimburse the four secretaries should they choose to accept the abolition of the duties of their charges: Torcy accepted 800,000 *livres*, but la Vallière (Huguenots) kept his title, Pontchartrain (Marine and Royal Household) passed his to his son (the count of Maurepas, then only 15), and Voysin, although his secretaryship (War) was abolished, remained chancellor. The Regent did disgrace Desmarets and his chief collaborators (the six intendants of finances and the intendants of commerce); the controller general consoled himself by adding to his recently purchased *hôtel* (for which he paid 220,000 *livres* in 1710); Philip allowed la Vrillière to attend the Council to take the minutes but did not allow him to speak.

Philip brought in a massive cohort of dukes and princes, the revenge of the feudal aristocracy, if we are to believe Saint-Simon. Although leadership of the Polysynod councils passed into the hands of ancient aristocrats – Noailles, Villars, Huxelles, d'Estrées, d'Antin, and even Villeroy – nothing of the sort happened. The Regency Council itself quickly became a mob scene, growing in size from the dozen of 1716 to 29 by 1719 and to 35 by 1722, virtually all of them from the high aristocracy. As the Council's size grew, however, its importance diminished: the number of meetings declined from 165 in its first year to only 57 in its fourth. Philip obviously ran the government elsewhere, in his tight little circle of advisors. By September 1718, he abandoned the Polysynody approach and reverted to the old mechanisms, reestablishing the secretaries of state for War and Foreign Affairs and dividing up the provinces of the kingdom among the secretaries (thus effectively abolishing the Interior Council as well). After the collapse of John Law's system (see pp. 170–72), the Regent restored the positions of the controller general and his chief assistants.

In short, the famous experiment of the Polysynody institutionally changed nothing. The same secretariats, the same controller general's office, the same organization came back to life but without the Colbert and Le Tellier clans. This remarkable changeover in personnel should alert us to what had happened. The traditional element of French state administration, the role of personal connection, remained firmly in place. When the king died, those whom he protected lost their jobs (whether it was Sully in 1610 or Desmarets in 1715). What Colbert, Louvois, and their successors had created, however, was a new state bureaucracy that could not be dismissed. The ministry system had such firm control over the functions of state that even when the ministers could be disgraced, the system they represented could not be discarded. The Regent unwittingly informs us, by his dual action of successfully disgracing the ministers and unsuccessfully suppressing the ministries, that Louis XIV had created a new form of government. The new ministers came from the former assistants of the old; thus Orry, former clerk of Desmarets, became controller general in 1730.

The transition away from Colbert and Louvois created a permanent institutional framework for governmental development. Given the overwhelming connection between individuals and institutions in early modern France, the ministerial system might have collapsed after the deaths of Colbert and Louvois. That it did not partly explains why Philip failed to eliminate the ministerial system thirty years later. People leave, but the state remains.

The ministerial system reflected fundamental transformations in the reality and the theory of government. In hindsight, we can easily see that the ministerial arrangement presaged the development of modern, bureaucratic government. The government evolved from a system dominated by councils and by great Crown officers – the constable and colonel general of the infantry, the superintendent of finances, the chancellor – to one conducted by ministers, the heirs of the secretaries of state of Richelieu's time. Louis XIII and Louis XIV abolished many of the old offices (like constable and superintendent of finances) and even the chancellor lost much of his power, save in judicial matters.

The reduced role of the chancellor shows us the interplay of theoretical and actual elements in royal government. The chancellor represented the old state, the old notion of kingship: the king as judge. In the transition from the king as judge to the king as lawmaker, the chancellor did not lose his power. So long as the state remained a matter of law, of justice, the chancellor had to remain at the center of the royal government. As we have seen, the king of France gradually shifted the emphasis of his function from that of judge (dominant in the Middle Ages), to that of legislator (dominant after Francis I), to that of administrator.

Louis XIV represented the final step in the second transition: the king himself as superintendant of finances; the king himself as first minister in a government run by ministries; the king as unquestioned source of law, hence the elimination of the Parlements' right to preregistration remonstrances on royal edicts and the change in their official title from sovereign courts to superior courts. The royal councils lost much of their power, except the Council of State. The chancellor did not sit by right in that council, although individual chancellors, usually men who had first been secretaries of state, received invitations.

Some French historians refer to this evolution as the shift from a "judicial state" (*état de justice*) to a "financial state" (*état des finances*). The phrase has much to recommend it, if we keep in mind that it refers to the *emphasis* of the state, not to some exclusionary categories. The new structures did not come mainly from financial expediency: the rising power of the ministers came about because of the increased demands on the central state. Those demands required routinization. The larger the enterprise, the more it must rely on routine procedure to function. Louvois and Colbert, if they represented anything, represented the attempted triumph of routine. Lest we get carried away by the apparent novelty of their administration, however, we should recall the response to the Breton rebellions (see chapter 3) and the extremely personal nature of their interaction with subordinates.

How did these governing structures handle the crises of the second half of the reign? The traditional view has long had it that the great innovators of Louis XIV's reign – Colbert, Louvois, Le Tellier – served in its early stages. That view needs substantial revision, yet, to date, has not attracted much serious historiographical attention. Certainly, Colbert and Louvois attempted widespread reform of the French government. Colbert standardized use of the intendants, reduced the direct taxes, increased indirect taxes, and unified the tax farms. Louvois streamlined the military administration, attempting to introduce uniformity and order, for example in supply networks, particularly for troops on the march in France.

These reform programs took time to mature. Colbert's successor as controller general, Le Peletier (1683–89), permanently reestablished (1686) the Royal General Tax Farm (abolished in the aftermath of Colbert's fall) and introduced an intendant into Brittany (1689). Le Peletier, Pontchartrain, Chamillart, and Desmarets standardized many of Colbert's more ad hoc policies.

In some cases, they moved in new directions. Colbert abhorred the use of subdelegates. His successors understood that the intendants had to have such assistants; they went beyond passive support for the use of subdelegates and created geographic subdelegations within the intendancies. Where Colbert tried to follow the principle of constant shuffling of intendants, to prevent the official from developing close local ties, Pontchartrain, Chamillart, and Desmarets tended to keep effective intendants where they were (such as Basville in Languedoc). They understood that local ties, although a potential threat, also enabled the intendant to work more effectively.

Each of the three attributes of early modern government we have discussed – the justice system, finances, and the military – underwent fundamental change in this period. In fact, Lavisse's dictum should be turned on its head. The great period of reform and change under Louis XIV came not early in the reign, under Colbert and Louvois, but at its end, under the influence of Desmarets, Pontchartrain, and the other central administrators. Let us examine each traditional aspect of the state in turn to get some idea of how those changes affected the long-term evolution of the French state.

Louis XIV and the system of justice

Louis XIV's most famous acts toward his judicial system came early in the reign, when he restricted (1667) and then abolished (1673) the Parlement's right of preregistration remonstrance, having removed the term sovereign from their name (1665). The Parlements now had to register all royal edicts *before* they could send their objections to the king. No more long delays in registration; no more need to send arbitrary registration letters (*lettres de jussion**) or to hold royal sessions (*lits de justice**), with the king in person forcing the Parlement of Paris to register an edict. The abolition of the right of preregistration remonstrance shifted the focus of the Parlements to more specifically judicial matters. Indeed, that reemphasis on their judicial role fitted in perfectly with one of the more fundamental changes of Louis's reign: the substitution in most of the country of royal for seigneurial courts. The 1670 criminal code revision accelerated the decline of these courts by shifting much of their criminal case load to royal tribunals.

The justice system changed very little with respect to the structure and practice of the royal court system itself: the hierarchy of Parlement–presidial–bailiwick remained the same and the chancellor maintained his role at the apex of the judicial pyramid. The volume of cases in royal courts, however, expanded enormously at the expense of seigneurial jurisdictions. The king rarely suppressed seigneurial jurisdictions: when he sought to do so in Paris in 1674, he failed. The judicial clientele simply voted with their feet. In the Norman lordship of Pont-Saint-Pierre, local participation at the court sessions declined precipitously between the sixteenth and eighteenth centuries. In the 1580s, the seigneurial court met once a week and dealt with an average of 32 cases per session. The court met 43 times in 1661 but only 37 times in 1681, 30 in 1740, and a mere 17 in 1760. The number of cases per session dropped from 32 in the 1580s to 10 in 1700. In short, a seigneurial court that heard over 1,500 cases in 1580 heard only 370 in 1700 (and 201 in 1740). The value of the clerkship of the court, which peaked in 1651 at 300 *livres* (and 24 pounds of sugar!) remained 220 *livres* as late as the 1670s. In the 1680s, it dropped to 130 *livres* and to 100 *livres* at the turn of the century.[14]

Elsewhere in France the situation looked much the same. In Brittany, the value of clerkships in royal courts rose dramatically in the seventeenth century, indicating that royal courts made great inroads even in an area of extremely strong seigneurialism. In terms of the impact on ordinary French citizens, the shift from seigneurial to royal courts during the seventeenth century must rank as one of the most dramatic changes of the period. Royal courts had firmly established their ability to hear appeals from seigneurial courts by the sixteenth century, but most peasants still went, in the first instance, to a seigneurial rather than a royal court. By the end of the seventeenth century, most peasants avoided the seigneurial court and went instead directly to a royal one. The great lords, such as the Rohans of western Brittany or the members of the royal family, and the landlords of the Midi offered the most effective seigneurial resistance to this loss of authority. The letters of the intendants to the controller general demonstrate the geography of the matter: in 1683, the intendant of the Auvergne complained of the "great authority gentlemen and their officers of justice still have over the people" and of their interference in the repartition of the *taille*. By way of contrast, the intendant of Paris wrote in the same year that the local nobles did not interfere in the

[14] J. Dewald, *Pont-St-Pierre, 1398–1789* (Berkeley: University of California Press, 1987), 254–55, tables 51 and 52.

division of the tax burden. In Caen, the intendant went so far as to say that "there is not a province in the kingdom in which the seigneurs have less authority, where the peasants are better informed about their rights and about how to maintain them."[15]

The number of jurisdictions varied sharply from one region of the country to the next. The *élection* of Paris alone had 460 seigneurial courts; Brittany had more than 1,000 high justiciars. Upper Normandy (Rouen), however, had so few high justiciars that the king created new ones in 1702, to help maintain order in the countryside. Such an action may seem contradictory, in light of the clear royal effort to supplant seigneurial authority in the countryside, but we should bear in mind that the first premise of royal action remained the maintenance of order. If that meant creating new seigneurial jurisdictions (whose powers and prestige, to be sure, were much less than those of existing ones), then so be it. In many areas, royal courts met far from outlying villages, so that, even from governmental eyes, a seigneurial court remained the best solution. The peasants sometimes saw a need for seigneurial courts; in some regions, the village *cahiers* of 1789 demanded the revitalization of the local courts.

The seigneurial courts, about which we know very little, often met on market days. Virtually everyone involved, including in many cases the judge, was a peasant. The few studies we do have indicate that more than 95 percent of the cases involved peasants; in fact, almost all cases involved one peasant suing another one. These seigneurial courts served an important function in maintaining order in village communities; the *cahiers* that demanded their revitalization had this function in mind. The peasants cast a wary eye on the seigneur's own use of the court: where the records survive, they indicate that in disputes between the lord owning the court and the peasants, the lord won. The *cahiers* opposed to seigneurial courts focused on this problem. The government, too, often sided with the peasants, because the cases typically involved matters that bore directly on the parish's ability to pay its taxes. In the eighteenth century, at least in Burgundy, the intendant frequently supported parish communities against landlords.

The second great change in police activities came in Paris, where the king created the lieutenant of police (1667). The lieutenant of police combined a wide range of powers, giving one official, for the first time, authority over most (but not all) of the capital. The first two lieutenants of police, La Reynie and Voyer d'Argenson, gradually created a larger administrative structure for the city but the main changes wrought by the

---

[15] A. de Boislisle, *Correspondance des controleurs-généraux avec les intendants de province, 1683–1715* (Paris, 1874–79), 3 vols., I, 11 (Auvergne), 23–24 (Paris), 37 (Caen).

lieutenancy took place later in the eighteenth century (and are discussed in chapter 5).

Policing the poor

The third change, like the first one, involved the acceleration of a preexisting trend, not a radical transformation such as the lieutenancy of police in Paris. Louis XIV greatly expanded and intensified the policing of "marginal" groups. Three groups stand out above all in this renewed repression: women, Protestants, and the poor. After the Revocation of the Edict of Nantes (1685), the state kept careful watch on these Protestants: intendants wrote frequently to the controller general about the "Catholic" worship by former Protestants. The official outbreak of war in 1689 led to renewed fears of internal French Protestants (in part because some French Protestant nobles, such as marshal Schomberg, who had left in 1685, fought in foreign armies). Protestant Europe, especially England, painted the war as a holy crusade; Catholic France responded in kind.

The worst excesses of the repression took place during the War of the Spanish Succession. The poor Protestant peasants of the Cévennes Mountains, known as the Camisards, resisted efforts to convert them to Catholicism and supported an underground Protestant church. On occasion, they resisted with force the attempts to arrest the wandering pastors. Louis XIV sent dragoons into the mountains, there to destroy the hillside Protestant communities with fire and sword. In what ranks with the destruction of the Palatinate as the most odious deeds of Louis XIV's reign, the soldiers massacred peasants by the thousands.

The Camisard War, like so many repressive actions, demonized an entire group of people, the Protestants of the Cévennes. The reporter of the provincial estates of Languedoc wrote that the Camisards led

an abominable life, since the girls sleep freely and shamelessly with the boys that they love . . . At Escoplier, one of them lay with two men, and at Saumanes, two girls were with four boys, claiming that since they had spoken to God, there was no harm in it.

Little wonder that the local authorities blamed the inevitable "vagabonds and faithless men," the "unknown people." Jean Velay, a local notable, thought the ruthless repression a good thing, because it would "teach to posterity how great a crime it is to rebel against one's sovereign."[16] The government targeted the local poor, especially the rural artisans, for special repression; local elites tried to make arrangements with the government, to protect their goods and lives.

[16] P. Higonnet, *Pont-de-Montvert* (Cambridge, MA: Harvard University Press, 1971), 42 for both quotations.

Demographic catastrophe: the famines of 1693–1694 and 1709–1710

The second police problem, the treatment of the poor, had special urgency between 1690 and 1715 because of the desperate material conditions of the "mini Ice Age." Two dramatic crises interrupted the demographic growth of the seventeenth century: the famine of 1693–94 and the great freeze of 1709.

The generally cold weather of the late seventeenth and early eighteenth century meant a series of bad harvests, of which the worst took place in 1693, 1698, and 1709. The weather brought on the crises in most regions. In 1693, Mme. de Sévigné tells of her Breton estate ruined by hail just on the eve of the harvest, her farmer unable to pay his rent. The hail shattered the windows of her chateau and damaged his roof, obliterated the wheat and hay; and, in some regions, the hail killed the poultry. The entire summer passed in rains, leading to a catastrophic harvest (coming on the heels of a poor harvest in 1692).

The price of grain mounted steadily, rising in Paris from 10 *livres* the *setier* in July 1691 to 20 in November 1692 and then to 42 in August 1693. Riots broke out in Paris and other cities. In Paris, the king ordered the construction of special ovens in the court of the Louvre, ovens which produced 100,000 loaves of bread a day for sale at below-market prices. Later, the king had the parish priests distribute the bread (so the rich could not buy it); he then switched to direct subsidies. These efforts, at Paris and elsewhere, attenuated the crisis in certain regions: in the north and west, and the Seine-Loire region, the population declined but slightly. In the distant Midi, however, government action did not mitigate the general catastrophe (harvests there suffered more than in other regions and previous stocks were lower). Marcel Lachiver estimates that more than 660,000 people died, nearly 26 percent of the population. In France as a whole, almost 6 percent of the population disappeared, dropping the total from 22 million to 20.7 million virtually overnight.[17]

In May 1693, the intendant from Rouen wrote that more than 20,000 people received alms each day in the city and 3,000 more begged in the streets. In many regions of France, intendants wrote of people flocking to the cities for bread, of peasants reduced to eating grass and tree roots. Death rates soared in certain areas; marriages virtually ceased; births declined.

Who would wish to have a child in such a year? At the parish of Mouy, near Beauvais, 30 of the 43 children born between October 1693 and

[17] M. Lachiver, *Les années de misère. La famine au temps du Grand Roi* (Paris: Fayard, 1991), regional figures on 207.

September 1694 died before their first birthday (the normal rate would have been "only" 15). At Amiens, people died of hunger in the streets, like the two unidentified women, one 17, the other 50, reportedly from the village of Dury, who died on the doorstep of the convent of the Soeurs grises. In poor parishes, the death rate climbed to as much as eight times its normal level in August 1694 and to 4.5 times its annual rate in 1694.[18] In the richer parishes, the death rate climbed more slowly, perhaps doubling. The increase in mortality even in rich areas alerts us to the dual nature of the crisis: in poor areas, some people died of malnutrition; throughout the city, people died of infectious diseases, whose rapid spread was related to the reduced resistance of the malnourished poor. Disease, not hunger, killed most people, but hunger magnified the impact of disease far beyond its usual murderous level.

The winter of 1708–09 remained proverbial for its severity, yet the weak harvest of 1708 caused trepidation even in the spring of 1708. The king wrote to all intendants in June, asking them to take a census, so that he would know the relief needs of the country in the "coming famine." Once again, weather, this time extreme cold led to harvest failure. The unusually harsh winter of 1708–09, when the temperature dropped below $-10°C$ all but two days in a two-week period of January and reached record lows again in late February and mid-March, destroyed crops, killed livestock, and froze people to death. Even in the palace at Versailles, bottles burst in the antechambers, their contents expanded by freezing. Peasants found their huts so cold that the bread froze, forcing them to cut it with axes. Wine casks froze in the cellars. Fruit and olive trees split open; the low temperatures destroyed the entire olive cultivation of Languedoc.

At Lyons, the intendant Trudaine wrote in June that beggars stretched from one end of the street to the other. "At first they demand alms with some sort of decorum but after several days of begging they become insolent, so bold that our merchants fear to go to the Exchange, to avoid the words and propositions they make. Despair makes them this way."[19] A month later, the workers of Rouen rioted, stoning the home of the intendant and pillaging two houses. The dreaded dragoons put a stop to the rioting a few days later. Nonetheless, the government had learned the lessons of 1693–94. This time, the ministers acted forcefully to buy grain, even for outlying regions. They also actively sought out hoarders. France suffered terribly again – about 800,000 people died – but the losses remained far lower than in 1693.

[18] P. Goubert, *Beauvais et le Beauvaisis de 1600 à 1715* (Paris: EHESS, 1960, reedition 1982), 56–57; and P. Deyon, *Amiens, capitale provinciale*, 14.
[19] Boislisle, *Correspondance*, III, 169.

In periods of crisis, such as 1693, 1698, or 1709, authorities became increasingly hostile to beggars and wanderers. The sheer numbers involved led to a pervasive climate of fear, a fear intermixed with compassion, to be sure. The same mentality that led to the Camisard massacres stood behind the repression of the poor: anything that threatened order had to be eradicated. Many aspects of the repression followed traditional lines: ordinances banning begging, edicts threatening incarceration (sometimes in the galleys) of wanderers. Try as they might, however, the authorities could not keep up with demand: in January 1694, the two main hospitals of Paris held 13,000 people, 8,000 of them simply incarcerated poor. Jean Guérin, in his *Discourse on the Confinement of the Poor* (1662), summarized the elite attitudes of the time: "They [the poor] were but the refuse and dregs of the world, and if one may put it thus, the excrement and the ordure."[20] Guérin and many others, including the king, suggested that the state lock them up, to turn them, by labor, into productive citizens. As we shall see in chapter 5, the state tried just such an approach on a wide scale in the 1720s.

The great famines of 1693–94 and 1709–10 traumatized contemporaries. Historians have recently reevaluated the overall consequences of these events. We long believed that the population of France declined between 1690 and 1720, yet the work of Jacques Dupâquier has shown that conclusion to be false: the population stagnated (at about 22 million). At Amiens, people may not have married in 1693 or 1694, but those who did not merely put off the ceremony until 1695, when the number of marriages made up for the deficit of the previous years. The population recovered its losses within ten years of the 1693–94 famine, and even more rapidly after that of 1709–1710.

The most remarkable aspect of the Old Regime demographic crises remains their localism. Grain could not be efficiently moved over land, so that those areas cut off from river transport suffered starvation even as the neighboring regions had a surplus. The large areas affected by the famines and associated epidemics, however, set apart the crises of 1693–94 and 1709–10. France lost its demographic momentum in these hecatombs: nearly two million people died in the two crises. When one combines these losses with those associated with the wars, we can see that the trough 1690–1720 separates long periods of population growth in the seventeenth and eighteenth centuries.

People somehow survived the famines, relying on the charity of Church and state. The central government played a much greater role in poor relief in 1661, 1693, and especially 1709 than it had ever done before

[20] T. Adams, *Bureaucrats and Beggars. French Social Policy in the Age of the Enlightenment* (New York: Oxford University Press, 1990), 30.

but the Church remained the main bulwark of the poor. The crisis of 1693 gave way to the bountiful harvest of 1695, one so large that peasants complained they could not sell their grain. They wanted to pay their taxes in kind. Three years later, several intendants (in Limousin, Champagne, and Bordeaux, among others) wrote that the harvest led again to famine. The 1698 harvest in the Southwest demonstrated the problem: Gascony had a good harvest; Quercy and Rouergue suffered from a famine as bad as that of 1693. Countrywide, the situation looked similar: the Soissonais and Champagne had no grain, while Brittany had a surplus. The problem, of course, was to move Breton grain to starving consumers in Soissons or Reims.

The bitter winter of 1709 had other effects, ones hidden by the simple demographic calculation that people managed to survive. All over France, tenants lost their leases, unable to pay the rent. Outside of Nantes, at the *métairie* of La Chapelle aux Moines, the Baboneau family, which had held the lease since 1611, suffered foreclosure on 15 August 1710, because they had been unable to make their rent payment of October 1709. On the other side of France, in the hills of western Burgundy, the peasants of Alligny-en-Morvan suffered the same fate in record numbers: the male heads of household declined from 162 in 1709 to 125 in 1710. Philibert Donat, a royal sergeant who visited the parish in June 1709, described the misery he saw everywhere, from the house of Léon Lepage, where his two children had died and his brother had left to beg, to that of the widow of François Regnault, where four orphans lived alone, subsisting since Easter on nettles, to that of the widow of François Nidellet, who had sent her children out on the roads, to beg the mercy of "faithful Christians." Most of those who dropped of the tax roll, like the widow Regnault, came from the poorest segments of the population (the tax roll described her as a beggar as early as 1705), but many of the richest peasants lost their leases in the aftermath of 1709.[21]

Women and the state

As the case of the widow Regnault reminds us, women made up a disproportionate number of the poor. Poor women, however, had a more complex fate than their adult male counterparts. Prostitutes, "women of bad life" or "debauched girls" as the contemporary documents called them, suffered increased repression, particularly after Louis XIV's 1684 ordinance mandating the incarceration of such women in Paris at the Salpetrière. Louis stated that: "order and the public police desire

---

[21] AD Côte d'Or, C 6194, tax rolls of Alligny-en-Morvan. On the Baboneau family, AD Loire-Atlantique, H 275.

principally that one punish such women." All over the kingdom, local authorities increasingly locked up prostitutes, following the example of the lieutenant general of Paris. Adult male paupers, too, increasingly ended up in a workhouse/poorhouse/hospital (variously called *maison de travail* or a *maison de force*). In 1712, at Grenoble, the city's beggars gathered together at the *place* Grenette for a meal at the expense of the town fathers. After eating, they marched to the General Hospital, there to exchange their rags for new clothes and their freedom for confinement.[22]

Confining the poor proved to be a daunting task, simply because there were so many of them. The harsh tone of the 1684 ordinance gave way to a more understanding attitude in a 1698 text, in which the king (and his council, consisting of an entirely different group of ministers than in 1684) spoke of "the girls whom libertinage or necessity has engaged in disorder." Others, too, began to modify their harshness. In Lyons, in Grenoble, in Aix-en-Provence, the Church leaders and the town magistrates began to deal more systematically with the poor. Part of the bureaucratization came from the massive challenges to poor relief offered by the crises of 1693 and 1709. Relief authorities dealing with men increasingly followed the techniques used by those who helped women.

The deserving poor, largely women and children, had long received attention from the Catholic Church (primarily from nuns) and from well-intentioned upper-class women. Society "divided [relief] into two categories: the business of social control, in the sense of the supervision and training of the able-bodied poor, and charity pure and simple, such as the care of the sick and the obviously helpless. The former became the preserve of men, the latter of women."[23] The wives and daughters of the local civic leaders – usually of the royal officials – collected alms for the poor. In the late sixteenth century, women had taken control of the poor relief collections from the local tax collectors or church vestrymen. They gave the money to other women, especially to widows with children. By the second half of the seventeenth century, they gave home relief (money or bread) in secret to poor but "honorable" families, such as those of artisans ruined by bankruptcy or fire. The Church and state authorities followed their example, helping to feed large segments of the population, even in non-famine years. By the late eighteenth century, something like one-fifth of the population received regular relief.

The expanding public role of women came at a time of increased male efforts to limit that role. The French state consistently acted against women's rights in the sixteenth and seventeenth centuries. The state

[22] K. Norberg, *Rich and Poor in Grenoble, 1600–1815* (Berkeley: University of California Press, 1985), 81.
[23] Rapley, *The Dévotes*, 77.

sought to limit a woman's right to choose her husband; first, in the sixteenth century, the king required young women (under 25) to obtain paternal permission to marry; later, in 1639, the king required *all* never-married women to obtain permission to marry from a male guardian. That French women ignored these laws is beyond question; however, fathers and other male guardians could use them to force women into marriage or to prevent unwanted unions. The single largest use of the infamous *lettres de cachet* (arbitrary orders for arrest) was to incarcerate recalcitrant women. Husbands, fathers, or brothers would lock up their wives, daughters, or sisters in convents until the women broke down. We do well to remember that convents served not only as places of prayer and repose but as female prisons.

The patriarchal nature of the French state grew stronger as the century wore on. Louis XIV placed renewed stress on the traditional image of the king as the father of the people. Louis, following the Aristotelian biological beliefs common in his time, accepted the premise that the male provided all the genetic material for the children, that the women served merely as an empty vessel. His most striking affirmation of such belief came late in 1714, when he forced the Parlement of Paris to accept the right of his sons in a dual adultery, the duke of Maine and the count of Toulouse, to inherit the throne. Louis took these actions in the aftermath of the death of his son, grandson, and great-grandson (1711–12) but they show how far his personal egotism had taken him by the end of the reign. Louis also stipulated, in direct contravention of the Peace of Utrecht (although in keeping with French law), that Philip of Spain stood next in line of succession, after the toddler who would become Louis XV. In 1713, only these two remained among Louis's legitimate direct male descendants. After his death, the Parlement of Paris struck down Louis's will, as it had his father's and grandfather's.

That Louis's personal actions sprang in part from his response to the women question (the *querelle des femmes* as it was then known) will come as little surprise to anyone familiar with seventeenth-century French literature. Molière ridiculed the "old-fashioned" men who wanted to dictate choice of spouse to women. François Poullain de la Barre published, in the 1660s, a tract on the "Equality of the Two Sexes." Powerful patronesses dominated the Parisian salons, at which political and intellectual careers could be made and unmade. The king was surely sensitive to charges that his second wife, Mme. de Maintenon, had too much influence on policy; indeed, he often met with individual ministers in her apartments, with her present (although, by all accounts, not participating directly). In the latter part of the reign, the heritage of the powerful ministerial clans – Louvois and Colbert – passed through daughters to sons-in-law. These women, and others like them, had an enormous, although unofficial and indirect, influence on policy and appointments. The letters of Mme. de Sévigné bear abundant witness to the importance of women in the patronage networks of Louis's Court.

In the less exalted realms of society, much the same took place. Women everywhere became more prominent, despite the increasing legal efforts to repress them. More women appeared on tax rolls in the late seventeenth century; in Burgundy, their numbers nearly doubled between the 1620s and 1670s. More women ran businesses. Again and again in the towns, one encountered the two-income family; wife and husband had independent businesses or shared one. In the countryside, women increasingly appeared as co-signers on leases. All this transpired in a period in which women lost a wide range of legal rights, from that of choice of husband to that of hiring apprentices. These laws, vain efforts to hold back social change, failed miserably. Exogamy rates climbed steadily at the end of Louis's reign; in the eighteenth century, they skyrocketed. By the middle of the century, roughly half of all women married outside their own village, obviously to men not chosen by their families. By way of contrast, in the 1670s, 80 percent of rural women had married within their own parish.

Women offer an outstanding example of the legalistic fallacy of absolutism. Many historians have examined the laws issued by the government and seen greater repression and greater control, in short, absolutism. The social reality looked rather different. In some cases, the law could stunt or channel social and economic evolution (trade restrictions, for example), but in most cases the king and all his men could not put Humpty together again. Many rural women moved to cities (often to work as servants); in the city, the fortunate among them earned enough for a dowry (the least fortunate servants often ended up as prostitutes). With enough money for their own dowry, they had independence from their parents, who could no longer threaten to withhold the dowry as a means of forcing a young woman to marry against her wishes or of preventing her from marrying a stranger. What is more, the young woman had a very powerful ally: the Catholic Church. The Council of Trent (1545–63) had strongly reaffirmed the traditional Catholic doctrine of freedom of choice in marriage. When the king's laws came up against social and economic reality, particularly in combination with the protection of a powerful political force such as the Church, they had no chance of success.

The military under Louis XIV, 1688–1715

The other two realms of government, the military and financial, show much the same pattern. Le Tellier and, especially, Louvois instituted wide-ranging reforms in the early part of the reign but they had only partial success in implementing them. Louvois's remarkable subordinate, Jules-Louis Bolé, marquis of Chamlay, continued the efforts to improve the supply system of the army. Louis had long since dispensed with offices such as the constable, the admiral (later reinstated but without the old powers to name officers), and the colonel-general of the infantry. Their abolition made the ministers of War and the Marine, and their network of collaborators such as Chamlay, dominant figures in French military administration; indeed, one can say that the abolition of the great traditional offices like constable made possible the success of ministerial government. The hired mercenary companies of the Thirty Years' War had given way to a national army. The government actively sought to keep the French regiments of the army French by discouraging the recruitment of foreigners (the foreign regiments – Swiss, Scots, Irish, and others – made up about one-sixth of the army).

The long military revolution of early modern times took firm root only during Louis's final two wars. The government slowly introduced standardization: of weapons and munitions, of uniforms, of training. The changed battlefield tactics of the seventeenth century, with their emphasis on volley fire, encouraged the move to more standardized training. If the six- or ten-file square were to maintain its volleys, its men had to be trained to march and counter march in step, to load and fire in unison. The French borrowed these tactics from the Dutch and Swedes but by the end of the seventeenth century, other nations were borrowing training techniques from the French. The superior organization of the French told in their favor from the 1670s through the 1690s but the other armies had caught up by 1700. Quite apart from the unfortunate consequences of the leadership of incompetents such as Villeroy, Marsin, or Tallard, the French armies of the War of the Spanish Succession faced, for the first time in two generations, opponents as well trained and well organized as themselves. Even in the hands of a capable soldier such as Villars, the outcome of battles remained doubtful. The French won almost all the pitched battles of the 1670s, 1680s, and 1690s; they lost many of those of the 1700s.

Louis changed certain fundamental elements of the French military. He first created a large Navy, likely the strongest in the world by the 1680s, but then allowed it to decline, particularly during the War of the Spanish Succession. Navy spending peaked between 1691 and 1693 (about 27 million *livres* per year) and then declined to about half that amount during the second part of the Augsburg War and during that of the Spanish Succession. In contrast, the army grew ever larger, up from about 280,000 men during the 1670s to perhaps 360,000 men in the early

1700s. Military spending rose rapidly; in the second half of the reign, peacetime military spending averaged about 65 to 70 million *livres* per year, while wartime annual spending reached 150 million *livres*. The central government figures likely underestimate the actual costs; the 1707 budget figure for food and forage, 14 million *livres*, represented only about a third of the real cost for an army of 360,000 men. Troops in the field made up the difference on their own. In the hunger year of 1709, Villars's troops seized over 9,000 sacks of grain (the entire discoverable harvest) in the Cambrésis.

The vast numbers of troops required constant replenishment due to desertion, retirement, sickness, and battlefield death. The king constantly reformed existing regiments and created new ones. In 1702, he added 107 regiments; in 1705–06, he created 37 more. Within regiments, he added units, such as the fourth squadron put in each cavalry regiment in 1702 (a total of 20,000 men). Recruiting proved a daunting task: André Corvisier estimates that the army needed more than 650,000 new soldiers between 1702 and 1713, either in replacements or in new recruits.[24] Louis XIV introduced, in 1692, one important change in the recruitment of these poor souls: he specifically outlawed abduction and force. He threatened officers who violated the ordinance with loss of their position and prison. During the war, however, the government rarely enforced the edict (except in cases of public violence); in 1716, it took its full effect, which it kept throughout the eighteenth century. The king also reinstituted the militia, a forced levy of soldiers on the parishes that enrolled nearly a quarter of a million men during the Spanish war. The king used many of these men as replacements in the regular army. Finally, Louis created the first Veterans' Hospital, the Invalides in Paris, to care for his old and wounded veterans.

More men meant more officers, particularly when the king created new squadrons, companies, and regiments, rather than merely replenishing existing ones. The composition of the officer corps changed somewhat. Nobles from the old landed families continued to dominate – 48 of Louis's 54 marshals held the title of duke, count, or marquis – but demographics alone led to more rapid social escalation of robe noble families. At the outset of the War of Spanish Succession, Louis issued a massive series of promotions, at all levels of the army. He created 11 new marshals (more than doubling their number), 24 lieutenants general, 25 marshals-de-camp, and 30 brigadiers. These high-ranking officers tended to be from older noble families, but many sons of *robins* made it into the ranks below marshal. At the lower levels of the officer caste – the

[24] A Corvisier, *L'Armée Française de la fin du XVIIe siècle au ministère de Choiseul* (Paris: Presses Universitaires de France, 1964), 2 vols.

commands of squadrons, companies, and even certain regiments – sons of noble judges enrolled in ever-increasing numbers, in part because their families had the capital necessary to purchase one of these positions (in law non-venal, but in practice requiring a payment to the outgoing officer).

The fighting took a terrible toll on all these families: twenty years later, observers noted the scarcity of men in their early forties. The casualties struck noble families hardest, because Louis created an atmosphere in which the "true" noble had to serve, had to pay the tax of blood. French tactics – the frequent use of bayonet and sabre charges (as at Neerwinden) – exacerbated the problem. Just as noble families died out in droves during the Hundred Years' War and the Wars of Religion, so too they left the scene in the last two decades of the reign of Louis XIV. As in the middle of the fifteenth century and the late sixteenth century, social mobility accelerated to make up the loss. Jean Meyer has estimated that scarcely one-fourth of the French nobility of 1789 could trace their lineage back 100 years; the appalling losses of the last two of Louis's wars are one reason.

The War of the Spanish Succession, 1702–1713

The second of these wars, the War of the Spanish Succession, provided the ultimate test of Louis's monarchy. The childless Charles II of Spain had three possible heirs: the duke of Anjou (Philip, Louis XIV's grandson), who had (by means of his father's renunciation of his rights) the best claim, archduke Charles of Austria, and Joseph Ferdinand of Bavaria. France and the maritime powers (England and Holland) tried to negotiate a division of the Spanish empire to keep the peace. Their first agreement collapsed when the chosen heir to Spain and most of the empire, the Bavarian Joseph Ferdinand, died. William III and Louis XIV reached a second agreement (1700) but both Charles II of Spain and the Emperor refused to accept it. Just before his death (1 November 1700), Charles II named the duke of Anjou as his successor, a decision ratified by the Spanish Council of State.

The impossible had happened. The Bourbons now ruled the two great empires, France and Spain. Philip took over a vast empire, one whose extent we easily forget: Spain, the Southern Netherlands, the Kingdom of Two Sicilies, the Milanais, several small states in Italy, and the massive empire in the New World. Louis XIV and his grandson controlled the European coast from Antwerp to Palermo, save for Portugal and a few isolated pockets in Italy. Once Louis agreed to support Philip's claim, war became inevitable.

Poor Louis. By all accounts, he did not want such a war. He knew the kingdom needed peace. He did not desire the vastness of the Spanish empire, only a few of its pieces. Yet Louis was a man of overwhelming personal pride, with a powerful sense of his and his family's grandeur and honor. Philip, his grandson, had legitimately inherited the Spanish empire. Although Louis had signed agreements about the disposition of the Spanish holdings, his personal sense of honor and obligation to his family made it impossible for him to repudiate Philip and honor the treaties of partition.

The War of the Spanish Succession, like its predecessor, took place all over the globe. This time France had allies: Spain, Bavaria, Cologne, and briefly, Savoy and Portugal (both of whom deserted to the other side once the war broke out). The old coalition – England, Holland, Austria, the Holy Roman Empire, and Prussia – re-formed against France. The economic spoils – the right to trade in the Spanish empire – promised to be even greater than those of Ryswick. The key prize for England was the *asiento*, the right to trade slaves to the Spanish empire, a fitting symbol of the emerging world economy driven by the European powers and their conflicts. Those powers fought for the right to take people from Africa and sell them in South America, just as they fought in India for the right to export spices, tea, and cotton goods.

Seldom has a war encompassed such wild swings of fortune. France began victorious on most fronts. Philip received a tumultuous welcome in Spain. Catinat and Vendôme defeated the Austrians in a series of battles in northern Italy, while marshal Villars routed the Imperials at Friedlingen and Höchstadt. In 1702, the Austrians even captured Villeroy, an event immortalized in popular song:

> Frenchmen, give thanks to Bellona,
> Your happiness is without equal;
> You have conserved Cremona
> And lost your general.

Unfortunately for France, the king ransomed Villeroy, who soon played a central role in two military catastrophes. In 1704, the hapless duke lost track of the English army facing him, allowing its commander, the duke of Marlborough, to race down the Rhine, joining up with the Imperial army led by Prince Eugene of Savoy. Their forces together annihilated the Franco-Bavarian army, which lost 30,000 of its 50,000 men in the disaster of Blenheim. Blenheim, that rare battle that transforms an entire war, revolutionized European attitudes about the French army, much the way Rocroi had broken the mystique of the Spanish *tercios* sixty years before.

From 1704 to 1706, disasters followed one upon the other. In 1705, Marlborough, back in the Low Countries, routed the ubiquitous Villeroy at Ramilies and swept through Brabant and Flanders. Desperate to save his northern frontier, with Catinat dead and Villars in disgrace, Louis recalled Vendôme from Italy. At Turin, Prince Eugene routed Vendôme's inept successors, Marsin (one of the bunglers of Blenheim) and La Feuillade, and drove the French from northern Italy. How typical of the highly structured political culture that Louis had created that La Feuillade, an excellent corps commander but an incompetent army general, could not rely on the siege warfare advice of marshal Vauban, who had requested to serve under him as a volunteer. Because of Vauban's rank as marshal, he could not serve when the lower-ranking La Feuillade refused his approval. Deprived of a competent siege director by matters of etiquette, the French lost an army.

In Spain, the English carried all before them, but then lost everything save Barcelona and Gibraltar by year's end. In 1707, Villars and Vendôme restored stability in the Rhineland and the Low Countries; the Allies failed in a disastrous attack on Toulon. Throughout these ups-and-downs, Louis sent out peace feelers to his enemies, offering to give up large segments of the Spanish inheritance; the English and Dutch stood firm against compromise. The following year, disaster again overtook the French, this time at Oudenaarde (11 July 1708). When Louis's grandson, the duke of Burgundy (then second in line for the throne) overruled marshal Vendôme and ordered a withdrawal after the indecisive fighting on the 11th, the retreat turned into a rout, as was so often the case in early modern armies. Prince Eugene and Marlborough, always quick to follow up victories (a rare quality among generals of that time), advanced into France and captured Lille, the cornerstone of the northern frontier. Ghent and Bruges surrendered to the Allies within days.

One can hardly imagine a more complete picture of defeat than France in 1709. Driven from the Low Countries, the entire country staggering under a terrible famine, France seemed ready to collapse. The king's council agreed to seek peace at any cost; the minister of Foreign Affairs, Torcy, himself departed in secret to Holland to obtain terms. The Dutch offered a harsh peace: Louis would have to give up Strasburg, Toul, Verdun, Savoy, and Newfoundland; he would have to recognize Charles III of Spain; he would even have to send his own troops against Philip, if the latter refused to give up. For this he would get only a two-month suspension of fighting, after which the allies could make new demands.

Louis could not accept the last demand, that he fight against his own grandson. He took the extraordinary step, in June 1709, of writing a letter to the French public (through the intermediary of the intendants, who were to publish it everywhere, and the parish priest, who read it from the pulpit) explaining why he could not accept the Dutch terms. He wrote to his subjects that: "I share all the evils that the war has made such faithful subjects suffer ... [but] I am persuaded that they would themselves oppose the acceptance of conditions equally contrary to justice and to the honor of the name French."[25] Louis hung on. Seizing the Spanish bullion fleet when it arrived in Saint-Malo, he used the 20 million *livres* in gold to fit out a new northern army for Villars. Villars fought a brutal draw with Marlborough and Eugene at Malplaquet, one in which they won the battle but suffered 23,000 casualties, twice the number of the French losses. Paraphrasing Pyrrhus, Villars wrote to the king that "if God gives us the grace to lose another such battle, Your Majesty may count on his enemies being destroyed."

The war bogged down again into a series of indecisive victories. The stalemate began to crumble in 1710, when the Tories captured the government of England from the Whigs. Merchants in England and Holland demanded peace. The broad outlines of a settlement began to take shape. The Austrian archduke would get the Low Countries and the Milanais; Philip would keep Spain and the New World. England would get Gibraltar, Newfoundland, and the *asiento*. Philip would have to give up any right to the French throne; his brothers (and their heirs) would have to renounce their rights to that of Spain. Louis XIV would have to give up a bit of territory in the north (such as Tournai) and give back Savoy and Nice, but he would keep his earlier conquests, including Lille and Strasburg. As if to assure the French position, marshal Villars won one last battle, at Denain (24 July 1712). Perhaps Louis had reason to remember the sage counsel of François Eudes de Mézerai, offered in 1667: "People have always remarked that in war the last event determines everything; it does little good to win four or five battles if one loses the last one."[26]

The War of the Spanish Succession presented a monumental challenge to France: war against a coalition of all the other major (and most of the minor) powers of Europe. Such a task called for desperate measures. As so often happened in French institutional history, the remedies of desperation soon became ordinary medicine. Like a person suffering pain, France became addicted to stronger and stronger pills. The remedy that first seemed so drastic came to appear mild. When the cause of the pain subsided, breaking the addiction to which it led proved to be too difficult. Above all, the king sought new remedies for financial problems:

[25] Bluche, *Louis XIV*, 799–800.
[26] O. Ranum, *Artisans of Glory* (Chapel Hill, NC: University of North Carolina Press, 1980), 218–19.

paying for the War of the Spanish Succession forced dramatic changes in the third leg of traditional government.

Financial revolution?

The third leg of our governmental stool, finances, underwent bewildering changes and counter changes. The two wars stretched Louis's financial capacity beyond its limits. He tried virtually every conceivable approach to "revenue enhancement." In 1690, his basic taxes brought in a "gross" of about 120–125 million *livres*: half from the indirect taxes (paid by the General Tax Farm), a third in *tailles*, and the rest from the *pays d'Etats*, the clergy, the demesne, and the venal officers. Local expenses – judges, financial officers, tiny local garrisons – and the debt service reduced the tax revenue by about 22 million *livres*, leaving disposable income of 95–100 million *livres*. In fact, local expenses exceeded 22 million *livres* because the central accounts did not carry everything; some revenues (such as certain demesnes) paid for local courts. More importantly, intermediate bodies such as provincial estates and the clergy borrowed money for the king. The capital invested in these off-budget loans ran into tens of millions of *livres*.

The king needed far more than 95 million *livres* for ongoing expenses, so he had to find other ways to raise money. Louis had four basic options: (1) he could create new taxes or raise existing ones; (2) he could sell more offices; (3) he could sell more annuities (*rentes*); and (4) he could manipulate the currency. During the War of the League of Augsburg, he followed all four options.

The government sold massive amounts of annuities: in 1684, it raised 48.7 million *livres*; during the Augsburg war, it issued well over 100 million *livres*. At the end of the war, in 1699, it tried to consolidate the war debts in one big wave of annuities – 310 million *livres*. Such tactics had an obvious shortcoming: they crippled future revenues. In 1685, for example, interest costs rose 3.7 million *livres* to cover the costs of the annuities and offices sold in 1684. The "charges" against the regular tax revenues rose astronomically: from 22 million *livres* in 1683 they reached 48 million *livres* in 1699, 63 million *livres* in 1706, and, on paper, perhaps 90 million *livres* by 1713. In wartime, the king often suspended payments on the annuities; at the end of the War of the Spanish Succession, most *rentiers* had not received any payments in more than two years.

The king also created many new offices, ranging from inspectors of every conceivable product made in France to hereditary mayors of all walled towns. He obtained over 100 million *livres* from the sale of new offices and of increased *gages* or new rights to existing officers during the

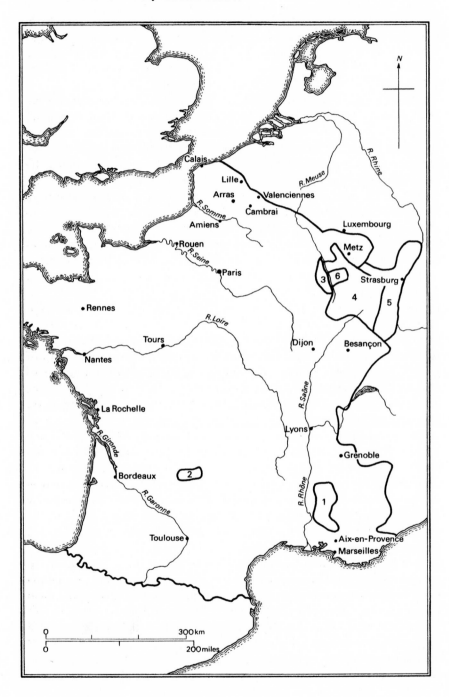

N

Calais

Lille
Arras   Valenciennes
Cambrai
Amiens   Luxembourg

R.Meuse

R.Somme

R.Rhine

Rouen   Metz
R.Seine
Paris   3 6   Strasburg
                4   5

Rennes

R.Loire

Tours   Dijon   Besançon
Nantes

R.Saône

La Rochelle

R.Gironde   Lyons

Bordeaux   2   Grenoble

R.Garonne   *R.Rhône*   1

Toulouse   Aix-en-Provence
                    Marseilles

0 ————————— 300 km
0 ————————— 200 miles

Augsburg war. In most cases, the affected parties – such as town governments or guilds – paid for the suppression of the new offices, so that the "offices" functioned more as forced loans. Given the widespread urban exemption from the *taille* and similar exemptions to many of the indirect taxes, these forced loans represented taxation.

One of the least understood aspects of Old Regime fiscality is precisely the relationship between the urban middle and upper classes and taxation. These people did not pay many of the regular taxes but, in times of war necessity, they provided a ready source of tax income. They preserved their tax privileges, yet the king obtained their money by means of "extraordinary" measures such as the sales of new, useless offices. The king sought to create offices that would be such an affront to the dignity of the urban privileged that they would demand the right to pay to abolish them. The venal mayors provide an obvious example, but the inspectors of guild-produced goods opened corporate pockets just as quickly. One dramatic change appeared at the end of the Spanish war; the king stopped selling so many offices. Indeed, during the eighteenth century, the government sold scarcely any offices.

In order to understand the nature of the changes during the last part of the reign, let us start with the figures from a representative wartime year, 1706. As Table 4.3 indicates, the king raised about 120 million *livres* in regular taxes and another 30 million *livres* from the new capitation, of which he could dispose of only about 61.5 million *livres* because of advanced spending and "charges" (usually interest or repayment for short-term loans). Given that his "official" expenses ran to 170 million *livres*, he fell far short of his needs. He sold new offices, created new taxes (thus raising about 41 million *livres*), and manipulated the currency (raising a similar amount). He shunted expenses forward, onto the revenues of 1707 and 1708, and issued still more annuities.

How like the days of Richelieu and Mazarin this all sounds: anticipating revenues, borrowing through annuities, selling offices, creating new

---

Map 4.1   France in 1715: 1. Avignon and Comtat Venaissin: owned by the papacy. 2. Viscounty of Turenne; 3. Duchy of Bar; 4. Duchy of Lorraine; 5. Alsace and Philippsburg salient. The other powers permanently recognized French sovereignty in Alsace at the Treaties of Utrecht (1713) and Rastatt and Baden (1714); Philippsburg remained under military occupation. The principality of Dombes, while the king's possession (and thus not outlined by the cartographer), remained outside the royal demesne; 6. Toul enclave, to France. In reality, the enclave was smaller than shown here.
Source: Rizzi-Zannoni, *Atlas historique de la France Ancienne et Moderne* (Paris: Desnos, 1766), plate 30: "Etat de la France à la fin du règne de Louis XIV."

Table 4.3 *Taxes and spending in 1706*

Regular taxes	Revenue	Charges against[a]	Anticipated in 1705[b]	Disposable in 1706
tailles	39.85	14.9	9.1	15.85
General Tax Farm	59.5	43.6	8.1	7.8
pays d'Etats	10.95	2.2	1.85	6.9
clergy	6.0	0.0	1.45	4.55
sale of wood	1.9	0.8	0.0	1.1
venal offices	1.8	0.0	0.0	1.8
New Tax				
capitation	30.2	0.0	6.7	23.5
Total	150.2	61.5	27.2	61.5

[a] local and regional expenses, including some interest.
[b] income from 1706 already assigned to expenses from the budget of 1705.
Source: A. de Boislisle, *Correspondance des contrôleurs généraux des finances avec les intendants* (Paris: Imprimerie Nationale, 1874–98), 3 vols., III, appendix.

taxes, augmenting the *gages* of existing offices. What interests us here is not so much these elements of continuity but the elements of change. Three elements stand out among the revenue enhancements: the sale of a new type of annuities, the manipulation of currency, and the creation of universal direct taxation, the capitation.

The king had issued annuities (*rentes*) for centuries. Prior to the late seventeenth century, he issued perpetual annuities, typically bearing interest of between 4 and 8 percent (here simplifying grossly for the sake of brevity). At the end of his reign, however, Louis turned to new methods: lifetime annuities (*rentes viagères*) and tontines. In the former, the king agreed to pay the annuity as long as the designated individual remained alive; the beneficiary of the annuity did not have to be the same person specified as the "life" in question. Merchants used this loophole to buy annuities against the lives of their children (or even those of others). The tontines paid a fixed amount of benefits to a pool of purchasers; as the purchasers died, the survivors received increased benefits. Both types of annuity proved ruinously expensive, not so much because French financiers did not understand how the annuities worked, but because the king needed to offer especially attractive terms to attract investors. These favorable terms made the real rates of interest on French government securities substantially higher than those paid by their opponents.

Louis introduced the universal capitation (head tax) in 1695. He created twenty-two classes of taxpayers, ranging from the first class, which included the Dauphin, the princes of the blood, the controller general, and the Farmers General, to the twenty-second, which encompassed soldiers, day laborers, servants in small towns and villages, and shepherds. The members of the first class paid 2,000 *livres* each, those in the twenty-second only one. The capitation raised about 24 million *livres* a year. Louis, true to his word, cancelled the tax after he signed the Peace of Ryswick (1697). Only the clergy escaped the capitation. Louis had originally included them, but they convinced the king to allow them to purchase exemption for a large grant (4 million *livres* a year).

The capitation takes us into an entirely new state structure, one in which all inhabitants must pay taxes. The capitation did not quite become a universal head tax because of the exemptions, but it was remarkably close to one for the time. When the king reinstituted the capitation, in 1701, he did not return to the system of classes. In the *pays d'élection*, each regional district paid a fixed sum, apportioned along the lines of the *taille*. For the vast majority of French taxpayers, the capitation became merely an augmentation of the *taille*. In the towns, the intendant cut deals with the various corporations, such as guilds, who paid a lump sum and then themselves apportioned it among the members. The intendant also set, with a noble assistant, the amounts paid by all nobles. The clergy continued to buy its exemption.

The nearly 600 categories of the original capitation primarily dealt with government officers, ranging from the controller general (class 1) and the First President of the Parlement of Paris (class 2), down to the archers of the mounted constabulary and sergeants in seigneurial courts (class 21, 2 *livres*). Most ordinary people did not appear until class 18 (10 *livres*), which included artisans owning their own shop in a large city and some "farmers and ploughmen." In fact, the first occupational category came only in the 11th class, wholesale merchants (100 *livres*). Landlords did not suffer much; town-dwelling *rentiers* appeared only in the 13th and 15th classes (depending on the size of their city), paying 60 or 40 *livres*. Nobles fell into six broad categories (listed above, on p. 134).

The 1701 system, with intendants setting noble assessments, likely represented little change (the fulminations of historians to the contrary notwithstanding) except for rural ploughmen, whose contribution surely increased when the capitation shifted from a fixed assessment to one based on *taille* contribution. After 1701, nobles paid a fixed assessment based on an agreement between the individual and the local commission (intendant and two or three leading local nobles). These new assessments differed little from the old ones, except for those in favor at Court, who often received exemptions.[27]

---

[27] I base this assertion on my own research using the capitation rolls in Burgundy and Normandy.

Despite the abuse of exemptions (clergy, some high-ranking nobles), Louis established an extraordinary principle with the capitation: that all had to pay direct taxes. He took this action in a climate ripe for change, one that looked across the sea to England and Holland to see why these tiny countries could raise more money than mighty France. Many writers proposed head or revenue taxes; the most famous such author, marshal Vauban, suggested the abolition of most royal taxes and the substitution of a royal tithe (*dîme royale*). Louis repudiated Vauban's ideas when the few copies appeared in 1707; indeed, he ordered the lieutenant general of Paris to seize and destroy all copies of Vauban's text. Four years later, he adopted a modified version of Vauban's *dîme*. Vauban wanted the proceeds collected in kind, the king's *dixième** was, theoretically, based on income and was paid in cash. Like the capitation, the *dixième* supposedly fell on all. Once again, the clergy bought an exemption, as did several of the *pays d'Etats*, whose estates paid a lump sum for the exemption.

The third major innovation, the manipulation of the currency, scarred France for generations. The monarchy had often manipulated the coinage; whenever tax revenues fell short, the king would issue an ordinance revaluing the money. In extreme cases, he would call in all coinage in circulation and remint it using a lower percentage of precious metal, as in 1692–94, when he made 50 million *livres* from the reminting (which included the melted-down royal silverplate). Louis XIII and Mazarin had regularly practiced such techniques; however, Colbert convinced Louis XIV to abandon currency manipulation. After his death, his successors followed a different policy. In 1689, 1693, 1701, 1704, and 1709, the controller general's office simply declared that all coins in circulation were worth a different amount (in 1689, for example, a tenth more than they had been).

Merchants denounced these manipulations, claiming that they greatly harmed French commerce. Des Casaux du Harlay, the deputy from Nantes on the Council of Commerce, wrote to the controller general in 1701 that the government's manipulation of the currency led, in part, to the shortage of cash. As he said, people had no incentive to bring *écus* in for reminting when the mint paid them 30.5 *sous* for the *écu* and sold it back at 36 *sous*. He further suggested that currency manipulation dried up credit, because the 8-percent reduction in specie value wiped out the interest profits on short-term loans. Given that the king was France's largest debtor, that was, of course, precisely the idea. In the 1720s, however, the government realized the value of sound money, having learned the lesson from England. Save for the Revolutionary period, French coins maintained their value from the 1720s to the 1920s, evidence of the enduring national obsession with sound money.

The second French monetary obsession, the abhorrence of paper money, also has its roots in the period 1690–1721. Most historians give the impression that France did not have paper currency under the Old Regime. In a strict sense, it did not, but the king issued a wide range of credit instruments that served the function of money. Private merchants had long used letters of exchange to balance their debts, particularly for long-distance trade. Royal tax collectors also used letters of exchange drawn on private merchants and financiers to move capital from the provinces to Paris because shipping cash was both expensive and dangerous. In hard times, the government demanded more cash and less paper; by the Augsburg war, regional receivers complained that the government no longer accepted letters of exchange as payment. They argued that it would be impossible to pay the taxes without them.

The government itself issued paper to pay its debts. The most common such documents were the *mandements de l'Epargne* and the *rescriptions de l'Epargne*, payment orders from the Central Treasury. The controller general (in the king's name and with his signature) would authorize a payment to a creditor, saying that he had the right to collect 50,000 *livres* on the *taille* receipts of, say, Rouen. The creditor could then sell the *mandement* for cash (at a discount), usually in Paris. In the seventeenth century, the central government regulated most of its transactions through these paper exchanges. One expense, however, required hard cash: troops. Those people, such as the clergy or the tax farmers, who could provide the government with hard cash, could (and did) drive hard bargains. In times of war or difficulties of collection, the Treasury orders sold at larger discounts.

In 1701, Louis XIV decided to expand his offering of what was, in essence, paper money, by issuing the infamous coin certificates (*billets de monnaie*). The director general of the mint, when he received old coins for reminting, would issue coin certificates, legally valid as cash, in lieu of new coins because he could not keep up the pace of reminting. He issued small amounts, a mere 6.7 million *livres* by the end of 1703. In 1704, however, the government realized that it could issue these coin certificates in much larger numbers, unbacked by real precious metal stocks. The government also recreated a loan treasury (the *caisse d'emprunts*) in 1702, carrying interest of 6 to 10 percent. Here we see a case of an idea of Colbert (who founded the first *caisse d'emprunts* in the 1670s) repudiated by his successor, Le Peletier (as part of the general dismantling of Colbert's financial network), and resuscitated by a later controller general, Chamillart, under the influence of Colbert's nephew, Desmarets. The government sought, by these means, to create a genuine national debt and, to some degree, a national bank (French financiers understood the English and Dutch advantage in having central banks).[28]

The government soon offered interest (7.5 percent) even on the coin certificates. By the end of 1706, when the system of certificates first collapsed (certificates sold on the open market for less than half of their face value), the government had over 180 million *livres* of them in circulation. In a typical trick of Old Regime financing, the government forced individuals to convert most of these bills into liens on various other revenues, into annuities, and into new certificates, legally defined as cash in the Paris region. Only the return of Desmarets turned the tide.

Desmarets struggled to find sufficient credit to keep the government moving. He reminted the currency in 1709 (using the Spanish gold seized at Saint-Malo) and created the ingenious *caisse Legendre* (December 1709) to create new credit. This *caisse* pooled the resources of twelve receivers general, who then issued interest-bearing paper instruments backed by the income from various taxes (sales of exemption from the capitation, the *paulette*, the clergy, and eventually many others). In five years, the *caisse Legendre* issued notes worth 400 million *livres*, enabling the government to stay in business.[29] By the end of the war, the government had almost 600 million *livres* of paper instruments (excluding the old annuities) to repay. The total debt contracted during the war likely exceeded one billion *livres*. The government had already spent the regular receipts of 1716 and 1717 by September 1715. In short, the kingdom faced fiscal disaster.

The greatest currency reform effort, which took place under the Regency of Philip of Orléans (1715–23), can only be understood against the backdrop of the mass of paper "money" created by Louis XIV. The government, one need hardly say, had no way to repay all this debt. The duke of Orléans first followed the time-honored device of disgracing the controller general and his entourage: he dismissed Desmarets and all of his chief assistants. Orléans then created a Chamber of Justice to investigate all of the financiers associated with Desmarets, following a precedent established by Colbert (investigating Fouquet's men in the 1660s) and Louvois (instigating Le Peletier to do the same to Colbert's clique in the 1680s).

[28] The Bank of Amsterdam, a private concern, had no direct connection to the national government, but served the States General as a substitute for a state bank, like that of England, when it came to borrowing money for government expenses.

[29] G. McCollim, "The Formation of Fiscal Policy in the Reign of Louis XIV: The Example of Nicolas Desmaretz, Controller General of Finances (1708–1715)," Ph.D dissertation, Ohio State University (1979), 277–85. This (unfortunately unpublished) dissertation contains some of the best information on the fiscal policies of the end of the reign, as well as an excellent section on some of the bureaucracy, notably the intendants of finance; the remarks below on these officers are also based on this work. My thanks to Dr. McCollim for a copy of his thesis.

The situation of 1715 differed from earlier ones in that the two main ministerial clans – Colbert and Phélypeaux – *both* lost power, thus the two rival financial networks also fell into disfavor. Thus Crozat's network, with its close ties to Pontchartrain, could not take advantage of the fall of Desmarets (and his bankers). Antoine Crozat himself faced a fine of 6.6 million *livres*, while the chief supporters of the Colbert clan, the Hogguer family of Geneva (and Lyons) went into bankruptcy (although a branch of the family resurfaced as successful bankers in Amsterdam). The Chamber assessed the Pâris brothers for 1.2 million *livres*, the seventh-highest fine. The total fines of 220 million *livres*, like those of earlier Chambers, could not be collected: the state received about 50 million *livres* in real income from the investigation. Many of those under suspicion, such as the Pâris brothers, later returned to prominence in the 1720s.

The Regent turned next to a Scottish financier, John Law, to solve the problem. Law combined three separate projects into one: (1) he created a national bank; (2) he founded a massive monopoly company for trade and tax collection; and (3) he issued paper money. The bank (privately founded in 1716 and serving only Paris) worked very well at first: issuing silver certificates, offering low discounts on letters of exchange, paying interest on deposits. The company came next: first (August 1717) a trading monopoly for the western hemisphere and Africa, the Compagnie de l'Occident, usually known as the Mississippi Company; then other trading monopolies, such as the East Indies in May 1719; next the tax farms (tobacco in 1718, the General Farm in July 1719, displacing the syndicate led by the Pâris brothers). Law sold shares in these companies for government certificates. Soon, the private bank at Paris became a Royal Bank (December 1718); not long afterwards, the government banned the use of silver for purchases of more than 600 *livres*, requiring instead the use of certificates. The Company now controlled all non-European commerce, all tax farming, and the issuance of money. Law sold the shares for 5,000 *livres* each but their trading value rose steadily in 1719, peaking at 18,000 *livres*.

Acting on his belief that more currency in circulation meant economic growth, Law rapidly increased the volume of certificates: 150 million *livres* in 1718; 160 million *livres* more by June 1719. In July 1719, however, Law began to issue staggering quantities of certificates in order to keep his enterprise afloat. At this point, the Company had become something like a pyramid scheme, requiring ever more capital to keep the cycle going and satisfy investors. In July, he issued 220 million *livres*; between July and December 1719, he gave out a total of about 820 million *livres*. In the first five months of 1720, he added 1.7 billion *livres* of certificates to the amount already in circulation. As one might expect, the frenzied pace indicated serious trouble; the Mississippi shares plunged in value. Panic gripped investors. By the summer of 1720, the Law System lay in ruins. Law managed to convince the Regent to make a last effort to save it in that summer but to no avail; by December 1720, Law had escaped to Brussels. The final accounting of the disaster revealed unpaid debts of 2.5 billion *livres*, of which the Mississippi shares represented a tenth. After the usual forced conversion of debts, the debt service returned to about its level of 1718, some 51 million *livres* of annuities per year. Law thoroughly discredited the idea of a central bank in France (Napoleon created the first one) and helped create the long-standing French distrust of paper money (a distrust enhanced by the *assignats* of the Revolution), one that has lasted to our own day.

One of the Law System's unanticipated effects involved debtors other than the king, notably the village communities. At Lourmarin, in Provence, as in so many other villages, the community itself and the leading peasants used the certificates to pay their debts in 1719 and 1720 for a fraction of the real value. All across France, village communities and rich peasants freed themselves from a burden that had long prevented agricultural growth. Surely this elimination of the debt burden on the peasantry bears some responsibility for the economic growth of the 1720s and after.

The return of the old borrowing and banking structure meant the return of the old administration of finances as well. Controller general Desmarets's key subordinates returned to high positions. These men came from the usual well-connected families: Bignon de Blanzy, intendant of finances for the *pays d'élection*, was a nephew of Pontchartrain; Lefèvre de Caumartin, responsible for the salt taxes, came from a high robe family we have encountered above; Lefèvre d'Ormesson, intendants of finance who controlled the collection of many of the direct taxes until the 1770s. Caumartin later became intendant for Paris, while other subordinates of Desmarets became dean of the king's council (Le Peletier de Souzy), Keeper of the Seals (Armenonville), and even controller general (Philibert Orry, one of Desmarets's personal clerks). When the old Desmarets–Colbert network (minus any members of the family, to be sure) came back into power in the 1720s, they brought their old financier supporters, such as the Pâris brothers and the Genevan bankers, with them. Little wonder that the entire financial apparatus, from the controller general down to his clerks and out to the bankers, reembraced the ideas of Colbert and Desmarets.

Louis XIV and the French monarchy

Louis XIV, the "God-given" (so called because of his seemingly miraculous conception, more than twenty years after his parents' marriage), did more than any other king to undermine the sacral nature of French kingship. Such a statement may seem odd, given Louis's traditional association with Divine Right monarchy, but, as we have seen, Divine Right monarchy provides a very poor insight into Louis's kingship. Louis's constant religious problems helped to drive a wedge between French political society and the Catholic Church. The persecution of the Huguenots harmed Louis's standing among some French elites but he alienated far more of them because of the split with the Papacy in the 1670s and 1680s, which fundamentally compromised Louis's position with respect to the internal divisions within the French Catholic Church.

The religious quarrels had two major aspects: the king's own fight with the Pope and the Jansenist–Jesuit split within the French Church. Louis had crushed the Jansenist *curés* in the 1650s but their influence spread beyond Paris, informing the piety of many late seventeenth-century French people. The judges of the Parlements had especially close ties to the Jansenists; the female leaders of the Port-Royal convent, center of Jansenism, came from Parlementaire families, like those of the founder Arnauld (relative of Arnauld de Pomponne). The king needed the support of his own political elites in the quarrel with Pope Innocent XI; the Pope, neatly seizing the subtleties of the situation, sided with the two Jansenist bishops in their quarrel over the *régale* with the king (and, by extension, his Jesuit confessor). At the same time, the French clergy issued the famous Four Gallican Articles, effectively saying that Church Councils had supreme authority in France and that the French Church did not have to follow the dictates of the Pope.

After twenty years of negotiations and bulls from various Popes, Louis and Pope Clement XI finally reached an effective understanding in 1713. Clement would denounce all ideas remotely associated with Jansenism by means of a bull condemning Pasquier Quesnel's *Moral Reflections on the New Testament* (reissued in an expanded edition in 1699); Louis, by soliciting a papal bull on Jansenism, would directly attack the Gallicanism of the French Church and implicitly assert the Pope's supremacy in matters of dogma. Louis promised the Pope that he would obtain the approval of a French Church Council for the bull. Predictably, the bull *Unigenitus* outraged many in the Church and in the Parlements; some of its strongest opponents were not Jansenists but Gallicans, such as the king's own chief attorney at the Parlement, d'Aguesseau, and the bishop of Paris, Cardinal de Noailles. After Louis's death, the Regent placed Noailles in charge of the Council of Conscience and d'Aguesseau became chancellor (1717), bringing the Gallican opposition to *Unigenitus* into the highest levels of the government itself. The inept combination of Gallicanism and Jansenism in the bull created a progressively more united front between the two groups, particularly in the Parlements.

Unigenitus, more than any other action taken by the kings of France, undermined the sacrality of the throne. The political nation, most particularly the judiciary, moved away from an ideology tying the king to the Church because that combination threatened both their idea of the real Church (the Gallican one) and, in some cases, their Jansenist leanings. They associated the Jesuits with authoritarianism, itself a direct attack on the Parlementaire belief in their role in the French state. Constitutional thought and religious belief therefore came together in the Parlements, encouraging the growth of a very different theory of state and kingship. The Parlements, once they rejected in part the sacrality of the monarchy, cast into doubt the inviolability of the contracts on which the French state rested. God's law protected contracts; the king, as God's anointed, above all men was bound to God's law. As soon as doubts about the sacrality of monarchy took root, the members of political society sought new means of guaranteeing their position. They sought such guarantees in law, a law created by the combination of the king and his Parlements. This struggle between the king and his ministers and the Parlements and political society helped define the evolution of the French state from the death of Louis XIV to the fall of Louis XVI.

The Regent paved the way for these changes because he opposed so many of Louis's final acts. Philip needed the Parlement to break the king's testament; he offered them in return the renewed right of preregistration remonstrance, which they would use to great effect throughout the remainder of the Old Regime. He brought in avowed Gallicans like d'Aguesseau and Noailles at the moment when the anti-Jansenist forces lost some of their leaders (Fénelon and Beauvillier had both died by January 1715).

Philip had widespread popular support for his actions. Louis XIV, the Sun King, the God-given, the Apollo of the 1660s, died little mourned in his own capital. His loyal officers, knowing the popular opinion of the king, brought his body from Versailles to Saint-Denis in the dead of night, leaving at 8 PM. All Paris lined the route, lighting it with the lanterns of their carriages, yet observers commented on how shallow a grief they expressed, particularly in contrast to their wild show of joy for the boy-king, Louis XV, earlier in the day. Soon the capital filled with insulting epitaphs, often focused on Louis XIV's heavy taxation: "Here lies the king of tax collectors/ The partisan of usurers."

Louis XIV left a more complex legacy than the songs suggest. He did undermine the "mandate of heaven" so important to monarchical government, yet he also left something of substance to his successor. As Louis himself said on his deathbed, "I am leaving but the state will live forever." The king always chose his words carefully; let us take note that he did not say the nation, he said the state.

5   A new France, 1720s–1750s

War markiz yaouank Pontkaleg
ker koant, ker drant, ker kalonek
–Traitour! ah! Malloz dit

(Oh the marquis Pontcallec
so handsome, so lively, so full of heart
–You who have betrayed him, be damned

The miserable marquis of Pontcallec and three of his fellow Breton
nobles lost their heads to the executioner at Nantes in March 1720.
Caught in the web of international politics and local dissatisfaction with
the Regency government, they led a tragi-comical uprising whose main
act of defiance was a petition signed by 500 mostly minor nobles of
western Brittany. Oddly enough, Pontcallec became a popular hero,
remembered in countless Breton songs, such as the *Gwerz* (lament)
above. He stood for the popular sense of outrage that the government had
lost touch with real life. The fiasco of the Law System, the particular
disgust against the forced exile (to Louisiana) of "colonists" (i.e., the
vagabond poor and others unfortunate enough to fall into the hands of the
guardsmen), the normal instability of a royal minority, the last appearance of the plague (1720–21 near and in Marseilles) – all these combined
to make the beginnings of Louis XV's reign inauspicious.

Such appearances hid a deeper reality of profound, largely positive
change. The France of the 1750s differed fundamentally from that of the
1710s. France had a larger and more genuinely urban population;[1] it had a
new economic structure superimposed on the old one; it had an open
political conflict among its elites; it lived in a new intellectual universe.
How did so much change so fast? Let us examine the structural changes in
French society between the end of the seventeenth century and the
middle of the eighteenth century before we turn to changes in the state
itself. Pierre Goubert, in his classic book, *The Ancien Régime*, offers the

---

[1] More urban but still overwhelmingly (80 percent) rural.

176

defining dates of that entity as 1600 to 1750. Given that generations of historians thought (and still think) of the Old Regime as something that lasted until 1789, we must begin looking at changes in the social system of the Old Regime. For Goubert and historians like him, the deeper social structures of France define historical time; let us, too, move away from the old political chronologies and look deeper into the mists of social time.

A new society: France, 1720–1750

Who are you? When the tax collector asked an early modern French person that question, he meant, what do you do? Unless you were tax exempt, your work defined you, at least insofar as the government cared to know about it. The question, or rather the answer, appears on isolated French documents in the seventeenth century. Here and there village tax rolls give the taxpayers' occupations; they sometimes even give the amount of land owned or rented by the taxpayer. These exceptions stand out in a sea of simpler listings: the tax collector noted the individual's name and contribution, nothing more (save, on occasion, for widows, who might appear in their own name with the notation, widow of "X"). Toward the end of the century, things began to change; more and more often, the tax collector wanted to know what you did. These categories are notoriously slippery, particularly for the poor. One year François Regnault of Alligny might call himself a day laborer (*journalier*), the next he might be an artisan of some sort, most often a roofer (*couvreur*). A poor woman might be a widow one year, a day laborer (*journalière*) the next, and a beggar the third. The tax collector knew who were the big fish, the ploughmen – that was a status defined by your possessions, not your whimsy.

Yet new patterns, new self definitions slowly emerged. In the Caux region of Normandy, the poor defined themselves as day laborers in the early eighteenth century; by the middle of the century, the poor called themselves weavers (often of cotton). The number of weavers increased from 1700 to 1730 and then jumped even more rapidly, rising from about 13.5 percent of the taxpayers of the *élection* of Argues in 1735 to 23.8 percent in 1789.[2] Certain towns and villages had a much higher percentage of weavers, even exceeding half of the adult population. In the late seventeenth century, a poor person living partly from day labor, partly from some artisanal work, and partly from relief believed him or herself to be a day laborer; fifty years later, living from the combination of artisanal weaving, agricultural day work, and relief, the same person thought her or himself a weaver.

[2] G. Lemarchand, *La fin du féodalisme dans le pays de Caux* (Paris: Editions du Comité de Travaux Historiques et Scientifiques, 1989), pt. II, ch. 3.

We would do well to take these people at their word, to give credence to what they thought of themselves. Indeed, two related factors dramatically altered French society between 1700 and 1750: the great increase in manufactured production and the massive impact of colonial trade. The increased manufactured production did not immediately suggest an industrial revolution – that lay well in the future for France – but the old economic structures of non-agricultural production began to shift inexorably.

First of all, the scale of production increased. In sector after sector, one sees the increased size of enterprises. In shipping, larger ships replaced smaller ones. That process, evident in Normandy in Colbert's time, accelerated in the eighteenth century. At Bordeaux, one of the three greatest French ports of the period, total tonnage shipped doubled from 1720 to 1785 (283,000 tons) and the average capacity of ships rose from 42 tons in 1700 to 112 tons by 1782. Even the coastal traders, dominion of the small merchant and modest captain, more than doubled in size between 1720 and 1782. The other great Atlantic port, Nantes, had a modest fleet of 107 ships in 1727, of which 96 carried under 200 tons; the flagship carried only 350 tons. By 1790, Nantes had 203 ships, 60 of which could carry more than 400 tons (14 of them more than 600 tons). The total capacity of 1727 (about 16,000 tons) would easily have fit in the 34 ships of 1790 that carried 500 tons or more.[3]

The other sectors of the economy looked much the same. In the hatting trade at Paris, more than half of the masters surveyed in 1739 (33 of 63) employed 4 or fewer journeymen; only 2 employed more than 40 people (16 percent of the total labor force). In 1790, no masters employed fewer than 5 people and 15 masters, employing 40 or more people each, gave work to 58 percent of the labor force. Even given the structural variations in the two surveys, the differences startle. The Paris printing trade evolved in the same way. The number of journeymen stayed roughly stable from 1666 to 1701 but the number of shops declined from 83 to 36; in the eighteenth century, the trend to larger shops continued. In Beauvais, in 1656, 64 of 103 cloth workshops employed only one or two journeymen and 98 of them employed fewer than 5. By the early eighteenth century, a typical workshop had 5 to 8 workers and many of them had 15 or more. In place of the old mythical workshop of master and journeyman working side-by-side, more and more large city workshops had a master removed from the shop floor, with an overseer-foreman and a workforce of 10 or 15 or even more journeymen. Such concentration happened first in the clothing and printing trades; it spread much more

[3] J. Meyer, L'armament nantais dans la deuxième moitié du XVIIIe siécle (Paris: Ecole Pratique des Hautes Etudes, 1969), ch. 5.

slowly into other sectors.[4] It also spread more slowly into certain regions.

France had always had highly regional economies; the inability to move goods, especially food (grain) from one region to another formed one of the critical weaknesses of Old Regime society. In the second half of the seventeenth and in the eighteenth century, however, a second, broader pattern developed in the French economy: the creation of two geographic sectors, one tied to the growing international economy, one not; one advanced, one backward; one expanding, the other stagnant. Little wonder that economic organization looked different in the backward than the dynamic regions.

The regions of growth ran along the seacoast, especially near the great ports (Rouen–Le Havre, Nantes, Bordeaux, Marseilles), up the great rivers (Seine, Loire, Gironde, Rhône) and into areas of rapid manufacturing expansion, such as Normandy, Picardy, or parts of Champagne. In the region of Rouen, cloth production (largely cotton) rose 700 percent between 1715 and 1743. Towns tied to the colonial trade or to the burgeoning textile sector rapidly expanded their populations. Nantes grew from 40,000 in 1700 to 80,000 in 1790; Bordeaux increased from about 55,000 in 1715 to 66,000 by the middle of the century and more than 100,000 by 1790. Textile areas showed similar growth. Caen's population rose 50 percent between 1725 and 1775; Lille increased 16 percent in the first 40 years of the century. After 1740, local population growth in the Lillois region shifted increasingly to the textile "suburb" of Roubaix, whose population rose 166 percent during the eighteenth century. Other tiny textile towns, such as Elbeuf, had similar rates of increase. Paris, the grand metropole, also shared in the demographic upsurge, growing from just under 500,000 to more than 600,000 people.

The backwater towns faced a different fate: Vannes, scarcely 100 kilometers from Nantes, declined from 1,830 taxable households in 1704 to 1,642 in 1760 and to 1,492 by 1783. Even large cities outside the mainstream of economic currents stagnated or fell back. Rennes, whose population had long equalled or exceeded that of its rival Nantes, declined from its traditional 40,000–45,000 people to under 35,000 by 1750. Limoges, lost in the mountains of the Midi, remained stable at 20,000. Beauvais, so close to Paris, faced a similar fate; it had no more people in 1836 than in 1700. Even once-prosperous Toulouse, one of the dominant towns of southern France, felt the wave of the future pass it by.

[4] M. Sonenscher, *Work and Wages in Eighteenth-Century France* (Cambridge: Cambridge University Press, 1991), offers the most up-to-date scholarship on this issue. Figures on hatters come from his book, *The Hatters of Eighteenth-Century France* (Berkeley: University of California Press, 1987); those on printers from R. Darnton, "Workers Revolt: The Great Cat Massacre of the Rue Saint-Séverin," in *The Great Cat Massacre and Other Episodes in French Cultural History* (New York: Vintage, 1984), ch. 2.

While its rival Bordeaux's population nearly doubled, that of Toulouse rose only 16 percent, barely enough to make up the losses of the sixteenth and seventeenth centuries. Toulouse had no more people in 1790 than it had in 1500; Bordeaux had nearly five times as many.

Two Frances: the vibrant, thriving one of the new world, the stagnating one of the old world. Even a royal court, a Parlement, could not rescue a city from stagnation, as both Rennes and Toulouse testify. The new world demanded new products: cotton cloth, sugar, coffee, tobacco. Concentration of production meant many small producers had to disappear, to be replaced by imported, mass-produced goods; thus Strasburg's brewers, who had only produced for a local market in the seventeenth century, suddenly became large exporters of eighteenth-century "Kronenbourg" (the same family makes the contemporary beer of that name). We need not overemphasize such changes; the vast majority of French producers still did so at a modest level. Local trade dwarfed long-distance trade in volume. Yet growth in the long-distance sector invariably led to growth in local trade as well. Most artisans in a city, such as Nantes, that exported sugar, did not work in any trade related to sugar. They produced other goods – cloth, paper, metal, brandy – that could be traded for the slaves exchanged for the sugar or that could be exchanged for the sugar (or indigo or coffee) itself.

The structure of population in the two Frances tended to diverge more and more as the century wore on. In the stable old world of towns such as Vannes, the occupational distribution tended to remain much the same. In 1704, 12.5 percent of Vannes's taxpayers worked in textiles; in 1783, 13.2 percent did so. The other major trades – foods, building, and leather – tended to remain stable. Châteaudun looked much the same in 1667 or 1767. In the growing cities, as one might expect, the occupational structure of the population changed: more and more textile workers, often laboring for a steady wage. That pattern held true in Roubaix or Elbeuf, Reims or Troyes, Caen or Grenoble. The commercial towns – Bordeaux, Nantes, Paris, Strasburg – did not have a rapid increase in textile output. Their local economies tended to be more varied. In the great ports, the number of dockworkers, sailors, and porters expanded rapidly.

The non-industrial towns, especially the administrative centers, had legions of domestic servants. Large industrial or commercial towns, such as Lyons or Marseilles, had few servants: in the eighteenth century, servants constituted only 4 percent of their inhabitants. In mixed commercial and administrative centers like Bordeaux, Paris, or Toulouse, their numbers could go much higher: 8 percent or more of the population. In an administrative town like Aix-en-Provence, the figure reached 16 percent.

Everywhere we see movement. We see tens of thousands of people shifting residence. Small-town inhabitants moved to the bigger towns. Medium-sized towns either grew with economic change, like Caen, or lapsed into demographic (and economic) stagnation, like Limoges. Peasants, too, took to the roads in unprecedented numbers. Endogamy rates declined virtually everywhere, although most of all in those areas able to send their migrants to the regions of growth. Parishes whose inhabitants married each other 80 percent of the time in the second half of the seventeenth century, now found that scarcely half of their marriages involved two parishioners. Women, especially, had new-found mobility. Many rural women moved to cities, there to work as servants and amass a dowry (the less fortunate among these female servants often had to resort to prostitution). In Lyons, 95 percent of the servants in the eighteenth century came from outside the city; according to their marriage contracts, two of every three Lyonnais female servants were the daughters of farmers. At Lyons, as at Toulouse, these female servants originally married more farmers than any other group; by the end of the century, however, they married into an urban (usually artisan) family.

The rural-to-urban movement alerts us to the growing disequilibrium in French economic life. Agricultural growth rates lagged behind industrial ones. Even in agriculture, the period between the 1720s and 1750s marked something of a break with the past. Per capita growth probably sustained itself at about 0.3 percent a year, an unusually high long-term level for the pre-industrial European economy. The population, too, rose steadily, by about 80,000 people a year between 1700 and 1740. Following a period of demographic stagnation between 1740 and 1750 (due to a combination of poor harvests, related epidemics, and war), the steady rise began again. France had some 21.5 million inhabitants in 1700, 23.2 million in 1720, 24.6 million in 1740, and 25.7 million in 1760. For the first time since the late sixteenth century, the French economy grew fast enough to cover demographic growth and to provide a further surplus in per capita output.

Agriculture certainly lagged behind in this economic transition, from the long-term stagnancy of earlier periods (a stagnancy due not to lack of growth but rather to its intermittency) to the sustained growth of modern times. As one would suspect, given the division of the country into zones of advanced and backward commercial development, agricultural output, too, varied sharply by region. In the *pays* of Caux, near Rouen, the new income provided by textile weaving allowed peasants to make greater investments in agriculture. A sample of 23 parishes shows a 53-percent increase in numbers of horses and a 42-percent increase in cattle between 1697 and 1789. The Norman parish of Avremesnil had 25 livestock owners in 1695, possessing 33 horses and 33 cows; in 1745, 41 people owned an animal and the herds had risen to 66 horses and 51 cows. More livestock meant more fertilizer; more fertilizer meant greater grain output per hectare. By way of contrast, a backward region such as the Vannetais saw no such change: the average number of cattle listed on wills stayed virtually the same from 1732 (4.1) to 1780 (4.0) as did the broader indicator of cattle listed in estate inventories (1.1 in 1745 as against 1.0 in 1780).

Two rural Frances: the increasingly prosperous rural regions such as Caux, with their burgeoning livestock populations, their manufacturing employment for the peasants (both poor and well off), and their rising output; and the dead-end regions such as the Vannetais, with their stable population (due to out-migration), lack of sufficient employment, lack of investment, and stagnant output. More and more we can see the influence of the market on rural France. We can see the growth of a consumer class sufficiently large and wealthy to sustain a host of new commercial activities and products. The colonial products are an obvious example: who in the seventeenth century drank coffee or ate sugar?

French products, too, changed substantially in response to international and national demand. The first *grand cru* wines date from the second quarter of the eighteenth century, whether in Champagne or in Bordeaux. The names of Dom Perignon and Château Haut-Brion have come down to our own days as synonymous with luxury French wines; both had their origin in these decades of the eighteenth century. The change at Bordeaux revolutionized its wine trade. The total volume of wine exports went up only 50 percent between the 1720s and 1780s (and the figures of the 1780s did not exceed the levels of the 1680s, which had peaked at over 100,000 tons) but the value of the wine exported tripled in the same period. Even allowing for the general inflation of wine prices, Bordeaux wines more than doubled in price, in large measure due to the introduction of higher quality wines: a wine from the chateaux of Lafite, Latour, Margaux, or Haut-Brion sold for 15 to 20 times the price of an ordinary wine.

Such wines formed part of an entirely new pattern of consumption. Europeans had always (with rare exceptions) drunk young wines, wines consumed in the year of their production. The great wines of a Latour or an Haut-Brion required ageing and storage. They became part of a culture of consumption, a culture that dominates western civilization to this day. Eighteenth-century elites wanted refinement, wanted new and exotic products. Aged wine was as exotic an idea as coffee; the same social classes consumed them both.

Society at large demanded a vast array of new products, from light cotton cloth to sugar, coffee, and tobacco. Ordinary people consumed these products: in 1675, the Breton peasants of the Bonnets Rouges rebellion listed as one of their fourteen demands that "tobacco be given out with the blessed bread at the Mass, for the satisfaction of the parishioners." The value of sugar imports quintupled between 1730 and 1790 and French consumption tripled. Popular consumption of sugar became so ordinary a fact of everyday life that Parisian artisans rioted for cheaper sugar during the French Revolution. Light cottons from India proved so popular that the central government and local authorities (Parlements, town councils, etc.) tried fruitlessly to ban them. Eventually, French producers stepped in to meet the demand, leading to cries of outrage from the wool cloth industry.

What a tricky business it must have been to govern such a society. Marseilles booms with trade and increased production; Aix, scarcely fifty kilometers away, stagnates. Nantes doubles its population and its wealth; Vannes, one of its traditional trading partners, withers on the vine. One country area hums with economic activity, perhaps in textiles or, in the north or east coal or metallurgy; that activity draws capital to the region, places much of it in the hands of peasants, who invest in agriculture and increase agricultural output too. Another country area, perhaps only 50 or 100 kilometers away, cries out in economic pain. Its population grows too fast for its output. Thousands take to the roads, often reversing traditional patterns of migration. Thus Brittany, long a destination for immigrants from neighboring provinces such as Normandy, starts to send its children east, to Normandy or Paris. Mountain regions like the Auvergne or the Limousin, far from the markets that bring prosperity, send long columns of laborers or masons off to Paris or Lyons each year.

Modern historians cannot make up their minds about the eighteenth-century French economy. Did it grow rapidly, ushering in a wave of prosperity, or did it stagnate? As this brief survey suggests, it did both. Side by side, we have the economic prosperity of some and the ruin of others (not unlike the experience of the Anglo-American world in the 1980s). Government officials could observe the rising prosperity in certain industries (some textile sectors), new luxury trades (like the *grands crus* of Bordeaux), and an enormous growth in colonial trade, particularly in the reexport trade, as the discrepancy between the increases in the value of sugar imports and in French consumption suggests. At the same time, they could also see widespread misery, perhaps not so pronounced as it would be in the late 1780s but real all the same. Some historians estimate that by the late eighteenth century, one-fifth of the French population needed poor relief each year and that one-half of it received such aid at one point or another in their lives.

A growing economy, newfound prosperity, new levels of material well-being, yet more poor people, intractable regional economic differences, and unprecedented mobility – how frightening a combination for the government to face. The eighteenth-century French government reacted as most governments do to such circumstances: they increased repression or, more accurately, they increased the rhetoric of repression. This problem, the "police" as they called it, takes us to the heart of the modern state. All modern states in economically developed countries must resolve the conflict between liberty and property. In eighteenth-century France, the conflict between these two values posed exceptionally complicated problems because neither liberty nor property had a clear definition. At the beginning of the century, few doubted the unequal distribution of all human qualities, whether they be rights/privileges or property. At the end of the century, the perfect correlation between unequal rights and an unequal distribution of property had broken down. Intellectually, the breakdown took place before the Revolution; politically, the situation collapsed only after the Revolution began.

The confusion about liberty and property, more particularly about the relationship of the state to liberty and property, led to some unusual political coalitions and to remarkable changes in the nature of the state itself. The transition to the modern state, in terms of the actual activities of the state, took firm root in the second quarter of the eighteenth century. The three main attributes of the old state (military, financial, and judicial) still dominated governmental thinking and expenditure but new concerns grew in importance. Four elements of new state activity stand out in the first half of Louis XV's reign: the police, poor relief, education, and public works. Political society came to expect the government to do something about such matters. As the government expanded its efforts in those directions, it substantially expanded the functions, size, and interventionist capacity of the central state. Alexis de Tocqueville's description of the Old Regime state as an interventionist yet ineffective leviathan can take us no further back than Louis XV, because the eighteenth-century French state differed so fundamentally from its seventeenth-century predecessor. Let us start with an examination of the new state and then turn to our familiar trinity in order to understand the elements of change and continuity.

The new state in eighteenth-century France

In early modern France, people used the term "police" to mean administration, particularly the administration of a city. They combined social, economic, political, and moral oversight into this one entity known as the police. Nicolas de la Mare, in his extremely influential *Treatise on the Police* (1705), stated that:

the Police includes in its objectives all those things that serve as a foundation and a rule to the societies that men have established among themselves ... Religion is the first and principal, one might even add the unique object of the Police.[5]

Such sentiments jar our modern ears: how can religion be the main object of the police? Here we can see the close interrelationship among religious, political, and social order so typical of early modern societies. In France, religion meant Roman Catholicism. The police made sure all French people practiced officially sanctioned versions of Catholicism, as well as assuring other forms of public order. Yet de la Mare's observation in 1705 described more accurately the past and the present, not the future. In the eighteenth century, the police spent very little time on religious matters.

The obsession with the well-ordered police state extended beyond France's borders into many other areas of continental Europe. These administrative states came to interfere more and more in the daily life of their inhabitants. People came to expect the central state to act for a variety of causes. They turned to the central state for new services, services that had never before formed part of the central state's obligations in France. Mercantilism offers one obvious example of such a policy – state-sponsored economic activity – but poor relief affords another. Local problems, like poor relief, came increasingly to be defined as national problems. Lest we get caught up in the myth of absolutism, we do well to remember that *local elites* demanded help from the national government to meet relief obligations. The impetus for state intervention in poor relief did not come solely from the top down, it came from the bottom up.

Poor relief did not exist as an isolated issue; it overlapped everywhere with the maintenance of order. The "deserving" poor – widows, the aged, children – provided an obvious target for relief efforts, but able-bodied men, the "undeserving" poor as some called them, stimulated a far different response from the authorities and from civil society as a whole. In Paris, the lieutenant general of police began greatly to expand his operations. He represented the extraordinary confusion of functions one official might have in Old Regime France. The lieutenant was a judge – rendering judgment every Friday at the Châtelet of Paris; he was a supervisor of economic life – overseeing the guilds, watching the markets (especially the all-important grain trade); he served as the chief censor; he was the main guardian of religious orthodoxy in the capital; he was, in effect, the intendant for Paris; he ran the police force of the city; he

[5] N. de la Mare, *Traité de la Police* (Paris, 1705), 267.

directed its fire brigades. His judicial functions tended to fade away – they mattered little after 1740 – but his position as chief administrator of Paris gave him more and more power as the century wore on. Of the fourteen men to sit as lieutenant general of police in the eighteenth century, five became royal ministers and the other nine councilors of state.

So powerful a man had vast responsibilities. Keeping watch on a city of 500,000 (later 600,000) people required many subordinates. At the beginning of the century, the forces at the lieutenant general's disposal can only be called pathetic: 150 men of the watch, a venal company that had long outlived its usefulness by 1700, and 43 men in the mounted city guard. In 1719–20, the royal government realized the absurdity of the situation and added two new companies to the guard. By 1760, the guard had 725 men; in 1788, it had more than 1,000. In those same reforms of 1719–20, the government decided to change the basic structure of the city's police force, creating the first permanent post (in what is now the *place* Vendôme); by 1754, the city had 15 permanent guard posts, by 1789 something like 50. The police could also call upon the units of the royal army stationed in and around Paris – the two units of the king's personal troops (the French and Swiss guards), with perhaps 7,500 men. As the Paris guard grew, the role of the army in Paris declined. Here we can see one of the fundamental differences between modern and pre-modern governments: the existence of a professional police force separate from the army. The numbers of men involved make it clear that, to the extent that Paris had much of a police force in the seventeenth century, the French guards, that is the royal army, formed the heart of that force. In the eighteenth century, however, Paris began to resemble a modern city, with a non-military police force.

The city began to possess other attributes of modern administration as well. Paris had no genuine fire department prior to 1716, when the first company of 32 men received royal sanction. In 1722, the company grew to 60, then to 160 (1770), and finally to 221. The fire department had pumps, permanent stations manned 24 hours a day, and 400-gallon water wagons. Serious fires declined; the skeptical public, initially little disposed to call in this new royal service, came to accept and finally to welcome the new service.[6] That a reliable fire department represented a revolutionary break with the past was only too clear to any well-informed French person of the time: one had only to look at Rennes, which virtually burned to the ground in 1720 or across the Channel to London, devastated by the massive conflagration of 1666. As the example of Rennes suggests, provincial cities did not have so full a complement of

[6] A. Williams, *The Police of Paris, 1718–1789* (Baton Rouge: Louisiana State University Press, 1979), provides the basis for this summary of police and fire services in the capital.

services as the capital; fire departments spread slowly in the provinces, often not forming effective companies until the nineteenth century.

The police, too, lay thin on the ground of provincial France. While Paris had its 1,000 or so guardsmen and the French guard, provincial France had only municipal guard companies in large cities and the mounted constabulary (*maréchaussée*) for the countryside. As in Paris, so in the provinces, the government of the early 1720s – again, the Regent Philip of Orléans – sought to modernize and standardize the police force. In 1720, the Regent reorganized the companies, creating one for each *généralité*, standardizing the staffing, introducing requirements for service (such as a minimum of four years' prior military experience), and shifting the new brigades out into the lesser towns of each district (rather than keeping the entire company in one city, as had often been the case). By 1730, the mounted constabulary had about 3,000 men, a tiny force for a nation of 24 million people and more than 300,000 square kilometers, but certainly the largest of its kind in Europe at that time.

So tiny a force obviously required assistance in order to police so vast a territory. They had many tasks to perform: their most common job required them to supervise the so-called "provostal crimes," those judged in the special mounted constabulary (provostal) courts. Their first responsibility, indeed the raison d'être of the original mounted constabulary created in the Middle Ages, involved the capture and return of military deserters. They later came to have authority over all vagabonds, as well as crimes committed on the main highways, offenses against public order: assault, theft involving use of force, and violations against the general tranquility such as grain riots. The mounted constabulary also policed fairs and larger markets. In the major towns, a local police force would assist them; indeed, in the great provincial cities such as Bordeaux, the mounted constabulary scarcely dared to show their faces. One poor trooper who arrested a Bordelaise in 1726 himself spent time in the local prison for exceeding his jurisdictional authority. A city like Bordeaux would have its own watch, of 50 or 100 men, to serve at its police force. These watches remind us of the extraordinary mixture of new and old in French state institutions. Paris and much of the countryside had modern police forces by the middle of the eighteenth century; the great provincial towns still relied on an essentially medieval institution, the civil guard or watch.

In all of France, the government could rely on about 1,000 Parisian policemen, just under 3,000 members of the mounted constabulary, and an often rag-tag assortment of members of municipal watches. Particularly in these large provincial towns, we cannot escape the fact that Old Regime France was a self-policed society. Neighbors would chase a thief as quickly as they would a tax collector. When the good citizens of Ribérac caught Alexis Faye stealing, they stoned him and beat him with clubs; the standard popular punishment for a thief in the Périgord was to be pummeled with clubs and to have half of his or her head shaved clean. The constabulary caught very few thieves; private citizens invariably turned over the offender, after giving him or her a suitable beating. In some areas, such as the mountains of the Midi, the population did not bother with the constables; they simply took the law into their own hands.[7]

The relative scarcity of crime attests to the effectiveness of community policing. In the southwestern district of Libourne, with a population of just under 100,000 people (1790), the authorities prosecuted about one murder and ten assaults a year; in the district of Périgord, the constabulary dealt with twenty-four murders in the 1720s and only two in the 1730s. Actual murders far exceeded such numbers, but remained relatively infrequent by contemporary American standards. The two most common other crimes were theft (the most common) and assault. The boundary line between them often blurred, as many crimes of violence might better be considered crimes related to property. In a society in which court cases dragged on forever, many people tried to resolve property disputes by private means. Such means could be violent. As the century wore on, however, more and more cases of theft came to the attention of the authorities, whether in the north (Normandy) or in the south, such as Périgord, where the number of theft complaints doubled in the 1770s and 1780s.

The precise reasons for the change are difficult to determine; the increase probably came about because of an actual rise in thefts (especially after 1770) and because people now more readily turned to the authorities to capture and punish thieves. We see here at work in rural France the same mental shift we earlier noted in Paris. Just as Parisians came to accept the fire brigade as a basic institution of everyday life, and became more willing to seek its aid, so, too, rural French people developed a more positive attitude toward the mounted constabulary in some regions. In general, northerners – as in Normandy – turned more readily to the police than did southerners: in the Auvergne, rare indeed was the peasant who would call on or assist the constables. The thief's identity provided the key factor in the community's attitude: those from the community usually received intra-community admonition; vagabond thieves could expect to be brutalized and turned in to the police.

Vagabonds had always frightened French people, especially those in

[7] I. Cameron, *Crime and Repression in the Auvergne and the Guyenne, 1720–1790* (Cambridge: Cambridge University Press, 1981).

the country, because of the threat they might pose to property and security. The vagabond poor had long ceased to be holy; by the sixteenth or seventeenth century, an able-bodied beggar had become an object of fear, not of pity or reverence. Royal and local ordinances consistently sought to repress vagabonds. In the sixteenth or early seventeenth centuries, expulsion provided the main weapon against vagabonds: town authorities (councils, even Parlements) would periodically order all unauthorized beggars to leave town within 24 hours, on pain of flogging or other harsh punishments. The dance of poverty would begin again; the beggar would leave Châlons and head for Reims, leave Reims for Troyes, leave any city to go into the countryside. In the eighteenth century, authorities tried a new technique: incarceration.

The great cities of France, Paris and Lyons above all, had long had special institutions for housing the poor and sick. The General Hospital of Paris cared for about 9,000 people in 1720, the Charité of Lyons about 2,000 adults and perhaps 6,000 infants (who lived with wet nurses). The efforts at incarceration started in earnest in the early 1660s but continued intermittently, and mainly in Paris, under Louis XIV. Under the Regency, the government decided on a new approach, sending able-bodied beggars off to Louisiana as "colonists." The authorities first looked to the two key elements of the General Hospital of Paris, the Salpetrière (for women inmates) and Bicêtre (for men). An initial wave of support for the deportations – some citizens even recommended their own family members for emigration – gave way to popular revulsion, culminating in Parisian riots that left ten deportation guardsmen dead and the house of the lieutenant general himself, Marc-Pierre d'Argenson, under siege. The government backed off from so incendiary a policy. Four years later (1724), however, the government decided to step up efforts at arrest and incarceration, this time in the country as a whole, not merely in Paris.

The edict creating the new policy sounded distressingly familiar: the "deserving" poor would receive shelter, food, and assistance; the "undeserving" poor would have two weeks to find a job; any able-bodied person unemployed more than two weeks after the publication of the edict would be imprisoned and forced to labor at a work house. In practice, the situation looked a bit different. Each parish had its resident poor: the tax rolls invariably list some people as beggars and they often remained in the same parish for years on end. Local people had little interest in turning these people over to the authorities; the wrath of repression fell on the wandering poor. They wandered often into towns, and there the authorities met and arrested them. In Lower Normandy, Caen had 500 inmates in its General Hospital before the 1724 incarceration edict.

These inmates worked; at Caen, they produced over 11,000 *livres* in income.

When times worsened, when the price of bread rose rapidly, the numbers of beggars would quickly dwarf these figures. One-quarter of the population of Bayeux begged in the streets in 1725. The city responded by locking up 104 beggars; nearby Caen confined more than 300. Hospital populations soared, then leveled off somewhat, but at much higher levels than before 1724. In 1733, when the government decided to back down from its confinement policy, numbers dropped much more sharply. Confinements between 1726 and 1733 tended to vary with royal financial support. The main flow of new inmates continued to come from voluntary enrollment: children, above all, flocked to the hospitals in times of high bread prices. Some towns, such as Bayeux, took a harsher view than others, like Caen, so that the pattern of repression tended to vary in part due to local factors, but those towns that received more money from the central government, locked up more people. If the figures from Lower Normandy and southeastern France are any indication, nearly twice as many people found themselves in poorhouses/hospitals in 1733 than had done so in 1724.[8]

Before we get carried away by such figures, however, we must stop to consider who these people were. Overwhelmingly, in all cities, the hospitals confined children and the aged infirm. At Grenoble, nearly 75 percent of the inmates were under 20 or over 60; authorities described more than 85 percent of those over 60 as ill. One could cite similar figures for Lyons or Aix, Caen or Bayeux, even for Paris, which had the highest proportion of able-bodied adult beggars.

Since the pioneering work of Michel Foucault, historians have called the late seventeenth and eighteenth centuries the period of the Great Confinement. Certainly the policy of confining able-bodied beggars took root in this period, beginning with Louis XIV's 1661 ordinance and continuing through the enhanced incarceration efforts of 1724–33 and 1768–89. The government and local authorities did confine more people, but they confined relatively few able-bodied beggars (particularly able-bodied male beggars, who formed the main rhetorical target). One study of Paris shows that in a group of 3,370 beggars arrested by Parisian police commissioners between 1700 and 1784, fewer than 800 were adult men, and some of those men were severely ill or physically handicapped. The same study demonstrates that nearly two-thirds of the commissioners had little or no interest in making such arrests.

Who, in fact, did the police lock up? More children and old people.

[8] R. Schwartz, *Policing the Poor in Eighteenth-Century France* (Chapel Hill, NC: University of North Carolina Press, 1988), on treatment of the poor in Normandy.

Even at Bayeux, which had a reputation for ruthlessly locking up adult beggars, the city locked up only 104 people in 16 months of enhanced repression; given that the authorities claimed 1,800 beggars swarmed in the city, and given that a goodly number of the 104 internees were children, rare indeed was the adult male beggar locked up in the Bayeux Hospital. The situation looked much the same everywhere else. At Caen, fewer than 75 adult men aged 20–50 spent time in the hospital in the first great wave of confinement between 1724 and 1733 (this in a city of well over 20,000 people).

The hospitals had become something quite different than the royal edicts of 1661 or 1724 would suggest: they had become "a kind of repository for the detritus of society, for those who were old, weak, and useless, and whom no one else would take in."[9] In reality, the hospitals of Old Regime France, far from being an instrument of confinement for the able-bodied poor, had become the first national example of socialized care for the aged and for poor children. Traditional society had long assigned the family the task of caring for its "dependent" individuals (those under 15 and over 60); in the face of dramatic social change in the eighteenth century, that tradition began to collapse. David Troyansky has generalized the findings of those such as Pierre Goubert who pointed out a generation ago that more people lived past 60 or 70 in the mid and late eighteenth century than had done so before.[10] In Goubert's sample of five rural parishes in the Beauvaisis, slightly more than a third of adult burials listed the age at death as over 60 during the seventeenth century, whereas 52–60 percent of adults dying in the 1770s and 1780s had passed sixty. Indeed, a higher percentage of adults had reached 70 in the latter period than had reached 60 in the earlier one. This dramatic change required a reexamination of the way in which French society regarded old age and care of the aged.

More and more, the French state took on the responsibility of caring for those unable to care for themselves. Such care took place in an often puritanical environment of forced labor, mandatory prayers, and regimentation, but it replaced the growing spectacle of indigents lining the streets of cities. The able-bodied unemployed men stood out among the group because they struck fear in the hearts of the well-off citizenry. The royal ordinances invariably spoke of such "worthless" men when discussing the purposes of the hospitals; in the real world, however, the hospitals served primarily to house, feed, and care for those even the authorities would call the "deserving poor." The mix of people locked up by the authorities changed dramatically – to able-bodied youths and men

[9] Norberg, *Rich and Poor in Grenoble*, 180.
[10] D. Troyansky, *Old Age in the Old Regime* (Ithaca, NY: Cornell University Press, 1989).

– in the second great wave of repression (starting in 1768), as we shall see in chapter 6.

The state itself sometimes employed these able-bodied poor men, most particularly in road construction. The genuine poor of eighteenth-century France included the day laborers, of city and country. Those in the country lived a mixed existence, working during the harvests, later flailing the grain, heavily occupied during parts of the spring, often unemployed in the early fall or mid-winter. The sedentary among them spent part of this time working for the royal government (without pay, except during the famine of 1739–41) on the road system. The French government had long ignored the country's infrastructure; other than Sully and Colbert (whose main project, the Canal du Midi, did not involve roads), no French minister had devoted real attention to the nation's roads and bridges. In 1720, the government decided to do something about the situation, sending an edict to the intendants spelling out in great detail the standards to be applied to road upkeep. Given the necessity for a labor force to carry out the work, the intendants interpreted this edict as establishing, *de facto*, a royal *corvée** or forced labor requirement on roads.

Philibert Orry, intendant of Soissons, carried out the edict with exemplary skill. He required ploughmen to provide fifteen days of labor a year; day laborers had to work three days. Property owners had to maintain the shoulders (usually ditches) on their road-abutting property. Orry established clear accounting methods for building the roads (either with cobblestones or crushed stones) and for peasant eligibility for the *corvée*: all those living within about fourteen kilometers had to work. When Orry later became controller general (1730), he applied his system to the country as a whole.

How typical of Old Regime government that a jurisdictional conflict tied Orry's hands. In the seventeenth century, Colbert had held the positions of both controller general (a commission) and superintendent of buildings (a venal office). When he died, the office of superintendant passed, as family property, to one of his sons; the king named a new controller general, so that the two positions became separate. The superintendent of buildings later became known as the director general of roads and bridges. By the 1720s, the director general of roads and bridges and the controller general shared responsibility for the transportation network. Not until the (forced) resignation of the director general Dubois did Orry obtain full control of the situation and shift responsibility for the roads and bridges back to the controller general's office, where it would remain until 1789.

The results spoke for themselves. Orry spent 2.5 million *livres* a year (about 1 percent of the budget) on the transportation network, apart from the cash value of the *corvée* labor. The *corvée* spread to most of France; in fact, Orry had to write to some intendants to ease up on their construction projects because the labor demands hurt the agricultural economy and thus the direct tax receipts. Orry managed to get the intendants to send him a complete survey of all roads in France; the government published maps of all these roads in 1751. Everywhere, the roads, bridges, levees, and dikes improved. Rare indeed was the seventeenth-century traveler who did not complain of French roads; in the eighteenth century, those same roads often received compliments.

The largest public works projects, however, remained royal buildings. The complex at Versailles occupied thousands of artisans, as did the upkeep of the vast network of palaces scattered throughout the country, especially near Paris. Town governments, too, employed workers to keep up their streets, their walls, and their bridges. In large parts of the countryside, along the flood plains of rivers, doubtless village communities employed their poor to maintain the network of dikes and levees. The central government often supported these projects, either directly or indirectly: villages that had to maintain large levees received tax relief from the *taille*. One remarkable element of French local public works stands out: the tiniest parish, seeking to repair one of its roads or its church steeple, had to obtain royal government permission to raise the money to do so. This principle, that only the king could approve any taxation, gave the central government control over local spending, a pattern that has continued in French political life ever since.[11]

In the last of the four new areas of action, education, one cannot really speak of the government's separate initiative. In eighteenth-century France as in England or elsewhere in Europe, the establishd Church ran the educational system. Yet the government encouraged the spread of primary education, first in the cities, then in the countryside. The results in the first three quarters of the eighteenth century were, in northern France, astounding. In the 1680s, only 5 of the later 83 departments of France had literacy rates as high as 40 percent. One of the best areas, that around Reims and Châlons, showed the way of the future; Reims had schools for both boys and girls and Châlons also had a *collège*. Two key groups had their origins in Reims, the Sisters of the Holy Infant Jesus and the Christian Brothers. Each group focused on educating the lower and lower middle classes, such as artisans. The Sisters, and other female orders like them, introduced many of the basic elements of modern pedagogy. Building on the work of the Sisters, the Christian Brothers

[11] As always, one must note exceptions to this rule: in Provence, for example, the *communes* had the right to levy local taxes without royal permission.

(whose founder, Jean-Baptiste de la Salle, first served as protector to the Sisters at Reims) introduced the great innovation of seventeenth-century teaching: simultaneous instruction. Teachers no longer taught each student, one at a time; they now faced large classes, separated by skill level and subject, and taught 30, 40, 50, or more students at one time.

The Christian Brothers soon spread outside Reims. La Salle established a training college for country schoolmasters at Reims (1687), relying heavily on the support of Bishop Colbert (brother of the late controller general). Eleven years later, la Salle and others, among them Mme. de Maintenon, convinced the government to issue an edict mandating that *all* children between the ages of 7 and 14 enroll in a Catholic school. The guild of writing masters sued the Brothers to stop the spread of the schools; despite considerable support among the wealthy burghers of certain towns, the suit failed. The Brothers introduced many revolutionary practices: they used simultaneous instruction; they educated the poor; they taught in French, not Latin. Little wonder that those areas in which the Brothers established their schools had the highest literacy rates. By the 1780s, most of the later departments north of the line running from Saint-Malo to Geneva had male literacy rates over 50 percent, and all exceeded 40 percent. Two Norman departments had rates exceeding 80 percent; in some areas, more than 90 percent of the men could sign their name.

Again, our two Frances stand out clearly. Urban, modernizing France had an increasingly literate population. By the late eighteenth century, virtually all male artisans could read a bit and sign their names and more than half of urban women of that class could as well. In the countryside, especially in the south and in the isolated areas, virtually no one could sign. In Normandy, more than two-thirds of the population could sign its name in the 1780s; in nearby Brittany, fewer than 20 percent could do so. Indeed, in the backward Vannetais, the rate fell to under 10 percent. Such figures remind us not only of the economic differences within the country but of the linguistic ones. Vast areas of France did not speak French in the eighteenth century. In western Brittany, everyone spoke Breton; in the Midi, people spoke dialects, some of which, like Auvergnat, might be considered separate languages. Along the Mediterranean, many country people spoke Occitan or Provençal; in the Alps, it would be Italian; in the Pyrenees, Basque, Catalan, or Spanish; in the north, many spoke Flemish or Picard; in the east, all of Alsace spoke a German dialect. The progress of French came slowly to most of France. The real limits of *popular* French were the core of the Ile-de-France, the Loire valley, Champagne, western Lorraine, southern Picardy, Burgundy, the Lyonnais, and Normandy. Elsewhere, townspeople knew French but the country people often did not. Those who did not know how to speak French, of course, had not learned how to read it.

The government expanded slowly into these new areas, poor relief, police, public works, and education. In poor relief, the government worked extensively with the Church, which remained, despite the new governmental initiatives, the dominant source of poor relief before the Revolution. Nonetheless, the idea that the government had an obligation to do something about the poor, particularly provide food and shelter for the old, the infirm, and the very young, took firm root during the eighteenth century. As for the police, more and more citizens looked to the mounted constabulary for help. They had come to accept the principle of state intervention into what had traditionally been community and personal issues.

The government took contrasting actions in public works and education. In public works, the government finally took seriously its long-standing obligation to renew the infrastructure. One element of the decision surely was the rapid decline of seigneurial authority under Louis XIV and Louis XV; the seigneur had traditionally claimed authority over local roads. With seigneurs out of the way, the royal government could act. How typical of Old Regime France that it did so by adapting one of the classic elements of seigneurial feudalism, the *corvée*, to the task. In education, the state offered legal and, in certain cases, financial inducements but took no role itself in the process. The king, or other body (such as provincial estates or a town council), could make a grant to an educational institution; often the local bodies made such grants at the expressed order of the king. The government also tried to offer a special inducement to teachers: exemption from the *taille*.

The new state – the modern state, with its combination of social welfare and military apparatus – took root in the eighteenth century. The new elements – such as the poor relief or the broader police efforts – took up a very small percentage of governmental revenues. The eighteenth-century state remained primarily what the seventeenth-century state had been: an institution based on the old triumvirate of military, financial, and judicial apparatuses. Let us turn away from the elements of change back to those of continuity for, in truth, the state still largely defined itself in terms that would have been quite familiar to Louis XIII.

The old state: military, financial, and judicial developments

Militarily, the period 1721–54 offers relatively little of interest; no doubt the economic growth of the period owes something to that happy circumstance. France fought in two wars: a brief flurry during the War of the Polish Succession (1733–35) and some hard fighting in the War of Austrian Succession (French participation, 1741–48). The main trend in military affairs started at the end of the War of the Spanish Succession: the French army got much smaller. In 1715, the king abolished 200 of the 320 regiments; the French units of the army, which held about 300,000 men in 1710, had only 110,000 men by 1717. In peacetime, that figure did not change much until after the War of the Austrian Succession, when it rose to 130,000 (1751). The annual budget much appreciated this eighteenth-century peace dividend.

The structure, organization, and use of the French military evolved relatively little between the end of the War of the Spanish Succession and the start of the Seven Years' War. As always in peacetime, the percentage of noble officers increased because the army needed fewer officers. The basic outlines established under Louvois and his successors took firmer root. The army now had uniforms, standard-issue weapons and ammunition, and an elaborate system of stores and arsenals. One significant improvement did take place; municipal governments, acting largely on their own, constructed barracks for the troops. The existence of such barracks took the soldiers out of the homes of ordinary citizens and surely improved civil–military relations during peacetime.

The success of the diplomacy of Cardinal Dubois (under the Regency) and of Cardinal Fleury (under Louis XV) meant that the king had little use for either his army or his Navy. Here dynastic considerations played a role all over Europe. In England, the Hanoverian line replaced the Stuarts in 1714; the supporters of the latter (called Jacobites after the Stuart Pretender, James) formed a formidable threat to the Hanoverians until the 1740s. In France, the legal heir to the throne until 1729 remained King Philip V of Spain (barred from the succession by the Peace of Utrecht but, in French law, indisputable heir until Louis XV had a son). Simple dynastic elements had played a key role at Utrecht: after the death of his brother, Holy Roman Emperor Joseph I, Charles became Emperor; this accession made him a much less attractive candidate for the Spanish throne, for which he had been in line. The elaborate tangles among Bourbons (Spanish and French), Habsburgs, Wittelsbachs, Stuarts, Hanoverians, and Hohenzollerns, to say nothing of dynastic problems in Russia or Poland, had a strong continuing impact on the maintenance of peace or war in Europe. Dubois and Fleury after him believed in maintaining the status quo as the best protection of France's interests, so that the country enjoyed a long period of relative peace (1715–40).

The one exception came in 1733, when Louis XV's father-in-law

Stanislas Leszczynski, obtained the throne of Poland (which he had claimed earlier in the century but then lost to Augustus II of Saxony) from an assembly of nobles. A Russian army quickly marched into Poland, captured Warsaw, and oversaw the election of the Russian and Austrian candidate, Augustus III of Saxony (son of Augustus II). Leszczynski fled to France. During the War of the Polish Succession, the French army, under the aged generals Berwick and Villars (commanders during the Spanish Succession war) fought primarily in the Rhineland and in Italy. They defeated the Austrians and their allies in both regions, even capturing (with their Sardinian–Savoyard allies) Milan. France had a total diplomatic victory: the Spanish Bourbon house inherited the Kingdom of Two Sicilies and the Savoyards (Sardinians) obtained territorial gains in Italy, although the Austrians regained the Milan region. France obtained Lorraine for Leszczynski, who had already renounced the Polish throne; at his death, the duchy would revert to France, which would finally end up with Lorraine, after centuries of dealing with the independent duchy. In return, France recognized the Pragmatic Sanction, which allowed Emperor Charles's daughter Maria Theresa to succeed him (in direct violation of the law in such matters); Austria would convince Marie Theresa's fiancé, duke Francis of Lorraine, to give up Lorraine in return for Tuscany.

The larger war, of the Austrian Succession, began as a conflict between Prussia and Austria over Silesia. France played no direct role in the first stage of the war, providing only subsidies to the Prussians, but quickly joined in when Austria seemed in dire straits. France on one side meant England on the other, so the war spread from Europe to the Americas and Asia.

The entry into this war marked the effective decline of power of Cardinal André-Hercule Fleury, chief royal minister from the mid-1720s until his death in 1743. Fleury always stood for peace and, to the extent possible, for an Anglo-French entente. Fleury had been Louis XV's tutor; he maintained a similar role when the king came to adulthood and his own kingship. So long as Fleury dominated royal councils, France preferred peace to war. In the 1730s, Fleury faced a war party led by Germain-Louis de Chauvelin, the foreign minister. Chauvelin had strong ties to the traditional hawk party: many members of the upper nobility, such as the d'Epernon and la Trémoille families, and the hawk leader of the moment, the marquis of Belle-Isle, grandson of the disgraced superintendant of finances Fouquet. Belle-Isle commanded one of the French armies in the Polish war and agitated for new action in the 1740s. Fleury lost out in the arguments about the Polish succession (in large measure because Leszczynski was Louis XV's father-in-law) but he successfully started the peace negotiations early in the war and maintained his most vital foreign policy objective: peace with England. Fleury believed in a rapprochement with both England and Austria, and he had similarly inclined counterparts in both England and Austria. Unfortunately for the peace of Europe, these factions did not prevail in the councils of 1740.

Eventually, the opposing forces wore down the aged (octogenarian) Fleury's objections. The war made precious little sense to Fleury; he disagreed with the arguments of the hawks: that France could destroy forever the power of the Austrian Habsburgs and capture the southern Netherlands (modern-day Belgium). He foresaw correctly that war with Austria meant war with England, and thus the repudiation of his greatest diplomatic achievement. The early fighting proved disastrous for France; a French army captured Prague but then lost the city and conducted a dispiriting retreat across Germany because the Prussians reached a separate agreement with the Austrians. In June 1743, the duke de Noailles (an ardent member of the war party) made the same blunder Villeroy had made some forty years before, allowing the Austrian and English armies to combine. Their forces defeated the French at Dettingen but failed to follow up on their advantage.

The English troops fought at Dettingen despite the lack of open war between England and France (the declaration of war came only in 1744). English troops fighting in western Germany had two purposes, one national – the preservation of the Austrian Netherlands against French aggrandizement – and one dynastic – King George II also ruled a small western German state, Hanover, threatened by France and its Prussian ally. The War of the Austrian Succession brought together all of the classic elements of a dynastic conflict and a national one. Germany had three important dynastic families: the Habsburgs, the Hohenzollerns (rulers of Prussia and of a smattering of small territories in the west), and the Wittelsbachs, rulers of Bavaria and of three Rhenish territories. France supported the two other families against the Habsburgs, in an effort to destroy their power in western Germany. The French did succeed in electing the duke of Bavaria, Charles Albert, as Holy Roman Emperor in 1742 (the first non-Habsburg in more than 300 years), but he died in 1745, to be succeeded by Maria Theresa's husband, Francis of Lorraine.

For France, the key contest began with the declaration of war against England in 1744. In America, the New England colonists, on their own initiative, mounted (1745) a successful expedition to capture Louisbourg, at the mouth of the St. Lawrence river. Fortunately for France, England's allies on the continent took to quibbling about what to do next and failed to achieve any military success in 1744. In that year, the Prussians resumed their war against Austria, allowing the French the respite that enabled them to reorganize and resume the European offensive in 1745. In Flanders, an army under the marshal Maurice de Saxe and Louis XV himself routed the English at Fontenoy (1745). De Saxe soon captured most of the important towns: Ghent, Bruges, Tournai, and, in 1746, Brussels. In England, Bonnie Prince Charlie (Charles Stuart) successfully invaded from his Scottish highland base, forcing England to withdraw troops from the continent. The troops subsequently crushed his Highlanders at Culloden (1745).

At the peace negotiations of Aachen (Aix-la-Chapelle), the French gave back the southern Netherlands to Austria. Despite their triumphs there and in India, the French ended up with an agreement simply restoring their status quo. Maria Theresa did not get back Silesia, leaving her with a powerful grudge against Frederick of Prussia, one that would lead Europe into war again a few years later. France recognized the Protestant succession in England and forced Charles Stuart to take up residence in Italy. In a grim foreshadowing of events to come, France's diplomatic weakness probably reflected its financial inability to pay for military activity, although the situation at the end of the War of the Austrian Succession was by far the best of that following any of the great wars of the period 1715–74. Peace also allowed France's overseas trade, devastated during the war, to recover.

Financial restructuring: Orry and Machault

Given a generation of relative peace, one would expect a series of internal reforms to rectify the unstable long-term financial situation. In some ways, however, the long peace allowed the state to function in its traditional way, because the annual resources more or less met expenditures in most peacetime years. The Regency government and its immediate successors enacted a wide range of reforms, as we have seen. The government reformed poor relief, the police of Paris and of the countryside, and parts of the financial system. One financial reform lasted over a half century: in 1726, the government finally stabilized the *livre tournois* and stopped manipulating the currency for income. The *livre* remained stable until 1785, a remarkable achievement when one considers Louis XIV's monetary follies and the long monarchical tradition of irresponsible coinage manipulation.

The basic tax system itself seemed in flux; indeed, one cannot imagine a better time to have enacted wide-ranging reform. Louis XIV had established the principle of universal lay tax eligibility. Two taxes symbolized this momentous change, the capitation and the *dixième*. The revised capitation, with its extensive exemptions and its modified format, survived the War of the Spanish Succession, despite the royal promise to abolish the tax after the war was over. The *dixième*, created in 1710, followed a much more checkered path. Abolished in 1721, the government reestablished it in 1733 to help pay for the Polish war; miraculously, the king kept his word and abolished it at the end of the war. In 1741, a new war meant another *dixième*, this one, too, abolished after the war ended. The effort to raise a royal fiftieth, in kind, failed in the mid-1720s; this tax, so obvious a copy of the clerical tenth, elicited violent reaction among elites. The difference between the fiftieth and the ongoing tenth was that the latter was based on declarations of revenue provided by the taxpayers themselves. For those subject to the *taille*, the government did not have to rely on such declarations; the *dixième* could (and did) become a proportional supplement to the *taille*. For those exempt from the *taille*, the nobles and many bourgeois, however, the state had to rely on the declarations. Little wonder that the *dixième* produced so little, perhaps 20 to 25 million *livres* under Louis XIV, rising to 35–40 million *livres* during the War of the Austrian Succession.

The Regency government and, later, Orry's ministry tried another variation on the *dixième*, one which they called the *taille tarifée*, or indexed *taille*. Rather than relying on the arbitrary decisions of the village tax-collecting council, the intendants would travel through their districts to establish tax rates based on land and possessions in all parishes. With a solid knowledge of plough teams, land holdings, and other essential economic data, the villages could establish rates fixed to such criteria. Such a system existed already with respect to land holdings in southern France, where the *taille* fell on all those holding non-noble land (the *taille reélle*). Southern French parishes had cadasters (land registers) that listed the value of each plot; the parishioners simply apportioned the taxes according to the proportional value of the land. The 1716 effort at establishing such a system in the north worked well in the *généralité* of Paris but soon fell afoul of elite resistance. Starting in the late 1720s in Champagne, the government tried the same experiment everywhere in the *pays d'élection*. Only Champagne and Limousin actually succeeded. Everyone agreed that the *taille tarifée* was a better system and would help overcome the greatest complaint against the direct taxes, their inequity; the constellation of political forces, however, defeated every effort at reform. The *taille tarifée* never lasted more than a few years outside of Champagne, the Limousin, and the Ile–de–France.

The tax system thus looked somewhat different than it had in the late seventeenth century. The direct taxes included the *tailles*, the capitation, and, during wars, the *dixième*. To these, we might add the burden of the corvée and the annual levy for the militia (usually 30,000 men, but, in wartime, as many as 60,000). The parish had to provide a man or two for the royal militia, which did not serve in peacetime but did so during the war; the parish itself outfitted the soldier, which required an additional direct tax. The capitation involved the nobility and townsmen, although many towns, provinces, and corporations purchased exemption. The largest such exemption fell to the clergy, which had paid 25 million *livres* for the privilege: as with the capitation, so, too, with the *dixième*. In this case, the exemptions were much more widespread. In provinces such as Brittany and Languedoc, where nobles (and others) paid the capitation, the provincial estates purchased exemption from the *dixième*. During the War of the Austrian Succession, for example, Brittany paid 1.8 million *livres* a year and Languedoc 1.5 million.

The overall resources of the monarchy did not much exceed what they had been in the early eighteenth century but, in sharp contrast to the fiscal irregularities that produced the money in, say, 1706, the income came from set and established taxation. The total revenue in the late 1730s and early 1740s came to about 200 million *livres*, of which 91 million came from the General Tax Farm, 41 million *livres* from the *tailles*, 33 million from the capitation, and about 16.5 million from the old *pays d'Etats* and the newly conquered provinces (excluding Lorraine, whose 8.5 million *livres* still went to Leszczynski). The rest came from the demesne, sale of offices, coinage, the postal system, and other assorted income. The king spent this money much as he had always spent money: the military absorbed 55 million *livres*, the king's household another 30 million, interest took 45 million, payments to officers a further 20 to 25 million. Basic expenses ran to between 175 and 195 million *livres*, leaving a small surplus for "unforeseen" expenses. Such expenses need not be small; in 1739, the king spent 30 million *livres* on his eldest daughter's wedding. Unable to pay such a sum at once, he borrowed it from the Farmers General. When war broke out, military spending devoured any surpluses.

The little war of the Polish Succession more than doubled customary military and foreign spending. The military budget jumped to more than 110 million *livres* and the spending through the Foreign Affairs ministry increased from 14 to 38 million; much of this foreign affairs spending paid subsidies to troops put in the field by French allies. A serious war, like that of the Austrian Succession, meant even greater expense. All told, the king raised 757 million *livres* in "extraordinary" revenues between 1741 and 1748; the total cost of the war likely came to a billion *livres*. These "extraordinary" taxes included the *dixième* (again abolished at the end of the war) as well as new indirect taxes, such as new duties on goods entering cities, notably Paris. These taxes did not cease at the end of the war. The king borrowed large sums of money, so that he had new debts of 200 million *livres* by 1748, yet total debt service had risen only by 5 or 10 million *livres* at the end of the war.

The fiscal situation of the monarchy remained fairly solid under Orry's successor, Machault d'Arnouville. Machault abolished the *dixième* in 1749 but immediately after doing so introduced another tax on revenue, the *vingtième*★ (twentieth). Once again, taxpayers had to make declarations about their income; the royal commissioners demanded to see documentation (such as copies of rental contracts) to justify the declarations. The edict specifically stated that the *vingtième* would be used only to reimburse the state debt; indeed, the money would go to a separate treasury, created for that purpose. The *vingtième* supposedly fell on all; once again, the privileged orders sought exemption. At first, the government resisted strongly, forcing even Languedoc and Brittany to pay. Only the clergy held out. The bishop of Rennes, speaking for the Assembly of the Clergy in 1750, told the king: "Our conscience and our honor do not permit us to consent to see changed into a necessary tribute that which can only be the offering of our love." The clergy also had some regard for their financial interest in the matter. In the end, the king settled for the usual expedient, a fixed grant. On the eve of the Seven Years' War, the government, typically short of cash, conducted a fire sale of *abonnements*,★ fixed contributions in lieu of actual assessment. The estates of Languedoc and Brittany, those of Artois, Provence (Assembly of the Communes), and Burgundy, all quickly agreed to fixed payments; in each case, the new payment was substantially less than the old.

Why would the monarchy deliberately agree to lower its income from the *vingtième*, particularly on the eve of a war that would surely increase the state debt to be paid off? Cash. The monarchy of Louis XV, every bit as much as that of Henry IV, never had enough cash. Lacking a central bank, the French government had to find credit wherever it could in times of crisis. Those with ready cash could drive hard bargains, to obtain special financial privileges or higher rates of interest. The Farmers General usually settled for the latter. They would advance the king money at the beginning of their six-year lease or lend him vast sums (such as the 30 million of 1739) on short notice. In return, they got lenient treatment of their management of the tax farms and large payments of interest. In 1741, they had to give an advance (uncounted in the payments of the regular lease) of 25 million *livres* and received interest at 10.5 percent; in 1755, they provided 60 million *livres* at 5 percent. Their net profit from the transaction was much smaller, because they, too, had to borrow the money (typically at three-fifths of what they charged for it).

The *pays d'Etats* and other corporations sought special privileges more than interest. The privilege could be honorific but usually (as in the case of the clergy and the *vingtième*) involved both honor and income. The king and his ministers were not fools; they had little leverage against the Farmers General but could be much more hard-line with provincial estates. We must remember that the king wanted revenue above all; he would always sacrifice to provincial elites the right to choose how to tax, so long as they paid him what he wanted. There were a few unusually good deals – Provence's contribution to the *vingtième* dropped from 700,000 to 400,000 *livres* because of its Assembly's accord with the king – but in most cases the king likely got more money from such an agreement. What is more, he got it immediately. In many cases, the estates would pay the king an advance on the forthcoming income of the *vingtième* and would borrow this money at their own expense.

The exemption deals on the *vingtième* reflected a broader policy extensively pursued by the eighteenth-century French government: let corporations do as much of royal borrowing as possible. These corporations – the General Farm, provincial estates, guilds, town councils, and the clergy – had much better credit ratings than the king; they borrowed at rates of interest often half those available to the central government. The king's use of such intermediaries made perfect sense in light of the structure of government finance. The king got the money he needed; he paid less in interest than he would have paid on the open market; he tied important elites to the success of the government (they wanted to get their money back); and he provided those same elites with an important source of profits.

When the king made a deal with, say, the estates of Brittany, cutting the Breton contribution from 1.46 million *livres* (1753) to 1.25 million *livres*, he received many advantages. He got this money in advance, which meant no royal costs of collection, no worries about non-payment, and an immediate sum to spend. Given that the costs of collection of taxation ran to 15 percent in almost all cases, we can see that the reduction represented simply the king shifting those costs from the royal administration to the estates of Brittany. His net income from the *vingtième* in Brittany probably went up, even though the amount officially carried on the accounts went down.

This Alice-in-Wonderland quality to eighteenth-century French finance – what goes down actually goes up, what goes up may be going down – touched every facet of the administration. The tendency to see the political life of eighteenth-century France as a struggle between the king and his ministers and a traditional old guard, centered on the Parlements, poses substantial dangers. These ministers invariably came from the

Parlementaire elite; they had – *had to have* – close personal and professional ties to that elite. Nowhere can we see such ties more clearly than in the interrelationship between the controller general and the General Tax Farm, itself a frequent target of Parlementaire ire, yet directly tied to that institution.

We need not go into great detail about these interactions. Let us take the case of Jean-Baptiste de Machault, count of Arnouville, who became controller general in 1745, keeper of the seals in 1750, and secretary of state for the Navy in 1754. He resigned as controller general in 1754 to take over the Navy; in 1757, the king disgraced him, so he lost both the secretariat and the seals. Machault was the classic eighteenth-century ministerial "reformer." He introduced the *vingtième*, at first taking the hard line on any exemptions. The Parlements even registered the edict without great difficulty.

Like so many eighteenth-century reformers, Machault had impeccable Parlementaire credentials. He had been a councilor there from 1721 to 1728, when he became a master of requests of the king's household. His grandfather had been a councilor, his father a master of requests, councilor of state, and, briefly, lieutenant general of the police of Paris. Machault had close family ties with a wide range of Parlementaire and financier families. His great-grandfather married Françoise Lefèvre de Caumartin, member of one of the greatest Parlementaire dynasties at Paris. That family connection involved financiers as well; the Lefèvre de Caumartin had intermarried with the Fieubet family, Central Treasurers under Louis XIII. Machault's wife, Geneviève Louise Rouillé de Coudray, was the granddaughter of a director general of finances, great niece of the Attorney General of the Parlement, and granddaughter of the Grand Master of *Eaux et Forêts* of France. We could draw similar affiliations for every important eighteenth-century minister.

Court life under Louis XV

Machault participated extensively in the social life of the Parisian elite. He witnessed the marriages of several children of Farmers General and stood as godfather to the son of Farmer General Jean-Joseph Chicoyneau de la Valette. The godmother was none other than Jeanne-Antoinette Poisson, Mme. de Pompadour, all-powerful mistress of Louis XV. Here we enter into another of the Wonderland qualities of French government in the middle of the century: the dominant position of royal mistresses. Mme. de Pompadour held the strongest position. As her presence at the christening suggests, she sponsored Machault; he owed his position as controller general in part to her. When he lost her favor, in 1757, she quickly engineered his disgrace, even though he still had the favor of the king. She protected the Farmers General, even when her protegé Machault turned against some of them. She was the granddaughter, niece, and wife of Farmers General. Indeed, many courtiers believed she was the illegitimate child of Farmer General Le Normant de Tournehem or of one of the powerful financier Pâris brothers, for whom her father worked. If the former was true, then she married her cousin.

Mme. de Pompadour represents the pinnacle of influence of mistresses on royal policy. Because of her extensive ties to the world of finance, she had a large family to promote. She favored one set of Farmers General, or even sub-farmers, over another; her favorites rewarded her with splendid presents and bribes. Not that they forgot the royal ministers: Machault received an official bribe of 300,000 *livres* when he renewed the General Farm lease in 1749, his right as controller general.[12] He could also get social rewards: he tried, unsuccessfully, to marry his brother-in-law to the daughter of one Farmer General. Not one to give up easily, he then married the young man to the niece of another financier, whom he convinced the king to add to the list of Farmers General. Machault had enough power to make sure his supposed client, Etienne Bouret, received the General Farm in 1750, yet what a coincidence that Bouret's brother, François, married Mme. de Pompadour's first cousin virtually the same day that the lease took effect. Parisians suspected that Mme. de Pompadour owned shares in the farm: indeed, the rumor had it that the king himself bought shares in his tax farms (using a valet as a front man) because the profits were so attractive. The General Farm brought in something like 4 to 6 million *livres* a year in profits for the farmers; they also obtained substantial benefits from the interest (6–10 percent) paid on their obligatory advance to the king at each new lease.

Popular opinion thought little of the financiers. Mme. de Pompadour was the object of particular disdain because of her dual association with the world of debauchery and that of finance. Popular songs highlighted the association:

> Once good taste came to us from Versailles,
> Now it's the *canaille* (vermin) . . .
> But why be astonished,
> Isn't it from the market
> That fish comes to us?

[12] These official "gratifications" to relevant officials had long been standard practice in French tax leasing, from the General Farm all the way down to local ones (the treasurers of France in Brittany, for example, had the right to a "gratification" at every renewal of the Breton import–export duty farm).

> Daughter of a blood sucker and blood sucker herself,
> A fish [Poisson] in that palace, of extreme arrogance
> Has had put up everywhere, without shame and without dread
> The skins of the people and the disgrace of the king.

His liaison with Mme. de Pompadour only served to deepen the moral offense Louis XV offered to his people.

Louis XV combined many contradictory traits, somewhat like the Regent Philip of Orléans. Both men possessed considerable intelligence; both actively participated in the business of governing; both lost themselves in regular debauchery. Louis attended the Council of State, indeed all of his councils; these meetings took place a minimum of four days a week. He also met individually with the chancellor (or Keeper of the Seals) and with the individual ministers. Louis rarely spoke at the councils; he often struggled to speak in public and all his contemporaries noted his extreme timidity. He greatly preferred to work by himself, pen in hand, correcting memoirs and edicts sent to him by his officials. In this he followed an unusual course, making the written notations himself, rather than ordering a secretary to do so, as the other monarchs of his time (and his ancestors) did. Louis prided himself on his attention to detail. In a typical letter to the Parlement of Rennes, he wrote:

I read your remonstrances . . . You say there that I was not informed, but nothing is more false. I read everything that you wrote and no one has sent you anything that I did not order myself.[13]

Louis's personal habits, however, did much to undermine his kingship. He possessed a fanaticism for hunting. He often hunted three or four times a week and spent long stretches of time at the small royal hunting chateaux surrounding Paris. The king's frequent absences from Versailles surely had one unintended consequence: they accelerated the shift of the social Court from Versailles to Paris.

Louis remains famous, of course, for his lamentable personal morality, demonstrated by his constant search for new mistresses. Popular opinion thought poorly of these women; in 1744, when the king fell deathly ill at Metz, the bishop of Soissons, called to the king's bedside, refused to bring the viaticum unless Louis's current mistress, the duchess of Châteauroux, left the city. As she made her way across France, the population fired stones and mud at her carriage. Already in 1739, Louis's confessor had refused him communion because of his open consorting with another mistress, Mme. de Mailly. Because he could not receive communion at Easter, the king could not perform the ceremony of the king's touch, at which he touched those afflicted with scrofula, so they might be healed. The king

---

[13] M. Antoine, *Le conseil du roi sous le règne de Louis XV* (Geneva: Droz, 1970), 616.

likewise suffered this public humiliation at Easter 1740 and Christmas 1744; no doubt, he found more forgiving confessors thereafter. The damage, in popular eyes, had been done in 1739.

Elites took a very different view of the situation. Some of them had intimate ties with the world of the Court, even with the General Tax Farm. Two of the great *philosophes*, Helvétius and Lavoisier, were themselves Farmers General. Other leading intellectuals, such as Montesquieu, benefited from the protection of high-ranking Court figures; Montesquieu sought and obtained some help from Mme. de Pompadour in a controversy surrounding his *Spirit of the Laws*. The wives of financiers and their friends ran salons in Paris; this group financed the *philosophes* and often fed them as well. When the duke de Croÿ went to find the marshal de Saxe at the home of Farmer General la Pouplinière, he found Voltaire instead. After he gave up his position as Farmer General, Helvétius often gave weekly Tuesday dinners to a group that included Diderot, d'Alembert, d'Holbach, Condorcet, and Turgot – in other words, the core group behind the Encyclopedia. Given that those who would purchase the Encyclopedia belonged to the same world of high society, the connection should not shock us.

The shift to Paris began immediately after Louis XIV's death. Under Philip's Regency, high society stayed in Paris. Once established there, it never fully returned to Versailles. Courtiers who lived at Versailles in Louis XIV's time merely visited the Court of Louis XV. When the king left the palace (a frequent occurrence – in 1750 he spent only fifty-two nights in Versailles) courtiers and ministers alike fled, "like schoolboys let out on vacation," to Paris. As Jean-François Solnon has suggested, Louis XV preserved the forms of Louis XIV's Court but not its spirit; most of all, he and his Court merely mimicked the styles of the past without understanding the deeper meanings behind the ceremonial gestures. The Court slowly lost its ascendancy over Paris, especially in literary matters, which little interested either Louis XV or Louis XVI. Playwrights now wrote for a Parisian audience, not one at Court. "Failing to encourage letters, the Court no longer mastered opinion."[14] Opinion, public opinion, the new master of the age, formed outside of the Court, in Paris, at the salons, among the *philosophes* and their readers.

Philosophy and the state

The Encyclopedia and the *philosophes* bring us to the most remarkable change in the monarchy during the second quarter of the eighteenth

[14] Solnon, *La cour de France*, 473.

century: the collapse of a philosophical consensus about the nature of the monarchy and of the state itself. There had long been dissidents who objected to the officially promulgated version of the social myth, including the relationship of the state to society, but the official monarchical position remained dominant in public discourse until the 1720s. From the 1720s until the 1750s, the officially sanctioned social myth – the society of orders, the absolute monarchy – rapidly eroded. By the 1750s, it stood in complete ruin; only the king still believed in his absolute power. The Parlement of Paris, in its "Great Remonstrances" of 1753, made that abundantly clear:

When there is a conflict between the king's absolute power and the good of his service, the court respects the latter rather than the former, not to disobey but in order to discharge its obligations.[15]

How had matters come to such a pass? What intellectual currents had overwhelmed the political order? We can isolate two related, although separate currents: (1) the ongoing religious controversy over the bull *Unigenitus*; and (2) the increasing secularization of elites. The controversy over *Unigenitus* had not ended with Louis XIV's death. Cardinal Fleury strongly supported the bull and he sought by every means to have it accepted. Fleury's position mirrored that of Louis XIV; he saw the opponents of the bull as a political problem as much as a religious one. They represented a threat to order, to the king's absolute power. He had little sympathy for the view expressed as early as 1713 by d'Aguesseau and Joly de Fleury (the king's attorneys at the Parlement of Paris) that the bull itself threatened the king's power by giving the Pope too much authority over the French Church.

Fleury began his campaign against the Jansenists well before he became chief minister (1726). As a member of the Council of Conscience, Fleury – who had the full confidence of Louis XV – established veto power over all ecclesiastical appointments.[16] He used that power ruthlessly to exclude all opponents of *Unigenitus* from high ecclesiastical office; he even used arbitrary arrest orders (*lettres de cachet*) to imprison, or force into exile, opponents of the bull who already held benefices. Once

---

[15] J. H. Shennan, *The Parlement of Paris* (Ithaca, NY: Cornell University Press, 1968), 309–10.

[16] Under Louis XIV, the Council of Conscience, in charge of suggesting nominees for ecclesiastical positions – bishops and abbots – faded out of existence. By the 1680s, the king and his confessor (always a Jesuit) alone made the choices, although always within the legal fiction of the council. The Regent created a Council of Conscience, primarily to deal with Jansenism, but he abolished it in 1718. In 1720, he created another Council of Conscience to deal with religious matters. Dubois dominated at first but by the mid-1720s Fleury had taken over. He used the Council to attack the Jansenists everywhere.

in power as chief minister, Fleury stepped up his campaign. He particularly targeted the parish clergy of the diocese of Paris, whose ties to Jansenism went back to the Fronde. A pamphlet war, not unlike that of the 1650s, broke out in 1727; two pamphlets, one detailing the efforts of Fleury and the Pope to convince Cardinal de Noailles of Paris to end his waffling about *Unigenitus*, and the other presenting the position of the Parisian *curés*, caused the government particular embarrassment.

At the same time, Fleury obtained an opportunity to strike another blow at the Jansenists. When Jean Soanen, bishop of Senez, issued a pastoral instruction that denounced *Unigenitus* and praised Quesnel, Fleury had Soanen's provincial archbishop (of Embrun) convene an assembly to rebuke the old Jansenist. They did so, suspending him from his bishopric and pronouncing *Unigenitus* a dogmatic judgment of the Church. The king responded by exiling Soanen to an isolated monastery; the Pope issued a pronouncement late in 1727. The opponents of *Unigenitus* did not rest. Jansenists flooded Paris with pamphlets and even founded a weekly journal of religious news, the *Nouvelles ecclésiastiques*. Despite the royal prohibition against the *Nouvelles*, it continued in print throughout the rest of the Old Regime. More than 1,500 churchmen signed petitions against the actions of the Embrun council; Cardinal de Noailles publicly denounced the sentence against Soanen. The solicitors (*avocats*) of the Parlement published a condemnation of the council's action that focused on the broader point, explicitly denying that *Unigenitus* was either a dogmatic judgment of the Church or a law of the realm. Their objections went to the heart of the broader opposition to *Unigenitus*, because they attacked it from the Gallican perspective. The Parlement of Paris, and some of the provincial ones, had Jansenist judges, to be sure, but overwhelmingly they opposed *Unigenitus* on Gallican principles.

Fleury obtained a short-lived victory in the ongoing struggle when the wavering archbishop of Paris, Cardinal de Noailles, retracted his opposition to *Unigenitus* in 1728. Noailles died in 1729, allowing Fleury to name a hard-core Constitutional (i.e., *Unigenitus* advocate), Charles-Gaspard-Guillaume de Vintimille, as archbishop of Paris. Vintimille quickly commanded all priests in his diocese to accept *Unigenitus*, but initially showed some forbearance with those who did not. The opponents of *Unigenitus* kept up their harsh rhetoric against him, however, and he and Fleury increasingly took a hard line. The opposition found a popular cause on which to rally in the strange case of François de Pâris, an unofficial popular "saint" adopted by the Jansenists.

François de Pâris had been the deacon at Saint-Médard (rue Mouffetard) in Paris. In his lifetime, he received universal renown for his piety, his charitable works, and for his remarkable asceticism. He always wore a hairshirt and frequently used other devices of self-torture, such as a spiked belt. He fasted often; in Lent of 1724, he abstained from food altogether, leading him to develop severe convulsions. Pâris unswervingly opposed *Unigenitus*; indeed his extreme personal piety and asceticism were Jansenism carried to the *n*th degree. When he died in 1727, his parishioners and other Parisians thronged to the funeral, even taking his household goods and relics – bits of his hair, nails, or clothing – from the coffin. Soon all Paris heard of miracles taking place at his tomb in the cemetery of Saint-Médard. Given Deacon Pâris's obvious Jansenism, the "miracles" of Saint-Médard quickly became a political issue. The government grew increasingly hostile. The cemetery's attraction simultaneously grew with each passing day. Soon thousands of pilgrims gathered at the tomb, many of them following Pâris's example by lapsing into convulsions. The convulsionaries went far beyond what the Jansenist heirs of Pâris's tradition had intended, losing some Parlementaire support in the process. Finally, in January 1732, the Paris police abruptly closed the cemetery by force.

The ongoing disputes poisoned the general ecclesiastical atmosphere. Vintimille eventually suspended over 300 parish priests; the public outcry was such that the king felt obliged to issue yet another royal defense of *Unigenitus*, this time a declaration ordering all ecclesiastics to accept without reservation or condition the bull "as a law of the Church . . . [and] a law of our kingdom" and eliminating all right of appeal to the Parlement for cases involving the bull. The Parlement registered the edict only in a *lit de justice*.

In the early 1730s, the Parlement jousted continuously with Fleury about these matters: going on strike, publishing a decree stating that the temporal power existed independent of any other, such as the spiritual, and essentially positing the supremacy of temporal over spiritual power. Although Fleury forced them to rescind the decree, what it represented could not be rescinded. We can see here already the desacralization of the monarchy, the definitive decoupling of Church and state. If the state no longer rested on some sort of divine benediction, on the king's role as God's anointed, then it could only rest on law. Once elites had accepted the idea that the state rested on law, not on a preordained divinely sanctioned order of which the "absolute" monarchy was a part, then the key political conflict of the eighteenth century became obvious: who would make the law?

In this sense, the dispute over *Unigenitus*, although itself profoundly religious in character (as the example of the convulsionaries of Saint-Médard makes clear), took on a secular context. The elites became increasingly secular; they tended to move away from the organized Church, which they saw as a bastion of venality and corruption, and toward a more personal religion. The organized Church itself contributed to the process by its violent attack on the legitimacy of the miracles attributed to Pâris. They questioned the veracity of any human testimony about miracles, inadvertently contributing to doubt about all miracles, even those officially recognized by the Church. In the twentieth century, the perpetual conflicts about *Unigenitus* – at the end of Louis XIV's reign, in the early 1720s, the early 1730s, and the early 1750s – are difficult to understand. The bull struck at the very heart of the French monarchy: at its sacerdotal quality. To the king, opponents of *Unigenitus* supported disorder and dissent within the Church, which could lead to political dissent. To the Gallicans of the Parlement, the postulation that the Pope could excommunicate the king and could issue binding pronouncements about religion in France violated the Four Gallican Articles of 1682 and offered a direct affront to the French *nation*, represented by the king's person. To the Gallicans, no outside power could dictate to the French nation; if the king went along with such an assertion, he was simply wrong, even though he himself embodied the nation and spoke for it.

One man brought all these currents together in his writings, François-Marie Arouet, known to posterity as Voltaire. Voltaire offered the French reading public a new vision of the world, beginning with his *Letters on the English* (1733), the fruit of his three years' stay in England (1726–29). In it, he described England as the land of liberty, where privilege had no part. All paid taxes; each person could choose their own religion; everyone could seek material gain without fear of confiscation; merchants received honor, not opprobrium, from society. He exaggerated, of course, yet he did so for effect. He wanted to show French people that their government was arbitrary, that their values needed to change in a changing world. The government took a different view: it burned *Letters* in 1734 and Voltaire went into exile.

His subsequent career in letters demonstrates the extent to which eighteenth-century intellectuals had an ambiguous relationship with those in power. Voltaire devoted himself to science in the 1730s, returned to favor in the 1740s (sufficiently so to be one of the official royal historians), went to visit Frederick II of Prussia in the early 1750s, and published his largely laudatory history of Louis XIV in 1751. He turned his satiric pen away from the state and society and focused on the Church. Indeed, the main focus of the Enlightenment in the middle of the century was not the state as such but the separation of Church and state. In 1758, he published his most famous novel, the satirical *Candide*. In it, the hero of the title goes off to El Dorado, the earthly paradise, in which there are no law courts or suits, in which the largest government building is the ministry of science, in which all children attend school at government expense, through which merchants travel freely, staying at government-sponsored inns. Every clergyman in the novel is a moral reprobate – sexually promiscuous, thieving, ethically bankrupt. Voltaire lampoons war and religion and, by his description of good government in El Dorado, the French state. He promulgates a new version of the state, one whose function does not lie in making war but in enabling its citizens to obtain the good life. The state sponsors education, commerce, science, and industry. The people of El Dorado practice a singular religion: they get up each morning and thank God for their blessings. No organized Church; no monasteries; no ecclesiastical hierarchy; no church buildings. *Candide* provided a powerful (and funny) summary of intellectual currents of the previous generation.

Charles Louis de Secondat, baron of Montesquieu, the other towering intellectual figure of the second quarter of the century, came from an old robe noble family: he served as a president of the Parlement of Bordeaux. He had published his *Persian Letters* in 1721: in it, Persian travelers criticized the court of France for the excesses of a tyrannical monarchy. In the 1730s, he attacked again, this time choosing the Romans as his subject. The Roman Republic became the font of all virtues, the Roman Empire the root of many evils (including the fall of Rome itself). The literary public understood the real target: a monarchy that did not rest sufficiently on its laws.

Montesquieu moved from the historical to the philosophical in his greatest work, *The Spirit of the Laws*, published in 1748. The book enjoyed enormous success, which demonstrates the extent to which its ideas had an audience in mid-century France. Montesquieu established principles that would profoundly affect French developments and those elsewhere. His belief in a division of powers – that the legislative and executive powers had to lie in different hands – formed the basis for the political debate in late eighteenth-century France and one of the foundations of the U.S. Constitution. Montesquieu greatly admired English government (he, like Voltaire, spent time there), with its balance among the two houses of Parliament and the king. He wanted French Parlements to be more like their English namesakes, that is, he emphasized the Parlement's role in *making*, not simply judging law.

Here we have a fundamental shift in the self-perception of the Parlementaire elite: they now wanted a share in the lawmaking power. If one could no longer accept the premise on which the absolute state rested – that divine law offered protection to the king's subjects because he had to respect it – then one had to seek protection in man-made rather than divine law. Montesquieu, so different from the French political philosophers of the seventeenth century like Bossuet, placed the law in the realm of man, not of God. Once one had accepted that premise, leaving the lawmaking authority in the king's hands did not make sense. French propertied elites, like English ones, needed control over the lawmaking process to protect their property. They also needed to come up with a coherent definition of property itself, because eighteenth-century France had several varieties of property. In rural areas, the conflict among these varied property rights often hamstrung economic development.[17] In the broadest sense, we should view the works of authors such as Voltaire or Montesquieu less as determinative of intellectual (or, more particularly, political) developments than as evidence of the changing nature of the French intellectual climate.

The intellectual rebellion of the Parlementaires and other members of the elites had profound consequences out in the provinces as well. As we saw in chapter 4, during the reign of Louis XIV, the titled nobility moved en masse to Paris and Versailles, where they remained in the eighteenth century. Their absence left the Parlementaires, many of them now bearing titles of their own (most often baron or marquis), at the apex of provincial society. When Louis XV squared off against his Parlements, he no longer faced royal judges against whom he could play off the local titled nobility; he faced royal judges who had displaced that nobility at the pinnacle of provincial political, social, and cultural life. Provincial society had no other elite to whom the king could turn; even the intendants often had direct ties to the Parlementaire elite of their province. Opposition from the Parlements meant the immediate collapse of royal authority.

All these developments came to a head in the early 1750s, perhaps most clearly in the affair of the refusal of communion. The hard-line, pro-*Unigenitus* bishops ordered their parish clergy to refuse to give communion to parishioners who could not produce a certificate of orthodoxy from a recognized Constitutional priest.[18] When several such cases, involving known Jansenist ecclesiastics, took place in Paris, the bishop held firm. The Parlement supported the Jansenists, ordering the arrest of several carriers of the viaticum. The Parisian people sided even more strongly against the Church, many rejecting the organized Church altogether. Secretary of state d'Argenson wrote in his memoirs that by 1753 he could no longer defend the clergy in polite society, for fear of

---

[17] J.-L. Rosenthal, *Fruits of Revolution* (Cambridge: Cambridge University Press, 1992), provides clear evidence of the impact of fuzzy property rights on economic development in rural Provence and Normandy.

[18] When near death, Catholics received the sacrament of extreme unction, which included communion. All Catholics in good standing, physically able to receive the viaticum, were supposed to perform this sacrament and to receive absolution for their sins.

bearing the shame of association with the "Inquisition." Once again the king ordered the Parlement to desist; once again they refused and he exiled them. The senior councilors (the *Grand'Chambre*), whom he had not exiled, took such umbrage that they demanded the same fate as their brothers. In the end, the king relented. The Parlement, and the lower courts, intervened effectively against the refusing clergy.

The Pope finally put an end to the difficulty by abolishing the communion certificates (1756), but the Parlement of Paris, heady with success, pushed onward. They did so at the most inopportune of moments, the start of the Seven Years' War. The government, as always at the start of a war, had need of money, so it had a series of financial edicts to register. In another *lit de justice*, the king forced the Parlement to accept a wide range of edicts, not least of them a reduction of the court itself. He eliminated two of the five Chambers of Inquests; that is, he got rid of the youngest, most rebellious magistrates. Machault, the old Parlementaire, stood behind the edicts, just as Maupeou, former First President of the Parlement, would stand behind the effort to abolish the court in 1771. Most of the Parlement resigned in response to Machault's coup. What is more, the provincial Parlements, so often at odds with that of Paris, stood behind their fellow judges. In doing so, they supported a principle expounded by the Parisians in 1755, that all of the Parlements formed one Parlement (the so-called *union des classes**). Only the attempted assassination of the king by the madman Jacques Damiens resolved the situation. Each party became more transigent. The king dismissed Machault and restored the officers (although not the abolished Chambers; the court apportioned the judges among the other three Chambers). The Parlement supported the fiscal edicts, so desperately needed in the midst of so great a war.

Viewed from a distance of two centuries, the ballet of king and Parlement seems almost farcical. The entire process somewhat resembles a Japanese kabuki production, with its elaborate, ritualized, unchangeable gestures. The king issues an unpopular edict; the Parlement sends back its remonstrances; the king holds a *lit de justice*, forcing the Parlement to register; the Parlement resigns; the king exiles the Parlement; the two sides are reconciled. When the king failed to follow the script, as in 1753, the unexiled judges had to demand that he exile them, lest they lose face. Despite the appearance of theatre, at times even of comedy, substantive matters lay at the root of the disputes. In 1759, the Parlement wrote to the king:

All administration in the state is founded on the laws. That involves free registration, preceded by verification and examination . . . [T]he people's trust

. . . which the supreme power, however just, cannot inspire alone, is a result of this free scrutiny, after which the verification of the law testifies to the justice of its motives and to the need for its execution.[19]

In other words, the king and the Parlements (who, in the *union des classes* ideology, formed, in reality, one Parlement) together make the law. That single statement sounds the death of the Old Regime, as historians traditionally define it.

What would take its place? Whither the state in the 1750s, in the midst of the crisis of the Seven Years' War? Should the ministers reform the state, sweeping aside the detritus of centuries, discarding useless institutions, establishing a state based on principles of reason? Or should the ancient institutions, such as the Parlements, press their case to act as checks upon the power of monarchy? Should political society follow the wise counsel of Montesquieu, seeking above all to keep the legislative and executive powers in separate hands? If the state took the first course, attacking the corporations on which it lay, how would it reconcile that attack with its ongoing (and growing) financial dependence on those same corporations? If the ministers would not lead the reform, who would? Could the old corporations put aside their corporate interests and create a state that would serve the interests of a new entity, one whose name came often into play in the emerging political discourse of the eighteenth century: the nation.

[19] Shennan, *Parlement of Paris*, 312.

6   Reform, renewal, collapse

There is a philosophical wind blowing toward us from England in favor of free, anti-monarchical government; it is entering minds, and one knows how opinion governs the world. It could be that this government is already accomplished in people's heads, to be implemented at the first chance, and the revolution might occur with less conflict than one thinks.[1]   Minister of state d'Argenson

The master metal workers of Nantes complained regularly to the local court, to the mayor, even to the Parlement at Rennes about their unruly journeymen. It seems these disreputable and disorderly souls organized "cabals" among themselves, swore secret oaths (borrowed from the Freemasons), intimidated journeymen who would not join them and boycotted masters who would not heed them. They wanted to control their own labor, not to submit to the work bureaux run by the masters. The frequent complaints make it clear that the journeymen succeeded. We have other evidence, such as the journal of Jacques Ménétra, a Parisian glazier who took his *tour de France* between 1757 and 1764, that journeymen everywhere controlled their labor. In every town, Ménétra goes straight to the first journeyman for work, never to the work bureau.

The language of the offended masters of Nantes alerts us to the death of the Old Regime. It passed away, as most social systems do, in its sleep, leaving its citizens unaware that it was gone. No society more fully reflects Hegel's dictum that the Owl of Minerva flies only at dusk; few people in eighteenth-century France understood that the Old Regime was no more. Curiously enough, historians misled by the apparent continuity of so many elements of French society are reluctant to notice it, either. Institutions and social structures do not change overnight, they evolve into new patterns. Abrupt changes provide the exception, not the rule.

Let us consider briefly four elements of French life in the second half of

---

[1] K. Baker, ed., *Inventing the French Revolution* (New York: Cambridge University Press, 1990), 21.

the eighteenth century: the economy, social structure, political life, and patterns of thought. The Old Regime structures lingered on in each one. In the economy, agriculture ruled, seconded by manufacturing focused on textiles. Guilds still ran production in most towns. The social structure looked much the same as ever: nobles, lawyers, merchants, guild masters, and others. In politics, the king still ruled a ministerial administrative state, his power to make law undiluted. People still believed in religion, in the king, in the social order around them.

Yet such appearances hid the new reality. Let us return to Ménétra whose journal provides such rich testimony to the complexity of eighteenth-century French life. Ménétra traveled France from 1757 to 1764. He followed traditional routes, leaving Paris to wander down the Loire valley to Nantes, down the Atlantic coast to La Rochelle, Bordeaux, and Bayonne, across the mountains to the nesting of Mediterranean towns, and then up the Rhône to Macon, thence to Dijon, Auxerre, and Paris again. What did this intrepid wandering journeyman find on his *tour de France?* Ménétra's observations provide us with a clear picture of the extent of change in late eighteenth-century France. He himself shows many characteristics of the changes in urban popular attitudes: he detests the Church, preaches toleration of Protestants and Jews, and struggles against the forces of order.

He fights constantly against the authorities and against the Gavots, adherents of the journeymen's association rival to his own (the Devoir). We see him working for many widows – a reaffirmation of the importance of women in the French economy – and in mostly small shops. Yet we also see him, later, in Paris, working as a subcontractor, engaging in activities illegal but burgeoning. Ménétra shows us the continuing importance of the traditional guild structure, yet he also shows the strains on that structure and its elements of change.[2]

He often works in small shops outside Paris, yet we can see that a limited number of masters dominate glassmaking in Paris itself. This trend to larger and larger enterprises, which began in the late seventeenth century, accelerated after 1750. The fastest changes came in the cloth trades. The trend toward concentration, noted above for the late seventeenth and early eighteenth centuries, accelerated. By the 1770s, at Reims or Sedan or Troyes, the workshop looked completely different: the share of the labor force of masters employing 20 or more workers had risen to 75 percent at Sedan and to 50 percent even at Reims, a center of the more conservative woolen manufacture, where Ponce Jean Nicolas

[2] J. Ménétra, *Journal of My Life*, ed. D. Roche (New York: Columbia University Press, 1986).

Ponsardin had 100 looms and employed 1,000 workers and Jean-Baptiste Sirot had 60 and 600, respectively. At Troyes, where cotton was king, the wave of the future had washed over the town: instead of the 350–400 masters and merchants owning looms in Reims, only 50 merchant–manufacturers produced cloth. Some owned as many as 60 looms and employed up to 1,500 workers. Whatever else such production may have been, it was certainly not traditional guild work.

Ménétra shows us too the elaborate world of ceremony in which ordinary people lived. When he leaves a town, the journeymen give him a send-off, complete with feast and procession through town. On appropriate holidays, such as the feast of Saint Luke (patron saint of glaziers), the journeymen host elaborate feasts for journeymen in other trades, as well as a parade, with musicians and a dance. Again and again, the journeymen copy the rituals of established society, yet modifying them, mocking them, turning them to their own meaning. In Paris, Ménétra spends his youth fighting the police but his middle age as a member of the fire department. How typical this must have been of a guildsman's life: the wandering youth of the rebellious journeyman, followed by the stable, sedentary middle age of the guild master. Always, we find two defining elements in his life: age and women. We see the typical roles of the man and woman: he does the production; she runs the shop. He squanders money (especially in his youth); she saves it. Ménétra also bears witness to the complexity of men's attitudes toward women and sex. He treats certain women, those holding property, with some respect; defenseless women, such as servants or peasant women, he often rapes. His contempt for rural women extends to all peasants; he, like most urban dwellers, views the peasants as a semi-savage race apart.

Ménétra takes us, too, into another bastion of everyday life, the tavern. On the road, like most journeymen, he lives in dormitories attached to taverns, run by the "mother" of the journeymen. He invariably conducts business over a glass of wine. He visits his neighborhood tavern to socialize, to conduct business, to meet friends; he never does these things at home. On Sundays, he sometimes goes out to Ramponneau's, the famous *guinguette* on the edge of Paris (outside the duty barriers, so offering cheaper wine). How like most Parisians he was. The artisans especially frequented the taverns: in one sample of judicial records about taverns, roughly half of the clientele of Parisian taverns described themselves as artisans, masters, or journeymen. By way of contrast, very few nobles – virtually none after 1731 – could be found in these "caverns of debauchery," as the police called them. Here again we find an emerging pattern of social separation. The occasional noble wandered into neighborhood taverns in the early eighteenth century (and *chez* Ramponneau even at its end); most nobles went instead to the café after 1740.[3]

The police, ever larger in Paris as we saw in chapter 5, likely presented more of an annoyance to the artisanal customers than ever. To the artisan, the tavern formed part of his home; to the police, the tavern was public space, in which they had to prevent real or potential evil (even the fomenting of insurrections). Surely this immediate presence of "ministerial despotism" provided a political object lesson for the Parisian population. When they supported the Parlementaires in the latter's resistance to that despotism, they had in mind the increasing interference in daily life – perhaps best symbolized by the construction of the tariff wall around Paris in 1785 – so vexing to them. One of the most important developments in eighteenth-century French political life was precisely the elaboration of a specific set of meanings for volatile new words – such as liberty – by people such as those in the taverns. The temporary alliances of Parlementaires and people should not deceive us into believing they meant the same thing when they said the same thing, whether it be an attack on "despotism" or a defense of "liberty."

Ménétra also demonstrates another radical change in eighteenth-century French life: many workers could read and write. Ménétra himself, educated at a church school for several years beyond the norm (because, he tells us, he sang well and performed in the choir), does represent an exception, in that he wrote an entire journal. Surely his several positions as first journeyman of the town reflected his writing abilities. Yet he was not alone. At Lyons, three-quarters of the bakers, of the cabinet makers, and even of the semi-proletarian silk workers could sign their names in the 1780s. In 1780, 40 percent of the estate inventories of Parisian servants listed books, as did a third of the inventories of even the poorest workers, the day laborers (*gagne-deniers*, literally the penny earners).

What did France look like in the 1750s? How did it change between the 1750s and the 1780s? Economically, the balance of production shifted more toward manufacture; France remained primarily an agricultural country, but the portion of national output produced by the primary sector certainly declined. International trade grew by leaps and bounds. We have already noted the rapid increase at Bordeaux and Nantes; other ports, in different regions, also expanded. Marseilles, tied both to colonial and Levantine trade, underwent unparalleled growth. Coffee imports jumped from one million kilograms in 1737 to seven million by 1785. Cotton imports (from the Near East) rose from 5,000 quintals in 1688 to 90,000 in

---

[3] This and other information on taverns and drinking comes from T. Brennan's fine study, *Public Drinking and Popular Culture in Eighteenth-Century Paris* (Princeton, NJ: Princeton University Press, 1988).

1789; the exportation of finished cotton goods rose in the same period from 1,200 "pieces" to 63,000. The colonial trade did not reach every town, far from it, but those areas it touched, it transformed completely.

The growth of agricultural output continued until about 1770, when a period of uncertain fluctuation set in, one with some extremely bad harvest years, such as 1788. The long-standing pattern of capital flow toward the countryside – due to urban investment in land, to relatively low (and stable) direct taxation, and to a steady rise in agricultural prices – began to reverse. After 1760, capital likely flowed in the opposite direction, most notably in the form of higher rents. Contemporaries believed land rents had doubled in the two decades before 1787; if we move the starting date back to 1760, that estimate would hold true in many regions of France: Languedoc, Normandy, the Ile-de-France. At Pont-St-Pierre, for example, the Roncherolles's income went up from 15,574 *livres* in 1740 to 32,192 *livres* in 1780, an increase typical of most of France. In most cases, the 1760s provided the great increase. As in the seventeenth century, the sudden increase in rental income led to reduced peasant investment and to lower output, although the two great famines (1770 and 1788–89) had more traditional climatological causes. The increased tax burden on landlords – through the *vingtièmes* and the capitation – surely provided a strong impetus to their efforts to raise rents.

The agricultural growth of the period up to 1770 slowed in most sectors (such as grain) and reversed sharply in others, especially wine. Wine-growing regions – particularly those producing cheap wine – greatly expanded production in the 1760s and 1770s; overproduction led to a crash from 1779 to 1787, when wine prices collapsed, ruining many of the small producers of Languedoc. The textile industry, too, suffered in the 1780s. Reduced internal consumption, due to reduced purchasing power of many consumers (wine growers, peasants renting land), overproduction (at Reims and Troyes, production rose 77 percent between 1783 and 1787), and the immediate effects of the trade agreement with Britain in 1786, abolishing protective tariffs, combined to lead to a production crisis in textiles, especially cotton. The intendant wrote to the government that

the position of manufactures in [Troyes] is becoming more critical than ever; the journeymen and workers are beginning to grumble, and they are even putting up placards in which they threaten to burn down the merchants who refuse to buy.[4]

Little wonder the journeymen grumbled: by October 1788, more than 10,000 of them had lost their jobs. Reims, tied to woolen cloths, had a lesser reduction, but 3,000 people joined the unemployed.

[4] L. Hunt, *Revolution and Urban Politics in Provincial France. Troyes and Reims, 1786–1790* (Stanford, CA: Stanford University Press, 1978), 41.

The France of 1787 differed sharply from that of 75 years before. It had far more textile workers and therefore was much more sensitive to industrial problems. It had a much improved network of roads, begun by Orry but fully implemented by his successors (using engineers trained in the Paris school). News traveled much faster; between 1660 and 1760, the average speed of the postal couriers doubled. News of Paris now reached Rouen in a day and a half, Lyons in six days, Bordeaux in five and a half. Goods still poked along, lucky to travel 20 kilometers in a day (as against the 80 of the couriers). The better main roads allowed more reliable, consistent movement and thus considerably encouraged trade; the secondary roads in underdeveloped regions like the Auvergne remained appalling and significantly hindered local trade. The improved road system likely had a greater political than economic effect, because it tied the provinces more tightly to political events in Paris.

The towns connected by these roads changed in one of two ways. Some grew rapidly, with expanding populations of textile workers (most particularly in the surrounding villages). In these expanding towns, one often found the emergence of the large workshops, with their implicit destruction of the traditional artisanal production unit. In the smaller towns, those less tied to new goods, the opposite pattern seems to have continued: individual masters with one or two workers dominated production. Even in some large towns, such as Lyons, in which a given trade – in Lyons, silk – dominated production and maintained the old structures, the master at his bench, working beside his journeyman, remained the norm.

The social tensions in the modernizing towns stretched the abilities of the authorities to respond; the seasonal unemployment of so many textile workers particularly led to difficulties. Unlike the repression of the 1720s, the waves of repression that started in 1768 locked up adult and young adult men: an average of 10,000–12,000 of them each year, most of them between the ages of 15 and 30. In the Caen district, more than half of these men were either agricultural laborers (27 percent) or artisans (24 percent), usually textile workers. Authorities, who as late as the 1760s arrested people for begging, now shifted focus to vagrancy. As they did so, they found a readier ally in local populations: the percentage of prisoners discovered through public reports more than doubled in Caen between 1768 and 1774 and remained close to the higher figure (just under half of total arrests) into the 1780s. Civil society, at least in Normandy, took a progressively harder line toward outsiders.

The rising economic power of the merchants also created political stress. These merchants often found allies among the town lawyers, resentful of the dominance of royal officials on town councils. The councils of towns as disparate as Troyes and Vannes (one a thriving cotton manufacturing center, the other a withering agricultural and administrative town) had sharp political conflicts in the 1760s, local parallels to the conflicts taking place on the national level. At Vannes, the conflict pitted the presidial court against the council; at Troyes the merchants fought the bailiwick officials for control until an uneasy truce of 1773. In almost all French towns, from Lille to Toulouse, the merchants lacked full representation on the town council; indeed, in many cities, such as Nantes or Toulouse, a place on the town council ennobled the alderman and his descendants (the much despised *noblesse de cloche* or belltower nobility). That privilege tended, above all, to attract royal officials.

In the countryside, massive changes had taken place. Everywhere, the seigneurie declined; seigneurial courts lost power to royal ones. Noble income came increasingly from ground rent, not from seigneurial obligations. Even though some seigneurs tried to increase their income from the old sources, the far greater strain on the peasants came from the increased land rents. Many parts of the French countryside now came to be jumbles of manufacturing and agriculture. The combination provided new prosperity in many regions, and likely fueled the purchase of land by peasants in the second half of the century. In other regions, however, the new employment possibilities encouraged pauperization (a sort of early proletarianization), especially after 1770.

In some regions the peasantry owned far more land in the 1780s than they had owned in the 1680s, yet in others, such as the area near Toulouse, they owned less. Everywhere peasant property tended to be in small units, typically encompassing a house and a garden and little more, but a small minority of peasants did amass a farm with 12–25 acres of land. These people, the ploughmen, dominated the economy of rural society. They produced the grain surplus to feed the country. They obtained their larger holdings through rental contracts, leasing land owned by the urban elites, by nobles, and, in some regions, by the Church. In the Norman parish of Avremesnil, the skewed land distribution remained a constant from 1695 to 1787: in 1695, the twelve largest renters held 83 percent of the rented land. Among the 169 taxpayers, 107 rented no land and 31 others rented either one or two acres. In 1787, the situation looked much the same: the twelve people who rented more than 10 acres held 76 percent of the land. As for peasant ownership, the tax rolls suggested that only nine people owned their house in 1695 and that the taxpayers collectively possessed only 9 of the parish's 702 acres. In 1787, things had improved a bit: 16 taxpayers owned a house and the group held 39 of the 670 total acres.[5] The

---

[5] AD Seine-Maritime, C 1738, tax rolls of Avremesnil.

country probably had no more than one million ploughman families, even if we are generous in our definition of ploughman. In comparison, France had four or five million cottager and day-laborer families. In Lorraine, the percentage of ploughmen declined from 17.5 percent in 1737 to 13.4 percent in 1761, a pattern that continued in the 1770s.[6] Despite these difficulties, however, the overall standard of living certainly increased until the 1760s.

The rising standard of living in town and country led to new patterns of consumption. Ordinary people ate sugar and smoked tobacco. The better-off of the towns ate new foods (such as exotic vegetables), drank better wines, sipped coffee. In the cafés where they consumed their coffee and sugar, they read newspapers (another innovation of the eighteenth century), periodicals, and pamphlets; quite naturally, they discussed politics. These discussions created a genuine, fairly broad-based political society – public opinion – something that had never existed in France before. Even in the villages, people began to consider larger political issues. The comparison of the *cahiers de doléances* for the Estates Generals of 1576 or 1614 and those of 1789 shows how much more likely eighteenth-century French villages were to discuss national issues than their sixteenth-century predecessors had been.[7]

These 1789 *cahiers* also show us other dramatic changes. They rarely attack seigneurial courts, focusing much more typically on dovecotes and mills. They rarely mention soldiers, whose depredations had been one of the leading causes of complaint in 1576. They provide stunning evidence of the effectiveness of the reforms of Louvois and Choiseul that created barracks for troops and established a military supply system. They scarcely consider the Church, save to ask for the abolition of the tithe or for its use in poor relief. No more looting soldiers; no more widespread complaints of seigneurial abuse of power; no more recommendations for reform of the Church. The peasants of 1789 wanted tax equality: they wanted to create a land tax to replace other levies. Some of them, no doubt

---

[6] The overall figures come from a comparison of the total population, of the rural percentage of population, of tax rolls, and of the figures offered by marshal Vauban in his *Dîme Royale*. The figures on Lorraine come from M. Morineau, *Les faux-semblants d'un démarrage économique: agriculture et démographie en France au XVIIIe siècle* (Paris: Cahiers des Annales, 1970).

[7] J.-M. Constant, "Les idées politiques paysannes: étude comparée des cahiers de doléances (1576–1789)," *Annales ESC*, vol. 37 (1982), 717–728. The 1576 *cahiers* of 50 parishes in the area around Chartres are found in Bibliothèque Nationale, Mss. Fr. 26,324; *cahiers* for 1614, for the Troyes region, have been published by Y. Durand, *Cahiers de doléances des paroisses du bailliage de Troyes* (Paris, 1966) and commented upon by R. Chartier in several articles. Many of the *cahiers* of 1789 are published, in sources too numerous to mention here.

strongly influenced by the lawyers among them, demanded permanent Estates, which would vote taxes.

Let us not be fooled by the traditional language of such as the master *taillandiers* (metalworkers) of Nantes. They did not want traditional structures; they wanted new ones – in their case, control of the labor market. Everyone called to tradition in the second half of the eighteenth century, but let us remember that the same word has different meanings in different contexts. A call for a representative assembly in sixteenth-century France bore little resemblance to a similar demand in 1787. At the Estates General of 1614, the nobility forced the Parlementaires to sit with the Third Estate; in 1789, the Parlementaires proved to be the staunchest defenders of noble privileges – no one questioned that they would sit with the Second Estate. In 1614, bishops, cathedral canons, and abbots represented the First Estate; in 1789, parish priests provided more than half of the clergy's deputies. The name of the body was the same – the Estates General – but to suggest that the Estates of 1789 bore any substantive resemblance to those of 1614 is foolish. Those fighting to make the Estates look like those of 1614 had no chance of success, as the Parlement of Paris amply demonstrated in its anachronistic decision of September 1788, that the Estates should follow the rules of 1614.

One obvious sign that the Old Regime died long before 1789 is the frenzy of reform that the monarchy attempted between the 1750s and the 1780s. These reforms sought to bring the political system into line with the changed economic and social reality; they failed. We start the tale of the transition from one society to another with the Seven Years' War, which began – a perfect symbol of the changed world order of the 1750s – in the wilds of what is now western Pennsylvania.

The Seven Years' War

On 9 July 1755, two regiments of British regulars and an assortment of American colonial troops, engineers, road builders, and camp followers made their way through the dense forest near the Monongahela River, approaching the French Fort Duquesne. The sight of European regular troops of the line in the American wilderness must have seemed incongruous to some; to others, "a finer sight could not have been beheld, the shining barrels of the muskets, the excellent order of the men."[8] An hour later, these regulars loosed a volley at a handful of Canadian French and their Indian allies; the Canadians mostly fled, while the Hurons, Wyandots, and Shawnee scattered into the woods surrounding the

[8] P. Kopperman, *Braddock on the Monongahela* (Pittsburgh: University of Pittsburgh Press, 1977), 18, citing contemporary account of Thomas Walker.

British line of march. Three hours later, those 650 warriors and the handful of remaining French had annihilated a British–American force of 1,300, killing or wounding more than two-thirds of them. Braddock's Defeat touched off the greatest of the Old Regime wars, known in America as the French and Indian War and in Europe as the Seven Years' War.

The war burst upon a France in full economic boom, a surge in part fueled by the need to meet the internal pent-up demand for colonial products and colonial demand for French goods after the end of the War of the Austrian Succession. Sugar imports fluctuated wildly with the cycles of war and peace but the long-term trend moved sharply up; overall foreign trade increased from 190 million *livres* in 1726 to 484 million *livres* on the eve of the Seven Years' War. Industrial production, too, jumped rapidly in coal, iron, and especially, cloth: cloth production at Rouen doubled between the late 1730s and the early 1750s. Grain prices remained fairly stable, so that the years between the two great wars seemed a Golden Age to many a French worker or peasant.

That Golden Age did not long survive the start of the war. Once full-scale war with Britain broke out (1756), trade with French colonies dried up: sugar imports dropped 90 percent and overall commercial activity declined by more than half. Many of the workers hired in the late 1740s and early 1750s lost their jobs; iron, coal, and cloth production all plunged. Textiles in particular suffered a dramatic decline, with the loss of their African and American markets.

The dramatic trade fluctuations represented mercantile response to anticipated political events. On the eve of war, merchants built up stocks, so that real decline only set in by about the third year of hostilities. Much of the fanatical trading of the immediate postwar years merely reflected pent-up demand. The economic malaise evident by the third year of war had a dramatic impact on government policy; by year five, the economy (and royal finances) would be in disastrous shape – French military fortunes suffered the consequences (in the Americas, 1759, the fifth year of colonial fighting, proved fatal for France).

The Seven Years' War brought with it a diplomatic revolution: France allied with its traditional enemy, Austria – that is, the two great warring dynastic families, Bourbon and Habsburg, now found themselves on the same side. Britain and Prussia, now a full-fledged Great Power, provided the opposition. Russia, for the first time, became seriously involved in a central European land war. As the tale of the unfortunate armchair general Edward Braddock suggests, the war took place throughout the world, wherever the French and British empires clashed. The first conflict took place in what is now Pennsylvania, in 1754, but the empires fought informally elsewhere: Admiral Boscawen captured two French ships off the Grand Banks in June 1755 and Admiral Hawke, in official privateering, captured 30 million *livres* in prizes. Key fighting took place in Canada, the West Indies, and India. The French lost almost all the key battles. Although France and Britain did some fighting in Europe, their real war concerned colonial empires. The Seven Years' War proved decisive in the evolution of European imperialism; henceforth, there could be no question that Britain would be the dominant imperial power.

In Europe itself, the war was a tragic farce. At the beginning, Prussia faced three Great Powers: Austria, France, and Russia. The fighting favored first one side, then the other. Frederick the Great of Prussia, widely considered the best general of the day (although he lost nearly half of his major battles), routed a combined Imperial and French force at Rossbach (November 1757) and annihilated the Austrians at Leuthen a month later. He appeared on the verge of victory, yet the forces opposed to him finally wore him down. He lost battles to the Austrians and Russians – the latter even burned Berlin – and appeared on the edge of defeat in 1761. The death of the Tsarina Elisabeth and the succession of Tsar Peter III, a personal admirer of Frederick, led to rapid reversal; Russia withdrew its alliance from Austria and sent aid to Prussia. The tragedy whimpered to an end in 1762, leading to the treaties signed at Hubertusburg (ending the German fighting) and at Paris (Britain and France) in 1763.

Seldom have so many died for so little. The European fighting restored the territorial status quo. That result did mean the balance of power had a new, permanent player: Prussia, now firmly in possession of Silesia and of Great Power status. In addition, the war marked the permanent entry of Russia into central European politics. The Seven Years' War marked the beginning of 150 years of stability in the composition of the five Great Powers: until 1918, they would remain Austria, Britain, France, Prussia, and Russia (albeit in changing power configurations).

For the French, the most important fighting took place in America, India, and on the seas. The British Navy demolished the French Navy, most critically off the coast of Brittany (Quiberon Bay, 1759). The French and their Native American allies routed the British on all fronts in 1757, yet a concentrated effort by the American Colonies themselves and by the British government (after 1757 under the control of the effective hard-liner, William Pitt the Elder) bore fruit in 1758 and 1759. British expeditions captured Louisbourg and Québec City. By 1760, Britain controlled all of Canada and the Ohio River valley system. In India, Robert Clive captured virtually all of the French enclaves. The French army in Europe also gave a dismal account of itself, certainly its worst overall performance in any war fought by the Bourbons.

The Treaty of Paris, unlike the Peace of Aix-la-Chapelle, was a victor's peace. In 1748, no one had been happy: the French did not like giving up the southern Netherlands, the British (especially the American colonists) felt cheated when they had to give back Cape Breton and Louisbourg. In 1763, there would be none of that. The British got almost everything: Canada, the northern Atlantic islands (except two tiny, albeit economically vital ones kept by the French so they could continue to fish the Grand Banks), India (save Pondicherry), and Sénégal. France got back only two of its lost Caribbean islands, Martinique and Guadaloupe; Britain got the others (Tobago, Saint-Vincent, and Grenada). Spain traded Florida to Britain for Havana and received French Louisiana in compensation.

The Seven Years' War touched off a wave of national soul searching in France, much like the Franco-Prussian debacle of 1870 would do a century later. The war cost a staggering 1.5 billion *livres*. The government's finances never recovered from the shock, not only because of the size of the debt but because of the way the government managed it. The financial albatross of the Seven Years' War hung around the monarchy's neck until its death. The monarchy had a sound financial footing in the early 1750s: direct taxation increased, with the introduction of the permanent *vingtième* in 1750, to a total of 100 million *livres* a year. The indirect taxes, leased to the General Farm syndicate, produced about the same in the early 1750s but considerably more after the end of the Seven Years' War. French financial resources rose steadily after 1740, reaching 250 and then 270 million *livres* a year. Annual ordinary government spending ran about the same – indeed, in most years, slightly more. How could one finance a war costing 1.5 billion *livres* from such resources?

The obvious answer was that one could not. As in all early modern wars, the government resorted to one of two extraordinary (i.e., short-term) means to raise the money: they could raise taxes or borrow. In a policy remarkably familiar to Americans who lived through the final stages of the Cold War, the government chose to borrow rather than to tax. Jacques Necker, later director of the king's finances, explained the rationale for such a policy:

A need of 100 million comes up in a society. There are two ways to obtain it, either by ordering a tax contribution for that sum or by borrowing it, and establishing a tax which merely pays the annual interest on 100 million. When [public] confidence permits the success of the second method, it is the easiest and most commodious for all of society.[9]

[9] Cited in H. Lüthy, *La banque protestante en France de la Révocation de l'Edit de Nantes à la Révolution* (Paris: S.E.V.P.E.N., 1961), II, 466.

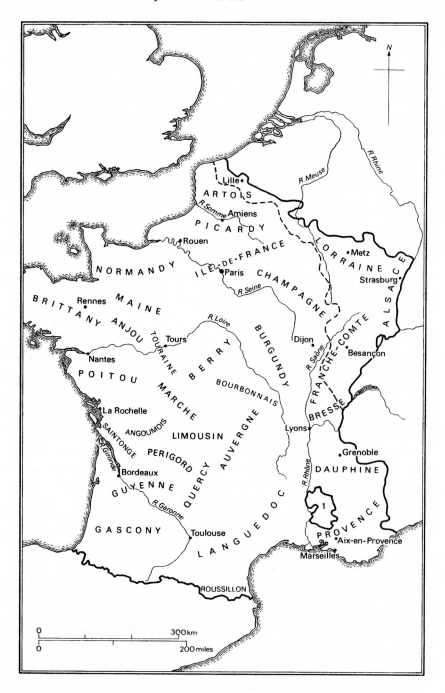

The end result of such borrowing looks rather familiar, too: ever-mounting interest payments fueling steadily increasing deficits. The French government did raise taxes – notably by means of added *vingtièmes* and new grants from corporations such as the Church – but nearly two-thirds of the money needed to pay for the war came from borrowing, either in straightforward loans (59 percent) or in sales of offices (5 percent). The use of credit peaked early in the war; in 1757 and 1758, 86 percent of the extra money came from borrowing. As the realization set in that the war would last, new taxes appeared ever more inevitable. Lenders also became more suspicious of subscribing royal loans, given the French king's long track record of partial bankruptcies. Wary lenders demanded higher interest; rates offered to the government rose between 50 and 100 percent during the war. Whenever possible, the government sought to use an intermediary – the General Tax Farm, the provincial estates, or towns – to borrow, because those bodies had better credit ratings (and thus paid lower interest). In many cases, the inter-mediaries themselves paid the interest bill, even though they could not list such payments as part of their contribution to the royal treasury.

The Seven Years' War, more than any other event, created the precipitant cause of the government's eventual collapse: financial insta-bility. The previous two centuries had hardly been a period of fiscal stability, so why did the financial burden of the Seven Years' War have such different consequences than burdens created by earlier wars? In the earlier cases, the government defaulted on a substantial portion of its debts, either by straightforward non-payment or by consolidation at lower rates of interest. The enormous debt burden created during the War of the Spanish Succession increased debt service payments by only 20 percent; why could not the government handle the debts from the Seven Years' War in the same manner? Because failed financial reforms provided a leitmotif for public debate throughout the final four decades of the monarchy, we must first summarize the developments in French government finance between the Seven Years' War and the meeting of the

---

Map 6.1 France in the middle of the eighteenth century: 1. Avignon and Comtat Venaissin: owned by the papacy. Broken/dotted line indicates boundary of France in 1643; note that France had also added all of the enclaves, except the Comtat.
Source: Rizzi-Zannoni, *Atlas historique de la France Ancienne et Moderne* (Paris: Desnos, 1766), large map, outside of the text, supplemented by plate 33. Map bears the title "La France Renaissante sous le Règne heureux de Louis XV le Bien-Aimé" (France reborn under the happy reign of Louis XV, the Well-Beloved."

Estates General (1787), before we examine the dramatic changes in political culture during the 1750s and after.

The legacy of failure: government finances, 1754–1789

The lynchpin of governmental reform had to be financial reorganization. During the Seven Years' War the government relied on traditional devices: first on loans, then on increased direct taxes (a second *vingtième* – a tax of one-twentieth on income, mainly on income from land, such as rents), then on new indirect taxes and fees. Some of these loan policies proved particularly onerous; the state relied more and more heavily on life annuities, at high rates of interest. In 1758, the government first sold these annuities on two lives, for slightly lower interest (the rate varied from 10–14 percent for one life; it remained fixed at 8 percent on two lives). In 1759, the "reforming" controller general, Etienne de Silhouette, even managed to issue a loan guaranteed by the excess profits of the General Tax Farm. Dizzy with the success of this venture, he introduced a broad package of tax reform: suspension of *taille* exemptions for bourgeois of privileged towns and for royal officers (except those serving in Sovereign Courts, such as the Parlement), suspension of the *gabelle* privileges of several provinces, and a wide array of new taxes on the rich (taxes on liveried servants, on carriages, on coffee, etc.). He also suspended payments on the Royal Treasury. His disgrace followed quickly upon these unpolitic gestures.

His successor, Henri Bertin, lieutenant general of police in Paris, suspended Silhouette's "reforms," and introduced some of his own: a third *vingtième*, a doubled capitation for the privileged, and a 5-percent surtax on indirect levies. By 1763, the state owed something like 2.3 billion *livres*. When Bertin tried to register an edict that would preserve some of the wartime taxes in order to pay off some of the debts, the Parlements refused. Bertin, too, resigned, to be replaced by one of the leading councilors of the Parlement, Clément de Laverdy. We can easily contrast the relative ministerial calm of the first half of Louis XV's reign – two controllers general from 1730 to 1754 – with the frenzy of the second half: between 1754 and 1774, Louis XV employed Séchelles (1754–56), Peyrenc de Moras (1756–57), Boullogne (1757–59), Silhouette (1759), Bertin (1759–63), Laverdy (1763–68), Maynon d'Invau (1768–69), and Terray (1769–74) as finance ministers. Little wonder that fiscal policy lacked continuity.

The tale of constant ministerial turnover demonstrates the extraordinarily close relationship between the state apparatus per se and the Court. At every level of the administration, high-ranking officials had clients, often relatives, who honeycombed the ranks of the officers and *commissaires*. This pattern existed already in the seventeenth century; nearly half of the *commissaires des guerres* during Louvois's administration were his blood or marital relatives. In the eighteenth century, close ties between the controller general and the financiers (notably the Farmers General) paralleled the personal system existing in the finances of Colbert's time. Louis XIV had been a master at playing off the different factions of his time; Louis XV had much less success in that endeavor.

One must distinguish between two distinct elements of the central state apparatus: the highest echelons, such as the office of controller general, and the permanent administration. The permanent administration, such as the intendants of finance, tended to remain quite stable. The one exception to that pattern came, interestingly enough, in the early 1750s: four of the six offices changed hands, and a fifth one passed definitely from a father to a son, with whom he had shared it between 1740 and 1756. The *families* did not lose out: Boullogne and Trudeau passed their offices to sons and Taschereau gave his to a kinsman, Peyrenc de Moras (who passed it a year later to a cousin, Moreau de Beaumont). Nevertheless, the fact remains that the central financial administration lost four of its six intendants between 1751 and 1755; that rupture surely explains much of the loss of continuity of policy during the 1750s.

The intendants of finance, unlike the controller general, lived and worked in Paris. The Lefèvre d'Ormesson, for example, held one of the offices from 1722 until the intendants of finance were abolished in 1777; their office oversaw all matters related to the receipts general. The Lefèvre d'Ormesson chaired a weekly meeting (at their home) of the major receivers general; Lefèvre d'Ormesson then informed the controller general of what he and the receivers general – who were, with the Farmers General, the state's bankers – had decided. The Farmers General, too, lived in Paris, and met regularly with an intendant of finance. These three groups of people – intendants of finance, receivers general, and Farmers General – really decided state financial policy. We might profitably divide the central government into two parts: the permanent administration, installed in Paris, and the ministerial leaders, who split time between Paris and the Court (Versailles).

The personal factor played a critical role in the instability at the highest levels of French government after the death of Fleury. The cardinal's *personal* influence over Louis XV helped to maintain a certain stability in governmental policy and personnel – Orry, for example, served as controller general from 1730 until 1745. Orry, in a pattern soon to become all-too-familiar, lost his position because the king's mistress, Mme. de Pompadour, speaking on behalf of her relatives, the financier

Pâris brothers, agitated for Orry's dismissal. As controller general, he placed too much scrutiny on military supply contractors (i.e., the Pâris brothers). Orry's successor, Machault, lost his ministerial posts in 1757 because of a similar falling out with Mme. de Pompadour (and, not coincidentally, the Farmers General). Later, in the 1760s and early 1770s, the Court would be divided along personal lines; dismissed ministers had invariably lost the confidence of the permanent administration in Paris. Policy considerations aside, personal intrigue at the Court provided one of the dominant motifs of French state development in the eighteenth century.[10]

Nowhere does this private impact on state development come through more clearly than in international affairs. Louis XV carried on two parallel diplomacies, one through his regular foreign minister, and the other through a private channel, known as the "Secret." Louis allowed his cousin, Louis François de Bourbon, prince of Conty, to carry out a separate, secret diplomacy through much of the 1740s and 1750s. Conty reported personally to the king about the results of his negotiations. The secret efforts began with Conty's attempt to obtain election as king of Poland (1745–46), but continued into the diplomatic maelstrom of the Seven Years' War. Conty, although the originator of the "Secret," lost his special place in late 1756, when the king forced him to stop his private diplomacy.

In fact, Louis did not end the private diplomacy, he merely transformed it into the "Secret of the King." The directorship of the "Secret" fell to Charles François, count of Broglie, then ambassador to Poland. Broglie's chief ally was Jean-Pierre Tercier, first clerk of the foreign ministry. In 1759, the new War minister, the duke of Choiseul, obtained the resignation of Tercier, but this disruption of the link between the two diplomatic channels only drove the "Secret" further into the private sphere of Louis XV, interested as ever in the election of a new Polish king (1760).

Louis continued this secret diplomacy through the end of the reign,

[10] Peter Campbell, in his stimulating presentation of certain issues, *The Ancien Régime in France* (London: Blackwell, 1988), argues that "the court was also the centre of power, the nerve-centre of the realm" (67). Campbell's argument here, in my view, underestimates the powerful role of the permanent administrative apparatus in Paris. What we need to do is to combine an understanding of the interest group politics being played out in Paris and the personal politics to which it gave rise at Court. Unfortunately, we do not have any scholarly studies of the inner workings of the Court, such as monographs on the first gentlemen of the king's bedroom and other important Court posts. The possessors of these Court posts had daily access to the king and played a central role in Court, and thus state, intrigue. Lacking detailed monographic studies on which to rely, the synthesizer can only point out the importance of Court intrigue and hope that future scholars will bridge this gap.

conducting private negotiations with Britain and Austria, among other powers. In the end, the jealousy of the foreign minister and the discovery that the Austrians had intercepted much of the correspondence of the "Secret" combined to lead first to Broglie's disgrace, and then to the disintegration of the "Secret" network itself, abandoned after Louis XV's death. This private diplomacy, which sometimes worked in conjunction with that of the foreign ministry but at other times (as in the early 1760s) worked directly against it, highlights the worst aspect of the personalized system of power established by Louis XV.

The desperate financial and diplomatic situation of 1763 prompted a public outcry and a genuine public debate, clear evidence that a meaningful "public opinion" had come into being during the 1750s (a matter to which we will return below). The program set forth in one prominent pamphlet, Roussel de la Tour's *Richesses de l'état*, touched off a conflict over the best means for dealing with both the long- and short-term financial problems. His main suggestion – raise taxes on the rich by taxing landed wealth irrespective of the status of its owner – looked quite similar to certain aspects of what Silhouette proposed. Roussel (like Orry before him) demanded an accurate national land register (cadaster). He further demanded the abolition of the General Tax Farm, which he claimed paid the king only a third of what it collected.[11]

Roussel set forth two of the three basic complaints about the tax system that dominated discussion of reform for the next three decades: elimination of privileged exemptions and state control of state finances. Large segments of the royal administration itself had no difficulty accepting either argument. The powerful forces arrayed against these two changes included the General Tax Farm and those privileged people who believed that preservation of the old order provided their sole defense against heavy taxation. As for the third element of reform, public presentation of the government's accounts, the royal administration simply refused to divulge its secrets. To do so would have been to admit that public opinion, not royal will, was the final arbiter of national policy.

In 1770, Louis XV tried again, this time combining radical institutional reform of the judiciary with a new assault on the financial problem (the judicial reform is treated below). The new controller general, Abbé Terray, convinced the king to take some decisive steps. He began with a partial bankruptcy, transforming the ruinous tontines into simple life

---

[11] The claim had some merit. The General Tax Farm subleased to regional tax farmers, who, in turn, subleased to local ones, who often subleased to still others (down to the level of the parish). Even assuming an entirely honest administration (certainly not a valid assumption), profits of 10 percent at each level of subleasing would have diminished the king's share to under 50 percent, allowing also for legitimate costs of collection such as paying staff, rent of offices, and writing expenses.

annuities, reducing the rate of interest on most other annuities, suspending payment on rescriptions and General Tax Farm notes, carefully
leaving to one side the *rentes sur l'Hôtel de Ville de Paris*, widely owned by
members of the Parlement of Paris. These economies reduced the deficit
from 100 to 30 million *livres*. The Parlement actually agreed to the
rescheduling of the debt, a policy its members favored over new taxes.

Terray had other tax-related changes in mind; before he introduced
these edicts, certain to be less than popular in the Parlement, he and
chancellor Maupeou engineered the disgrace of their ministerial colleague, Choiseul. Maupeou then convinced the king to issue an edict
reaffirming the absolutist principles he set forth in the 1766 Seance of the
Scourging. The Parlement responded by suspending judicial operations.
This political crisis led to the abolition of the Parlements and their
replacement by a new court system. With the Parlements out of the way,
Terray could introduce his new taxes, especially the new verification
system for the *vingtième*, now a permanent tax. Even the new Parlements
raised some objections to the threat to their property but, eventually, they
acquiesced.

Terray's reform of the *vingtième* declarations improved them only
slightly. He did manage to introduce a remarkable change, however; he
successfully ordered the intendants to collect accurate data on annual
births (baptisms). For the first time, the government would begin to have
accurate data on population. He also abolished a number of the payer-
treasurers, such as those for the Parlements, and cut some supernumerary
paymasters in the royal household and administration. Finally, Terray
responded to public outcry about high grain prices by abandoning the
deregulation policy of Laverdy and reregulating the grain trade. In 1774,
however, the unpopular Terray and Maupeou lost power when Louis
XVI succeeded to the throne.

The state immediately lurched forward to another "reform" program,
this time under the well-known *philosophe* and Physiocrat, Anne-Robert-
Jacques Turgot. Turgot's father, Michel, had been provost of the
merchants (chief municipal officer) of Paris; he himself was a fourth-
generation master of requests. He had served as intendant of Limoges,
where his experiments with the *taille tarifée* and with other "reform"
policies had won him great praise. He belonged to a group of economic
thinkers known as the Physiocrats, who believed in free markets and in
the dominance of agriculture in economic life. As one might expect of
such a man, he quickly rescinded Terray's new grain controls, once again
allowing free shipment of grain under most circumstances. Like
Maupeou and Terray or Silhouette or Machault, he attacked corporate
society. He tried to improve the collection of the taxes that could hit the

rich and privileged (the capitation and *vingtième*) and he abolished the guilds. The guilds, like the Parlements, represented privilege; like the Parlements, they had powerful financial tools to protect their interests. When Turgot fell, his replacement had little choice but to revive the guilds, from whom the government borrowed so much money.

Turgot suffered disgrace because the king would not stand behind the changes. The parade continued: Clugny and Taboureau de Réaux in 1776 and 1777, Jacques Necker from 1776 to 1781, quickly followed by Joly de Fleury, Lefèvre d'Ormesson, Calonne, and two nonentities standing in for Loménie de Brienne and later for Necker again.[12] We can see poor Louis XVI lurching from one extreme to the other: Necker was a Swiss Protestant banker; Joly de Fleury and d'Ormesson came from two of the most prominent Parlementaire families; Calonne was a man universally detested by the Parlements for his role in the La Chalotais affair in the 1760s; Brienne admired Necker and followed many of his reforms. These ministers followed wildly different policies; in many cases, those policies stemmed less from conviction than from political expediency. No matter where he turned, Louis XVI had no more success than his predecessor in establishing a consistent policy.

Necker tried the most radical institutional reforms. He abolished a wide variety of disbursement officials, trying to create a small number of officials with the authority to make payments. He created single treasurers for the Royal Household as well as for the army and the Navy; the latter two replaced the twenty-seven military disbursement officials. Necker even abolished the receivers general, the extraordinarily powerful receiver-bankers who collected and disbursed the income from direct taxation. This abolition, which would have overturned the entire fiscal system, did not survive his disgrace in 1781.

As an administrative reformer, Necker pursued admirable policies; as a finance minister, paying for actual expenses, he followed disastrous ones. Politics intervened to create greater fiscal burdens on the state. The American colonies revolted against Britain in 1775; they turned to Britain's ancient enemy for support. France first provided some financial support but then (1778) entered the war on the American side. Most of the fighting between France and Britain took place at sea – in the West Indies, off the coast of North America, in India. In a clear testimony of the effectiveness of the Choiseul–Praslin reforms, the French Navy acquitted itself admirably, gaining some notable victories (especially

---

[12] Neither Necker, Joly de Fleury, nor Brienne held the portfolio of controller general, even though they clearly set royal fiscal policy in the years in question. Necker, as a Protestant, could not legally hold the office; the king named him director general of finances, a title also used for Joly de Fleury and Brienne.

those at Yorktown and in India). French naval success, and the French expeditionary force fighting beside the American army, helped the Americans to gain their independence at the Peace of Paris (1783).

Successful though it was, the war cost money, lots of money. Necker borrowed to pay for it, using all of the discredited methods of his predecessors, particularly the onerous lifetime annuities. Foreign investors, such as the Genevan bankers, flocked to buy the annuities; in 1779, they could get 10-percent interest on an annuity guaranteed by one life, 8.5 percent on an annuity guaranteed by two lives: as long as the designated person(s) remained alive, the government would have to pay the annuity. The government did not reimburse the principal. By choosing young healthy "lives" (a ten-year-old girl was ideal for the purpose), bankers would make a fortune. Genevan bankers created the ultimate sophisticated manipulation of the system: they bought 60 million *livres* of lifetime annuities, 2 million *livres* each on the lives of 30 young girls (1784). They then sold combined shares in the 30 separate annuities, allowing investors to spread their risks. When poor little Pernette-Elisabeth Martin died in July 1788, taking two million *livres* of capital with her, all Geneva mourned her loss.[13]

Mlle. Martin's early death notwithstanding, the French government lost a fortune on these annuities, making payments into the 1790s on loans taken out during the Seven Years' War. The American war merely added to the burden: a total cost of between 1.5 and 2 billion *livres*, most of which the government simply borrowed, paying interest that often reached 10 percent. Year in, year out, the situation got worse. Annual income now ran to more than 350 million *livres* but expenses, other than war, reached more than 400 million, about 40 percent of it for interest. The government expanded its old technique of borrowing through intermediaries: the estates of Languedoc, Brittany, Burgundy, and Provence together borrowed 100 million *livres* in 5 years. The town government of Lille, which had paid 264,000 *livres* for debt service in 1770, paid 431,000 *livres* by 1787. Yet borrow as they might, the government and its intermediaries could not keep pace with war expenses. By 1781, the state once again tottered on the brink of bankruptcy.

Necker, recognizing his precarious position, decided to take an unprecedented action: he published his *Compte Rendu au Roi* – a report to the king on his finances. The book proved an instant success, selling 6,000 copies the day it appeared. For the first time – so Necker claimed – the public had accurate information about the state of the kingdom's finances. Necker offered a disingenuous picture, excessively praising his

[13] Lüthy, *La banque protestante*, II, 478–81.

own administration and its economies: he even stated that the regular budget showed a surplus of 10 million *livres*. Such figures had little to recommend them. The real deficit likely ran to 50 million *livres*.[14]

Some of Necker's other points, while exaggerated, rang truer. He excoriated the excesses of the Court, pointing out that pensions cost 28 million *livres* a year, a figure that shocked his contemporaries (he even had the temerity to list many of the individual ones, causing tremendous infighting at Court – which, among other shocks, learned that Marie-Antoinette's favorites, the Polignac family, received 700,000 *livres* a year). His figures, when carefully examined, showed how much money disappeared long before it reached the Central Treasury: excluding money from loans, 40–43 percent of the tax money had to be paid out at the local or regional level, or to special treasurers who reimbursed annuities (such as those guaranteed on the General Tax Farm). By 1788, this figure had risen to 55 percent.

The massive loans continued under Joly de Fleury: 180 million in 1781, 120 million in 1782 – a total of 653 million in five years. Again the state used lifetime annuities; again it paid absurd rates of interest – 10 percent in 1782, rising to 12 percent for those over 60; even 9 percent on two lives. As James Riley has pointed out, these exorbitant rates of interest did not represent real interest; they represented a risk premium, an advance against a suspected future government bankruptcy. Riley convincingly argues that the lack of fiscal soundness in French borrowing practices – for example, the inability to apply basic (known) life expectancy tables and amortization rates – did more to undermine the finances of the state than any other factor. The state paid massive risk premiums but then refused to carry out the bankruptcy for which it had paid in advance.[15]

In 1787 and 1788, the ministers in charge (Calonne, then Brienne) offered information about the financial situation. Calonne's figures for 1787 indicated revenues of 475 million *livres* and expenses of just under 600 million, of which more than half went for interest. In April 1788, Brienne provided another *Compte rendu* to the king, one that gave, for the first time, genuinely accurate information. Several historians erroneously call this the first real "budget" of the monarchy; we should rather refer to

[14] R. Harris, *Necker, Reform Statesman of the Ancien Régime* (Berkeley: University of California Press, 1979), has tried to argue that Necker's figures do add up but Necker's distinction between regular and extraordinary expenses (a distinction Harris accepts) is illegitimate. By this means Necker could hide expenses whose existence could be taken as a given, but whose precise size remained unknown at the start of the fiscal year. If one adopts such criteria, the budgets of much of the eighteenth century would balance.
[15] J. Riley, *The Seven Years' War and the Old Regime in France* (Princeton, NJ: Princeton University Press, 1986).

it as the first public budget of the monarchy. The documents on which Brienne relied, the preliminary statements of revenue and expense (the *états du roi*) had existed for centuries; in many cases, the government had very precise information about total expenses and revenues (under Sully, to cite but one example). The 1788 public budget, however, was the first one of its kind. It met one of the most insistent demands of the government's opponents: full disclosure of financial matters. The 1788 budget also called for two other reforms: the creation of a single central disbursement treasurer and the use by that treasurer of standard double-entry bookkeeping. The second of these measures – the use of double-entry bookkeeping – may seem a small technical matter, but it certainly was not. Without sound accounting principles, the government could not keep accurate track of its financial situation. To show the backwardness of France's fiscal system, we can remember here that Italian merchants had used double-entry bookkeeping since the thirteenth century, that Dutch ones had done so since the sixteenth, and that the Dutch and British governments had been doing so for well over 150 years.

The first measure, the creation of a genuine Central Treasury, culminated two decades of reform efforts. John Bosher has rightly emphasized the importance of the great reforms of 1787–88, which abolished virtually all of the great *caisses* – disbursement treasuries.[16] Henceforth, only five officials would dispense money: the new Central Treasurer, the treasurers of War and of the Marine and Colonies, the treasurer for Pensions and Debt (except the Paris *rentes*), and the Miscellaneous treasurer (responsible for the Royal Household, the police, most expenses in Paris, and various other expenses). These new administrators (although all of them previously held a similar position) no longer had venal offices. They no longer had the right to lend the king his own money: prior to 1788, as we have seen, the king's own disbursement officials would "advance" him the tax monies in their possession, at interest. This system of rescriptions had essentially collapsed by 1787, in part because several of its most important players – the receiver general of Rouen, one of the two War treasurers, and one of the two treasurers of the Marine – declared bankruptcy in the first half of the year.

One can hardly imagine a more desperate fiscal crisis than that facing the French monarchy in 1787–88. The annual budget carried a deficit of 25 percent; debt service amounted to a crushing burden, one that went up each year; anticipations of future revenues, which reached a record 240

---

[16] J. Bosher, *French Finances, 1770–1795* (Oxford: Oxford University Press, 1970).

million *livres* in 1788, consumed *half* the annual revenue; and several major receiver–treasurers declared bankruptcy. The government needed to do four things to solve the problems: (1) reschedule the debt at lower rates of interest; (2) expand the tax base; (3) get control of expenditures; and (4) reform the administration of taxes. Whatever criticisms one may offer of Necker, Calonne, and Brienne, they did try to remedy some or all of these problems. Necker focused on problems three and four; Calonne on problems two and three; Brienne on two through four. The failure effectively to address problem one undermined all these efforts, as we shall see when we return to the crisis of 1787.

Here we must leave the realm of finances and move into the broader perspective of political society. The government could not use the most obvious solution to the fiscal crisis, defaulting on its debts as it had in the past. Its inability to do so poses two questions: (1) to whom did the government owe the money? and (2) why could it not default on debts to these people? The most alluring possibility lies in question one. Perhaps the government could not default in 1765 because the people holding the debt differed from those who had done so in 1661 or 1721. Unfortunately, this simple answer does not work. Whether we examine the lists of *rentiers* in Brittany in the 1570s or those in Paris in the 1770s, we find the same social groups. Royal officers come first in line, followed by widows of royal officers (not only as heirs but as purchasers in their own right), merchants, *rentiers*, and Court nobles. Women held a substantial portion of the royal debt because they had such difficulties finding investment opportunities. When the king sold royal annuities in small enough denominations, people from the artisanal class, even servants, bought them. These people would form a syndicate, pooling their meager resources to buy a share in a royal annuity. In the seventeenth and eighteenth centuries, with the French capital market clearly having shifted to Paris, a disproportionate number of those holding royal debts lived in Paris. One of the largest elements of that debt, the *rentes sur l'Hôtel de Ville de Paris*, consisted of annuities paid by a special treasurer working for the city of Paris, so the capital's citizens felt themselves uniquely protected.

In the seventeenth and early eighteenth centuries, the government had few qualms about defaulting on its debts to these people. The government always made exceptions during the defaults: some people did not lose anything, others lost only a small portion. When the government reduced the rate of interest on annuities, royal letters often specifically exempted the annuities owned by powerful individuals. Similarly, when the king cut back on the *gages* of royal officers, he did not reduce all *gages* by the same percentage; the Parlement of Paris, in particular, often benefited from special treatment. By softening the blow to the most powerful, the king could ease its political ramifications. Even in the Law System bankruptcy, some members of the elite (such as high nobles) obtained inside information that enabled them to amass enormous profits by cashing in their shares for bullion just before the collapse. The entire situation eerily resembled the bankruptcy of 1634, when unprecedented numbers of financial officials sold their positions just before the edict reducing their *gages* and other payments. The consistent pattern of the big fish getting away at just the right moment makes one suspicious, yet no hard evidence remains to suggest a conscious policy or collusion among certain officers and the government (either in 1634 or 1721).

If the identity of the creditors remained the same – royal officers, town governments, guilds, merchants, some nobles, in short, those with cash – why then could the king no longer consider bankruptcy as a serious option in 1763? Because the political system had changed, those holding the debt now had sufficient political power to protect their interest. In a monarchy theoretically absolute, in a political system in which the government was incontestably more powerful than it had ever been, how could such a thing have been possible? Let us continue our examination of the death throes of the monarchy with that question, with a look at the confluence of political action and political ideology in the middle of the eighteenth century.

Political discourse and political action, 1750s–1780s

All the ministers whom I have had have always formed the project to put order in my household, but terrified in the execution [of their plan] they have abandoned it ... Calm yourself and allow to subsist an incurable vice.[17] (Louis XV, speaking to Choiseul)

The old quarrel over *Unigenitus* provided the dominant political issue of the 1750s; this time it manifested itself as the controversy over the refusal of sacraments. Without a certificate from a Constitutional priest, one could not receive communion. When the Constitutional clergy refused the viaticum to several dying Jansenists in Paris, the opposition clergy demanded, and got, intervention on their behalf from the Parlement of Paris. When we broke off from that quarrel in 1756, the king had forced the Parlement to register three draconian edicts, one of which abolished two of the Chambers of Inquiries; the Parlement, in response, had resigned en bloc. Many observers felt the actions of the two sides out of all measure with the importance of the issues. The duke

---

[17] On Louis XV's Court, see Solnon, *La Cour de France*, ch. 17.

of Choiseul, later to be the chief royal minister, wrote that to solve the problem, "it would require a king who had some strength and a bit of intelligence, and ministers who were not occupied with intrigues and their own interests. France had neither one nor the other."[18] Most of Louis XV's other councilors would not have questioned his intelligence; they would likely have agreed with Choiseul about the king's lack of strength.

In January 1757, scarcely a month after the mass resignations, Jacques Damiens, an unemployed servant (one who had worked for several of the leaders of the Parlementaire opposition), stabbed Louis XV with a four-inch knife. The king, at first fearing the worst, survived. In this hour of crisis, with full-scale war just broken out in Europe itself and the king apparently at death's door, the Parlement proposed a compromise, which the government accepted. Two and a half months after the attempt, the state mercilessly tortured Damiens to death on the *place* de Grève in Paris. Damiens's attempt to remind Louis XV of his duty (his stated reason for the attack) did accelerate political events. Not only did the king reach a rapprochement with the Parlement, he disgraced Machault and, shortly thereafter, d'Argenson, the secretary of state for War, and Rouillé, the Foreign Secretary. The king's ostensible reason for dropping Machault was that the minister had "betrayed" Mme. de Pompadour but surely the Parlement, against whom Machault had taken so hard a line, also agitated against him. He might have withstood the attack from one side, but could not survive both.

One "reforming" minister gave way to another. The historiography of eighteenth-century France is most remarkable in this respect: virtually every minister sought "reform"; many sought systematic reform, a dramatic break with the past. In finances, virtually the only controller general who is not called a reformer is Orry. First Machault, then his successor Silhouette, later Terray, Turgot, Necker, or even Calonne – all are "reformers." Elsewhere in the government, we find more of the same: Rouillé reforming the Navy; Machault reforming the Navy; Choiseul and Praslin reforming the Navy; Saint-Germain and Choiseul reforming the army. The problem in most cases (and the military reforms of Choiseul, Praslin, and Saint-Germain are notable exceptions) was one of reform tomorrow, reform yesterday, but never reform today.

What should constant "reforms" tell us? They strongly imply that the existing government had failed. Indeed, the conclusion is inescapable that the French government, in its most Alice-in-Wonderland stunt of all, managed simultaneously to get stronger and to collapse in the middle

---

[18] *Mémoires du duc de Choiseul*, eds. J.-P. Guicciardi and P. Bonnet (Paris: Mercure de France, 1982), 128.

of the eighteenth century. Administratively, the government possessed far greater strength than ever before. The administrative apparatus had become ever more like a real bureaucracy, one of routinized procedure and impersonal action, delving into the most private areas of life. Ideologically, the government had achieved a sort of philosophical bankruptcy. That philosophical bankruptcy prevented a financial one – the government did not have the moral authority to declare a politically risky default – and so made impossible a solution to the financial crisis within the existing political parameters. The government had lost the moral high ground, the legitimacy for action, to a new force in French political life: public opinion.

The ideological crisis involved the confluence of several independent yet related trends. First, the desacralization of the monarchy undermined support for the existing system. The king's personal behavior did much to undermine the monarchy. Many courtiers protested when the king allowed his mistress, Mme. de Pompadour, to be officially presented at Court; indeed, Louis had some difficulty finding anyone to present her. Many contemporaries deplored Louis's character. Choiseul, for one, blamed the king for the lack of morality at the French Court: "[T]he King . . . never thinks that his example authorizes all of the villainies that take place at the Court."[19]

Choiseul's personal losses (financial ruin after his disgrace in 1770) colored his judgment of some aspects of Louis XV's character, but the memoirs of the Court unanimously decry the moral turpitude of the king and his relationships with a series of official mistresses and with a staggering array of temporary partners. Each official mistress came from a lower social order than the previous one, a fact that progressively scandalized Court society; the final blow to the social order of the Court came in 1768, when the king took as chief mistress an illegitimate commoner from Paris: Mme. du Barry. He had even greater difficulties finding someone to present her at Court than he had for Mme. de Pompadour (not surprising, given that Court etiquette required that someone officially presented to the royal family prove their nobility back to 1400).

The desacralization involved more than the monarchy itself, even admitting that the king certainly accelerated its progress. The long-standing quarrel over religious matters with the Parlements called into question the sacerdotal quality of kingship. Public relations disasters such as the failure to perform the king's touch (1739) certainly added to the difficulties. Broader social and intellectual currents, however, also

---

[19] *Ibid.*, 65.

played a role. Many members of the elite turned away from organized religion. In the libraries of Parlementaires, works of theology declined from 19 percent of the books inventoried between 1734 and 1765 to only 6 percent between 1781 and 1795. A typical private library in Paris contained only 10 percent books on religion as against 25 percent on history and nearly one-half literary works. The aristocratic elite had a few more religious works – they formed 20 percent of the libraries of dukes and peers – but judges had 12 percent religious volumes and tax farmers only 6 percent. The judicial elite read more history than others; tax farmers read more specialized works on taxation, economics, and the sciences, as well as a much higher percentage of literature than other elite groups. Even among priests, the percentage of religious books in libraries declined, both in Paris and in the provinces. By the end of the Old Regime, a typical provincial priest's library had only two-thirds religious books; in Paris, the figure had fallen to 29 percent, fewer than the percentage of history titles. The share of religious titles among the books receiving official permission to be printed in Paris declined from 50 percent in 1700, to 33 percent in the 1720s, 25 percent in the 1750s, and only 10 percent in the 1780s. Meanwhile, the numbers of books in private libraries expanded enormously, especially among the upper and middle classes: nobles and legal men possessed an average of 300 books in the 1780s, as against the 20 to 50 of earlier in the century.[20]

The constant drumbeat of attacks by the *philosophes* against the Catholic Church had a tangential effect on elite adherence to the monarchy. If significant segments of the elite believed that the Church was a bankrupt and illegitimate institution, then the Church's special blessing on the king lost its value. If the king's adherence to God's law, as laid out by the Church, no longer protected elites because the Church no longer had the moral authority to proclaim its laws as God's law, then elites needed a new form of protection for that most vital of commodities, property. Many members of the educated elite turned outside the Church, joining secular clubs such as the Freemasons, a secret society that swept through the Atlantic world in the third quarter of the eighteenth century.

Unigenitus lasted so long as a political issue precisely because it summarized the key philosophical question of the time: what was the relationship of the king and the nation? In the beginning, people did not much concern themselves with the issue. Here we can remember that Louis XIV, on his deathbed, said that the state, not the nation, lasts forever. Yet Louis XIV (and Louis XV after him) erred in ignoring the

[20] R. Chartier, *The Cultural Origins of the French Revolution* (Durham, NC: Duke University Press, 1991), 69–71.

profound attack on the French *nation* embedded in *Unigenitus*. The Gallican opponents of the bull may have started as defenders of an ancient tradition – the independence of the French Church (i.e., Gallicanism) – but the changing political context of the eighteenth century turned that defense of an ancient tradition into something new, into defense of the French nation. The Parlementaires would never agree to a bull that they felt removed power from the French nation and gave it to an outsider – in this case, the Pope. When the king agreed to do so (or appeared to do so, because it came to the same thing), the Parlementaires and their allies began to think seriously about the relationship of the king and the nation. Even reactionaries now spoke about the nation in new ways; when the marquis de Grenolle demanded of Choiseul that the minister support Grenolle's cashiering of the commoner Lantier as an officer in 1763, he observed that the "military must be composed of the purest part of the nation."

By the early 1750s, with the dispute over the communion certificates, the Parlementaires had already reached radical conclusions about the meaning of nation. As War Minister d'Argenson wrote of the Parlementaires in exile in 1753:

All have applied themselves to studying the public law on the basis of the sources, and they confer about it among themselves as if in the academies ... In the general opinion, and as a consequence of the studies of these gentlemen, the opinion is being established that the nation is above kings, just as the universal church is above the pope. Anticipate what changes can occur in all governments as a result.[21]

We can see here the dramatically different flavor of new wine in old bottles. D'Argenson rightly reminds us of the ancient element involved in *Unigenitus*, the struggle within the Catholic Church over the relationship between the Church Councils and the Pope. The debate about conciliar versus papal supremacy lasted throughout the Middle Ages; secular theories of *royal* responsibility to representative bodies owed much to the medieval conciliarists such as Marsilio of Padua. By tying *Unigenitus* to that specific controversy, eighteenth-century Parlementaires tied their struggle with the monarchy to the medieval (and sixteenth-century) conflicts over the relationship of king and political nation. The new element, the idea that the nation is above kings, had powerful antecedents, in Britain and in sixteenth-century France, but the idea of the subordinate king represented a stunning break with the previous 150 years of French political tradition.

---

[21] Baker, *Inventing the French Revolution*, 33.

If the government had three basic functions – judicial, legislative, and executive – then the conflict would take place on all three fronts, on what Keith Baker has called the realms of justice, reason, and will.[22] The Parlementaires had long-standing rights to act as the king's judges; when the king tried to abrogate an entire category of cases from the Parlement, as he did with religious cases in the 1750s, they had to revolt. Similarly, when the king tried to express his arbitrary will, either by carrying out a policy by edict or by making law without consultation, the Parlement would object. Lastly, the Parlement called into question the monopoly of reason implicitly claimed for royal ministers. Richelieu had long ago established the maxim that reason guided the state, but all people's reason does not lead them to the same conclusions. To the Parlementaires, the king and his ministers suffered from what one might call the Platonist conceit: that the philosopher–minister would use his reason to provide the necessary solutions to the problems of government. The Parlementaires took the messier Aristotelian line, that the interaction of interested parties would produce the solution most amenable to civil society.

These two positions, profoundly rooted in deepest elements of western political culture, struggled for supremacy in late eighteenth-century France. One reforming minister after another claimed that he had the solution; the Parlements (and other corporate bodies) fought these reforms at every turn. They fought the reforms not only on purely selfish grounds – new taxes, to be effective, would have to have fallen on the rich – but on general, philosophical ones. Here our paradox makes sense. The Parlements fought so relentlessly against the reforms not because the government was weak, but because it was strong. Once the government got the reforms in place, it had the existing apparatus to enforce them. The reforms would overturn the *social* Old Regime as well as the political one. Corporatism, the very foundation of Old Regime society, would be destroyed. Given that obvious social and economic developments had undermined corporatism already, the government's abandonment of the corporate state could only be the final disaster for the privileged corporations. The one key weakness in the government's position vis-à-vis these corporations – its financial dependence on them – ultimately undermined the entire program of reform.

The political philosophers of the third quarter of the century alert us to the sharply different nature of political discourse. As Keith Baker, Mona Ozouf, Roger Chartier, and others have pointed out, French elites

[22] *Ibid.*, 25.

created a genuine public opinion in the 1750s.[23] No longer did members of political society address programs of reform solely to royal ministers, looking to the king as the ultimate source of political legitimacy and action; rather they now acted in what German scholar Jürgen Habermas has called the public sphere, a sphere defined by the culture of print.[24] They, like Roussel de la Tour, published pamphlets or articles in periodicals. Most frequently of all, lawyers arguing cases before the Parlement of Paris used a loophole in the censorship laws to publish their pretrial briefs, which could then serve as vehicles for discussion of government policy and even of a critique of the fundamental philosophical principles of the monarchy.

Many writers, like Voltaire, looked to Britain for a model. They did not see there democracy (far from it); they saw a system of government in which the dominant property-owning elites could protect their property and general interests from arbitrary government. In particular, those property owners had a clear say in lawmaking and in the manner and volume of taxation. The Parlementaires clearly belonged to this Anglophile wing of the reform. The effort to create a union of the Parlements in the 1750s marked only one stage in their efforts to establish themselves as the voice of the political nation. Throughout the second half of the century, the Parlements became increasingly vocal and strident in their assertion of the principle that the law stood above the king – a principle that negated the fundamental basis of "absolutism." In 1770, during the d'Aiguillon controversy (see pp. 250–56), the king's own *avocat général* at the Parlement of Bordeaux wrote that "royal orders which contravened the law, 'cannot but be considered as transient acts of a subverted will and not as permanent acts of a reasoned, free, and legal will.'"[25]

The most radical statements came from philosophers such as Jean-Jacques Rousseau, who took the current discourse on wills and made it a central theme of his *On the Social Contract* (1762). Rousseau distinguished three wills: individual, corporate, and general. Twentieth-century commentators usually focus on the contrast between the individual and general wills, yet Rousseau's contemporaries (and he himself in the text) feared the corporate will most of all. Corporations such as the

---

[23] By "public opinion," I do not mean the opinion of the entire population, only that of its politically active members. In the case of eighteenth-century France, that meant educated, fairly wealthy people – those who could write, or read and easily understand the printed political literature of the day. Such people deliberately set themselves off from the uninformed "people" or "populace," as Chartier and others have amply explained.

[24] J. Habermas, *The Structural Transformation of the Public Sphere* (Cambridge, MA: MIT Press, 1989).

[25] W. Doyle, *The Parlement of Bordeaux and the End of the Old Regime, 1771–1790* (New York: St. Martin's Press, 1974), 144.

Parlements, the Church, the *pays d'Etats*, the guilds, and the major towns
had special vested interests to protect: their privileges, that is, the private
laws that governed their relationship with the king and the state.
Rousseau believed that France had to destroy such privileges if civil
society were to become legitimate. Most Parlementaires did not take this
perspective. Caught between an ever-stronger government and the
apparent threat that government's enhanced potential for arbitrary action
posed, they sought protection in a traditional sphere, privilege, but
demanded a series of reforms that would adapt the English system to
French reality.

The most radical reformers invariably worked for the government
itself; for them, Rousseau's idea that the corporate wills had to be
destroyed made perfect sense. In the 1770s, a series of ministers sought to
destroy corporate wills by destroying corporations. The ministers also
felt quite comfortable with many of Voltaire's ideas; after all, Voltaire
essentially proposed a sort of philosopher–king, reform implemented
from the top down. The royal ministers may have disagreed with Voltaire
about the nature of the reforms to carry out, but they certainly agreed
about the methods for doing so. As the *Journal encyclopédique* said on 15
August 1763: "Everyone currently contests in wanting to be a Reformer." During the greatest effort at reform – chancellor Maupeou's
abolition of the Parlements in 1770–71 – Voltaire even wrote pamphlets
for the government.

The ideas of the Encyclopédistes – men such as Helvétius, Condorcet,
Diderot, even Rousseau – spread rapidly in elite circles. The people
discussing – not necessarily *accepting* – these ideas included the political
and social elite: Court nobles, Parlementaires, lawyers. The ideas of
reform especially attracted the young people. As we have seen, the king
recognized the old/young split in the Parlement of Paris; in his 1756
partial abolition of the Parlement, he eliminated two of the Chambers of
Inquiries, that is, the sections of the young judges. He (erroneously)
counted on the support of the senior judges, those of the *Grand'Chambre*.
The situation looked much the same everywhere; in Toulouse, Abbé
Audra wrote to Voltaire (1768) that:

I know Toulouse well enough to assure you that there is not, perhaps, another city
in the Kingdom with so many enlightened men. As for the Parlement and the
barristers . . . practically all under 35 are full of zeal and light.[26]

Many philosophes supported the Parlementaire party in the 1760s and
early 1770s, yet some of these same men supported Maupeou in 1771 and

[26] L. Berlanstein, *The Barristers of Toulouse in the Eighteenth Century* (Baltimore: Johns
Hopkins University Press, 1975), 121.

virtually all of them praised the elevation of Turgot to the ministry in 1774. The immediate aftermath of the Seven Years' War prompted near universal support for reform. In the changed political climate of the 1760s, with the newly created court of public opinion challenging the supremacy of the king, these reform proposals appeared not merely as memoirs on some minister's desk, but as pamphlets or other publications in the salons, cafés, and other elite gathering places of Paris and the leading provincial cities. Rousseau, after all, burst into prominence by winning an essay contest sponsored by the Academy of Arts and Sciences in Dijon, not in Paris. In the provinces, the Parlementaire elite dominated social, political, and intellectual life. Their unquestioned practical dominance of provincial life gave a new political meaning to their resistance to the king.

The white heat of events tempered these new political ideas, allowing the magistrates and others to forge them into a coherent alternative ideology. France had had only one tenable, coherent ideology for more than a century; by the 1750s, however, the royal monopoly on political discourse had ended. Rather than looking for causation between these new ideas and events, we do better to look at their interrelationship, at the gradual evolution of political ideas in response to political events, and of the influence of ideas on the course of events – and first on the actual reforms implemented by the various ministers.

Choiseul started with the army. He eliminated many of the regiments, fired large numbers of officers (virtually all of the commoners), and established a sort of grammar school for nobles wishing to attend the Military Academy at Paris (itself a creation of the reforming d'Argenson in 1751). Choiseul reformed the administration of the regiments: he created new treasurers, gave them real oversight authority, reduced the powers of colonels, removed recruitment from the captains, established full-time recruiting sergeants, tightened discipline, and established standardization more firmly. French troops, who had been relatively well supplied during the War of the Austrian Succession, suffered miserably in the Seven Years' War. Choiseul effectively mandated standard uniforms, better food rations, and better weapons. In the 1780s, the count of Saint-Germain would amplify these reforms, cutting down on the king's household troops, establishing Prussian methods of discipline, overhauling the artillery, and cutting superfluous positions (including those in the bloated militia). The reformed French army probably formed the most formidable force in Europe in the 1780s.

The Navy received the same treatment, first from Choiseul and then from his cousin, the duke of Praslin. The pitiful flotilla of 1748 grew rapidly during the Seven Years' War but the catastrophic losses of 1759 reduced the fleet once again. In the 1760s, the government continued to invest heavily, creating a real Navy of 45 ships of the line and 50 frigates by 1770, giving an enormous economic boost in the process to the royal Naval arsenals at Toulon and Brest. In 1769, Praslin even combined existing informal groups into a Naval Academy dedicated to the scientific study of ships and naval warfare. All this activity cost money; the king spent about 200 million *livres* on the Navy between 1755 and 1759. After a sharp decline at the end of the war, spending rose sharply again in the 1760s, putting further strain on the overall budget. Peacetime army spending, too, increased dramatically, especially under Louis XVI, reaching 124 million *livres* by 1788.

The state also reformed its economic activities, largely in response to the disastrous consequences of the war. The loss of Canada naturally eliminated French monopoly trade to the region; in fact, the government even repudiated two-thirds of the debt issued (60 million *livres*) to cover Canadian costs during the war. The monopoly company, the Company of the West Indies, lost heavily during the war, the value of its shares declining by more than 50 percent. Despite its successful efforts to float loans in the mid-1760s, the Company fell out of favor with the government, as the mercantilist principles it represented lost support. In 1769, the state abolished the monopoly of the Company of the West Indies. The government even allowed complete freedom (1764) in the circulation of the most heavily regulated commodity of the time: grain.

The ongoing reform problem – not whether to reform but how, most specifically under whose authority – first came up in 1763, when Bertin tried to register the edicts continuing the wartime taxes. The Parlements took the position that continuing the wartime taxes, in the absence of serious financial reform, made no sense. They claimed to defend the rights of the nation in refusing to register the edict: in Rouen, the Parlement's remonstrances referred to "the French Nation, whose mere name announces the liberty which is natural to it" when objecting to the edicts. Three years earlier, the same court had had the temerity to claim that, in the absence of the Estates General, the Parlements held the right to approve taxation. They had even begged the king: "Give us, Sire, our liberty; give us our Estates." Lest we misread such a demand, it should be noted that they likely meant the restoration of the defunct estates of Normandy, not the calling of an Estates General.

The Normans show how financial matters led to political ones. In fact, at the same time that the king sought to pass the "reforming" tax edicts, he confirmed a great victory for the Jansenists in the Parlement: the abolition of their chief enemies, the Jesuit Order. In 1761, during a lawsuit against the Jesuits by some merchants of Marseilles, the Parle-

ment condemned the Order to massive payments to creditors of individual Jesuits (and the Order itself) and then demanded a copy of the rules of
the Order (so did the king's council). One of the key members of the
Parlement's attack on the Jesuits, the judge who wrote the edict
condemning several Jesuit books and closing the Jesuit collèges, Laverdy, soon became controller general, an obvious royal effort to placate
the Parlementaires. The Parlement of Paris abolished the Jesuits in
France and ordered all members to leave France or to resign from the
Order and to swear allegiance to the Four Gallican Articles of 1682. The
provincial Parlements followed suit, led by the Parlement of Brittany,
whose *procureur général*, René de La Chalotais, issued a stirring denunci-
ation of the Jesuits.

Oddly enough, this final triumph of the Jansenists proved hollow.
Without the Jesuits, Jansenism became a non-issue. Indeed religious
toleration had spread so quickly and so widely, that Louis XVI seriously
considered offering a special promise of toleration to Protestants in his
coronation oath in 1774 (in the end, he did not). In 1776, Louis XVI even
named a Protestant, Jacques Necker, as head of his finances. The focus of
the struggle between the Parlements and the Crown now shifted from the
intersection of religion and politics to the realm of pure politics. The
struggle over *Unigenitus* had served for fifty years to focus debate on the
meaning of the term nation, and on the relationship of the nation and the
king. When the Parlement abolished the Jesuits, the debate could move
directly to the issue of the king, the law, and the nation. There can be no
more clear-cut symbol of this shift in focus than the entry of Laverdy and
Abbé Terray into the king's council as controllers general.

The Brittany Affair and the Maupeou "Revolution"

Laverdy and Terray alert us to the difficulty of viewing the political
conflicts of the eighteenth century in crude Crown-versus-Parlement
terms. Both Laverdy and Terray had long served in the Parlement of Paris;
Laverdy was one of its leaders. Yet each man readily abandoned the
Parlement to serve the king. Terray allied with no less a figure than the
First President of the Parlement, René Nicolas de Maupeou, in an effort to
destroy the Parlements. Problems in Brittany, involving attorney general
La Chalotais and the governor of the province, the duke d'Aiguillon,
provided the backdrop to the Maupeou "Revolution" of 1771.

The Brittany Affair involved all of the usual elements of eighteenth-
century French politics: personal enmity, patronage, Court intrigue, and
political principles. When the estates of Brittany resisted royal fiscal
demands (notably about road repair), the governor, the duke d'Aiguillon,

had the ill grace to offend La Chalotais, a client of Mme. de Pompadour and of the duke of Choiseul, then chief royal minister. When La Chalotais inserted language critical of d'Aiguillon into the registration of the royal financial edicts of 1764, d'Aiguillon protested to the king. Louis called La Chalotais and three compatriots to Versailles and sternly rebuked them, particularly La Chalotais (whose patroness, Mme. de Pompadour, had since died). When Laverdy introduced a special surtax without the consent of the estates (1764), the estates and the Parlement of Brittany opposed it. The government persisted, so the Parlement refused to render justice and then resigned en bloc. The king tried, with d'Aiguillon's support, to create a substitute Parlement; the old Parlement resisted, as did the local population. Anonymous letters attacking the king and the "*jean-foutres*" in the rump Parlement reached the secretary of state Louis Phélypeaux, count of Saint-Florentin (uncle of d'Aiguillon); someone accused La Chalotais of being the author. D'Aiguillon had him arrested and imprisoned at Saint-Malo. Rumors spread (not without foundation) that d'Aiguillon and the king himself wanted to behead the obstreperous old attorney general.

The other Parlements sprang to the aid of their Breton colleagues, reminding the king of his obligations to the nation; he responded (in a letter to the Parlement of Rouen) that he took his oath "not to the nation, as you dare say, but to God alone." The Parlement of Paris took up the cudgels for their provincial colleagues. In remonstrances of 2 February 1766, they stated the case, not simply of La Chalotais or the Parlement of Brittany, but of the entire social order they wished to defend. Protesting that the person of high royal officials (and noble peers) received protection from "a law of the state," they argued that:

If this law, Sire, can be infringed, all orders of birth and distinction, all bodies, all ranks, all dignities must henceforth fear the imperious force of absolute power . . . of sole power, to which all the legitimately established powers in the state would be subordinated.[27]

These remarks highlight the key issues for the Parlementaires: they wanted to defend a social order based on ranks and dignities (in which they included offices) and they no longer admitted that the "legitimately established powers in the state" (i.e., the Parlements themselves) should be subordinated to an "absolute" power. They took these positions on behalf of the "nation."

The king responded quickly. Without warning, he arrived at the Parlement on the morning of 3 March 1766, not to conduct a *lit de justice*,

[27] J. Rothney, *The Brittany Affair and the Crisis of the Old Regime* (New York: Oxford University Press, 1969), 173.

but to run Parlement personally. The duke de Croÿ, who witnessed the scene of the king crossing the Pont Neuf, called it a day that "was one of the most important and glorious of his life, and one which did him the most honor." Mincing no words, the king, at the Seance of the Scourging first denounced the "pernicious consequences" of the idea of Parlementary union (the *union des classes*) and the "erroneous principles" the Parlement advocated. He said it was only an illusion that the union of Parlements formed

the essence and basis of the monarchy; that it is the seat, the tribunal, the spokesman of the nation; that it is the protector and the essential depository of the nation's liberties, interests, and rights; that it is responsible to the *nation* for this trust ... that it is responsible, in all concerns of the public welfare, not only to the king, but also to the nation; ... that as a reciprocal guardian, it maintains the balance of government, repressing equally the excesses of liberty and the abuses of authority; that the parlements cooperate with the sovereign power in the establishment of laws [my italic].

The king reminded them that no one should

forget that the sovereign power resides in my person only . . . that my courts derive their existence and their authority from me alone; . . . that to me alone belongs the legislative power . . . that the public order in its entirety emanates from me, and that the rights and interests of the nation, which some dare to regard as a separate body from the monarch, are necessarily united with my rights and interests, and repose only in my hands.[28]

Louis had a clear idea of the issues at hand. The Parlement claimed to share in the sovereignty (i.e., in the ability to make law); it claimed to represent the "nation"; and it claimed that the interests of the nation superseded those of the king. The king, in contrast, believed that he held full sovereign power and sole ability to make law, that the interests and identity of the nation were coterminous with his own, and that the nation could not be superior to him. The later trial of d'Aiguillon (1770) in the Parlement of Paris brought out these straightforward philosophical differences. In the interim, the king had restored the Parlement of Brittany and withdrawn d'Aiguillon. The Parlement of Paris, not content with this victory, decided to try d'Aiguillon for malfeasance. The king withdrew the case from their jurisdiction.

Once again, we must pull back from the simple philosophical confrontation we would like to present. The First President of the Parlement in 1766 was none other than René de Maupeou, who, as chancellor in 1770, would lead the attack on the Parlement, along with another former

---

[28] *Ibid.*, 176–77 (for both quotations).

Parlementaire, Abbé Terray (now controller general). La Chalotais had lost his protectors: Mme. de Pompadour had died and Choiseul suffered disgrace in December 1770. Little wonder that the king would exonerate d'Aiguillon, now in favor with the ascendant Court circles; d'Aiguillon even joined the Council of State, as Foreign Minister.

In the late fall and winter of 1770–71, Maupeou and Terray convinced the king to precipitate a political crisis over the dual issues of financial reform and royal sovereign right to make law. As we have seen, the Parlement of Paris originally agreed to Terray's financial reforms but the abbé expected their opposition to his further changes. Maupeou then convinced the king to send an edict to the Parlement reaffirming the principles set forth in the Seance of the Scourging. The Parlement of Paris responded by suspending judicial operations.

To that point, the political kabuki of minister and Parlement had followed the familiar gestures: unpopular royal edict, remonstrances, royal rejoinder, suspension of justice by the judges. Even Maupeou's use of musketeers to demand a return to service, and the exiling of the judges after their refusal, had several precedents. Maupeou, himself the First President of the Parlement from 1763 to 1767 and a judge (and then president à mortier) for thirty years before that, decided to follow a new choreography. He created a new court. Finding himself boxed in by his hard line, he continued to push harder and harder: he added six conseils supérieurs (all in cities without Parlements) to hear the non-political cases formerly heard by the Parlement. In April, Maupeou's rump Parlement had to register an edict abolishing its offices and creating a new court to take its place. He then purged all of the provincial Parlements, abolished the Paris Court of Aids and even some bailiwicks.

Most of his contemporaries found Abbé Terray an odious character. Recent historians, such as John Bosher, have pointed out that Terray started reforms that tried to streamline the financial administration; they paint a more positive picture of him. The same is true of Maupeou. Most historians portray him as a fearless reformer, the saviour of the monarchy, the abandonment of whose reforms was a "tragedy."[29] Or was he the villain contemporary opinion made him out to be?

Historians generally fall into two categories. One group emphasizes the positive side of ministerial efforts at reform. To them, a given minister – a Maupeou, a Turgot, a Necker – represented the best hopes for solving the monarchy's difficulties at the end of the eighteenth century. Similarly, the Parlements represented reactionary obstructionism, obsessed as they

[29] A. Cobban, *A History of Modern France, Volume I: Old Regime and Revolution, 1715–1799* (Harmondsworth, Middlesex, and New York: Penguin, 1957), 99.

were with defense of their privileges and property. Other historians view the end of the monarchy through a different looking glass: to them, the ministers represented royal despotism and corruption. The Parlements become the defenders of more than their own privileges; they become the only bastion protecting the nation from ministerial despotism. The problem arises because each group of historians examines only part of the problem. The pro-ministerial group looks only at the specific policy issue – for example, Necker's reform of the financial administration. If this reform was a good idea (and surely it was), then Necker becomes a hero. The pro-Parlement group looks only at process: so long as the state would not fully disclose its finances, the Parlements, as the only representative of the political nation, had no business approving any changes in the tax or administrative structure. The Parlements thus become what they were for their contemporaries: the sole barrier to further fiscal oppression.

Let us examine more closely these different interpretations, ones held both by eighteenth-century observers and by modern historians. The Maupeou reforms succeeded in many ways. At Bordeaux, for example, the new reduced Parlement actually dispensed justice faster (and cheaper) than the old one. The new order had abolished the *épices*, the official bribes paid by all litigants, replacing this money with direct payments from the government to the judges. The Maupeou reforms suggested that the Crown could finally break the Parlements, those most powerful protectors of the corporate order, and thus destroy the corporate state itself. The new courts did work reasonably well but the edifice rested on shaky ground. The Maupeou reforms lacked depth and the all-encompassing vision necessary for a complete overhaul of the system. As William Doyle has suggested, the reforms often proceeded on an ad hoc basis: Maupeou did not have a fully elaborated plan; he adapted to circumstances.

The dispute of 1771–74 highlighted the impossibility of reform in late eighteenth-century France. On the one side stood the Parlementaires and their allies, the so-called Patriot party; on the other side stood the ministers and their allies. Both sides agreed on certain basic principles of reform: improved finances, including broader taxation; sharper lines of authority, so that local officials could act more efficiently; and an end to the dominance of special interests. They disagreed about other important matters: who should have that authority; who were the special interests. The ministers focused on the privileges of the elites – the Parlements and their allies; the Patriots saw those privileges as liberties, as their protection against despotism. The Patriots believed the Farmers General and other ministerial favorites were the special interests who acted against the general interest of the state; the ministers and their allies

believed that corporate society as a whole was the culprit. The Patriots
wanted what Durand Echevarria calls negative liberty, protection from
arbitrary (governmental) behavior; the ministers wanted to clear away the
institutional and customary barriers to government action.[30]

These philosophical disputes took place against a background of
intense personal dispute at the Court. Maupeou and Terray relied heavily
on the protection of Mme. du Barry. When Louis XV died (May 1774),
their days were numbered. The new queen, Marie-Antoinette of Austria,
detested Mme. du Barry; Louis XVI locked Louis XV's ex-mistress in a
convent. Marie-Antoinette also detested Terray and Maupeou, in part
because of her affection for the disgraced Choiseul (whose family had
long served her father's house in Lorraine and who moreover had
arranged her marriage to Louis XVI). Beset on all sides by enemies of
Maupeou and Terray – the Parlementaires, the Parisian people, some of
the *philosophes*, and Marie-Antoinette – Louis XVI quickly disgraced
both men (24 August 1774). He clearly could not maintain the policy they
represented after dismissing the ministers.

Terray had pushed for higher taxes on the rich, surely a necessary
reform, albeit an unpopular one with the politically powerful. His debt
rescheduling also made sense as an overall policy, although the specific
mechanisms he adopted did not follow sound actuarial practice. Terray
probably increased royal revenue by about 40 million *livres* a year and
reduced expenses (mainly debt service) by the same amount. However
laudable some of Terray's goals and policies may have been, the methods
he used provoked profound unrest. He certainly used unethical and
illegal methods to raise taxes and lower expenses; he and his allies
(notably Mme. du Barry) enriched themselves in dubious schemes. The
entire Court stank of corruption by the 1770s. The list of those owning
shares in the 1772 General Tax Farm included Terray's family, his
notary, two of the king's daughters, Mme. du Barry, and even the king
himself. Even granting Marcel Marion's point that owning a share of the
General Tax Farm gave Louis XV complete information about its inner
workings, how does one explain the feeding frenzy of members of the
royal family and the inner circle of the entourage? In such circumstances,
Parlementaire and public suspicion of the motives of "reforming"
ministers seems entirely justified.

Maupeou's reforms created widespread sympathy for the Parlementaires, who had always enjoyed considerable popular support in Paris. At
a distance of 200 years, we tend to separate the reforms of Maupeou and
Terray but surely their contemporaries did not. When they fell, in the

[30] D. Echevarria, *The Maupeou Revolution* (Baton Rouge: Louisiana State University
Press, 1985).

summer of 1774, celebrations broke out all over France. In Bordeaux, the First President Le Berthon received a hero's welcome. The procession bringing him back to the city contained more than 200 carriages; the local Freemasons constructed a triumphal arch for him; the people danced in the courtyard of his home, part of festivities that lasted a full week. In Paris, the crowd stoned Maupeou's carriage, feted the returned Parlementaires, and hanged Maupeou in effigy on the *place* Saint-Geneviève, alongside an effigy of Terray atop a funeral pyre. By way of contrast, Choiseul had received tumultuous outpourings of support after his disgrace.

After Terray came Turgot, who brought some new ideas, such as the Physiocratic belief in free markets. He, too, tried to reform the king's finances and to attack corporate society. Where Terray took on the Parlements, Turgot abolished the guilds. He, too, failed. The spiral spun ever downward in the 1770s and 1780s, in the sense that the political consensus had been shattered by the struggles of the 1750s, 1760s, and 1770s. The system did not call forth another consensus after the failure of Maupeou's "'Revolution." The successes of the American War of Independence and the strength of several sectors of the economy (textiles, colonial trade) in the late 1770s and early 1780s masked the critical nature of the situation. The financial problem, however, could not be resolved; it led to the final collapse of the monarchy in a crisis that began in 1787.

7   The crisis of 1787–1789

The parlements, the nobility, and the clergy have dared to resist the king; in less than two years there will not be any parlements, nobility, or clergy.

Keeper of the Seals Lamoignon, July 1788

I was enjoying myself and watching my days go by when the French Revolution came suddenly and revived all our spirits [sic] And the word liberty so often repeated had an almost supernatural effect and invigorated us all . . .

Jacques Ménétra, Parisian glazier

The fiscal crisis quickly turned political, with the calling of Assemblies of Notables in 1787 and 1788 and of an Estates General in 1789. The monarchy had not used an Assembly since 1627 or an Estates General since 1614, which gives some indication of the government's desperation. The specifics of the conflicts of 1787 through 1789 can be followed elsewhere; let us begin with a very brief summary of events and then focus on the broader lines of the dispute.[1]

The king, at Calonne's suggestion, called an Assembly of Notables, hoping to compromise with the aristocratic opposition by forging an agreement on the common grounds of the Patriot and ministerial positions. The government primarily sought to rally public opinion in favor of new taxes – a stamp tax and a land tax – by means of having the Assembly actually vote such taxes. Given that Assemblies of Notables had never had the right to do so, the assumption that this Assembly could do so proved a fatal mistake. Calonne made a second mistake, following in the footsteps of Vauban, Orry, and others: he proposed a land tax collected in kind. Creating a massive new player in the grain, wine, and timber markets, an in-kind tax would have devastated the economic

[1] Three works stand out for their detailed presentation of these events. The classic treatment is that of G. Lefebvre, *The Coming of the French Revolution* (Princeton, NJ: Princeton University Press, 1959), a translation of his *1789* (Paris, 1939). Lefebvre's interpretation has come under increasing criticism, so one should read the newer synthesis of W. Doyle, *The Origins of the French Revolution* (Oxford: Oxford University Press, 1980, 1988). For a detailed examination of events, one should turn to J. Egret, *The French Prerevolution, 1787–1788* (Chicago: University of Chicago Press, 1977), a translation of the French edition of 1962.

position of French landowners. Opposition in the Assembly combined with intrigues from rival ministers to lead to Calonne's disgrace.

Historians are too quick to criticize the Notables on the grounds that they wanted to preserve noble tax exemptions, conveniently ignoring the fact that nobles paid both the *vingtième* and the capitation; the surviving documentation on the former suggests that noble landlords paid substantial sums.[2] Calonne's successor, Loménie de Brienne, archbishop of Toulouse and one of the leaders of the Assembly's opposition, proposed a land tax levied in cash and administered by newly created provincial assemblies. The Assembly generally approved of this tax but did not actually vote to levy it, on the (entirely justified) grounds that they lacked the authority to do so.

The king sought, by means of the Assembly, to consult with the political nation; in so doing, he abandoned the ministerial form of government followed since the second quarter of the seventeenth century. That path ended in the 1770s, with the failure of the reforms of Maupeou, Turgot, and Necker. The Parlements and their Patriot party allies did not always object to the specific policies, but they objected to the unilateral action of the ministers, to what they saw as arbitrary or despotic government. Once the ministerial form of government could not reform, the king tried the only other available precedent, consultation through an Assembly and, later, an Estates General.

Brienne and the king did not get their vote of taxes but they did get tacit approval of the Assembly for a broad range of reforms. Brienne immediately followed the standard procedure for enacting these reforms: he sent edicts to the Parlement. The Parlement, meeting in this rare case as the Court of Peers (i.e., the Parlement of Paris, plus the princes of the blood and the thirty-four ecclesiastical and lay peers of France, most of whom had attended the Assembly), enacted some of the edicts. Here again, we look back with hindsight and see only the rejection of the tax edicts. The Parlement did enact many of the initial reforms proposed by the government (following the advice of the Notables). The Parlement approved the creation of provincial assemblies (June 1787), the reestablishment of free trade in grain, the conversion of the public works *corvée* into a cash payment, and the short-term loans.

Six major tasks lay ahead: the tax edicts, the reform of expenditures, the reform of the fiscal administration, the reorganization of the army and of the judiciary, and the granting of civil rights to Protestants. Before we turn again to the fight over the land tax, we would do well to remember that the Parlement eventually agreed to the expense reforms, to those

[2] AD Côte d'Or, C 5829, declarations for the *vingtièmes* by various Burgundian nobles in the 1740s and 1750s.

reorganizing the army and the fiscal administration, and to civil rights for Protestants. Two major sticking points remained: judicial reform and the tax bills.

In the midst of the internal political crisis, external events dramatically reduced the government's authority. France had held a strong diplomatic position in the early 1780s, due to the success of the American revolutionaries. Other powers noted, however, that France itself made only minor gains at the Peace of Paris (1783), a reflection of its fiscal exhaustion. In the mid-1780s, France's diplomatic position unraveled completely. In eastern Europe, Russia took the initiative, first seizing the Crimea (1783), then maneuvering the Ottoman Empire into war (1787). Closer to home, the Prussians invaded Holland (September 1787) to put down the Patriot party and restore the House of Orange; France, the ally of Holland (from the American war) and protector of the Patriot party, sat and watched, a humiliating example of the powerlessness induced, in large part, by financial problems.

Discredited abroad, stalemated at home, the drowning government of Louis XVI grasped at any available straw. The Assembly of Notables and, later, the Court of Peers, accepted the argument of the Marquis de Lafayette that only an Estates General, representing public opinion, could approve new taxes. Any reasonably astute observer could see this demand for what it was: an effort on behalf of the political classes to share sovereignty with the king. From voting the taxes, an Estates would move quickly to assert rights about lawmaking authority.

The king did not have the personal strength to create a firm policy in response to the conflicting demands placed upon him. Louis XVI lacked the qualities necessary for action. He had less intelligence than Louis XV and spent much of his time either hunting or tinkering with locks. Louis XVI failed to consummate his marriage to Marie-Antoinette for seven years (1770–77), making him the target of vicious satire in Paris (and throughout Europe). Court society waned even further; the real center of social life had long since shifted to Paris. Now Louis's cousin, the duke of Orléans, the richest individual in France, led the social whirl in his enclave at the Palais Royal. Orléans also became the focal point of political opposition: he played a major role in the Freemasons and served as protector to a reform society. Another such group, the Society of the Thirty, that included such high nobles as la Rochefoucauld and Lafayette, played a key role in the political events of 1788 and 1789, particularly in organizing a publicity campaign against the ministers.

Louis's queen, Marie-Antoinette of Austria, bore the brunt of most criticisms against the royal family. Louis's sexual inadequacies led to rumors of her infidelity; pamphlets and, later, pornographic illustrations, accused her of a wide range of sexual misconduct, including liaisons with the king's brother and with various of her female favorites. This unhappy couple stood at the center of events in 1787; neither of them had the will or the intelligence to organize a coherent royal policy toward events.

The king waffled in the face of demands, such as that for the calling of an Estates General (21 May 1787). That demand, first made by Lafayette at the Assembly, initially received little echo but, in the changed climate of the summer of 1787, it became the rallying cry of the Court of Peers, who issued a formal demand calling for the Estates in July 1787. Four months later, during the debate on yet another loan, Louis XVI announced to the Parlement of Paris that he would convene the Estates sometime before 1792. With that declaration, the end of the ministerial state and of the vestiges of the Old Regime were at hand.

An Estates General offered many potential pitfalls. The Estates had not met since 1614–15, so no one really had a clear sense of what its powers might be. In reality, the king had never recognized the principle that the Estates had to vote all new taxes, although the monarchy paid lip service to such a view in the late sixteenth century. The tax-approval demand of the Assembly and of the Court of Peers, cloaked as always in the vocabulary of tradition, in fact concealed a revolutionary meaning in the context of 1787–88. Indeed, some of the leaders of the Patriot party – people such as Lafayette or the duke of Orléans – seemed to have understood clearly the revolutionary implications of their demand.

The chronology of events in 1787 and 1788 followed the traditional lines. After the first Assembly, the king sent financial edicts to the Parlement, which refused to register them. The king held a *lit de justice*, the Parlement declined to implement the edicts thus registered, and the king exiled the Parlement to Troyes. Minister of State Malesherbes assessed the situation quite clearly:

I say that the Parlement of Paris is at this particular time merely the echo of the Parisian public, and that the Parisian public is the echo of the whole nation . . . We are dealing therefore with the whole nation.[3]

Brienne created a compromise tax package that the Parlement could accept and they came back, only to encounter another *lit de justice* about more financial matters (this time, loans). In January 1788, they even approved the dreaded land tax. We can note two vitally important differences in the traditional ballet of the king and the jurists: (1) the Parlement refused to register the taxes on the grounds that an Estates General had to vote them; and (2) as Malesherbes suggests, the Parlement stood not merely for itself but for an aroused public opinion.

[3] Egret, *French Prerevolution*, 98.

In May 1788, Brienne continued the offensive, introducing Lamoignon's plan for judicial reform. The plan stripped the Parlements of virtually all their cases. At the center, it created a Plenary Court for political cases, including taxation, by co-opting the senior magistrates of the Parlement of Paris (the *Grand'Chambre*), the peers, the senior crown officers, the princes of the blood, and various other high officials and personages. At the regional level, the reforms established Grand Bailiwick courts to handle in final judgment all civil cases involving 20,000 *livres* or less and all criminal cases not involving high-ranking individuals (such as peers or top royal officials). The reforms also abolished all torture and greatly modified the Criminal Code of 1670, as well as removing virtually all cases from seigneurial courts. Needless to say, the Parlements and their allies violently resisted. The nobility led the resistance in some provinces, such as Brittany, yet hung back in others, such as Burgundy or Dauphiné.

If we stop to consider the situation of the fall of 1788 for one moment, we can see why Egret and others consider it a "prerevolution." In Paris, the government had deprived the Parlement of its functions; completely reorganized the central financial administration; introduced several new taxes; drastically reduced the Court pensions; and reorganized the army. In the provinces, the government introduced the provincial assemblies into the *pays d'élection*, reduced the power of the provincial Parlements, and created the Grand Bailiwicks. A Frenchman leaving the country in 1780 would have been hard pressed to recognize its government in 1788. He would have recognized the frantic pace of reforms, one followed for nearly twenty years. He would have had one obvious question: will these reforms stick?

Historians usually seek the answer to that question in Paris, yet we likely can best locate it in the provinces. The ideas of the Enlightenment had percolated deeply into French society. People all over France subscribed to the *Encyclopedia*: in Paris to be sure, but also in Lyons or Toulouse (which ranked second and third in subscribers). Provincial cities developed their own newspapers, like the *Affiches et annonces de Toulouse*, which originally floundered in a series of lawsuits by corporations who felt attacked in its pages but then returned to offer literate Toulouse an outlet for its burgeoning political culture. Twenty-two French cities had Academies of Science; more than 6,000 men are known to have belonged to them during the century. As one might expect, more than half of the active members of these Academies (although only a quarter of total members) came from the royal judiciary.

The climate of reform in 1787 varied sharply from place to place. The provincial Parlementary cities – Rouen, Rennes, Bordeaux, Pau,

Toulouse, Aix, Grenoble, Dijon, Besançon, Nancy, Douai, and Metz – had an immediate and obvious stake in the judicial reforms of 1788. Even in 1787, the tax edicts had to go to these Parlements; that of Bordeaux proved so difficult that the king exiled them to Libourne. In 1788, things were much worse. Other cities, such as those with presidial courts that would not become Great Bailiwicks, also protested strongly: a town such as Vannes, in Brittany, seemed likely to lose the mainstay of the local economy with the loss of the presidial's caseload. In such a town, all local elites rallied to the side of the Parlement, the presidial, and the nobles (upset about the loss of seigneurial jurisdictions). In other towns, such as Reims or Troyes, the locals cared little for the political upheaval, save for the obvious sense that something was afoot.

The two worst scenarios played out in Dauphiné and Brittany. In Brittany, noble, popular, and, finally, Parlementaire resistance against the May 1788 edicts led to civil disorder (requiring the use of troops) and to the radicalization of the town governments of Rennes and Nantes, who urged their colleagues in other Breton cities to rise up against the nobles and the clergy in the next sitting of the estates of Brittany. In 1789, the polarization of Breton politics led to a boycott of the Estates General by Breton nobles and to the formation of the radical Breton Club of Third Estate deputies; the Breton Club later took the name of the Parisian convent in which it met, the Jacobins. In Dauphiné, order broke down in June 1788, leading to an armed confrontation between troops and the civil population at Grenoble, who rained roof tiles down on the soldiers (the Day of the Tiles, 7 June 1788). As in Brittany, popular resistance led to political radicalism. The leaders of the Third Estate organized an Assembly at Vizille (14 June) that demanded the revival of Dauphiné's provincial estates and the return of the Parlement from exile; it also promulgated two of the key demands of 1789: doubling of the Third and voting by head in the upcoming Estates General.

Politics had come to the people. It came, as it often does, through greater material prosperity and through education. Out in the provinces, as in Paris, people went to reading rooms, first attached to booksellers' shops. There they read periodicals, French and foreign newspapers, and legal briefs. As early as the 1750s in Millau, a small southern town, members of the local elite met almost every day to discuss the newspapers. In short, they discussed politics. They created, in so doing, a new, more broadly based political society. People became familiar with the general ideas of Voltaire, Montesquieu, or Rousseau, even if they had never read any of their books (or, in the case of Rousseau, had read his novels rather than his political philosophy). If Ménétra is to be believed, Rousseau even fraternized with artisans (such as Ménétra himself) at the

Café de la Régence in Paris. Ménétra claims they played chess (Rousseau won) and that they often discussed various matters. He informs us that "both of us had the same clothes but not at all the same [breadth of] knowledge. Between us [the difference] was like night and day." Although Ménétra was not a philosopher like Rousseau, and had a tenuous grasp of Rousseau's ideas, later the glazier would play an important role in the efforts to implement Rousseau's philosophy. Different, yes, but strongly connected in ways inconceivable a century before.

In the 1780s, Ménétra and people like him began to play an increasing role in politics, especially in Paris. The role could be symbolic, as in 1787, when the fishwives of Paris refused to go to Versailles to make their immemorial traditional salute to the queen on her birthday. Rumors of her loose morals had undermined public esteem for Marie-Antoinette; the fishwives made a powerful moral and political statement by staying home. The role could be physical, as in the frequent incursions of the crowd into the Parlement's meetings in the Palais de Justice.

The government hesitated, as always, in 1788. On the one hand, Brienne and Lamoignon enacted the May judicial reforms, eviscerating the Parlements, and they reshuffled the financial administration, destroying the powerful receivers general. On the other hand, the May edicts prompted widespread opposition from nobles as well as Parlements. The political climate of uncertainty, one largely created by the promise of an Estates General at an unspecified time, caused chaos in the credit markets. By the summer of 1788, the government had trouble obtaining short-term loans. In August, ever more desperate, the king recalled the financiers' favorite, Necker, and dismissed Brienne, who had lost the confidence of the credit markets. He also announced the date of the Estates General: 1 May 1789. A few weeks later, Keeper of the Seals Lamoignon, too, left in disgrace, and the Parlements returned. In the streets of Paris, the police and the people clashed daily, with unusual levels of police violence against the crowds.

Tempting though it might be to view the struggles of the 1780s as a continuum with earlier problems, they were not. By the 1780s, both sides in the traditional conflict had discredited themselves. Here the influence of intellectuals proved paramount. As we have seen, the *philosophes* stood on both sides of the king–Parlement conflict. In general, they looked to the Parlement for protection against despotism, yet they looked to the reforming royal ministers for the programs they would support. As the count of Mirabeau, soon to be a leader in the Estates, wrote in 1788: "[P]rivileges are useful against kings but detestable against nations." The Parlement, of course, stood precisely for the use of privilege to protect against the king. Many of their allies understood that in 1785 only privilege could protect the nation – that is, that only the privileged protecting their privileges could stand up for a nation with no other means of defense – but they also understood that, in order to create the means of protection they desired, a society based on law and individual rights, they would have to destroy the Parlement as well as the unrestricted king. Admittedly writing in hindsight, Ménétra offers an interesting perspective on the situation: "This revolution was supposed to secure the happiness of the French people by confining the king to his throne and returning to all the rights that the parlements the priesthood the nobility had usurped under the leadership of the ministers." Clearly, this perspective, that the ministers of the government and the Parlements represented merely two sides of the same despotic coin, had broad support. As Echevarria has rightly pointed out, the Maupeou crisis created a political climate in which neither of the two old parties – the Parlementaires and the ministers – could hope to achieve success. The crisis of the late 1780s brought into the open the third option, what Echevarria, following the work of Robert Palmer and others, calls the democratic party.[4]

Turgot (and his disciple Brienne) in particular enjoyed strong intellectual support for their programs, if not their methods, from the *philosophes*. When the system broke down completely in the summer of 1788, the *philosophes* and their sympathizers – many of them liberal nobles such as Lafayette, la Rochefoucauld, and various dukes and peers who had participated both in the Assembly of Notables and in the Court of Peers – did not support either the king or the Parlement. They saw the Estates General as a means to create a new form of government – for most of them something similar to what they thought Britain possessed – that would more faithfully mirror the new structures of French society. The barrister Lacretelle, in a pamphlet written for the government, had to wrestle with the question dogging everyone in the summer of 1788. What was the Estates General?

It is a vestige of ancient barbarism . . . it is a collision of all the false interests with the general interest . . . Let a king at the end of the eighteenth century not convoke the three Orders of the fourteenth; let him call together the proprietors of a great nation renewed by its civilization.[5]

How Rousseauian the barrister sounds, with his talk of the general interest. Lacretelle even called for the king to present a constitution to the

---

[4] Here meaning democratic in the sense of relying on a larger, broader public opinion, but by no means a genuinely democratic system that would give any real power to the lower classes or to other disenfranchised groups, such as women.

[5] Egret, *French Prerevolution*, 188.

assembly. Yet how unlike Rousseau, with his emphasis on the "proprietors"; of course, that was it precisely – the proprietors, the property owners, would come together to make rules (laws, a tax system) to protect their interests, their property, and, by extension, society itself. This position, in France as in America, represented the mainstream; in France, it would receive its clearest exposition in 1791, during the debate on the suffrage for the new Constitution, in speeches by Antoine Barnave and others.

Although mainstream public opinion would certainly have agreed with Lacretelle that the proprietors should control the Estates, the modalities of organizing the Estates and allocating its real power sharply divided elites. Public opinion, in the form of petitions, pamphlets, and private memoirs, surged to decide the issue. The princes of the blood sent Louis a letter demanding that he maintain all the traditional forms and the Parlement, in an historic blunder (September 1788) ruled that the Estates should follow the precedents of 1614. Towns all over France circulated petitions and sent them to the king, demanding a doubling of representation of the Third Estate. Some of them, following the lead of the assembly of the Three Orders of Dauphiné at Romans, also demanded voting by head. The king, as always, vacillated: he finally ruled in December 1788 that the Third would be doubled, that each bailiwick would have an equal number of deputies, that the orders could debate in common if they chose to do so, and that anyone (including a noble or cleric) elected by the Third could sit for them. He said nothing about voting by head or by order. Implicitly, the king recognized that the Third would represent the countryside, by means of a series of elections, starting at the parish (where all taxpaying men over the age of 25 could vote) and leading up to the bailiwick.[6] Each level of assembly could prepare lists of grievances (*cahiers de doléances*). The nobles and clergy would have separate bailiwick assemblies, at which they, too, would elect deputies to the Estates. In fact, the spring elections followed a bewildering variety of methods; they created an Estates with 654 deputies from the Third Estate (many of them lawyers and nearly 20 percent bailiwick officers), 282 nobles, and 302 members of the clergy, including 192 parish priests. In

[6] Although little noted in the literature about the prerevolution, the debate about who would represent the countryside was critical to the success of the Third Estates. The Second Assembly of Notables argued to the king that the noble and clerical landlords had traditionally represented the peasants and the Third only the towns; as noted in the introduction to this volume, that position was correct with respect to medieval Estates General and to most of the provincial estates. It was false with respect to the Estates General of 1614. Given the overwhelming preponderance of peasants in the country's population, this last demand gave substance to the other arguments of the Third, particularly to the argument that they represented the largest segment of the nation, and should therefore have more deputies.

some areas, such as Brittany, electoral disputes led to boycotts (by Breton nobles) and to harsh polarization along the line noble/commoner.

The political crisis of 1788–89 paralleled a terrible economic crisis, one which combined elements of the new and the old: an economic crisis of the capitalist type, involving *over*-production (textiles and wine) and one of the subsistence type, involving under-production (of grain). Such a crisis demanded new remedies, rather different than those of the traditional economy, remedies beyond the capacity of the existing government. The elections took place in a France with skyrocketing grain prices, massive recent layoffs in the textile industry, widespread ruin in the wine sector of the south, and spreading civil disorder, leading up to the Reveillon riots in Paris (late April).

Everyone expected radical change from the Estates. The consensus position – the minimum acceptable change – seems clear enough: the king would have to agree to a representative body of some kind that would have taxing authority. Nothing less would satisfy royal creditors, past and potential. Without a representative assembly, the king would not have been able to borrow money. Historians often focus on the role of force in the spring of 1789 – on the use or non-use of royal troops – yet to do so is to ignore the simple fact that the king needed money to pay these troops. Unless he agreed to an assembly, he would not be able to borrow that money.

When the Estates met on 5 May, all of the outstanding issues came immediately to the fore. The Third, as in 1614, had to put up with the humiliation of remaining standing for hours, while their privileged counterparts sat down. That gesture must have hardened many a heart. When Mounier proposed two days later that the Third demand the common verification of credentials (i.e., all three orders verifying credentials in common), the Third agreed not to constitute itself as a separate body. The nobles and clergy refused to meet with the Third, leading to an impasse over credentials that lasted a month. Despite royal efforts to mediate a compromise at the end of May, the hard-liners held out in each order. On 10 June, the Third decided to invite the other two orders to join it; the motion also stated that, if the other two orders refused, the Third would act alone. The nobles refused, so the Third fulfilled its threat. It began to check credentials on 12 June. The clergy voted (narrowly) to join them, but only a handful of deputies actually moved to the Third's chamber.

On 17 June 1789, the deputies of the Third Estate, joined by some twenty priests, declared themselves to be the National Assembly. Our story ends there. However one defines the Old Regime, a National Assembly had no part in it. The National Assembly represented everything the Old Regime was not: it meant a society with a written constitution, with laws written by a representative assembly, taxes voted by such an assembly, and a government responsible to that assembly. From that day to this, save for a few brief interregna, through a remarkable variety of governments, including such authoritarian regimes as the later manifestations of the monarchy, two empires, and the Vichy collaborationists, France has always had a representative assembly. By definition, that is a different state than the early modern one we have examined here.

Bibliography

The list of titles here only scratches the surface of the scholarship on the French monarchy. I do not assume readers know French, so I have concentrated on English-language titles. For those who do know French, I have added a select few French titles. The English-language scholarship listed here will provide full bibliographies of specialized French scholarship. In all sections, my goal is merely to get the reader started on the right path, using those books I have found most useful.

GENERAL SURVEYS

R. Briggs, *Early-Modern France, 1560–1715* (London: Oxford University Press, 1977).

P. Campbell, *The Ancien Regime in France* (London: Blackwell, 1988).

A. Cobban, *A History of Modern France, Volume I: Old Regime and Revolution, 1715–1799* (Harmondsworth, Middlesex and New York: Penguin, 1957).

W. Doyle, *The Origins of the French Revolution* (Oxford: Oxford University Press, 1980, 1988).

J. Egret, *The French Prerevolution, 1787–1788* (Chicago, 1977; translation of 1962 French edn.).

P. Goubert, *The Ancien Régime* (New York: Harper, 1970)
Louis XIV and Twenty Million Frenchmen (New York: Harper, 1970).

P. Goubert and D. Roche, *Les Français et l'Ancien Régime* (Paris: Armand Colin, 1984; in French), 2 vols.

J. R. Major, *Representative Institutions in Early-Modern France* (New Haven, CT: Yale University Press, 1980).

M. Marion, *Dictionnaire des institutions de la France aux XVIIe et XVIIIe siècles* (Paris: A. Picard, 1923, 1968; in French); be careful, Marion is not always accurate.

R. Mousnier, *The Institutions of France under the Absolute Monarchy, 1589–1789*, 2 vols. (Chicago: University of Chicago Press, 1979, 1982).

D. Parker, *The Making of French Absolutism* (New York: Cambridge University Press, 1983).

V.-L. Tapié, *France in the Age of Louis XIII and Richelieu* (New York: Praeger, 1974; translation of 1967 Paris edn.).

There are also three new short books on the French state in the sixteenth through eighteenth centuries, all in French:

F. Bluche, *L'Ancien Régime. Institutions et Société* (Paris: Editions du Fallois, 1993).

F.-X. Emmanuelli, *Etat et pouvoirs dans la France des XVIe–XVIIIe siècles. La métamorphose inachevée* (Paris: Editions Nathan, 1992).

M. Fogel, *L'état dans la France moderne de la fin du XVe au milieu du XVIIIe siècle* (Paris: Hachette, 1992).

ROYAL AND MINISTERIAL BIOGRAPHIES

(in chronological order) Limiting myself to one biography per king, I would select as follows:

J.-P. Babelon, *Henri IV* (Paris: Fayard, 1982; in French).

L. Moote, *Louis XIII. The Just* (Berkeley: University of California Press, 1989).

F. Bluche, *Louis XIV* (Paris: Fayard, trans. M. Greengrass (Oxford: Basil Blackwell, 1990; translation of French edn.; Paris: Fayard, 1986)).

M. Antoine, *Louis XV* (Paris: Fayard, 1989; in French).

J. Hardman, *Louis XVI* (New Haven, CT: Yale University Press, 1993).

On the chief royal ministers, the best biographies are:

B. Barbiche, *Sully* (Paris: Albin Michel, 1978; in French).

J. Bergin, *Cardinal Richelieu: Power and the Pursuit of Wealth* (Cambridge: Cambridge University Press, 1985).

P. Goubert, *Mazarin* (Paris: Fayard, 1991; in French).

D. Dessert, *Fouquet* (Paris: Fayard, 1987; in French).

A. Corvisier, *Louvois* (Paris: Fayard, 1983; in French).

R. Harris, *Necker, Reform Statesman of the Ancien Regime* (Berkeley: University of California Press, 1979).

Colbert does not have a fully satisfactory biography, nor do any of the eighteenth-century ministers save Necker.

FINANCES

R. Bonney, *The King's Debts* (Oxford: Oxford University Press, 1981).

J. Bosher, *French Finances, 1770–1795* (Oxford: Oxford University Press, 1970).

J. Collins, *The Fiscal Limits of Absolutism* (Berkeley: University of California Press, 1988).

J. Dent, *Crisis in Finance* (Newton Abbot, Devon: David and Charles, 1973).

J. Riley, *The Seven Years' War and the Old Regime in France* (Princeton, NJ: Princeton University Press, 1986).

The following four titles in French are essential for any serious knowledge of the financial system but they are quite detailed, and not easily accessible to the general reader:

F. Bayard, *Le monde des financiers au XVIIe siècle* (Paris: Flammarion, 1988).

D. Dessert, *Argent, pouvoir et société au Grand Siècle* (Paris: Fayard, 1984).

C.-F. Lévy, *Capitalistes et pouvoir au siècle des lumières*, 3 vols. (Paris: Mouton, 1969–80).

H. Lüthy, *La banque protestante en France de la Révocation de l'Edit de Nantes à la Révolution* (Paris: S.E.V.P.E.N., 1961), 2 vols.

CENTRAL ADMINISTRATION

M. Antoine, *Le Conseil du Roi sous le règne de Louis XV* (Geneva: Droz, 1970).

R. Bonney, *Political Change in France under Richelieu and Mazarin* (Oxford: Oxford University Press, 1976).

D. Buisseret, *Sully and the Growth of Centralized Government in France* (London: Eyre and Spottiswoode, 1968).

D. Echevarria, *The Maupeou Revolution* (Baton Rouge: Louisiana State University Press, 1985).

A. Hamscher, *The Conseil Privé and the Parlements in the Age of Louis XIV: A Study in French Absolutism*, Transactions of the American Philosophical Society, vol. 77, part II, 1987 (Philadelphia: American Philosophical Society, 1987).

J. M. Hayden, *France and the Estates General of 1614* (Cambridge: Cambridge University Press, 1974).

S. Kettering, *Patrons, Brokers, and Clients in Seventeenth-Century France* (Oxford: Oxford University Press, 1986).

F. Mosser, *Les intendants des finances au XVIIIe siècle: Les Lefèvre d'Ormesson et le "département des impositions" (1715–1777)* (Geneva: Droz, 1978).

O. Ranum, *Richelieu and the Councillors of Louis XIII* (Oxford: Oxford University Press, 1963).

Very specific aspects of the workings of the central government, especially royal councils, are also provided in many articles, notably those by B. Barbiche, M. Morineau, R. Mousnier, and G. Pagès, in such journals as *Revue Historique*, *XVIIe Siècle*, and the *Revue d'Histoire Moderne et Contemporaine*.

LEGAL SYSTEM

L. Berlanstein, *The Barristers of Toulouse in the Eighteenth Century* (Baltimore: Johns Hopkins University Press, 1975).

J. Dewald, *The Formation of a Provincial Nobility: The Magistrates of the Parlement of Rouen, 1499–1610* (Princeton, NJ: Princeton University Press, 1980).

W. Doyle, *The Parlement of Bordeaux and the End of the Old Regime, 1771–1790* (New York: St. Martin's Press, 1974).

J. Egret, *Louis XV et l'opposition parlementaire* (Paris: Presses Universitaires de France, 1970).

A. Hamscher, *The Parlement of Paris after the Fronde, 1653–1673* (Pittsburgh: University of Pittsburgh Press, 1977).

S. Kettering, *Judicial Politics and Urban Revolt: The Parlement of Aix, 1629–1659* (Princeton, NJ: Princeton University Press, 1978).

L. Moote, *The Revolt of the Judges: The Parlement of Paris and the Fronde, 1643–1652* (Princeton, NJ: Princeton University Press, 1971).

J. H. Shennan, *The Parlement of Paris* (Ithaca, NY: Cornell University Press, 1968).

B. Stone, *The Parlement of Paris, 1774–1789* (Chapel Hill, NC: University of North Carolina Press, 1981).

POOR RELIEF AND POLICE

T. Adams, *Bureaucrats and Beggars. French Social Policy in the Age of Enlightenment* (New York: Oxford University Press, 1990).

T. Brennan, *Public Drinking and Popular Culture in Eighteenth-Century Paris* (Princeton, NJ: Princeton University Press, 1988).

I. Cameron, *Crime and Repression in the Auvergne and the Guyenne, 1720–1790* (Cambridge: Cambridge University Press, 1981).

N. Castan, *Crime et répression en Languedoc au siècle des lumières* (Paris: Flammarion, 1980).

J.-P. Gutton, *L'état et la mendicité dans la première moitié du XVIIIe siècle* (Lyons: Centre d'Etudes Foreziennes, 1973); Gutton also has several other works on this subject, all of them of high quality.

O. Hufton, *The Poor of Eighteenth-Century France* (Oxford: Oxford University Press, 1974).

K. Norberg, *Rich and Poor in Grenoble, 1600–1815* (Berkeley: University of California Press, 1985).

S. Reinhardt, *Justice in the Sarladais, 1770–1790* (Baton Rouge: Louisiana State University Press, 1991).

R. Schwartz, *Policing the Poor in Eighteenth-Century France* (Chapel Hill, NC: University of North Carolina Press, 1988).

A. Williams, *The Police of Paris, 1718–1789* (Baton Rouge: Louisiana State University Press, 1979).

NOBILITY AND STATE

G. Chaussinand-Nogaret, *The French Nobility in the Eighteenth Century* (Paris: Hachette, 1986).

J.-M. Constant, *Nobles et paysans en Beauce* (Paris: Presses Universitaires de France, 1986).

J. Dewald, *Pont-St-Pierre, 1398–1789* (Berkeley: University of California Press, 1987).

F. Ford, *Robe and Sword* (Cambridge, MA: Harvard University Press, 1953; New York: Harper, 1965).

R. Forster, *The Nobility of Toulouse in the Eighteenth Century* (Baltimore: Johns Hopkins University Press, 1960).

J. Meyer, *La noblesse bretonne au XVIIIe siècle* (Paris: Ecole Pratique des Hautes Etudes, 1966), 2 vols.

Interested readers should note that there is an abundant and excellent literature on the nobility in the sixteenth century; among the authors one should consult are Denis Crouzet, Robert Harding, Mack Holt, Arlette Jouanna, Kristen Neuschel, and Ellery Schalk.

COURT SOCIETY AND POLITICAL CULTURE

K. Baker, ed., *Inventing the French Revolution* (New York: Cambridge University Press, 1990).

M. Bloch, *The Royal Touch* (New York: Dorsey, 1961, 1989).

R. Chartier, *The Cultural Origins of the French Revolution* (Durham, NC: Duke University Press, 1991).

The Cultural Uses of Print in Early Modern France (Princeton, NJ: Princeton University Press, 1987).

N. Elias, *The Court Society* (New York: Pantheon, 1983).

M. Fogel, *Les cérémonies de l'information dans la France du XVIe au milieu du XVIIIe siècle* (Paris: Fayard, 1989).

J. Habermas, *The Structural Transformation of the Public Sphere* (Cambridge, MA: MIT Press, 1989).

S. Hanley, *The* Lit de Justice *of the Kings of France* (Princeton: Princeton University Press, 1983).

R. Jackson, Vive le roi! *A History of the French Coronation from Charles V to Charles X* (Chapel Hill, NC: University of North Carolina Press, 1984).

C. Jouhaud, *Mazarinades: la Fronde des mots* (Paris: Aubier, 1985).

E. Kantorowicz, *The King's Two Bodies* (Princeton, NJ: Princeton University Press, 1966).

N. Keohane, *Philosophy and the State in France from the Renaissance to the Enlightenment* (Princeton, NJ: Princeton University Press, 1983).

J. Klaits, *Printed Propoganda under Louis XIV* (Princeton, NJ: Princeton University Press, 1976).

J. Merrick, *The Desacralization of the French Monarchy in the Eighteenth Century* (Baton Rouge: Louisiana State University Press, 1990).

J. Sawyer, *Printed Poison* (Berkeley: University of California Press, 1990).

J.-F. Solnon, *La cour de France* (Paris: Fayard, 1987; in French).

D. Van Kley, *The Damiens Affair and the Unravelling of the Old Regime* (Princeton, NJ: Princeton University Press, 1984).

LOCAL ADMINISTRATION

W. Beik, *Absolutism and Society in Seventeenth-Century France: State Power and Provincial Aristocracy in Languedoc* (Cambridge: Cambridge University Press, 1985).

J. Collins, *Classes, Estates, and Order in Early Modern Brittany* (Cambridge: Cambridge University Press, 1994).

F. Emmanuelli, *Un mythe de l'absolutisme bourbonien. L'intendance du milieu du XVIIe siècle à la fin du XVIIIe siècle* (Aix-en-Provence: Publications de l'Université de Provence, 1981).

V. Gruder, *The Royal Provincial Intendants* (Ithaca, NY: Cornell University Press, 1968).

R. Mousnier, *La vénalité des offices sous Henri IV et Louis XIII* (Paris: Presses Universitaires de France, 1945, 1971).

A. Rebillon, *Les Etats de Bretagne, 1661–1789* (Paris: A. Picard and Rennes: Plihon, 1932).

D. Roche, *Le siècle des lumières en province. Académies et académiciens provinciaux, 1680–1789* (Paris: Mouton, 1978).

H. Root, *Peasants and King in Burgundy. Agrarian Foundations of French Absolutism* (Berkeley: University of California Press, 1987).

R. Schneider, *Public Life in Toulouse, 1463–1789* (Ithaca, NY: Cornell University Press, 1989).

LOCAL STUDIES

G. Bossenga, *The Politics of Privilege. Old Regime and Revolution in Lille* (Cambridge: Cambridge University Press, 1991).

F. Ford, *Strasbourg in Transition* (Cambridge, MA: Harvard University Press, 1965).

D. Garrioch, *Neighborhood and Community in Paris, 1740–1790* (Cambridge: Cambridge University Press, 1986).

T. Le Goff, *Vannes and Its Region in the Eighteenth Century* (Oxford: Oxford University Press, 1981).

D. Roche, *The People of Paris* (Berkeley: University of California Press, 1986).

There are many fine local studies in French. For the countryside, one should start with either P. Goubert, *Beauvais et le Beauvaisis de 1600 à 1715* (Paris: EHESS, 1960, reedition 1982) or E. Le Roy Ladurie, *Les paysans de Languedoc*, 2 vols. (Paris: S.E.V.P.E.N., 1966: both the French pocket edition, published by Flammarion, and the English short version, *The Peasants of Languedoc*, published by University of Illinois Press, leave out the most important part of the book, so be wary of them); on towns (in French), P. Deyon, *Amiens, capitale provinciale étude sur la société urbaine au XVIIe siècle* (Paris, The Hague: Mouton, 1967), *Recherches sur les structures sociale à Châteaudun* (Paris: S.E.V.P.E.N., 1968), M. Garden, *Lyon et les Lyonnais au XVIIIe siècle* (Paris: Flammarion, 1978), and J.-P. Poussou, *Bordeaux au XVIIIe siècle* (Paris: EHESS, 1983), offer a fine start to the very rich literature.

RESISTANCE TO AUTHORITY

Here five classic titles stand out, all of them in French, although one is now available in a translation (alas without its supporting documentation):

Y.-M. Bercé, *Peasant Rebellions* (Ithaca, NY: Cornell University Press, 1989), a translation of *Histoire des Croquants* (Paris, Geneva: Librairie Droz, 1974).

M. Foisil, *La révolte des Nu-Pieds* (Paris: Presses Universitaires de France, 1970).

A. Jouanna, *Le devoir de révolte* (Paris: Fayard, 1989).

R. Pillorget, *Les mouvements insurrectionnels en Provence de 1595 à 1720* (Paris: A. Pedone, 1971).

B. Porchnev, *Les soulèvements populaires en France avant la Fronde, 1623–1648* (Paris: S.E.V.P.E.N., 1963; translation of the Russian edition of 1948).

In addition, readers will note that the works of Moote (*Revolt of the Judges*), Kettering (*Provincial Politics*), and Collins (*Classes, Estates, and Order*) cited above, along with Orest Ranum, *The Fronde* (New York: Norton, 1994), deal with resistance.

Index

absolute monarchy, 70, 76, 80, 114, 141, 210, 240; culture and, 119–21; definition of, 1–3; intendants and, 50, 54, 93; myth of, 185, 208; relationship to law, 10–11, 156, 212, 234, 246, 251; Revocation of Edict of Nantes and, 104–05

administrative monarchy, 2, 3

admiral of France, 15, 50, 54, 94, 157, 226

aides, 18–21, 110

Aix-en–Provence, 32 (map), 43, 96, 98, 154, 164 (map), 180, 183, 190, 199, 227, 228 (map); Parlement of, 7, 115–16, 262; revolts in, 52 (1630), 71–72 (Fronde)

Alsace, 7, 19, 30, 95, 104, 115, 123, 126, 128, 165, 194, 228; seizure of, 97–100

Amiens, 19, 30, 32 (map), 43, 96, 164 (map), 228 (map); courts of, 8–9 (table); famine of 1693–94, 151–52

Anjou, 9, 49, 79, 129, 134, 136, 159, 228 (map)

Anne of Austria (Regent of France, 1643–54), 44, 62, 79, 81, 95, 118; and Fronde, 65–76

annuities (*rentes*), 107; and 1634 bankruptcy, 51, 53; in 1640s, 67–69; under Henry IV, 24–25; in late eighteenth century, 234–39; during War of League of Augsburg, 163–66; and War of Spanish Succession, 170–72

army (*see also* military), 3, 5, 6, 23, 26, 28, 29, 33, 46, 57, 58, 59, 81, 86, 106, 123, 135, 136, 226, 235, 236, 241, 258, 259, 261; in 1720s, 196–99; final reforms of Louis XIV, 156–59; during the Fronde, 71–75; Louis XIV, early wars, 94–101; origins, 14–15; reform in 1620s, 48–55; reforms of Choiseul and

Saint-Germain, 248–49; and tax system, 16–19; Thirty Years' War, 61–66; War of League of Augsburg, 126–29; War of Spanish Succession, 159–62, 186

artisans, 4, 31, 34, 40, 42, 62, 74, 104, 117, 149, 154, 162, 167, 180, 183, 193–94, 218, 221, 262

Artois, 7, 30, 95, 115, 202, 228 (map)

Assembly of Notables, 202; of 1583, 22; of 1626–27, 47–50; of 1787 and 1788, 257–60, 262, 264–67

bailiwick, 8, 9, 38, 115, 116, 135, 138, 147, 222, 261, 265

ban et arrière-ban, 14, 62

Bavaria, 59, 126, 127, 159, 160, 198

beggars, state repression of, 34, 151, 152, 154, 189–91

Blois, Edict of (1579), 22, 47, 65, 136

Bordeaux, 7, 29, 32 (map), 43, 62, 85, 92, 115, 137, 153, 164 (map), 187, 212, 217, 219, 221, 228 (map); commerce of, 178–80, 182, 183; Fronde in, 66, 67, 73–75; Parlement of, 12, 115, 137, 246, 254, 256, 261–62; population of, 30

bourgeoisie, 1, 2, 12, 42, 132

Brienne, Loménie de, 235, 237–39, 258, 260, 261, 263, 264

Brittany, 7–9, 15, 22, 24, 38, 43, 48, 49, 63, 66, 68, 72, 94, 112, 136, 153, 176, 183, 194, 226, 228 (map), 239, 261, 266; estates of, 11–13, 28, 35, 52–53, 103n, 236, 262; justice in, 146–48; Parlement of, 11–13, 26, 86, 250–52 (Brittany Affair); revolts of 1675, 117–19; taxes in, 19–20, 106–08, 201–03, 205n

Burgundy, 7, 24, 30, 38, 43, 49, 66, 111, 112, 115, 116, 141, 148, 153, 156, 161, 167n, 194, 202, 228 (map), 261;

275

NEW APPROACHES TO EUROPEAN HISTORY

1 MERRY E. WIESNER
Women and Gender in Early Modern Europe
0 521 38459 1 hardback
0 521 38613 6 paperback

2 JONATHAN SPERBER
The European Revolutions, 1848–1851
0 521 38526 1 hardback
0 521 38685 3 paperback

3 CHARLES INGRAO
The Habsburg Monarchy 1618–1815
0 521 38009 X hardback
0 521 38900 3 paperback

4 ROBERT JÜTTE
Poverty and Deviance in Early Modern Europe
0 521 41169 6 hardback
0 521 42322 8 paperback

5 JAMES B. COLLINS
The State in Early Modern France
0 521 38284 X hardback
0 521 38724 8 paperback

6 CHARLES G. NAUERT, JR
Humanism and the Culture of Renaissance Europe
0 521 40364 2 hardback
0 521 40724 9 paperback

7 DORINDA OUTRAM
The Enlightenment
0 521 41522 5 hardback
0 521 42534 4 paperback

8 MACK P. HOLT
The French Wars of Religion, 1562–1629
0 521 35359 9 hardback
0 521 35873 6 paperback

9 JONATHAN DEWALD
The European Nobility, 1400–1800
0 521 41512 8 hardback
0 521 42528 X paperback

10 ROBERT S. DUPLESSIS
Transitions to Capitalism in Early Modern Europe
0 521 39465 1 hardback
0 521 39773 1 paperback